W9-DDJ-793

...For DUMMIES™

BESTSELLING BOOK SERIES

References for the Rest of Us!

Are you intimidated and confused by computers? Do you find that traditional manuals are overloaded with technical details you'll never use? Do your friends and family always call you to fix simple problems on their PCs? Then the ...*For Dummies* computer book series from IDG Books Worldwide is for you.

...*For Dummies* books are written for those frustrated computer users who know they aren't really dumb but find that PC hardware, software, and indeed the unique vocabulary of computing make them feel helpless. ...*For Dummies* books use a lighthearted approach, a down-to-earth style, and even cartoons and humorous icons to dispel computer novices' fears and build their confidence. Lighthearted but not lightweight, these books are a perfect survival guide for anyone forced to use a computer.

> *"I like my copy so much I told friends; now they bought copies."*
>
> — Irene C., Orwell, Ohio

> *"Quick, concise, nontechnical, and humorous."*
>
> — Jay A., Elburn, Illinois

> *"Thanks, I needed this book. Now I can sleep at night."*
>
> — Robin F., British Columbia, Canada

Already, millions of satisfied readers agree. They have made ...*For Dummies* books the #1 introductory level computer book series and have written asking for more. So, if you're looking for the most fun and easy way to learn about computers, look to ...*For Dummies* books to give you a helping hand.

IDG BOOKS WORLDWIDE®

1/99

Oracle8i™ For Dummies®

Cheat Sheet

BESTSELLING
BOOK SERIES

Enterprise Manager DBA Management Pack

Tool	Log in as	Uses
LaunchPad	None	Desktop path to tools; start other tools
Storage Manager	DBA	Create database files and tablespaces
Instance Manager	INTERNAL	Start and stop database; monitor activity
Security Manager	DBA	Create users and roles; assign privileges
Schema Manager	DBA	Create and edit tables, views, synonyms, indexes
SQL*Plus Worksheet	Table owner	Execute SQL commands
Console	Repository owner	Manage remote jobs; back up and restore database

Place Your Login Information HERE

Whenever you start up the Enterprise Manager's DBA Management Pack tools, you must log in. The first figure shows the standard login page that appears for every tool. If you set up the LaunchPad, you can save time because the LaunchPad remembers your first login of the session and reuses it when you choose the next tool. Typically, you will have three different Oracle user names: one for Instance Manager, one for SQL*Plus Worksheet, and one for all three other managers: Storage, Schema, and Security.

Fill in this chart to help you remember which user name goes with each tool. Keep your cheat sheet in a secure place. If you have no secure location, omit the passwords on the chart.

My Login Chart (place in the Username and Password boxes when logging in)

Tool	Username	Password
Instance Manager		
SQL*Plus Worksheet		
Storage Manager		
Schema Manager		
Security Manager		

Oracle8i™ For Dummies®

The Service box contains a unique name for your Oracle8i database. If you have multiple databases on your network, each one has a different Service name. Many businesses maintain two databases: one for testing and one for the "real" stuff. Use this chart to record the Service name (or names) that you need.

My Oracle Service names (place one in the Service box when you log in)

Service	Description

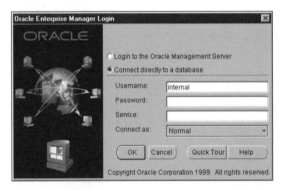

SQL Commands

SQL (Structured Query Language) gives you direct access to data in your Oracle8i tables. Use the following example to remind you of the correct syntax for a basic relational query:

```
SELECT SS.SAMPLE_ID, SS.SELLING_PRICE,
SS.SAMPLE_DESCRIPTION, TS.EDIBLE
FROM SEAWEED_SAMPLE SS, TYPE_OF_SEAWEED TS
WHERE TS.TYPE_ID = SS.TYPE_ID
ORDER BY SS.SAMPLE_ID;
```

IDG BOOKS WORLDWIDE

...For Dummies®: Bestselling Book Series for Beginners

ORACLE8i™

FOR

DUMMIES®

ORACLE8i™ FOR DUMMIES®

by Carol McCullough-Dieter

Foreword by Ned Dana
Principal Consultant and Toolmaster
Rare & Dear, Inc.

IDG Books Worldwide, Inc.
An International Data Group Company

Foster City, CA ◆ Chicago, IL ◆ Indianapolis, IN ◆ New York, NY

Oracle8i For Dummies®

Published by
IDG Books Worldwide, Inc.
An International Data Group Company
919 E. Hillsdale Blvd.
Suite 400
Foster City, CA 94404
www.idgbooks.com (IDG Books Worldwide Web site)
www.dummies.com (Dummies Press Web site)

Library of Congress Catalog Card No.: 99-63188

ISBN: 0-7645-0570-X

Printed in the United States of America

10 9 8 7 6 5 4 3

1B/QR/QX/ZZ/IN

Distributed in the United States by IDG Books Worldwide, Inc.

Distributed by CDG Books Canada Inc. for Canada; by Transworld Publishers Limited in the United Kingdom; by IDG Norge Books for Norway; by IDG Sweden Books for Sweden; by IDG Books Australia Publishing Corporation Pty. Ltd. for Australia and New Zealand; by TransQuest Publishers Pte Ltd. for Singapore, Malaysia, Thailand, Indonesia, and Hong Kong; by Gotop Information Inc. for Taiwan; by ICG Muse, Inc. for Japan; by Norma Comunicaciones S.A. for Colombia; by Intersoft for South Africa; by Eyrolles for France; by International Thomson Publishing for Germany, Austria and Switzerland; by Distribuidora Cuspide for Argentina; by Livraria Cultura for Brazil; by Ediciones ZETA S.C.R. Ltda. for Peru; by WS Computer Publishing Corporation, Inc., for the Philippines; by Contemporanea de Ediciones for Venezuela; by Express Computer Distributors for the Caribbean and West Indies; by Micronesia Media Distributor, Inc. for Micronesia; by Grupo Editorial Norma S.A. for Guatemala; by Chips Computadoras S.A. de C.V. for Mexico; by Editorial Norma de Panama S.A. for Panama; by American Bookshops for Finland. Authorized Sales Agent: Anthony Rudkin Associates for the Middle East and North Africa.

For general information on IDG Books Worldwide's books in the U.S., please call our Consumer Customer Service department at 800-762-2974. For reseller information, including discounts and premium sales, please call our Reseller Customer Service department at 800-434-3422.

For information on where to purchase IDG Books Worldwide's books outside the U.S., please contact our International Sales department at 317-596-5530 or fax 317-596-5692.

For consumer information on foreign language translations, please contact our Customer Service department at 1-800-434-3422, fax 317-596-5692, or e-mail rights@idgbooks.com.

For information on licensing foreign or domestic rights, please phone +1-650-655-3109.

For sales inquiries and special prices for bulk quantities, please contact our Sales department at 650-655-3200 or write to the address above.

For information on using IDG Books Worldwide's books in the classroom or for ordering examination copies, please contact our Educational Sales department at 800-434-2086 or fax 317-596-5499.

For press review copies, author interviews, or other publicity information, please contact our Public Relations department at 650-655-3000 or fax 650-655-3299.

For authorization to photocopy items for corporate, personal, or educational use, please contact Copyright Clearance Center, 222 Rosewood Drive, Danvers, MA 01923, or fax 978-750-4470.

About the Author

Carol McCullough-Dieter lives on beautiful Maui, Hawaii, with her family. She works as the Database Administrator for the Pacific Disaster Center, a federally funded project for aiding in disaster mitigation and recovery serving Hawaii and many Pacific Island countries.

This is the third update of *Oracle For Dummies,* and Carol has authored all of the editions. She also co-authored several other books on Oracle software for IDG Books Worldwide, including the *Oracle8™ Bible, Oracle8™ Developer's Guide,* and *Creating Cool Web Databases.*

If you have questions about this book, you can visit Carol's Question and Answer Page at

`www.maui.net/~mcculc/o8ifordum/Welcome.html`

Carol's personal Web site featuring unusual Christmas holiday traditions from the past has received several awards. Surf on over to Maui and see it for yourself at

`www.maui.net/~mcculc/xmas.htm`

Her e-mail address is `mcculc@maui.net`.

ABOUT IDG BOOKS WORLDWIDE

Welcome to the world of IDG Books Worldwide.

IDG Books Worldwide, Inc., is a subsidiary of International Data Group, the world's largest publisher of computer-related information and the leading global provider of information services on information technology. IDG was founded more than 30 years ago by Patrick J. McGovern and now employs more than 9,000 people worldwide. IDG publishes more than 290 computer publications in over 75 countries. More than 90 million people read one or more IDG publications each month.

Launched in 1990, IDG Books Worldwide is today the #1 publisher of best-selling computer books in the United States. We are proud to have received eight awards from the Computer Press Association in recognition of editorial excellence and three from Computer Currents' First Annual Readers' Choice Awards. Our best-selling ...For Dummies® series has more than 50 million copies in print with translations in 31 languages. IDG Books Worldwide, through a joint venture with IDG's Hi-Tech Beijing, became the first U.S. publisher to publish a computer book in the People's Republic of China. In record time, IDG Books Worldwide has become the first choice for millions of readers around the world who want to learn how to better manage their businesses.

Our mission is simple: Every one of our books is designed to bring extra value and skill-building instructions to the reader. Our books are written by experts who understand and care about our readers. The knowledge base of our editorial staff comes from years of experience in publishing, education, and journalism — experience we use to produce books to carry us into the new millennium. In short, we care about books, so we attract the best people. We devote special attention to details such as audience, interior design, use of icons, and illustrations. And because we use an efficient process of authoring, editing, and desktop publishing our books electronically, we can spend more time ensuring superior content and less time on the technicalities of making books.

You can count on our commitment to deliver high-quality books at competitive prices on topics you want to read about. At IDG Books Worldwide, we continue in the IDG tradition of delivering quality for more than 30 years. You'll find no better book on a subject than one from IDG Books Worldwide.

John Kilcullen
Chairman and CEO
IDG Books Worldwide, Inc.

Steven Berkowitz
President and Publisher
IDG Books Worldwide, Inc.

Eighth Annual
Computer Press
Awards ≥1992

WINNER
Ninth Annual
Computer Press
Awards ≥1993

WINNER
Tenth Annual
Computer Press
Awards ≥1994

WINNER
Eleventh Annual
Computer Press
Awards ≥1995

IDG is the world's leading IT media, research and exposition company. Founded in 1964, IDG had 1997 revenues of $2.05 billion and has more than 9,000 employees worldwide. IDG offers the widest range of media options that reach IT buyers in 75 countries representing 95% of worldwide IT spending. IDG's diverse product and services portfolio spans six key areas including print publishing, online publishing, expositions and conferences, market research, education and training, and global marketing services. More than 90 million people read one or more of IDG's 290 magazines and newspapers, including IDG's leading global brands — Computerworld, PC World, Network World, Macworld and the Channel World family of publications. IDG Books Worldwide is one of the fastest-growing computer book publishers in the world, with more than 700 titles in 36 languages. The "...For Dummies®" series alone has more than 50 million copies in print. IDG offers online users the largest network of technology-specific Web sites around the world through IDG.net (http://www.idg.net), which comprises more than 225 targeted Web sites in 55 countries worldwide. International Data Corporation (IDC) is the world's largest provider of information technology data, analysis and consulting, with research centers in over 41 countries and more than 400 research analysts worldwide. IDG World Expo is a leading producer of more than 168 globally branded conferences and expositions in 35 countries including E3 (Electronic Entertainment Expo), Macworld Expo, ComNet, Windows World Expo, ICE (Internet Commerce Expo), Agenda, DEMO, and Spotlight. IDG's training subsidiary, ExecuTrain, is the world's largest computer training company, with more than 230 locations worldwide and 785 training courses. IDG Marketing Services helps industry-leading IT companies build international brand recognition by developing global integrated marketing programs via IDG's print, online and exposition products worldwide. Further information about the company can be found at www.idg.com.   1/24/99

Dedication

For Blue, whose dedication to the S.W.A.N. (Stop Working All Night) campaign was a great success.

Author's Acknowledgments

Thanks again to the great team of editors, copywriters, artists, and office staff headed by Joyce Pepple, Greg Croy, Jeanne Criswell, Stephanie Koutek, Kim Darosett, Marita Ellixson, Carmen Krikorian, Megan Roney, E. Shawn Aylsworth, Jamila Pree, and others. What a crackerjack bunch of Dummies we all are! And proud of it, too.

Finally, thanks to my husband, Pat, who supported me as if his life depended on it. He is my ghost editor, saving me from my own terrible spelling and adding some great one-liners here and there. I'm not kidding!

Publisher's Acknowledgments

We're proud of this book; please register your comments through our IDG Books Worldwide Online Registration Form located at http://my2cents.dummies.com.

Some of the people who helped bring this book to market include the following:

Acquisitions, Editorial, and Media Development

Project Editor: Jeanne S. Criswell
   (Previous Edition: Tim Gallan)

Acquisitions Editors: Joyce Pepple, Greg Croy

Copy Editors: Stephanie Koutek, Kim Darosett

Technical Editor: Piroz Mohseni,
   Automated Concepts Inc.

Media Development Editor: Marita Ellixson

Associate Permissions Editor:
   Carmen Krikorian

Media Development Coordinator:
   Megan Roney

Editorial Managers: Rev Mengle,
   Leah P. Cameron

Media Development Manager:
   Heather Heath Dismore

Editorial Assistants: Jamila Pree, Beth Parlon

Production

Project Coordinator: Maridee V. Ennis

Layout and Graphics: Thomas R. Emrick,
   Angela F. Hunckler, Brent Savage,
   Barry Offringa, Kathie Schutte,
   Michael A. Sullivan, Brian Torwelle,
   Dan Whetstine

Proofreaders: Vickie Broyles, Nancy Price,
   Marianne Santy, Janet M. Withers

Indexer: Rebecca R. Plunkett

Special Help
   Darren Meiss, Pam Wilson-Wykes

General and Administrative

IDG Books Worldwide, Inc.: John Kilcullen, CEO; Steven Berkowitz, President and Publisher

IDG Books Technology Publishing Group: Richard Swadley, Senior Vice President and Publisher; Walter Bruce III, Vice President and Associate Publisher; Steven Sayre, Associate Publisher; Joseph Wikert, Associate Publisher; Mary Bednarek, Branded Product Development Director; Mary Corder, Editorial Director

IDG Books Consumer Publishing Group: Roland Elgey, Senior Vice President and Publisher; Kathleen A. Welton, Vice President and Publisher; Kevin Thornton, Acquisitions Manager; Kristin A. Cocks, Editorial Director

IDG Books Internet Publishing Group: Brenda McLaughlin, Senior Vice President and Publisher; Diane Graves Steele, Vice President and Associate Publisher; Sofia Marchant, Online Marketing Manager

IDG Books Production for Dummies Press: Michael R. Britton, Vice President of Production; Debbie Stailey, Associate Director of Production; Cindy L. Phipps, Manager of Project Coordination, Production Proofreading, and Indexing; Shelley Lea, Supervisor of Graphics and Design; Debbie J. Gates, Production Systems Specialist; Robert Springer, Supervisor of Proofreading; Laura Carpenter, Production Control Manager; Tony Augsburger, Supervisor of Reprints and Bluelines

Dummies Packaging and Book Design: Patty Page, Manager, Promotions Marketing

◆

The publisher would like to give special thanks to Patrick J. McGovern,
without whom this book would not have been possible.

◆

Contents at a Glance

Foreword ....*xxiii*

Introduction *1*

Part I: Road Map *7*
Chapter 1: A Quick Tour of Oracle8i 9
Chapter 2: Data Whaaaaat? A Database Primer 43
Chapter 3: SQL Nuts and Bolts 65
Chapter 4: Object SQL: The New Stuff 91
Chapter 5: Using the Enterprise Manager DBA Tools 107

Part II: Getting Started *121*
Chapter 6: The Relational Model and You 123
Chapter 7: Diagramming Your World 137
Chapter 8: Getting Familiar with Oracle8i Data-Dictionary Views 147
Chapter 9: Oracle's User 153

Part III: Putting Oracle8i to Work *167*
Chapter 10: Defining Tables, Tablespaces, and Columns 169
Chapter 11: Creating Object Types, Objects, and References 185
Chapter 12: Security Options: Roles, Profiles, and Grants 201
Chapter 13: Views and Synonyms: Do You See What I See? 221
Chapter 14: WebDB: The Best New Tool for the Internet 241
Chapter 15: Java and the Internet Database 259
Chapter 16: The Five Ws of Safeguarding Your Data 269

Part IV: Tuning Up and Turbocharging *289*
Chapter 17: What's Slowing Your Query Down? 291
Chapter 18: Speeding Up Queries with Keys and Indexes 301
Chapter 19: Correcting Flaws 325

Part V: The Part of Tens *343*
Chapter 20: Ten Tips for Good Design 345
Chapter 21: Ten Handy Oracle8i Features 359

Part VI: Appendixes..**365**

Appendix A: Glossary 367

Appendix B: About the CD 375

Index..**383**

IDG Books Worldwide End-User License Agreement **402**

Installation Instructions **404**

Book Registration Information ....**Back of Book**

Cartoons at a Glance

By Rich Tennant

page 289

page 167

page 7

page 365

page 121

page 343

Fax: 978-546-7747 • E-mail: the5wave@tiac.net

Table of Contents

Foreword...*xxiii*

Introduction 1

    Why This Book Makes Sense 1
    Some Basic Assumptions 2
    Quickie Overview of This Book 2
        Part I: Road Map 2
        Part II: Getting Started 2
        Part III: Putting Oracle8i to Work 3
        Part IV: Tuning Up and Turbocharging 3
        Part V: The Part of Tens 3
        Part VI: Appendixes 4
    Of Mice and Sven (Mouse Moves and Special Text) 4
    Icons Used in This Book 5
    About the Author vii

Part I: Road Map 7

Chapter 1: A Quick Tour of Oracle8i 9

    Discovering Oracle8i: The Program That Runs It All 9
        Oracle8i's core package 10
        Oracle8i's newest star: WebDB 12
        Enterprise Manager 13
        DBA Management Pack packs five all-star tools 13
    Starting Up Oracle8i 14
        Starting the database with the Instance Manager 15
        Starting Oracle8i using the Server Manager 17
    Looking Around with Schema Manager 18
        The Object window 19
        The other Schema Manager elements 21
        The Main Menu and Button elements 22
    Getting Acquainted with SQL: The Messenger Priestess of Oracle8i 23
        Starting and stopping SQL*Plus Worksheet on any platform 24
        Starting and stopping SQL*Plus on a desktop 27
        Starting and stopping SQL*Plus on a mainframe or a network 29
    Initializing the Enterprise Manager Console 30
        Creating a repository for Enterprise Manager Version 2 31
        Starting the Enterprise Manager Service 35
        Starting the Agent 36
        Taking a quick tour of Enterprise Manager Console 36

Getting Help: Let Your Mouse Do the Walking 38
Shutting Down Oracle8i 39
    Shutting down Oracle8i on a desktop 39
    Shutting down Oracle8i on a mainframe or a network 42

Chapter 2: Data Whaaaaat? A Database Primer 43
Dataspeak Definitions for the Techno-Impaired 43
Relational Database Concepts 46
    Users and roles 47
    Tables 49
    Columns and rows 52
    Relationships 54
Object-Relational Database Concepts 55
    An object defined 56
    The scoop on object types 57
    The connection of relational tables with objects 58
    Object reference 58
    Methods to their madness 59
    Nested tables 59
    Varrays 60
The Kinds of Database Things That You Can Do with Oracle8i 60
    Keeping track of a fishbowl (the easy example) 60
    Running a pet shop (the medium example) 61
    Tracking endangered species globally (the hard example) 62

Chapter 3: SQL Nuts and Bolts 65
Starting Up SQL Worksheet 66
Asking a Question in SQL 67
    The basic SQL query 67
    Some sample queries 68
    Some tips to help you write good queries 69
Using an Editor While Running SQL*Plus Worksheet 71
Pulling Out Data Without Breaking Anything 72
Combining Tables: The Meat and Potatoes of SQL 73
    Basic join query structure 73
    Examples of join queries 74
Using the Built-In Functions of Oracle8i 76
    Reformatting a date with TO_CHAR 76
    Concatenating columns with CONCATENATE (||) 77
Grouping and Summarizing Data 78
Making Power Changes in the Data 79
    Modifying data with the UPDATE command 80
    Inserting new rows with grace and style 85
    Deleting rows with distinction 87
Fixing Mistakes, or Where's the Brake?! 88
    The COMMIT and ROLLBACK commands 88
    Commands that can't be undone, even with ROLLBACK 89

Chapter 4: Object SQL: The New Stuff 91

Starting Up SQL Worksheet 93
Querying Object Tables in SQL 94
   The basic object-oriented SQL query 95
   Queries using a nested table 97
   Queries using a varray 100
Making Changes to Object Table Data 101
   Updating an object 102
   Updating one row in a nested table 102
   Inserting rows into an object table 102
   Inserting rows into a varray 103
   Inserting rows into a nested table 104
   Deleting rows from an object table 105
   Deleting a row from a nested table 105

Chapter 5: Using the Enterprise Manager DBA Tools 107

Managing the Enterprise Manager 107
Exploring Three Cornerstone Tools 109
   Storage Manager: The external viewpoint 110
   Security Manager: The keeper of the gate 112
   Schema Manager: The builder of tables 115

Part II: Getting Started *121*

Chapter 6: The Relational Model and You 123

Redundant Relational Database Redundancy 123
Keys Rule 124
   Considering types of keys 125
   Importing foreign keys 125
The Key, the Whole Key, and Nothing but the Key 128
One to Many: The Bread and Butter of Relational Databases 132
Objects and the Oracle8i Database 133
   Defining an object 134
   Connecting relational tables with objects 135

Chapter 7: Diagramming Your World 137

Getting Something Down on Paper 137
Using Tree Diagrams: Easy When You Know the Lingo 140
Hooking Up with Objects 143
Understanding the Basic UML Type Model Diagram 144

**Chapter 8: Getting Familiar with Oracle8i Data-Dictionary
Views** 147

Viewing Oracle8i's Data-Dictionary Views 147
Using Data-Dictionary Views 148
Looking at Data-Dictionary Views with the SQL*Plus Worksheet . . .150

Chapter 9: Oracle's User **153**

Playing a Role 153
What kinds of users are there? 154
What kind of user are you? 155
Creating a New User from Scratch 159
Changing Your Password 163
Changing your password in SQL*Plus Worksheet 163
Changing any user's password in Security Manager 164
Changing User Identity 165
Connecting anew in Enterprise Manager tools 165

Part III: Putting Oracle8i to Work *167*

Chapter 10: Defining Tables, Tablespaces, and Columns **169**

Tablespace: The Final Frontier 169
A Word or Two about Columns 170
Defining columns in Oracle8i 170
Allowing nulls or not 175
A Table of Your Own with SQL 175
Schema Manager's Wizard for Tables 178

Chapter 11: Creating Object Types, Objects, and References **185**

Types Need No Space 187
Defining an object type 188
Making a table type 191
Creating an array type 194
Objects Still Sit inside Tablespaces 196
Making an object table 196
Making hybrid tables 198

Chapter 12: Security Options: Roles, Profiles, and Grants **201**

Security Blanket Included 201
Roles Meet the Real World 203
Roles and Privileges with Security Manager 205
Creating a role 205
Assigning users to a role 207
Assigning privileges to roles 210
Roles and Privileges with SQL 212
Profiles: The Power Players 215
Creating a profile 216
Assigning a profile to a user 218

Chapter 13: Views and Synonyms: Do You See What I See? **221**

Views: Like a Table — Almost 222
Views that narrow 223
Views that tie everything together 227

Views with Schema Manager 228
Object views with Schema Manager 231
Synonyms: Nicknames for Tables and Views 236
Good uses for synonyms 238
A grant and a synonym combined 239

Chapter 14: WebDB: The Best New Tool for the Internet **241**

Exploring WebDB 242
Assigning WebDB Developers 244
Creating a Web Report 246
Going for a Form 252

Chapter 15: Java and the Internet Database **259**

Discovering Java Virtual Machine (JVM) 259
Using Oracle8i's JVM — some benefits 260
Introducing SQLJ 261
Creating a Stored Database Procedure with Java and SQLJ 261
Step 1: Writing Java code with embedded SQLJ 262
Step 2: Loading the Java into the database 264
Step 3: Creating a SQL wrapper for the Java code 265
Step 4: Using the SQL wrapper in a SQL query 266
Running a Java Stored Procedure from a Java Applet on the Web 267

Chapter 16: The Five Ws of Safeguarding Your Data **269**

Why Back Up — Onward and Upward! 269
What to Back Up 270
When to Back Up (Before You Go off the Cliff) 271
How to Back Up (Choosing Your Backup Weapon) 273
Data Manager 273
EXP and IMP commands 282
Where to Hide Your Backup Files 287

Part IV: Tuning Up and Turbocharging *289*

Chapter 17: What's Slowing Your Query Down? **291**

Helping the Optimizer Do Its Job 291
Moods and modes of the Optimizer 292
One command to analyze your entire schema 293
Personal attention: Analyzing one table at a time ..294
A hint . . . you're getting warmer 295
Getting Ahead While Testing and Tuning 296
Baby steps versus giant leaps 297
The SQL*Plus Worksheet's timing 297

Chapter 18: Speeding Up Queries with Keys and Indexes **301**

Why Create an Index? 302
Adding and Removing a Primary Key 303
 Adding a primary key 304
 Removing a primary key 308
Creating and Dropping Foreign Keys 309
 Adding a foreign key 309
 Removing a foreign key 313
Creating Your Own Indexes 314
 Adding an index 315
 Removing an index 317
Using Indexes with Object Tables and Nested Tables 319
 Creating an index on an object table 319
 Creating an index on a nested table 320
 Removing an index on an object table or a nested table 321
Oracle's Brain on Indexes 321
 Do you have an index? 322
 The infamous null value and the index 322
 Wildcards can throw everything off 323
 The logically illogical order of data 323

Chapter 19: Correcting Flaws **325**

Categories of Column Changes 325
Baby Bear: Easy as Porridge 327
Mama Bear: A Few Medium Steps 329
 If the column must be null. 329
 Column must not have nulls 332
Papa Bear: A Lotta Steps 333
Modification of Object Tables in Schema Manager 340

Part V: The Part of Tens *343*

Chapter 20: Ten Tips for Good Design **345**

Name Tables and Columns Creatively and Clearly 345
Look Before You Leap (Design Before You Build) 347
Go Ahead, Leap! (Build a Prototype) 348
Share — Don't Reinvent the Wheel 348
Remember that Primary Keys Are Your Friends 349
 Small keys take up less room 349
 Nonintelligent keys are easy to maintain 349
Use Caution When Modifying Table Definitions 352
Handle Derived Data Efficiently 352

Approach Security Roles in Practical Ways 354
    Low security 354
    Medium security 354
    High security 355
Be Smart about Test Data 355
Talk to Non-Techie-Type Humans 356

Chapter 21: Ten Handy Oracle8i Features **359**
ConText Cartridge 359
Network Computer Architecture 360
Web Assistant 360
Migration Assistant for Access 361
Data Migration Assistant 361
File Packager 362
Database Configuration Assistant 362
Net8 362
Performance Monitor 363
Sniffing Out and Mending Broken Relationships 363

Part VI: Appendixes *365*

Appendix A: Glossary **367**

Appendix B: About the CD **375**
Sample Schemas 375
    Build the AMY schema 375
    Create the AMYOBJ schema 377
    Create the BAKERY schema 378
Sample SQL Scripts 379
Additional Software 380
    SQL tools from Quest Software 381
    Web Design tools from Allaire Corporation 381
    Miscellaneous tools from 4Developers LLC 382

Index *383*

IDG Books Worldwide End-User License Agreement *402*

Installation Instructions *404*

Book Registration Information ....*Back of Book*

Foreword

● ●

*P*erhaps the subtitle for this book should be *An Aperitif,* because in a sense it is just that. Many volumes would be required to do justice to the entire Oracle8i meal because it consists of many courses and each one has a large array of spices and condiments to enhance the experience. But although developing an appetite for such a meal takes time, this book's taste of what's ahead is quick and fun and won't leave you feeling ill the following day.

My introduction to Oracle came during a 1980 interview at Relational Software, Inc. (as the company was then known) when Bob Miner was showing me a few things on his terminal. Distinctly brilliant and a great guy who was much loved by the developers, Bob was current Oracle CEO Larry Ellison's partner on the technical side. I remember being particularly taken by the elegance and simplicity of SQL when Bob explained that the output of any query (on a table or set of tables) was itself another table. The next year, I was helping Bob, Bruce Scott (who played a key role in early development — Bruce's cat's name is the password in Oracle's ubiquitous SCOTT/TIGER user), and others develop Oracle Version 3, a complete rewrite in the C language. This investment in portability was one of the early design decisions that enabled Oracle8i to become the best database on the market today.

If this book is your introduction to Oracle8i, you're in for a treat. Carol McCullough-Dieter covers complex and difficult material in a straightforward and conversational manner. But rather than boring you with details, she touches on key points and new features (like WebDB). Doing so not only gets you started but also inspires you. Carol's lighthearted style is backed by many years of experience.

If you're new to relational databases, you'll appreciate this book's many examples of simple database designs. In the two chapters on relational theory alone, you find many examples, ranging from doctor's office information to breadmaking. As you consider each example, you begin to get a feel for how relational databases are used to model real-world situations.

Carol McCullough-Dieter's background as a database administrator is evident when she discusses important issues such as backup and recovery, security, space allocation, and the way Oracle8i actually works inside. Sections on using indexes and tuning SQL statements are a definite plus.

So if you're hungry to find out about the database that gives Bill Gates indigestion, this snack — *Oracle8i For Dummies* — is a great place to start!

My company, Rare & Dear, Inc., is a Hawaii-based consulting group focused on the design and administration of Oracle databases in high-performance Web sites. As our name indicates, we're committed to excellence in our staff, the work that we do, and, of course, the place where we live! If you're interested in our company, you can reach us at 888-RareDear (888-727-3332) or check out our own (small) Web site at www.rare-dear.com.

Ned Dana

Principal Consultant and Toolmaster

Rare & Dear, Inc.

Introduction

● ●

Or-a-cle (noun) 1: a person (such as a priestess of ancient Greece) through whom a deity is believed to speak. 2: an authoritative or wise expression or answer. 3: an anagram of the name Carole.

That definition pretty much says it all, doesn't it? You've got Oracle8i. You've got the database to beat all databases. You've got the cream of the crop, the tip of the top, the best of the best, the oracle from which all wisdom and answers flow. And if you only had your own Greek priestess to consult, you'd have no problem figuring out how to use the pesky thing!

Besides being one of the best relational database packages around, Oracle8i is one of the most complex. Oracle8i does some very fancy things, but the easy things are sometimes tricky.

Fear not, for you have come to the right place. This book is the Oracle's oracle, written by the high priestess of database knowledge. Well, all right, I'm just a normal human being, but I have lots of experience as a database programmer and database administrator with Oracle7, Oracle8, and Oracle8i. I had to find out the hard way — on the job, bribing nerds with doughnuts, and even (shudder!) reading manuals. You can benefit from my experiences when you read this book, which easily guides you along the path to Oracle enlightenment with more fun than you're supposed to have at work.

This book focuses on Oracle Version 8.1 or higher. The vast majority of the subject matter applies to PCs, Macs, and mainframes and to all platforms from Windows to MacOS to UNIX. When appropriate, I show you how to use the Enterprise Manager, Oracle8i's desktop toolset. The Enterprise Manager comes as standard equipment with your basic Oracle8i database engine. All the figures used to illustrate the step-by-step instructions for the Enterprise Manager are shown on a Windows NT 4.0 computer. If you're using a different platform for Enterprise Manager, you may see some slight differences in the figures, but the steps should work on all platforms.

Why This Book Makes Sense

Oracle8i puts its entire software documentation — the manuals — on a CD-ROM. Putting the documentation on CD saves a lot of trees but doesn't help you much because the CD version is cross-referenced about as well as the old paperback volumes. If you know what the answer is before you start looking, the answer is really easy to find. If you don't know the answer, you may spend days trying to discover it.

This book gives you answers fast. Use it to get results quickly and easily. Hide it under your Oracle8i manuals and then dazzle your friends with your incredible know-how!

Some Basic Assumptions

To keep this book focused on database matters, I make some assumptions about your innate (or acquired) talents. You . . .

- ✔ Own or have access to Oracle8i and Enterprise Manager (on any platform)
- ✔ Use tables that others create and sometimes create tables yourself
- ✔ Use and create queries and reports and sometimes enter data
- ✔ Are comfortable using a mouse and Windows (not a requirement)

Quickie Overview of This Book

So that you can quickly and easily find topics that you want to know more about, I've divided this book into six parts. Here's a quick look at what's inside:

Part I: Road Map

In this part, you find important concepts and definitions that are used throughout the book. Chapter 1 is an introduction to Oracle8i; it includes a quick discussion of tasks that a database can (and can't) be used to accomplish. This part provides an in-depth look at SQL*Plus Worksheet, a utility that uses the SQL programming language to let you get at your data. Use it now and use it well.

Part II: Getting Started

An important aspect of using Oracle8i is knowing how an object-relational database puts together all the pieces of data that it stores. Even if you never design a table of your own, knowing a few of the basics helps you make better use of the database. Look in this part to find out how to read a diagram — you know, those strange-looking drawings with boxes and lines that look like a cross between a floor plan and a crossword puzzle.

I also explain the basics about objects and show you how Oracle8i uses them.

Part II also takes a look backstage at the props Oracle8i uses to keep track of you and all the things that you and others create. You find a bit of technical stuff here, but it's carefully contained with the proper hexes and spells, so don't worry.

Part III: Putting Oracle8i to Work

This part launches right into the heart of using Oracle8i. Here's where you find out how to create a table or two. After you create some tables, you may be upset if they get lost or get changed by some ham-handed programmer (possibly even someone who looks suspiciously like yourself). That's where the sections on security, backups, and sharing data come in really handy.

Finally, with tables in place, you're ready to find out if you can actually use the data in some way. Contrary to the opinion of many techno-systems analysts, data is actually intended for some purpose other than calculating disk storage space.

Part IV: Tuning Up and Turbocharging

After you give SQL a whirl, you're ready to find out why executing a three-line SQL command takes three days. Part IV looks at what's slowing you down, how to speed everything up, and what to do when you hit a speed bump, a wall, or some other obstacle that can slow you down.

Part V: The Part of Tens

The wonderful Part of Tens. Does this part remind you of grade school, when you had to count ten sticks, wrap a rubber band around them, and then repeat the process ten times to make a hundred? Only me, huh? The Part of Tens covers the same ground as the previous four parts but focuses on quick, really useful tips that can save you hours of research. Dazzle your toddler, your neighbor's dog, and maybe even your boss with your cunning.

Part VI: Appendixes

Appendix A contains a glossary, and Appendix B tells you what's on the CD-ROM that's attached to the inside of the back cover of this book.

Of Mice and Sven (Mouse Moves and Special Text)

For the most part, you don't need to do any special mouse functions because this book is mouse independent and covers Oracle8i on a lot of different platforms. Once in a while, I illustrate how to use the Oracle8i toolset for Windows: the Enterprise Manager. In these cases, your mouse does the walking. For clarity, here's the way I define mouse activities:

- ✔ **Select:** Highlight a word or phrase by clicking it. Sometimes you need to click, hold, and drag the mouse to the end of the word or phrase to highlight the entire section.
- ✔ **Click:** Select an object with the mouse by pointing at it and clicking one time with the left mouse button.
- ✔ **Double-click:** Point at an object and click twice with the left mouse button.
- ✔ **Right-click:** Point and click with the right mouse button.

So what does Sven have to do with it? Nothing, really. He's just a friendly fellow who wants to say everything clearly. He's here to tell you that when you see the kind of font on the next line, it means one of two things:

```
I am something you type into the computer.
```

or (where indicated)

```
I am what your computer says back to you.
```

Here's what words channeled from the little voice in my head look like:

You are so funny I could die.

Just kidding on that last one.

In the sections that talk about the Enterprise Manager tools, sometimes I tell you to use a menu command, like File⇨Open. You can execute this command by moving your mouse pointer up to the File menu, clicking it, and then choosing the Open command.

On a final note, Oracle8i is not case sensitive, so you may see table, row, or column names in uppercase or lowercase throughout this book.

Icons Used in This Book

All the *...For Dummies* books use icons to help you pick out the important details without having to read the fine print. Here are the icons that you find sprinkled like confetti around the pages of this book.

Watch for this icon to highlight new Oracle8i features. This version of Oracle includes some fun new Web-related features that you might like.

As you may have guessed, this icon marks some technical details that you can avoid or indulge in, depending on your mood. I take great pains to keep these sections to the size of your palm so that you can conveniently cover them up if you want.

This icon signifies hard-won information, from time-saving tricks to shortcuts.

Reserved for important and critical details, this icon is your cue to read carefully. Missing the stuff next to this icon can mean missing an important step and creating a query that never dies or some such freak of nature.

Watch out here. You may have to walk through a minefield to get to your goal. This icon shows you the safest route to take.

This icon alerts you to new terms and their definitions. Plain English gets you a long way in this book, but occasionally, I fall back on a commonly used technical term. When I do, I mark it with this icon and put the word in *italics*.

You can find lots and lots of examples in this book. This icon shows where the discussion ends and the action begins.

I use this icon to tell you about SQL— specific information — just the raw, bare facts of SQL code. The icon appears wherever clear and concise syntax must be followed for good results. I use a different font for SQL code and add this symbol to help set it apart.

 The Enterprise Manager has some really handy tools. Watch for this icon to see concrete examples of the various tools in action.

 I use this icon to tell you about related software included on the CD-ROM that comes with this book.

Bells and whistles that Oracle8i doesn't have

Perhaps you bought Oracle8i from the Oracle Store on the Internet. Perhaps you work with Oracle8i on the job. Whatever way you came to work with Oracle8i, I want to clear something up right now: You have at your command a truly versatile and complex database engine, but Oracle8i doesn't have all the niceties that software buyers take for granted in this age of plug-and-play technology.

Oracle8i by itself is not like Microsoft Access or Paradox, programs that include everything in one box, ready and easy to use. Oracle8i is very plain in appearance and has very few reporting or form-building features.

You paid for raw power. You don't get the nice, fun bells and whistles unless you pay more.

This book covers how to use the basic Oracle8i relational database engine using WebDB, the Enterprise Manager DBA Management Pack, and SQL. I show you how to tap the Oracle8i power at the source — and that knowledge enables you to better utilize the additional software tools that support Oracle8i.

Part I
Road Map

The 5th Wave   By Rich Tennant

AFTER DISCOVERING THE LAND OF LOST FILES, BILL AND IRWIN RUN INTO A TRIBE OF SQL NATIVES.

THIS IS GONNA BE TRICKY. THEY PROBABLY ALL SPEAK A DIFFERENT LANGUAGE.

In this part . . .

*B*efore I launch you full tilt into the brave new world of Oracle8i, Part I paves the way with bits of knowledge.

The motto of Part I is "Forewarned is forearmed!" I figure it's better to have some idea of what's in the refrigerator before you start making a birthday cake. Otherwise, you're running to the store in the middle of it all for a teaspoon of vanilla. With that in mind, Part I gives you a nice tour of all the tools that come as standard equipment with Oracle8i.

If you have a database to play with, this part also shows you how to create queries so you can see what you've gotten into.

Chapter 1

A Quick Tour of Oracle8i

In This Chapter

▶ Discovering what you've gotten into

▶ Starting Oracle8i

▶ Inspecting your tools

▶ Meeting Enterprise Manager

▶ Checking out the Schema Manager

▶ Landing in the Enterprise brig for "checking out" Schema Manager

▶ Glancing at SQL*Plus and SQL*Plus Worksheet

▶ Weaving through WebDB

▶ Shutting down Oracle8i

*W*ell, you lucky duck! Your world is about to expand into the great undiscovered country called Oracle8i. Actually, the territory is not really unknown because some of us have boldly ventured there and returned with a map. I suppose that you would have preferred Chinese takeout or doughnuts. Sorry, Charlie.

This chapter is your guide map. You look at what Oracle8i is all about and what components it includes; then you rev it up and give it a test drive.

Discovering Oracle8i: The Program That Runs It All

Once upon a time, back in the '70s, there was a man named Larry Ellison who built a great big software program called Oracle. The Oracle program lived in a giant mainframe, and when it fired up its boilers and started huffing and puffing, it expanded to the size of a house. Only the biggest mainframes had room for Oracle.

Then one day, a neighbor of Larry's saw what the big Oracle program could do and told Larry, "Hey! I want one, too, but my mainframe can't handle that really big program. If you make me a smaller one, I'll pay you big bucks."

Larry took the challenge and, in less than a year, created another Oracle program to fit into the smaller mainframe. He delivered it to his neighbor, who exclaimed, "It's a miracle!"

This exchange inspired Larry to think that other small-computer owners would want the Oracle program. So Larry went to all corners of the earth, found the best engineers, and gathered them together in the Promised Land of California to help him create Oracle for all sizes and shapes of computers.

Today, the Oracle engine is all that Larry dreamed it could be — and more. With Oracle8i, you're sitting on a database powerhouse. And they all lived happily ever after.

Oracle8i's core package

Figure 1-1 shows the Oracle8i database engine and the core utilities that are standard equipment with Oracle8i, regardless of your operating system or hardware. These core utilities and the database itself behave the same on all platforms. The differences are on the inside, where Oracle8i takes advantage of each computer's unique features for storage, reading, writing, and so on.

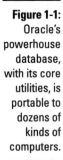

Figure 1-1:
Oracle's powerhouse database, with its core utilities, is portable to dozens of kinds of computers.

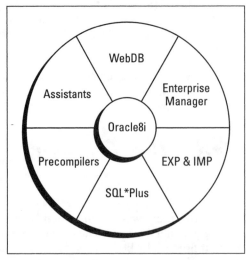

The core utilities are

- ✔ **WebDB.** Wait 'til you see what this can do! You can build Web pages that are stored as programs in the database and deliver on-demand data to the Internet or an intranet. I feature WebDB in several chapters of the book. Here's the best part: You don't need to know HTML, PL/SQL, or SQL to use this tool! You do need some kind of Web server (not included in the database . . . yet).

- ✔ **Enterprise Manager.** Oracle8i continues this feature, which was introduced as an add-on for Oracle7. This tool saves a great deal of code-writing by aiding you with menus and windows for many database-administrator tasks, such as creating new users and tables. The utility's easy-to-use tools make anyone a savvy *DBA* (database administrator) in no time! You'll love it! The latest edition of Enterprise Manager (Version 2) is packed with great tools, lots of documentation, and many advanced features I can't even get to in this book. So much data, so little time!

  Much of this book focuses on how to use this versatile and time-saving utility. Read on in this chapter for a better look at Enterprise Manager.

- ✔ **SQL*Plus.** This tool allows you to create and run queries, add rows, modify data, and write reports. To use SQL*Plus, you must figure out SQL, the Standard Query Language. You can use this language in nearly any relational database. The Oracle8i version is called SQL*Plus because Oracle embellished the usual SQL suite of commands. These embellishments allow you to customize reports, edit and save files, define variables, and do other cool stuff. You can even perform duties that are typically reserved for database administrators (DBAs), such as creating new users.

  I don't feature SQL*Plus directly, but I use SQL*Plus Worksheet, an Enterprise Manager tool, whenever I need to show you SQL commands. You see SQL examples that you can run in SQL*Plus in many of the chapters.

- ✔ **EXP and IMP.** You can export (EXP) data to or import (IMP) data from any Oracle8i database. You can use EXP on a PC to copy into a file data and tables that you created, for example. You can move this file to a UNIX computer, an IBM mainframe, or any other platform that has an Oracle8i database and then use IMP to place the information in that database.

- ✔ **Precompilers.** A bunch of precompilers are available; actually, there's one for each programming language, such as COBOL, Ada, C, C++, Pascal, and FORTRAN. The mix varies on different platforms (hardware/operating systems). I don't cover precompilers at all in this book; you need to know a programming language to use them.

✔ **Assistants.** Introduced in Oracle8, the assistants are wizards to guide you through tasks like migrating from Oracle7 to Oracle8i, moving an Access database into Oracle8i, and translating relational database structures into objects. There is an assistant to help you create Web pages and to help make network connections to Oracle8i databases.

✔ **Net8.** This tool is your key to communicating with a remote database. The tool comes with a wizard and assistant to help you configure your networked computer to reach any remote Oracle database on your network.

Oracle8i's newest star: WebDB

Larry Ellison was serious about making Oracle8i the Internet database! The WebDB tool is a melding of some older tools that required you to program a lot and some design tools that were not for the Internet. So, what is it? The really cool feature of WebDB is that all your work is done using Java-based Web pages that you run from your own browser.

WebDB consists of these parts:

✔ **Data browser.** Here is a way to see the data in your database without writing a query! And it's all in your Web browser!

✔ **Web page design toolset.** These tools are all run in your browser and use fill-in-the-blank boxes to guide you through the steps of creating various kinds of Web pages, such as reports, charts, and data entry forms. I give this a run for the money in Chapter 14.

✔ **Shared component toolset.** This part of WebDB allows you to create reusable objects, such as a list of values for a particular column in the database or a connection between a summary report and a detail report. The easiest parts of WebDB to use are the report-writing tools. I touch on this in Chapter 14.

✔ **WebDB administration toolset.** Here you tell WebDB who is allowed to create Web pages, what port to run the Web pages in, and other administrative details.

✔ **Site builder toolset.** This toolset is one of the newer features of WebDB and is both powerful and complex. I don't use it in the book.

WebDB has a lot of built-in templates that help you get a quick start on Web pages that have a polished look. You can also create your own templates, of course.

WebDB is aimed at professional application designers, so it has a lot of openings where you are free to add customized PL/SQL code if you wish. However, if you are just starting out, you can skip over those openings and still create great-looking Web pages.

Enterprise Manager

Whether you're working with Oracle8i on an IBM mainframe, Windows 98, Windows NT, or UNIX, you get this awesome toolbox: the Enterprise Manager. Enterprise Manager has a bunch of nice utilities that bring Oracle into the Windows world better than ever.

The Enterprise Manager, Version 2 (released in March, 1999), is based on Java clients that perform all the tasks. The new version has modified the components of Enterprise Manager quite a bit. You can now use the Enterprise Manager in three ways:

- ✔ **Access the DBA Management Pack locally.** This is the easiest way to use Enterprise Manager and requires minimal setup. I use this way of accessing the database throughout the book.

- ✔ **Access the DBA Management Pack via the Web.** You can run the DBA Management Pack from the Web only if you perform all the configuration steps required to run the Enterprise Manager Console from the Web.

- ✔ **Access the Enterprise Manager Console using a local Enterprise Manager Server.** Though this tool has been given a great deal more power to handle sites with multiple databases, it has also become more complex to configure and use. I show you how to start the console later in this chapter. However, most of the work is done outside the console.

- ✔ **Access the Enterprise Manager Console via the Web using a remote Enterprise Manager Server.** All the tools in Enterprise Manager are now Java-based, so moving them from running locally to running via the Web is a small step. Unfortunately, because this feature is very new, the exact setup must be done by hand rather than with wizards or installation setup scripts. Watch for vast improvements to this feature in later releases.

Here, I look more closely at the DBA Management Pack, which is the part of Enterprise Manager that I use the most in this book.

DBA Management Pack packs five all-star tools

The *management pack* is a new term used for add-on components for the Enterprise Manager. The DBA Management Pack is simply a rebundling of the primary database tools that were included in prior versions of Enterprise Manager. Oracle sells many other management packs.

Much of this book describes step-by-step instructions on how to use these tools to administer your database easily without requiring you to figure out SQL.

The DBA Management Pack includes these tools:

- ✔ **Schema Manager.** This tool allows you to see your database much like your Explorer (Windows NT) layout, using icons for tables, users, and other parts of the database. You can arrange all the objects in your database by type or by owner. You can add or change tables, indexes, views, keys, and columns here. I give you lots of examples of using this tool in the book.

- ✔ **Security Manager.** This tool makes creating users, setting and changing passwords, and assigning roles so easy that it's hard to make a mistake.

- ✔ **Instance Manager.** Sometimes, two or more Oracle databases are running on the same computer or within the same network configuration. Each database is called an *instance*. The Instance Manager allows you to see an overview of the activity on one instance at a time. You see who is logged on, what the user is doing, and whether the user is in trouble. Even if you have only one instance running, this tool is a troubleshooting aid. It is also a convenient place to start and stop the database.

- ✔ **Storage Manager.** Add more space to your database as easily as you create a new directory on your hard drive. This handy tool allows you to review and modify the data files and tablespaces that you use in your database.

The Storage Manager now has a direct link to the Backup Management Wizards and the Data Management Wizards. You can also access the Data Management Wizard through the Enterprise Manager console. I show how to use the Data Management Wizard in Chapter 16.

- ✔ **SQL*Plus Worksheet.** This tool replaces the SQL Worksheet found in earlier releases of Enterprise Manager. The worksheet is an alternative to running SQL*Plus from a line command or a plain window. You have a split window to use. The upper window allows you to type and edit SQL commands. The lower window executes your commands and displays the results. The SQL*Plus Worksheet makes editing SQL much easier than editing SQL in SQL*Plus. Use SQL*Plus Worksheet to run actual SQL commands that I show you in the book.

Starting Up Oracle8i

I know a lot of you are using Oracle8i on a mainframe or on a network. Oracle8i should be up and running as part of the initial startup routine for the computer. If not, you can use the Enterprise Manager. An alternative is to use the line command tool, Server Manager, as I describe in the section later in this chapter called "Starting Oracle8i using the Server Manager."

Starting the database with the Instance Manager

To get your Oracle8i database on its feet, follow these steps:

1. **Start up the Instance Manager.**

   If you have Windows 95, 98, or NT, choose Start⇨Programs⇨ Oracle HOME2⇨DBA Management Pack⇨Instance Manager.

   Note that the Oracle HOME2 label might have a different name, such as HOME1, on your computer. The exact name is designated by the person who installed the software on your machine.

   On UNIX, type the following command at an operating system command line:

   ```
   oemapp instance
   ```

   You see the initialization screen for Oracle Enterprise Manager, and then the login window appears, as shown in Figure 1-2.

Figure 1-2: The initial login window for the Instance Manager is the same for any of the DBA Management Pack tools.

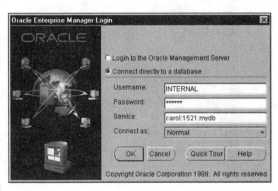

2. **Log in as INTERNAL.**

   Choose the radio button labeled "Connect directly to a database." Type **INTERNAL** as the user name and use **ORACLE** (or whatever your current password is) for the password. Either leave the Service box blank or type in the appropriate name of your Oracle network node.

   Take a moment to write down the login information on your cheat sheet! You can find the cheat sheet in the front of this book. It is a tear-out sheet with images and notes on it. Find the section labeled "Place Your Login Information HERE." It has a picture of the login screen that looks just like Figure 1-2, except the boxes are all blank. Use the charts to record the user name, password, and service entry that work for you. Keep the cheat sheet in a safe place! Don't tape it to your monitor. In fact, if you have any doubts, leave the password off and memorize it.

The next window you see is the Instance Manager's main page.

3. Click the Database label and observe the traffic light.

The Database icon is near the top of the tree shown in the left window. The icon becomes highlighted when you click on it. The traffic light graphic appears in the right window. If the light is green, your database is open and running. If the light is red, your database is closed and needs to be started. A yellow light means that the database is either started or mounted but not open for business. (There are certain recovery steps where you must have the database mounted but not open.) Figure 1-3 shows the Instance Manager window with a closed database.

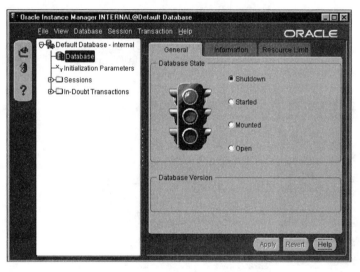

Figure 1-3:
When a database is shut down, the traffic light is red and the radio button labeled Shutdown is selected.

4. Start up the database, if needed.

If the traffic light is red, start up the database by clicking the Database Open radio button in the right window. Next, click Apply. You will be asked what initialization parameters to use. Click OK to use the default set of parameters. Then you get a status message saying that Oracle8i is running. Click OK and you now see the traffic light with a green light.

5. Exit the Instance Manager by clicking the X box in the upper-right corner.

Now you are ready to look around at the database.

Starting Oracle8i using the Server Manager

Do not start up Oracle8i without permission from your DBA every time. On mainframes, processes that require the database to be closed (such as a file backup) may be running. Check with your DBA, if you have one. The most common startup method, even for mainframe databases, is using the Enterprise Manager's Instance Manager as I describe in the preceding sections. Another alternative is to use the Server Manager. This startup method is probably more commonly used with mainframes but works on all the platforms. Here are the steps to start up the database with the Server Manager:

1. **Start up the Server Manager.**

   From the command line prompt on a computer that is running Oracle8i, type

   ```
   svrmgrl
   ```

   Press Enter. The Server Manager sends some status lines and starts up. Your command line prompt changes so you know you are running Server Manager. The prompt looks like this:

   ```
   SVRMGR>
   ```

2. **Connect to the database. Type**

   ```
   connect internal
   ```

   Server Manager replies

   ```
   Connected.
   ```

3. **Start the database.**

   Type

   ```
   startup
   ```

   Press Enter. The Server Manager starts up the database and replies

   ```
   ORACLE instance started.
   Total System Global Area 12071016 bytes
   Fixed Size                   46136 bytes
   Variable Size             11090992 bytes
   Database Buffers            409600 bytes
   Redo Buffers                524288 bytes
   Database mounted.
   Database opened.
   ```

The exact statistics you see may be different from the listing in this step.

4. **Exit Server Manager.**

Type

```
quit
```

Press Enter. Server Manager replies

```
Server Manager Complete.
```

Your prompt returns to its normal state.

Whether you use the Instance Manager or the Server Manager, you get the thing running! After the database is started, you can take a look around and see what the database looks like on the inside. The next section begins your grand tour.

Looking Around with Schema Manager

First, make sure your Oracle8i database is running by following the steps in the previous section. Then start up the Schema Manager by following these steps:

1. **Start the Schema Manager.**

If you have Windows 95, 98, or NT, select Start⇨Programs⇨ Oracle HOME2⇨DBA Management Pack⇨Schema Manager. The standard login window appears, asking for your input.

On UNIX, type:

```
oemapp schema
```

2. **Log in as a DBA Oracle user, such as the SYSTEM user.**

Choose the radio button labeled Connect Directly to a Database. SYSTEM is a built-in user name that comes with every Oracle8i database. The default password for SYSTEM is MANAGER. Use this or type in the user name and password of any valid Oracle8i user with DBA privileges. Leave the Service box blank to reach your PC's database or type in the instance name of the Oracle8i database on your network. Leave the Connect As box with the default of Normal.

Figure 1-4 shows the Schema Manager login window.

Get your cheat sheet out again. Find the section labeled "Place your login information here." Use the charts to write in the user name, the password, and the service entries that work for you. Remember, you're using a high-level login name and password, so protect them with your life!

Figure 1-4:
This login
window
looks just
like that
other login
window, but
you log in as
a DBA for
Schema
Manager.

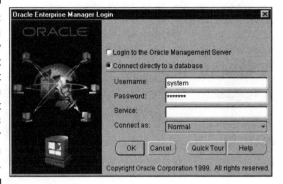

After you log on, you see the initial screen of the Schema Manager.

3. Double-click on the Tables folder in the left half of the window.

A list of tables appears on the right half. A list of schemas (table owners) appears under the Tables folder in the left half of the window. Your screen should look like Figure 1-5.

Notice how neatly the Schema Manager arranges the files, icons, and buttons you use to work with Oracle8i. This setup is certainly much neater than my husband's arrangement of tools, documents, and other assorted items on his workbench.

Figuring out the parts of Schema Manager that I highlight in Figure 1-5 helps you to get around like a pro. Think of the figure as a VCR manual. No, actually, it's a whole lot simpler than that. Just don't try to set the clock.

The Schema Manager window has two important groups of elements: the Object and Object Contents windows and everything else.

The Object window

The Object (left side) and Object Contents (right side) windows give you a visual representation of all the objects that you can access in Oracle8i. *Objects* are any of several kinds of things in a database, such as indexes, tables, packages, views, and synonyms. This book shows you many examples of how to use the Schema Manager to create and fix database tables, indexes, views, and synonyms. Some of the other objects — such as packages, procedures, and clusters — are beyond the scope of this book, and you don't need them for starters anyway. These objects come into play when you perform advanced DBA tasks that only a supergeek enjoys. (See the appendix for instructions on how to create your very own little tinfoil hat to protect you from the evil thought rays sent to you through your dental fillings by the government.)

Toolbar   Folder titles (double-click to expand or shrink folder)

Main menu   Object contents window

Object window   Column titles (click to sort by column)

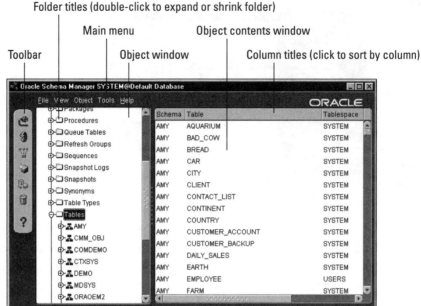

Figure 1-5:
Schema
Manager
manages
database
objects,
such as
tables.

The cool thing about the Schema Manager is that it uses many of the basics about getting around that you probably already know from Windows 95, 98, or NT Explorer. Here are some examples:

✔ The left frame shows a hierarchy of objects available for you to look at. The right frame shows the contents of whatever you select (via a mouse click) on the left side.

✔ Click the plus or minus signs next to the icons in the left frame to expand or contract the contents.

✔ Right-click an object to get a little menu that tells what you can do with the object.

✔ Double-click objects in the left frame to expand or contract them.

✔ Click the Table icon to see a list of all the tables owned by all the users in the database.

✔ Click the column headers in the right frame to rearrange the list, sorting by the heading that you click.

✔ Click the menu items across the top to see context-sensitive menu selections.

✔ Click and drag the edges of the window or dividing frame to change the dimensions of the window or frame.

✔ If you get lost, click the Help button, which offers context-sensitive instructions.

All the Managers that are available in the Enterprise Manager work in similar ways. As you discover how to use the Schema Manager, you develop skills that you can use later with the other Enterprise Manager tools.

By the way, if you have Windows 98 and are not familiar with it, check out *Windows 98 For Dummies* by Andy Rathbone (published by IDG Books Worldwide, Inc.) for a good start.

The other Schema Manager elements

The Object frame and the Object Contents frame are far from the only elements in the Schema Manager. Look for these additional goodies:

- ✔ **Control-menu button.** This barely noticeable button looks like the beginning of a genealogy tree. You can click this button to see a menu of standard controls — Exit, Move, and so on. Most of these controls are unnecessary when you know how to use the mouse and the Windows control buttons.

- ✔ **Windows control buttons.** These buttons are standard Windows controls for moving the window to the bottom taskbar, filling the entire screen, and closing the window. (Close the window; I feel a draft.)

- ✔ **Title bar.** If you are not sure where you are, the title bar tells you. If you are still not sure, go ask your mother. Also, if you click the title bar and drag, you move the entire frame. (I wish I could do that with the window over my sink; it's too close to the refrigerator. But I'm rarely in drag in my kitchen anyway.)

- ✔ **Main menu bar.** In this menu bar, you find the usual collection of menus, such as File, View, and Help. A click of any of them shows the options that are available.

- ✔ **Toolbar.** This bar shows little buttons of tools that you have available. You use most of these tools only occasionally. Nearly all the tools are available either by right-clicking or by clicking a menu bar. The buttons are (from top to bottom):

    - • **Change Database.** This button gives you a new login window so that you can switch to a different database instance without leaving your session.

    - • **Refresh.** Surprise! This button updates your windows with the latest data. Aaaaaaaah! How refreshing!

    - • **Show dependencies.** This button looks like an electronic circuit board to me. Use this button to find out how your table connects to other tables. Oracle8i goes hunting for foreign keys and lists the tables that reference the current table.

    - • **Create.** Creates an object of the type that is highlighted.

- **Create Like.** Copies something, such as a table or index.

- **Remove.** Drops the selected object from the database.

- **Help.** Provides context-sensitive help. This button seems to work only in the menu bar and toolbar. Otherwise, you get into the Help screens at the table of contents.

Try clicking some of the objects and see what appears.

If you are continuing with the chapter, keep the Schema Manager open and read on. If you are done, close the Schema Manager by simply clicking the X button in the top right corner of the window.

The Main Menu and Button elements

When you start digging into Enterprise Manager tools, you reveal another layer of detail. To reveal this layer, follow these steps:

1. **If needed, start the Schema Manager as I describe in the preceding section.**

2. **Double-click the Tables folder in the left frame.**

   A list of tables appears in both the left and right frames.

3. **In the left frame, click the first table in the list.**

   The right frame changes to display a tabbed window describing the highlighted table.

Figure 1-6 shows the components of this window. The basic structure that you see in the figure is common to most of the Enterprise Manager DBA Management Pack tools.

You get these buttons at the bottom of the window:

- **Apply.** Use this button to finalize any changes that you made in the window.

- **Revert.** Put the details in the window back to the state that they were in before you started messing around. This button does not reverse changes that you have already applied — only those that you have not yet applied!

- **Show/Hide SQL.** As you make changes, you create SQL code, and this code is run when you click the Apply button. Click the Show SQL button to open a small window displaying the SQL code that you generated. After you click the button, it transforms into the Hide SQL button. Click that button, and the code window shuts.

- **Help.** Click this button to zoom in on context-sensitive help.

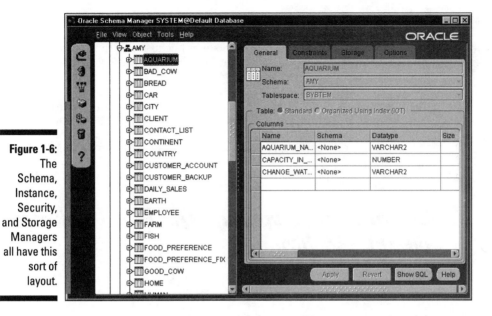

Figure 1-6:
The
Schema,
Instance,
Security,
and Storage
Managers
all have this
sort of
layout.

To close the Schema Manager, simply click the X button in the top right corner of the window.

Chapter 5 gives you a good review of the Schema Manager. Chapter 10 shows you how to create tables using the Schema Manager. Chapter 11 lets you create an object with Schema Manager. Chapter 19 shows you how to fix or change table layouts with the Schema Manager.

The next section shows you around one very important feature of Oracle8i: SQL*Plus Worksheet. Here is where you can use the powerful relational database language SQL to perform various miracles.

Getting Acquainted with SQL: The Messenger Priestess of Oracle8i

So how do you see and manipulate data stored in Oracle8i? You have two choices: The SQL*Plus Worksheet (one of the tools in the Enterprise Manager's DBA Management Pack) and a utility called SQL*Plus. Both tools require a knowledge of the relational database language called SQL (pronounced *sequel*).

SQL*Plus has been part of Oracle's software system from the start. The SQL*Plus Worksheet, on the other hand, is a relatively new player on the scene.

You can execute SQL commands in either the SQL*Plus Worksheet or SQL*Plus. In most of the book, I show you the steps for running most SQL commands only in the SQL*Plus Worksheet because it is more convenient. You can execute just about every example shown in the SQL*Plus Worksheet in SQL*Plus without any change.

Chapter 3 zooms in on the SQL*Plus Worksheet to show you how to write basic queries and how to add, remove, or change data by using SQL.

Chapter 4 rushes right in on how to query the new kids on the block: Oracle objects.

Starting and stopping SQL*Plus Worksheet on any platform

SQL*Plus Worksheet is one of the tools in the Oracle Enterprise Manager. To start SQL*Plus Worksheet, follow these steps:

1. **Select the SQL*Plus Worksheet menu option.**

   If you have Windows 95, 98, or NT, choose Start➪Programs➪ Oracle HOME2➪DBA Management Pack➪SQL*Plus Worksheet.

   Note that the Oracle HOME2 label might have a different number, such as HOME0 or HOME1, on your copy of NT.

   On UNIX, type the following command at an operating system command line:

   ```
   oemapp worksheet
   ```

2. **Choose the Connect Directly to a Database radio button.**

3. **Fill in a valid user name, password, and service in the security screen that pops up.**

   If you don't have your own user name, you can use Oracle8i's sample user name (SCOTT) and password (TIGER). The password shows up as asterisks (*) when you type. Leave the Service box blank if you work on a local database on your PC. If you don't, check with your DBA and type the name of the Oracle database to which you connect.

4. **Accept the Connect As box as Normal.**

   The SQL*Plus Worksheet appears when you click the OK button.

Figure 1-7 shows the SQL*Plus Worksheet window that you can use to type your commands. The window is divided horizontally into two frames. The top frame is the area in which you type SQL commands. The bottom frame displays the command and the results of the command. This tool is convenient because if you make a mistake (not *you*, the *other* readers!), you can fix the command and run it again. Your mouse works to position your cursor anywhere within a command or set of commands in the worksheet.

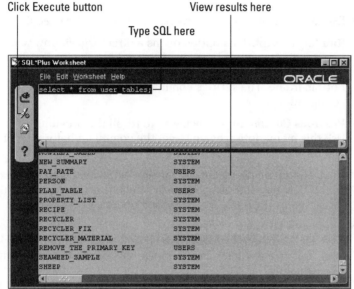

Click Execute button   View results here

Type SQL here

Figure 1-7:
The
SQL*Plus
Worksheet
window.

Here's a rundown of the components that you find dotted like constellations around the outer edges of the SQL*Plus Worksheet.

The menu selections along the top should look familiar if you use Windows. You use these controls to open and close the window, to resize and move the window, and to get help.

The File menu has a few extras that you see when you click it:

- ✔ **Change Database Connection.** Choose this command if you need to connect under a different user ID. While you're working in SQL, your view of the database changes depending on who you are. Each user ID has its own collection of roles and security access to other tables and sometimes its own tables, views, and indexes.

- ✔ **Save Input As.** Use this to save the commands that you have run.

- ✔ **Save Output As.** Use this to save the results of your commands, as seen in the bottom frame.

The Edit menu works with the context of your cursor to cut, paste, and so on.

The Edit menu contains a Clear All command that erases the contents of the current frame. If you're in the top frame and you choose this command, the top frame becomes blank. If you click anywhere in the bottom frame and then click Edit➪Clear All, you erase the contents of the bottom frame.

The Worksheet menu contains these selections:

- ✔ **Execute.** This menu option works the same as the Execute button.

- ✔ **Run local script.** This option opens a directory window where you can select a file from your local directories. After the file is selected, the script is brought into the top frame and immediately executed in the bottom frame. The script's commands are not stored in the worksheet command history.

- ✔ **Previous Command.** A quick way to recall the previous command. Use this menu option again to get the command before the one you just recalled.

- ✔ **Next Command.** Replaces the current worksheet with the next worksheet. This button does not predict the future; it works only if you have regressed to the past (by using the Previous Command button).

- ✔ **Command History.** Displays a list of commands in a pop-up window. You can select one with your mouse and place it into the worksheet area. You can also click the Command history button to get to the list of commands.

As a test, type the following SQL command:

```
select * from user_tables;
```

The SQL*Plus Worksheet requires one of these two symbols to end a command and allow it to execute:

- ✔ ; Use the semicolon at the end of the command.

- ✔ / Use the forward slash instead of the semicolon. The forward slash must be alone on the line following the end of the command.

For example, you can write the SQL query shown above as:

```
select * from user_tables
/
```

Now click the Execute button — the button that looks like lightning is about to strike a golf ball or a butter cookie or something. Don't mind me; I must be hungry. Just look for the yellow lightning bolt and click it.

You see results miraculously appear in the bottom half of the screen. (Captain! We're being hailed! On-screen, Mr. Data!) You should see something like Figure 1-8. Use the scroll bar on the bottom right side and on the bottom of the lower frame to scroll up, down, left, and right to view all the results, if necessary.

Close the SQL*Plus Worksheet by clicking the X button in the top right corner of the window. You see a window asking whether you want to save your worksheet. Click No to finish closing. That was easy!

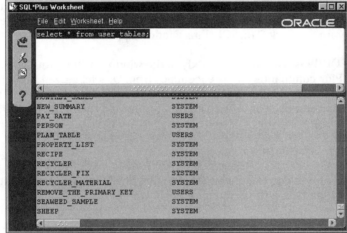

Figure 1-8: SQL*Plus Worksheet runs your commands and shows the results.

Starting and stopping SQL*Plus on a desktop

Unlike several Windows-based programs that are out today, SQL*Plus still works in ancient ways. No point-and-click mousing around with SQL*Plus — only command-line input is involved. You reach SQL*Plus outside the Enterprise Manager. To start SQL*Plus, follow these steps:

1. **Select the SQL*Plus program.**

   The icon has a yellow plus sign. If you have Windows 95, 98, or NT, choose Start⇨Programs⇨Oracle HOME1⇨Application Development⇨ SQL*Plus.

   Note that the Oracle HOME1 selection may appear as HOME0, HOME2, or some other name.

On UNIX, type the following command at the command prompt:

```
sqlplus
```

You are prompted to log in.

2. **Enter your user name and password in the security screen that pops up.**

   If you don't have your own, you can use Oracle8i's sample user name (SCOTT) and password (TIGER). The password shows up as asterisks (*) when you type.

   Leave the Host String box blank to reach the database on your PC. If you are working on a network, type in the name of the Oracle8i database on your network. The SQL*Plus window appears.

The SQL*Plus window is the body of the window, where you type and run SQL*Plus commands and see feedback from Oracle8i. Even though you're in a window, SQL*Plus is still an old-fashioned, line-by-line kind of utility. Go ahead and click anywhere in the window and then type this little one-line query:

```
select table_name from user_tables;
```

Press Enter to run the query. You see that SQL*Plus lists the results of the query right below the command, as shown in Figure 1-9.

To stop SQL*Plus, just close the window by clicking the Close box (the one with the X in the top right corner).

View results in same window

Press Enter to execute

Type SQL command here

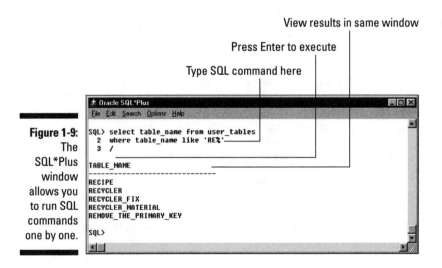

Figure 1-9: The SQL*Plus window allows you to run SQL commands one by one.

*Starting and stopping SQL*Plus on a mainframe or a network*

To start SQL*Plus on a mainframe or network, go to your operating-system command line and type the following command:

```
sqlplus username/password@net8name
```

Replace username with your Oracle8i user name. Replace password with your actual password. If you are not a person according to Oracle8i, you can impersonate the guy who has all the sample tables in Oracle8i; type **SCOTT** as the user name and **TIGER** as the password. If you are running a local database, you can leave off the @net8name. Otherwise, type the @ symbol and replace net8name with the name of the database to which you connect. You get a few status messages; then your prompt changes to this one:

```
SQL>
```

This prompt means that you are in SQL*Plus and are ready to go! Now you can create queries and tables and generally have fun to your heart's content. You can do one right now! Type in this line and press Enter to run it:

```
select table_name from user_tables;
```

Oracle8i lists the results on your screen, which look just like the results shown in Figure 1-9 earlier in this chapter, except without the window around it. When you're done, you leave SQL*Plus by typing the following command:

```
EXIT;
```

Then you press the Enter key. You return to your operating system, and the prompt returns to its normal state.

Many of the chapters in this book contain examples of SQL code that you can type in SQL*Plus and run (notice the SQL icon next to the code).

When running SQL commands in SQL*Plus, you must end the command with either a semicolon (;) or a forward slash (/). If you use a slash, it must be on a line by itself. The semicolon can be in the last line of the command. Either the semicolon or the slash is also required when you are running SQL commands in the SQL*Plus Worksheet.

Getting to know Oracle8i . . . and Scott and Tiger

Every Oracle database comes with demonstration tables that you may want to get familiar with. And if you do, you quickly notice references to Scott or Scott/Tiger. Perhaps you have already noticed these references in the Oracle8i documentation.

So who are Scott and Tiger? I hear that Scott is a real human (or was at one time). Now he's a legend whose name is engraved in every Oracle database around the world and whose name you can use as an acceptable user name. Scott's cat, Tiger, is a legend in his own right, now immortalized as Scott's password.

In the Oracle8i demonstration tables, Scott is one of only two highly paid analysts in a small company that is set on selling something. The head honcho's name is King. This company has four departments in four cities across America. All the salesmen get commissions, although one poor guy gets a zero commission. Nobody has ever earned a bonus. You can find out more about the people who work for Scott by typing these SQL commands in SQL*Plus:

```
select * from emp;
select * from dept;
select * from bonus;
select * from salgrade;
```

You can see that the boss lives in New York; the analysts, who all get paid more than their manager, live in Dallas; and the salesmen live in Chicago. Apparently, a puppet office exists in Boston — probably as a shady tax write-off. No doubt Tiger's behind it all!

Initializing the Enterprise Manager Console

You can do almost everything I describe in this book using Enterprise Manager's DBA Management Pack. You can access the DBA Management Pack either independently of the Enterprise Manager Console or through the Enterprise Manager Console. Generally speaking, bypassing the console is faster. However, if you get the console going, you may want to use some of its cool features, such as the job scheduler or the notifier (which can e-mail you if a remote database runs out of space, for instance).

Anyway, for those of you who like to tinker with everything, I include instructions on how to get the Enterprise Manager Console started.

You have to perform a few tasks to get it all set up, but you need to do these steps only once. After that, you can log straight into the Enterprise Manager Console. The tasks are:

1. Create a repository.

2. Start the Enterprise Manager Server.

3. Start the Intelligent Agent.

The next sections show how to do each of these tasks.

Creating a repository for Enterprise Manager Version 2

You may find that the task of creating a repository has already been completed during the installation of Enterprise Manager. Check with the person who installed Oracle8i if you don't have a clue. Pray that he or she does. Otherwise, better buy the person a copy of this book. Really!

If a repository already exists, skip to the next section. Otherwise, follow along with the bouncing ball. . . .

The database that stores the repository must have one of its initialization parameters adjusted: The processes parameter must be set to at least 200. The default is 59. You can modify this parameter by using the Instance Manager. Start up the Instance Manager, click the Initialization parameters icon, and then scroll down until you see the Processes parameter. Click the box and select 200. After you do so, follow the instructions in the last section of this chapter to shut down the database (be sure to save the parameters in a file). Restart the database, specifying the parameter file you just created as the parameter file you want the program to use. Now you are ready to continue with this section!

1. **Start up the Enterprise Manager Configuration Assistant.**

   Here's how to find it on a Windows 95, 98, orNT machine:

   Click Start⇨Programs⇨Oracle HOME2⇨Oracle Enterprise Management⇨Enterprise Manager Configuration Assistant.

   Note that the HOME2 part of the menu choice may be different on your machine. It may be HOME1, for instance.

   On UNIX, type this on the command line:

   ```
   vobui.exe
   ```

   After you select the assistant, the first window appears.

2. **Choose to create a new repository by selecting the first radio button. Click Next.**

   Figure 1-10 shows the first window of the assistant.

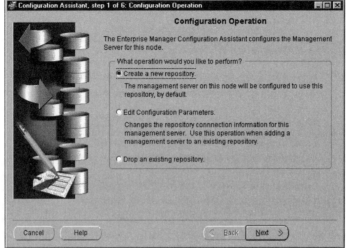

Figure 1-10:
Start a new
repository
now.

3. **Select a database for the repository.**

   The repository remembers who you are and what you've done when you next use the Enterprise Manager Console. The repository can reside in a local database or one that is remotely connected.

   In this window, you tell the assistant where to create the repository.

4. **Type in a valid Oracle user name and password.**

   Use one that has DBA privileges in the database. You can use the default DBA user name of SYSTEM. The default password for SYSTEM is MANAGER.

5. **Fill in the Net8 name of the remote database or the local name of the database.**

   Here is one case where you cannot leave the name blank. If you are using a local database or your Net8 is not configured for the repository database, type in the name as instructed in the tip shown at the bottom of the window.

   Figure 1-11 shows this page of the assistant.

6. **Click Next.**

7. **Specify the repository owner.**

   The assistant now wants you to define a brand-new user name and password. This user ID becomes the owner of all the repository tables. Do not use an existing user! Make up a new one. Figure 1-12 shows this page.

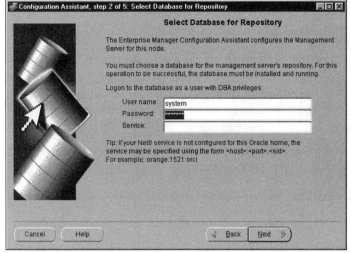

Figure 1-11:
The repository lives in one database that you name here.

8. **Click Next.**

9. **Choose a tablespace for the repository tables.**

You can simply accept the defaults for this page, as shown in Figure 1-13, or you can choose different tablespaces by using the pull-down selection lists provided.

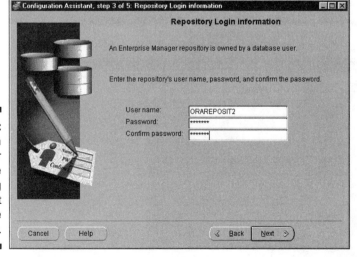

Figure 1-12:
Create a new user (don't use an existing user) that owns the repository.

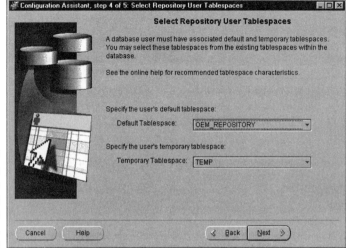

Figure 1-13:
Accept the
default
tablespaces
if you wish.

10. **Click Next.**

11. **The final step is simply to verify all the data you entered so far. Figure 1-14 shows this page. Verify the information and then click Finish.**

    The assistant goes about creating the repository for you. You can watch the progress in the status window as the assistant works away. When it is done, click Close.

Now you are ready to start up the Enterprise Manager Service.

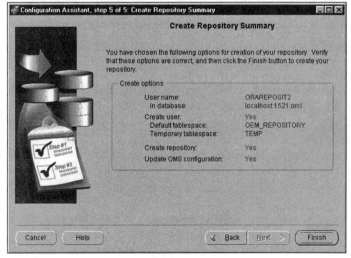

Figure 1-14:
The
assistant
displays
all the
information
you have
supplied.

Starting the Enterprise Manager Service

When you are using Windows 95, 98, or NT, start the service in the Services Panel. Follow these steps. If you are on UNIX, see the command after the steps.

1. **Go to the Control Panel.**

   Choose Start⇨Settings⇨Control Panel. This action opens a window of icons.

2. **Double-click the Services icon.**

   This action opens another window where you see a list of services.

3. **Start the service called OracleHOME2ManagementServer.**

   Note that the HOME2 part of the name depends on your installation. It may be HOME1 or some other HOME.

   To start the service, select the service and click the Start button. A status window appears, and after a few seconds, you return to the Services window. The service shows a status of Started, as shown in Figure 1-15.

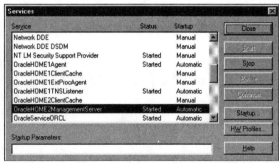

Figure 1-15:
The
Enterprise
Manager
Service has
been
started.

Under UNIX, type this command to start the service called Enterprise Manager Server:

```
oemctrl start oms
```

The final step of initializing the Enterprise Manager is to start up another service.

Starting the Agent

When you are using Windows 95, 98, or NT, start the service in the Services Panel. Follow these steps. If you are on UNIX, see the command after the steps.

1. **Open the Control Panel.**

   Choose Start⇨Settings⇨Control Panel. A window of icons opens.

2. **Double-click the Services icon.**

   This action opens another window where you see a list of services.

3. **Start the service called OracleHOME1Agent.**

   Note that the HOME1 part of the name depends on your installation. It may be HOME0 or some other HOME.

   To start the service, select the service and click the Start button. A status window appears, and after a few seconds, you return to the Services window. The service shows a status of Started.

On UNIX, type this command to start the Listener Agent service:

```
lsnrctl dbsnmp_start
```

Now you can start the Enterprise Manager Console!

Taking a quick tour of Enterprise Manager Console

Start the console and look around a bit.

To start the console on Windows 95, 98, or NT, choose Start⇨Programs⇨ Oracle HOME2 ⇨Oracle Enterprise Management⇨Enterprise Manager Console.

In UNIX, type this command:

```
oemapp console
```

You see the usual login window to log in to the console. Use the default administrator for Enterprise Manager: SYSMAN. The default password is oem_temp. The first time you use this password, you are prompted to change the password. Change it if you want and then press OK to continue.

Figure 1-16 shows the console and locates some of the major components.

I suggest that you click the Quick Tour button sometime to get a really good tour of the console. In a nutshell, the console has four parts, plus extras:

- **The Navigator.** Here you can see your databases and drill down into their components.

- **The Map.** Here you can add background maps to groups of databases. Cute, and perhaps even useful if you run a worldwide network of databases.

- **The Job Scheduler.** If you want to schedule a nightly backup, here is where you do so.

- **The Event Log**. Here you can monitor your database's activities, including when it was shut down and rebooted. You can tell the console to e-mail you or even call you on the phone (if you have the right combination of software, hardware, and technical support) when some disaster occurs to your database. For example, you probably want to know if the database fails to function on Thanksgiving night, right? Sure you do!

- **The Management Packs.** You can use the little icon to call up any of the DBA Management Pack tools (like the Schema Manager). In addition, if you spend money and buy other Management Packs, you can access them the same way.

The next section shows you how to get help. By now, you may need it.

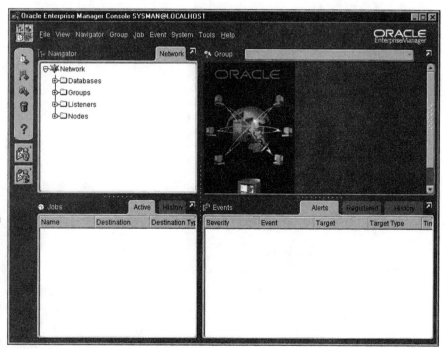

Figure 1-16:
The Enterprise Manager Console has a lot of parts.

Getting Help: Let Your Mouse Do the Walking

Oracle8i's tools always have a ton of documentation dragging along with them. The documentation actually holds a great deal of valuable information and is indexed and cross-referenced ad nauseum. Your mouse may get dizzy running the maze of trails through backtracks, side streets, riddles, and CMI (Completely Meaningless Information).

Here are several ways to find the Oracle8i documentation:

✔ Click the Help button that is located in almost every Oracle8i window.

✔ Select one of the documentation icons from the Start menu.

All the Help menus are now Java-based and use an outlined table of contents that lets you click open levels of headings, so click away.

The Index tab in the Help screens takes you to the window shown in Figure 1-17. The Index tab seems to be the fastest path to answers, and it works best if you know the special Oracle8i term connected with your problem. When you want to find out how to make a new table, for example, typing **create** or **table** gets you to the information fastest. Typing **make** gets you nowhere.

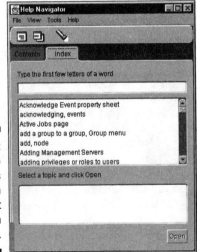

Figure 1-17: Help windows have an index that you can search.

For those of you who want to do a search, click the Flashlight icon. You can then enter the word you wish to search on and view the resulting hits in a window. To view the corresponding entry, just double-click it.

If you need additional help resources, call the Oracle Corporation at 415-506-1500 and scream "HEEELLLP!!" You can also reach the Oracle support Web page at

```
http://www.oracle.com/support
```

Shutting Down Oracle8i

The following sections show you how to shut down the database.

Be careful about shutting down your database, especially if you share the database on a network. Others may be using the database without your knowledge. Shut down Oracle8i only with permission from your DBA every time. If you are sure that everyone is finished with the database, go ahead and shut it down.

Another important guideline is to shut down the database before shutting down the computer that is running Oracle8i. A set of background processes run constantly while your database is running, and shutting down by using Oracle8i's utility assures you that the background processes all stop in an orderly fashion. This sequence prevents accidents.

Shutting down Oracle8i on a desktop

Oracle8i gives you a simple solution to shutting down the database. The Instance Manager can handle it for you. Follow these steps to shut down Oracle8i by using the Instance Manager.

1. **Start the Instance Manager.**

   If you are using Windows 95, 98, or NT, press Start⇨Programs⇨ Oracle HOME2⇨DBA Management Pack⇨Instance Manager.

   On UNIX, type this command:
   ```
   oemapp instance
   ```

   A login window appears asking for your input.

2. Log in as INTERNAL.

Fill in the boxes in the Login window with INTERNAL as the user ID and the current password for INTERNAL. The default password is ORACLE. In the Service box, type the name of your database instance. If you are running on a PC, leave this box blank. If you are using a network, type in the name assigned to the Oracle8i database on your network.

Figure 1-18 shows the main window you see when the Instance Manager starts up. The traffic light on the right side shows the status of your database. Green means the database is running. Red means it is already shut down.

3. Save the initialization parameters.

Perform this step only if you have changed your parameters or you have never before shut down your Oracle8i database from the Instance Manager. To save the parameters, click Initialization Parameters in the left frame. This step shows you the initialization parameters of your database. Click the Save button in the right frame. Figure 1-19 shows you the initialization details you see and illustrates the Save button to push. Oracle8i asks you to supply a file name. Type in a valid file name and click OK. You are returned to the Instance Manager. Click the database icon (near the top) in the left window to return to your view of the traffic light in the right frame.

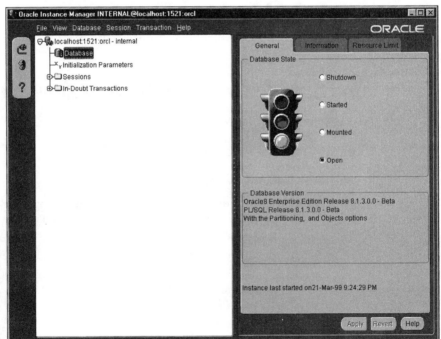

Figure 1-18:
Green light means you're running.

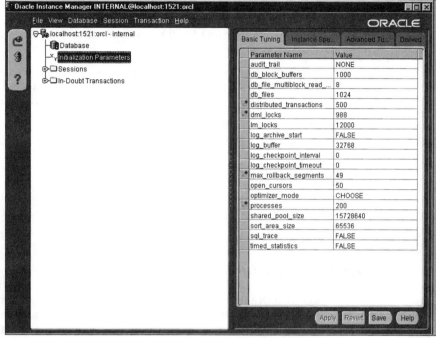

Figure 1-19:
Initialization
parameters
help you
fine-tune
your
database.

4. Select the Shutdown radio button and click Apply.

Oracle8i gives you a pop-up window of choices, as you see in Figure 1-20.
These are the different methods of shutting down the database.

Figure 1-20:
You
normally
select
Immediate
for shutting
down your
database.

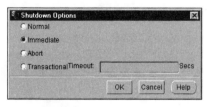

5. Select Immediate (default) and click OK.

The other choices for shutdown are:

- **Normal.** This choice takes longer, but it waits for all users to complete their work before shutting down the database. Use this when
you have given your users warning to log off and you want the
database to wait for them to complete their work.

- **Abort.** This choice is for times when your database refuses to shut down using Normal or Immediate. Use this when a previous shutdown was interrupted before completing or if the database does not respond to commands.

Oracle8i sends a message informing you that it will wait for everyone to finish before it shuts down. Click OK. Wait for Oracle8i to shut down. Oracle8i returns you to the Instance Manager, and the traffic light is red.

6. **Close the Instance Manager.**

Click the X box in the upper-right corner of the window.

Now your database is put to bed, and you can shut down your computer if you want to.

Shutting down Oracle8i on a mainframe or a network

Do not shut down Oracle8i without permission from your DBA every time. On mainframes, processes that require the database can be running — processes that you may not know about. (Some processes are scheduled to run after business hours so that they don't affect normal operations.)

Check with your DBA, if you have one. If you don't have a DBA, you may have to check the manuals that come with Oracle8i to find out the specific command to shut down Oracle8i. The most common shutdown method is done by going into Enterprise Manager's Instance Manager, as I describe in the preceding section.

Chapter 2

Data Whaaaaat? A Database Primer

In This Chapter

▶ Discovering the key terms of Dataspeak

▶ Exploring what databases can and cannot do for you

▶ Finding out about objects

▶ Using a small database, medium, or large database

So you just installed Oracle8i, you have the shiny new box sitting on your office shelf for your colleagues to envy, and you're ready to do some heavy-duty computing with databases. Good for you. That's great. But first — Ssssshh! Be vewy, vewy quiet! — wouldn't it be nice if you knew something about databases?

This chapter focuses on databases, tables, rows, and columns and how they all join to form one big, happy family. The chapter has a section on the new kid on the relational block: the object. For the most part, databases are designed to make your life easier. I offer lots of cute examples and scenarios in this chapter, just to show you how practical databases really are.

If, after reading this chapter, your head is spinning like that girl's in *The Exorcist,* please do not fret. Database development is as easy as . . . well, rocket science. After sifting through this book, you can create relational and object-relational databases in your sleep. Next stop: the very expensive sleep-disorder clinic. Better take a sleeping pill.

Dataspeak Definitions for the Techno-Impaired

Shakespeare wrote, "A rose by any other name would smell as sweet" — but when you order one over the Internet in today's world, you should probably call it a rose. Similarly, you should probably understand some common database terms, including

- ✔ Databases
- ✔ Users and roles
- ✔ Tables
- ✔ Columns and rows
- ✔ Relationships
- ✔ Object types
- ✔ Object tables
- ✔ Object views
- ✔ Methods
- ✔ Varrays
- ✔ Nested tables

Sections throughout this chapter provide an expanded look at each of these terms and how they relate to Oracle8i users.

Database — this general term has many meanings, depending on the context. In the world of *Oracle8i For Dummies,* this term refers to all the tables; all data inside the tables; and all the users, views, synonyms, and many more items that the Oracle8i software keeps track of for you. Your database has a name (or is called *default,* in the case of a PC with only one database installed). If your operation uses two databases, each has a unique name and each has its own set of tables, data, users, and so on. Each database is called an Oracle8i *instance.*

A *relational database* is a collection of tables connected in a series of relationships so that they reflect a small part of the real world.

An *object-oriented database* uses objects, rather than tables, to store information. Objects also contain *methods,* which are pre-defined ways to manipulate the data.

Oracle8i is a combination of a traditional relational database and an object-oriented database. I call this an *object-relational database.* So should you.

Databases are great for storing information for many reasons:

- ✔ Databases keep similar pieces of information, such as names and addresses, in one place so that you can use them in many places.
- ✔ Databases categorize, sort, filter, and pool items in multiple ways without duplicating the data.

You can harness databases to manage and reorganize your information. Suppose that you have two address books: one for clients and one for friends. Helen started as just a client but has become your friend. Would you copy her address into the Friends address book? Would you leave Helen's address in the Clients book and remember to look for her there? Would you give up and make a new book with both clients and friends in it? Would Helen really put up with all these address-book shenanigans? I think not!

If you have both address books in tables in Oracle8i, the program can combine the tables for you, as illustrated in Figure 2-1. Click a button, and Oracle8i opens with your friends' addresses, including Helen's, in alphabetical order. Close the file and click another button, and Oracle8i opens with your clients' addresses, including Helen's, in alphabetical order. Best of all, Oracle8i does not duplicate entries. You entered Helen's address only once, but you may feel as though you recorded it twice. How practical of you! Soon, you may need to start paying yourself twice.

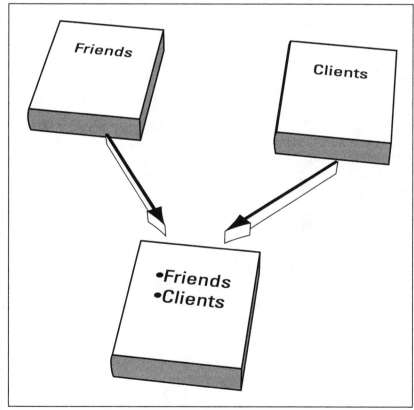

Figure 2-1:
Databases
make
managing
unrelated
information
easier.

Relational Database Concepts

The traditional relational database has been around for many years. It still is very popular for business applications from banking to airlines to manufacturing. Ask anyone! For example, airline reservation systems use relational databases.

Can a database darn my socks?

Who darns socks anymore? Your grandma probably did, and she couldn't rely on her database to help, either. For that matter, who actually uses the word *darn* anymore? This table shows database can-do and can't-do tasks:

Task	Can Do	Can't Do
Balance the checkbook	X	
Summarize by year or other criterion	X	
Configure your printer		X
Store and retrieve pictures, audio, and video	X	
Track sales calls	X	
Help you draw artistic pictures		X
Find your lost cat		X

Task	Can Do	Can't Do
Search for information embedded in text	X	
Decide the selling price for stock		X
Interact with the Internet	X	
Raid your refrigerator		X
Validate dates and numbers	X	
Sort your laundry	X	

This list of tasks barely scratches the surface. Databases are growing in popularity because they can do so much, both at home and in the workplace. Someday, Oracle officials will name their newest version C-3PO. The program will talk to you sarcastically and do the dishes.

Today, the relational database is still hot stuff as it finds its niche on the Internet. E-commerce, Internet banking, virtual shopping malls, and even dating services use relational database engines behind their Web sites. For example, the popular online bookstore Amazon.com uses an Oracle database to handle online searching and purchasing. Amazon.com also uses its database to display information related to a book — when you view the page for *Oracle8 For Dummies,* there is a list of other books that have been purchased by people who bought *Oracle8 For Dummies.*

This section describes the main ideas you should be familiar with when using a relational database.

Users and roles

A *user* is a unique login name in Oracle8i. Before any data goes into your database, you must have users to own the data. All users have these characteristics:

- ✔ A unique name that is 1 to 30 characters long.

- ✔ A password (which does not have to be unique) that is 1 to 30 characters long.

- ✔ At least one role assignment. *Roles* determine the capabilities and privileges that a user has inside the database. The database administrator (DBA) can add and remove roles. You can assign privileges to each user directly, but the easiest way to manage privileges is to assign them to roles. (I discuss users and roles in Chapter 9.)

Figure 2-2 illustrates the contents of all Oracle8i databases. The right side of the figure shows you the physical system. The physical system puts all the data in one or more files, which you name on the hard disk of your computer. Oracle8i stores data differently from, say, your word processing program, which stores the data saved to a document file in the same physical order as you see it displayed on-screen. Oracle8i, on the other hand, stores data by reserving portions of space for each table within the file. When Oracle8i uses that space, it reserves another slice of space in the file or in a different file. The two slices of space need not be next to each other. Even one row of data in a single table can be spread across several physical slices of file space. Chapter 10 goes into more detail about assigning space to tables and tables to tablespaces. The DBA role (which I explain later in this section) controls what Oracle8i does with its physical space.

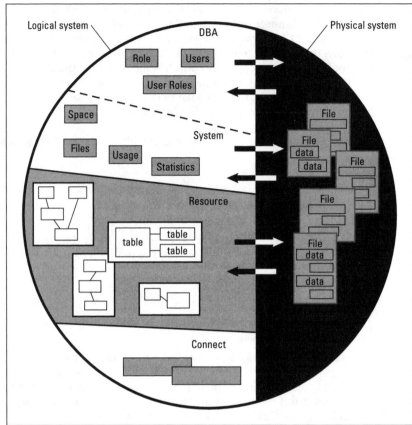

Figure 2-2:
This is your
brain on
Oracle8i.

The left side of the figure shows how Oracle8i logically (conceptually) divides the database by roles. The figure defines the logical system by the following roles:

✔ **DBA.** The most important job of the DBA (database administrator) is assigning roles to users. The DBA role also adds and removes users. Further, the DBA role controls the physical side of the database by adding new files and telling Oracle8i what can go into the files.

✔ **SYSTEM.** This role is a special section of the DBA role, an area inside the database where Oracle8i does a great deal of behind-the-scenes work, such as controlling how data is written into the physical files. The tables in the SYSTEM area show where everything else in the entire database gets stored.

✔ **RESOURCE.** This role allows users to create their own sets of tables and relate them into a unit *(schema)*. A user who creates a table is the owner of the table.

✔ **CONNECT.** This role allows users to gain access to the database. These users cannot create any tables of their own.

An Oracle8i user usually corresponds to one person in the real world. That person has his or her own user name and password. Sometimes, for convenience, several people share an Oracle8i user name, and all of them know the user name and password. This arrangement can have legitimate uses, such as in these situations:

✔ A team of programmers is working on one project. One Oracle8i user owns all the tables and other elements.

✔ You must give a large and continually changing group of people limited access to the database. Administering all the changes is too difficult. For convenience, you distribute a single user name and password to all these people. Generally, you do this only for a user name that has restricted access in order to prevent inadvertent damage to data.

✔ A large public or government bureau needs to find more effective ways to waste money on training everyone and his brother in how to log in to Oracle8i so that next year's budget will be larger.

Tables

A *table* holds information inside a database. Oracle8i stores the information in an orderly fashion, using *rows* and *columns*. A table is easy to sort, filter, add, average, find, combine, and otherwise manipulate. Every bit of information that goes into a relational database must also go into a table. Even Oracle8i itself keeps track of its own information in tables (see Chapter 8).

Tables are real-life objects and database objects. Table 2-1 shows the similarities and differences between the table in your dining room and the one in your computer.

Table 2-1	The Table versus the Table
Furniture Table	*Database Table*
Built of wood	Created out of thin air
Holds coffee cups	Holds the description and price of a coffee cup
Holds many kinds of objects	Holds information about only one kind of object

(continued)

Table 2-1 *(continued)*

Furniture Table	Database Table
Runs out of space	Runs out of space
Has four legs	Has at least one column
Usually, one exists per room	Usually, many exist per database
Gets scratched	Gets fragmented

Chapter 10 goes into nauseating detail on how to build a better database table. Oracle8i stores information about your tables and your data in its own system tables, which are tables of tables. See Chapter 8 to read more about tables of columns.

Every table has a name. Try to make table names singular nouns or noun phrases. Descriptive table names are helpful. A table named CAR probably has something to do with automobiles, or perhaps toy cars, or possibly train cars, or maybe even cable cars. A table named X1000 probably requires a comment explaining its contents. Without a comment attached, you may be reduced to asking someone for help, which could definitely interfere with your ultra-cool image at the office.

How to name any database object in Oracle8i

When you name a table, a column, an index, or any other database object, I have a few rules, exceptions, and suggestions for you. This table gives you a rundown:

Rules and Suggestions for Naming Anything in Oracle8i

Rule	Exception	Suggestion
Names must be no more than 30 characters long. A *character* is a letter or a single-digit number.		
Names must contain only these characters: A–Z, 0–9, $, #, @, and _.	You can use other characters, such as –, +, and blanks, if you always enclose the name in quotation marks.	Apparently, someone has bought the publishing rights to these characters. Use only A–Z, 0–9, and _ . For clarity, use _ (underscore) to separate words or acronyms in the name.

Oracle8i does not differentiate between uppercase and lower-case names.	If a name gets created by enclosing it in quotation marks, then Oracle8i recognizes it as case sensitive and allows other characters, such as spaces, to be used in the name. Names created this way must always be enclosed in quotation marks when used in queries.	Never use quotation marks when defining a name, and always use uppercase.
You cannot have two objects with the same name.	This rule applies only in narrow circumstances. Columns in the same table cannot have the same name. Columns in different tables can have the same name.	Use the same name for the same information unless this rule prevents you from using the same name. Even tables with different owners can have the same name.
name cannot be a reserved word. A *reserved word* is a word that Oracle8i interprets as a command, function, or variable. The list of reserved words keeps growing. Some of the more common ones that you may be tempted to use include *comment, access, date, default, definition,* and *resource.*		Do not include table names in the column names. Make up a standard and stick to it for column names— for example, "Always put _ID at the end of primary keys" or "Always add _DATE at the end of date columns."

Using these naming conventions simplifies reading a diagram, especially the relationship portions.

Tables always have columns and rows, which I cover in the very next section. Tables also have a *size*. Here are the main reasons for defining the size of a table:

✔ **To reserve room in the database for the table (initial space).** The database can store the table's data in one place, which makes the data more efficient to service. This arrangement is similar to going to a restaurant with a big group. If you call ahead and reserve space, the waiter seats your group together and can take your orders and deliver your food more efficiently. If you scatter yourselves all over the restaurant, the waiter works harder, and you have less fun. (On the other hand, watching the wait staff try to total multiple checks in a table configuration like this one is especially fun.) Keep your tables (and wait staff) happy and reserve the right amount of space for them.

✔ **To prevent a table from taking over the entire database (maximum space).** You may encounter a situation in which you are unable to predict how much information the table will store. All you know is that you want the table to stop growing when it eats up all the available database space. (This condition is known in some circles as the Rush Limbaugh syndrome.) Fortunately, a cure exists: the maximum space parameter. This method is not one of those dashboard buttons on the *Enterprise*. ("More power, Scotty!" "I'm givin' 'er all she's got, Cap'n! Any more, and she's going to blow!")

✔ **To control growth in a way that keeps the table from becoming scattered in the database (incremental space).** Some tables contain a great deal of data in one row. Tables containing video or graphics have rows that are much larger than the average bear. Larger tables benefit from having large chunks of space. Getting back to the restaurant example, suppose that your group grows in 50-person increments because members are arriving on buses. The wait staff would be wise to seat the group in one of the restaurant's larger areas instead of seating the group at random tables throughout the restaurant. If you use this method, be sure to add an automatic 15 percent gratuity.

Tables also usually have a primary key (a column or group of columns that uniquely identifies each row in the table), one or more indexes (see Chapter 18), and relationships (see Chapter 6).

Columns and rows

Columns are the vertical parts of tables. *Rows,* on the other hand, are the horizontal parts of tables.

Do other differences exist between the two? Absolutely. Columns and rows have different purposes in a table. A row holds different kinds of information about one item. The row for my Maui cruiser in Figure 2-3, for example, tells you that the car is a Buick Century, has four doors, and was made in 1982.

Columns   Rows   Columns

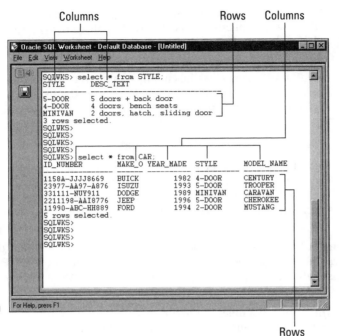

Rows

Figure 2-3:
Two tables
with labeled
parts.

A column holds the same kind of information about many items. One column in the CAR table in Figure 2-3, for example, tells you about the YEAR_MADE of all the vehicles in the table.

Columns determine all the information that you allow in a table. These items can be cars, animals, people, sales figures, or whatever you choose — but if you don't have a column for the item, you can't enter it in your table. You use the CAR table, for example, to gather only certain information about cars: the ID_NUMBER, MAKE_OF_CAR, YEAR_MADE, STYLE, and MODEL_NAME. Cars also have owners, color, options, tires, mileage, selling prices, and so on. You cannot place all this other information in the CAR table until you add an appropriate column for each one. As Figure 2-3 stands, you know only five distinct kinds of information about the cars in the table.

When you first create a table, the columns exist, but the rows don't. *Columns* are like ground rules, which must be in place before the game starts. As you can in some games, of course, you can later refine, add, modify, or even remove the rules (that is, the set of columns). See Chapter 19 for commentary on how to change your table's columns.

Each column holds one piece of information. You define a column by giving it a name and some guidelines about what it contains. Here are the components of a column:

✔ **Datatype.** This component describes the general class of data. High-class data own Cadillacs. (This situation tends to really pique Captain Picard. He, like you, is stuck with the *Enterprise.* Ready! Engage!) Actually, the most popular classes break down like this:

- VARCHAR2. This class has a funny name that stands for *variable character string, Version 2.* VARCHAR2 is used most often for any kind of text data, such as names, addresses, favorite colors, or eye colors.

- NUMBER. Obviously, this class holds numbers.

- DATE. Oracle8i keeps dates in a special format that enables it to perform date math faster. Some databases get flustered on a date, but not Oracle8i. The Oracle8i date contains not only a four-digit year (making the program Year 2000 compliant) but also the time of day if you need it.

✔ **Length.** You need this component for VARCHAR2 and NUMBER datatypes. If you leave length out, Oracle8i plugs in a big default length. Putting in a reasonable length prevents you from getting an enormous essay in the FAVORITE_COLOR column.

✔ **Null/not null.** *Null* means "unknown" or "missing." A row can be created in a table without all the columns filled in. Columns where no data has been entered are defined as containing a *null value.* Nulls are okay in any column except the primary-key column, which by definition cannot be null. You add the not null parameter to primary-key columns.

Chapter 10 goes into more detail on defining columns. Chapter 3 shows you how to make changes in data in your table by using SQL Worksheet. See Chapter 19 for complete instructions on adding columns to or removing columns from your tables.

Relationships

A database *relationship* is how two tables fit together. When two tables kiss, they're in a relationship. Even if they don't kiss, any connection between tables is a relationship, in database lingo.

Figure 2-4 highlights the relationship of the CAR and STYLE tables from the preceding section. The CAR and STYLE tables have the STYLE column in common. The relationship between the tables looks like this:

✔ A car in the CAR table can have one style, which exists in the STYLE table.

✔ A style in the STYLE table can be selected for none, one, or many cars in the CAR table.

Two cars have the same STYLE

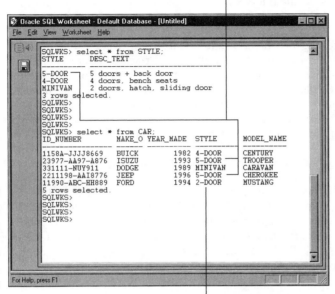

Figure 2-4:
Two tables
with their
relationships
labeled.

Every car has a STYLE found in the STYLE table

The key to the power of a database is the integrity of its relationships. When you say that a person has integrity, you imply that you trust him or her — that person does not say one thing and do another. *Integrity* in table relationships means that after you define the relationship, every row in both tables fits into the relationship. In the CAR and STYLE example, integrity means that no cars in the CAR table have a style that you do not find in the STYLE table.

The lines between tables in a diagram define relationships. Chapter 7 shows you how to accurately convey a wealth of information about the table relationships with a few lines and words in your diagrams.

Object-Relational Database Concepts

Oracle8i technically can be called an *object-relational database*. This term means that Oracle8i contains all the features of a relational database combined with some of the features of an object-oriented database. Because the program is a hybrid, it allows you to make some choices about how to set up your database design.

This section covers the basic definitions of Oracle8i's world of objects and describes the main ideas you want to be familiar with when using object-relational structures such as methods and object tables.

Only a few of the object-oriented features of Oracle8i can be used with plain SQL, which you see in this book. SQL (Structured Query Language) is an English-like set of commands for defining database objects and querying and modifying data in those objects. The features that cannot be used with plain SQL require you to use a programming language. The current release of Oracle8i supports Java, C++, and PL/SQL as languages in which you can program applications that use Oracle8i objects.

I very lightly cover programming in Java in Chapter 15, to demonstrate the Java Virtual Machine. Demonstrating C++ or PL/SQL is beyond the scope of this book. If you're interested, you can find out about C++ in *C++ For Dummies,* 3rd Edition, by Stephen R. Davis, and in *Foundations of C++ and Object-Oriented Programming* by Namir Clement Shammas, both books published by IDG Books Worldwide, Inc. My own recent book, *Oracle8 Bible,* also published by IDG Books Worldwide, Inc., shows you everything you need to know about programming in PL/SQL. Check it out.

An object defined

An *object* can be anything, sort of. In terms of Oracle8i, an *object* is a framework that defines

✔ How data is stored

✔ Where it is stored

✔ What kind of data it is

✔ How to put data together into logical whole parts

That last item is the part that's really interesting and unique to objects. In fact, if you prefer, Oracle8i allows you to define the first three items in the traditional relational database style and then gives you a way to map these relational tables into objects.

Think of an *object* as being a holistic set of concepts. Your object contains data about real-world things, such as car parts. On top of the data, your object contains information about what can be done with the data. It's like having the car-parts data and the assembly instructions for the car. An object can contain other objects. You may define one object called PERSONAL_ADDRESS, which contains up to three lines of a person's address. Another object, called PERSONAL_INFO, contains a person's name, Social Security number, and the PERSONAL_ADDRESS object for that person.

The scoop on object types

An *object type* enables you to extend the definition of datatypes (classes of data) into customized *user-defined datatypes*. Oracle calls these special datatypes *object types*.

An example of an object type is the FISH_TYPE in the sample database. This object type contains three elements:

- ✔ **Fish name** (datatype: VARCHAR2)
- ✔ **Date of birth** (datatype: DATE)
- ✔ **Date of death** (datatype: DATE)

Each of these are "normal" datatypes: VARCHAR2 and DATE.

Another example of an object type is the FISH_DESC_TYPE in the sample database. This object contains three elements:

- ✔ **Fish name, birth, and death** (datatype: FISH_TYPE)
- ✔ **Reference to the fish's aquarium** (datatype: REF)
- ✔ **A text description of the fish** (datatype: VARCHAR2)

In this example, the first element's datatype is the user-defined datatype FISH_TYPE. The second is a column with a REF datatype. REF is a datatype for connecting objects together. The third column has a "normal" datatype of VARCHAR2. This example shows how you can embed object types within other object types.

Object types are used in these kinds of places in Oracle8i:

- ✔ **As a column datatype.** Object types can be used in place of the usual datatypes when you define a column in a table. The column is called an *object column.*
- ✔ **As a definition for an object table row.** Object types are used in place of a list of columns when you define an object table. When you define an object table, you define it as a table of one object type. Each row of the object table contains all the attributes defined in the object type.
- ✔ **As an element in another object type.** Object types can be separated into modules and then composed into complex object types.

Chapter 11 shows you how to create and remove object types.

The connection of relational tables with objects

I mention previously that Oracle8i is a hybrid of both relational and object-oriented databases. To allow you to combine the two to get the best of both worlds, Oracle8i provides three bridges between relational tables and objects:

- ✔ **Object view.** An *object view* maps relational tables into an object table. Like relational views, the object view doesn't actually have data of its own; it's merely a way of looking at the underlying tables. The object view allows you to use existing relational tables in an object-oriented way. If you use the object view, the underlying data that resides in relational tables can be updated with the usual SQL commands or with object methods.

- ✔ **Object table.** An *object table* is a table whose rows are defined by an object type rather than explicit columns. The elements within the object type define what data is stored in the object table.

  In addition, an object table can have object methods, which perform data manipulation and are stored with the table's definition. In other words, object tables have both data and application functionality wrapped up into one object. Kind of like a corn dog.

  Object tables also can have primary keys (unique identifiers) and indexes (fast retrieval paths).

- ✔ **Object column in relational table.** A relational table that contains one or more columns defined by an object type as its datatype.

Chapter 11 demonstrates the creation of an object view and an object table. Getting a room with a view is my object when visiting relatives in the Far East.

Object reference

An object reference, or REF, is a special datatype created for object tables. It acts like a foreign key because it defines a relationship between two objects.

Say you have an object table called AQUARIUM_OBJ with a primary key. Another object table, the FISH_OBJ, has a column that connects the fish to its aquarium. This column is assigned the datatype REF, and the AQUARIUM_OBJ is named as the referenced object.

Unlike a relational table's foreign key column, the REF column is not directly readable by a normal SQL query. Even so, you can use the REF column to find details from the referenced object. For examples of how to use REF columns in queries, see Chapter 4.

Methods to their madness

An *object method* is a program stored in the database to perform special tasks on data in an object table. Object methods are great fun.

Methods are self-contained bits of programming code that travel with an object, delivering parts or modifying data according to the method code. Methods are the heart of object-oriented technology.

Suppose that you're working with an object-relational database schema (a set of related tables and objects) that contains information about making a model airplane. A model airplane has several subassemblies, such as the engine and the instrument panel, which are made up of individual parts. A change in any individual part may affect the assembly of the entire plane. If the fuel gauge in the cockpit is changed to a different diameter, for example, the hole drilled in the instrument panel must also be changed. You can use *object types* to define the individual parts, the subassemblies, and the entire airplane. *Object methods* define how these object types interact with one another. One program uses the object types and methods to handle changes in the data. Another program can use the objects and their associated methods to extract a complete instruction booklet for the plane.

Nested tables

Have you ever been stuck scribbling your friend's new cell phone number underneath her home, business, and fax numbers and e-mail address in your sorry little black book? What if you could magically expand that little one-line phone number spot so it could hold any number of phone numbers and then just tuck back into that one line when you didn't need it?

A *nested table* does this kind of cool trick. You can store multiple rows of one kind of data in a table nested inside the column of another table.

Nested tables are a form of *collection*, which means a table within tables. Another form of collection is the varray, which I describe in the following section.

Chapter 11 shows how to create a nested table. Chapter 4 shows how to query a nested table. Go for it!

Varrays

A *varray* holds a finite number of rows of data. A varray is a way to add repeated data into a row in a table. A varray is an alternative to defining two related relational tables.

The difference between a nested table and a varray is that the nested table has an unlimited number of rows whereas the varray has a predefined maximum number of rows.

Chapter 11 shows how to create a varray for your viewing pleasure. Chapter 4 shows how to query a varray, which happens to be an identical process to querying a nested table.

Databases, users, roles, tables, rows, columns, relationships, objects, nested tables, and varrays are not the only terms that are common to database development. Many more terms appear in this book and — if you're really brave — in the Oracle8i manuals. Look in the glossary in the back of this book for more definitions.

The Kinds of Database Things That You Can Do with Oracle8i

This section shows three scenarios that help you get a feel for what databases do in real life. I hope you enjoy these examples. Let your imagination run wild, and think about what you want your database to do for you.

Keeping track of a fishbowl (the easy example)

Why are aquarium fish so nervous when their world is quiet, rocking them in an endless cradle of gentle bubbles and waves? Well, I guess I would be nervous, too, if 12-foot eyeballs kept popping up in my picture window.

I have a small aquarium with one little gold guppy named Wesley, who was born on January 1, 1996. The aquarium once contained four guppies, but Wesley ate the other three. Your mission, if you choose to accept it, is to design a set of tables that accurately depicts the world of my aquarium.

When you create a set of related tables and all the database things that go with these tables, you create a *schema*.

Continuing with the aquarium example, here are the facts that you have to work with:

✔ I have one aquarium that holds one gallon of water, if my 7-year-old doesn't get to it.

✔ I feed Wesley once a day, whether he asks for it or not.

✔ I change the water once every 14 days, even if I can still see Wesley.

✔ Three fish died. Their headstones read:

  • Fish Two (black-and-tan female guppy), born 1/1/96, died 3/15/96

  • Fish Three (red-and-white male guppy), born 1/1/96, died 4/8/96

  • Fish Four (transparent guppy), born 3/1/96, died on an unknown date under very suspicious circumstances while I was out of town

You can easily track all this information in a simple two-table schema, as shown in Figure 2-5. I discuss the kind of diagram shown in this figure in more detail in Chapter 6.

Running a pet shop (the medium example)

I buy fish food at the pet shop around the corner from my house. The owner stocks the pet shop with bird cages, dog collars, flea powder, and a few hundred other items — including birds, rabbits, and even a monkey. Here are sundry activities that the shopkeeper handles with her database:

✔ Logging every item, purchase price, selling price, and number in stock

✔ Tallying tax on every sale

✔ Adjusting in-stock numbers on all inventory as sales occur

✔ Creating monthly accounting statements

✔ Creating annual tax reports

✔ Tracking names and addresses of customers

✔ Printing customized letters for advertising to customers

✔ Printing mailing labels

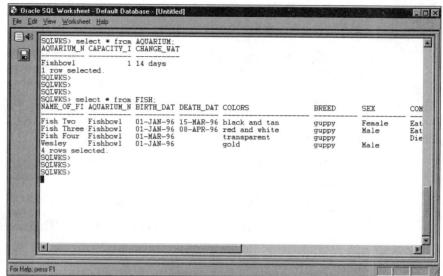

Figure 2-5:
My water
world.

Keeping tabs on the pet shop is a great use for Oracle8i! You get to use the power of the relational model so that you can store your data one time and use it in a variety of ways.

For your information, if you were to try implementing the pet-shop system by using only the Oracle8i database and the tools that are part of the basic package, you would have to do some advanced programming or get some additional tools. The portions that you cannot do easily with your Oracle8i database are

- **Automatically adjusting inventory.** This requires programming a database trigger, which is beyond the scope of this book.

- **Tallying tax on every sale.** You need a database trigger or an additional tool (such as Oracle Forms) to calculate tax at the time of the sale.

Tracking endangered species globally (the hard example)

Tracking endangered species globally is a worthy cause, for sure. If I were creating a database design for the effort, here are the features that I would include:

- ✔ Information-gathering from around the world by using the Internet
- ✔ Massive text archiving of news articles about both positive and negative activities
- ✔ Full text search capabilities
- ✔ Pictures of cute little animals to adopt by sending monthly payments
- ✔ Letters from cute little animals to their sponsors
- ✔ A Save the Guppies program, with a multibillion-dollar government grant
- ✔ Engraved identification tags for all card-carrying members of endangered species
- ✔ A clearinghouse of resources available to people and organizations, cross-referenced by needs, skills, locations, and funding
- ✔ Graphic maps showing populations of animals, color-coded by level of danger of extinction
- ✔ Internet search capabilities linked to graphic maps of areas — clicking the map zooms you to a more detailed map
- ✔ Maps that allow you to click an area and go to a screen that shows all the data about the animals, resources, organizations, and any other items related to the area that you select in the map
- ✔ Automatic coffee dispensers in every cubicle at state offices

Read Chapters 6 and 7 before diving in and designing your own relational database. Those chapters offer invaluable insights on how to put your world into the relational-database format. Remember — the best design for your situation may not be the obvious choice.

As you find out more about databases, you discover that you can fit many pieces of information into the database world. Just remember to allow the databases, like art, to imitate life. When you start expecting life to imitate your database, come up for air. You could turn into one of those nerds who write database books.

Chapter 3

SQL Nuts and Bolts

. . . .

In This Chapter

▶ Starting the SQL Worksheet

▶ Writing queries in SQL

▶ Editing files

▶ Using aliases

▶ Combining tables with joins

▶ Utilizing built-in functions

▶ Grouping and summarizing data

▶ Modifying your data

▶ Fixing things that go wrong

. . . .

$\boldsymbol{y}$ou're going to wear out the book flipping to this chapter so often. In this chapter, I cover information that spans about 300 pages of Oracle8i documentation. You may want to get your coffee pot going, put on your reading glasses, and break out the little tinfoil hat. (Hey! Put down the pocket protector! Easy, now! Just hand it over and there won't be any trouble.)

You may have heard rumors about Oracle8i being so new that you can just write Java scripts to create and run the entire database. Sorry; not quite! You still need a healthy helping of SQL.

This entire chapter is about SQL and relational tables. I include lots of examples for you to review and try out. Be brave. Enjoy yourself. Master the possibilities.

In this chapter, I first cover some background information about SQL. Then I show you how to get some great results by using this powerful tool. Chapter 4 has more SQL to dazzle and delight you. There, I show you how to use SQL to look at and revise data stored in object tables, nested tables, and arrays. Something to look forward to!

Starting Up SQL Worksheet

You may want to follow along by actually typing in the examples I show you in this chapter. To do so, you need to do two things:

- Add the sample schema from the CD-ROM that comes with this book.
- Start up SQL Worksheet.

You can find instructions on how to add the sample schema in Appendix B. After you complete the steps, you have a user called AMY with a password of AMY123 who owns a set of tables, indexes, views, and other goodies for you to use. Start up SQL*Plus Worksheet, and you're in business.

1. **Start up SQL*Plus Worksheet.**

   If you have your LaunchPad up, choose the SQL*Plus Worksheet from the DB: Administration menu. Otherwise, on Windows 95, 98, or NT, select Start⇨Programs⇨Oracle HOME2⇨DBA Management Pack⇨ SQL*Plus Worksheet.

   On UNIX, type this on the command line:

   ```
   oemapp worksheet
   ```

   If you come to a login window, go to Step 2. Otherwise, skip to Step 3.

2. **Log in with your own Oracle8i user name and password.**

   If you have installed the sample schema, log in with user name AMY and password AMY123. Leave the Service box empty if you are running your own personal copy of Oracle8i. Otherwise, fill in the name of the Oracle8i instance on your network. Leave the Connect As box defaulted to Normal. The SQL*Plus Worksheet window appears, as you can see in Figure 3-1.

Follow along and type in the examples shown in this chapter to get really familiar with SQL and the SQL*Plus Worksheet. This chapter goes from very basic to very powerful SQL examples in a few short, sweet pages. Hold onto your hat, tinfoil or otherwise.

To type in an example, click in the upper half of the screen and type. Press Enter to go to the next line and continue typing. Use your mouse to highlight and make corrections as needed. To run the command, click the Execute button (the lightning bolt). The command is copied into the bottom section and executed. The results appear in the top half of the window. To run the next command, simply highlight the old command in the lower half of the window, delete the whole thing, and start typing the new command.

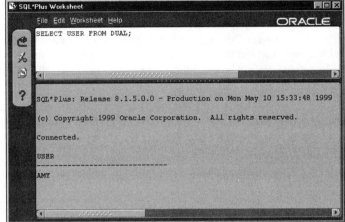

Figure 3-1:
Your
SQL*Plus
Worksheet
is ready
for you.

Asking a Question in SQL

In SQL, you ask a question when you write a query. The example queries in this book all begin with SELECT, which is your clue that they're queries. Your best weapon when you look at your data is a good knowledge of the *schema* (your set of tables) and how the tables relate to one another. You may want to read the stuff about diagrams in Chapter 7 and the stuff about keys in Chapter 6 before you go farther in this chapter.

Very simply put, anything that goes into tables in the database can come out when you use a query. With queries, you can do interesting things such as calculate average sales, find the highest-paid employee, sort by employees' middle initials, and so on.

Here's the magic formula for constructing queries: Know what you want and where it is. Knowing the proper syntax (format) of SQL queries also helps. One of the goals of this chapter is to give you a good working knowledge of how to construct some basic SQL queries for getting data out of a table.

The basic SQL query

A SQL query has five main parts (or clauses):

   ✔ SELECT: Put the list of columns that you want to see here. List all the columns, even if they are from several tables, and separate them with commas.

✔ FROM: Put the table name here. If you have more than one table, list them all and separate them with commas.

✔ WHERE (optional): Put comparisons, limits, and connections between tables here and list them with either AND or OR between each set. The WHERE clause is optional. When the WHERE clause is left out, all rows are chosen.

✔ GROUP BY (optional): Tell how you want data summarized here. You need this clause only for a query that summarizes data. See the "Grouping and Summarizing Data" section later in this chapter.

✔ ORDER BY (optional): List columns to use for sorting here. When there is no ORDER BY clause, rows are returned in no specific order.

A few other types of clauses can go into a query, but the preceding clauses are the primary ones.

Here's how the five parts fit together in a single SQL query:

```
SELECT COLUMN, COLUMN, ...;
FROM TABLE
WHERE CLAUSE
GROUP BY CLAUSE
ORDER BY CLAUSE;
```

Some sample queries

Pretend that you are ruler of the universe, and you're visiting Earth. Pour a glass of wine, have a little cheese, and light up that great contraband Cuban cigar. For all the property you've cataloged so far, you want a list that shows the ID number of the human who currently owns the property, the ID number of the property itself, and a short description of the property. The query looks like this:

```
SELECT HUMAN_ID, PROPERTY_ID, LAND_DESC
FROM PROPERTY_LIST;
```

Three columns are chosen from one table. The results may look like this:

```
HUMAN_ID    PROPERTY_ID LAND_DESC
----------  ----------- ----------

MA-0015487 A-100        LOT ON NORTH SIDE OF LAKE
NY-0000145 B-999        APARTMENT
MA-0015487 A-102        HOUSE IN TOWN
3 rows selected.
```

You want the list in order by human, so you add an ORDER BY clause like this:

```
SELECT HUMAN_ID, PROPERTY_ID, LAND_DESC
FROM PROPERTY_LIST
ORDER BY HUMAN_ID;
```

You execute the query, with this result:

```
HUMAN_ID    PROPERTY_ID LAND_DESC
----------  ----------- ---------
MA-0015487  A-100       LOT ON NORTH SIDE OF LAKE
MA-0015487  A-102       HOUSE IN TOWN
NY-0000145  B-999       APARTMENT
3 rows selected.
```

Suppose you want only the property owned by one human, the one whose ID number is NY-0000145. Add the WHERE clause to narrow down your selection. The WHERE clause comes between the FROM clause and the ORDER BY clause. When you use a word or phrase in the WHERE clause, you enclose it in single quotes. Any entry other than a number must be in single quotes. Otherwise, Oracle8i assumes that the entry is a column name.

```
SELECT HUMAN_ID, PROPERTY_ID, LAND_DESC
FROM PROPERTY_LIST
WHERE HUMAN_ID = 'NY-0000145'
ORDER BY HUMAN_ID;
```

Oracle8i looks for rows that have NY-0000145 in the HUMAN_ID column and then sorts the rows in proper order. Sorting does not do much when you have only one row, but there it is anyway.

```
HUMAN_ID    PROPERTY_I LAND_DESC
----------  ---------- ---------
NY-0000145  B-999      APARTMENT
1 row selected.
```

Some tips to help you write good queries

These tips may help you write good queries. Some of these tips are guidelines or hints for good form; others are simply possibilities — options you have available that you may not be aware of.

  ✔ List columns in the sequence in which they appear in your report. The SELECT clause is your only chance to specify which column comes first, second, and so on.

✔ Use the asterisk to select all the columns in a table to save yourself some typing time when you need all the columns (in the sequence they appear in your table) in your query.

```
SELECT * FROM HUMAN;
```

✔ List columns in the order in which you sort them. This is not a requirement, but it is logical — like listing people's names in the phone book with their last name first to facilitate quick visual searching.

```
SELECT COUNTRY, CITY, STREET ...
ORDER BY COUNTRY, CITY, STREET;
```

✔ Add words or phrases in your SELECT statement if you need them to make your report clearer, as in this example:

```
SELECT 'My name is', FIRST NAME
FROM HUMAN;
```

✔ Sort by multiple columns if you need to do so. List the columns in the ORDER BY clause, as in this example:

```
... ORDER BY COUNTRY, CITY, STREET;
```

✔ Oracle8i is sensitive to uppercase and lowercase in the words or phrases that you place inside single quotes.

```
... WHERE FIRST_NAME = 'Jane';
```

is not the same as

```
... WHERE FIRST_NAME = 'JANE';
```

✔ Oracle8i does not differentiate between uppercase and lowercase for column names, table names, and the select statement clauses.

```
SELECT TOWN FROM HUMAN;
```

is identical to

```
select town from human;
```

In fact, you can mix and match, which I do all the time. Oracle8i sees the following line as the same as the preceding two examples!

```
Select Town from HuMaN;
```

✔ Oracle8i does not care how you arrange your query as far as blank spaces and line breaks are concerned.

```
SELECT TOWN, COUNTRY FROM HUMAN ORDER BY TOWN;
```

is identical to

```
SELECT TOWN, COUNTRY
FROM HUMAN
ORDER BY TOWN;
```

Purely for aesthetics, my personal preference is to start each clause (SELECT, FROM, WHERE, and ORDER BY) on a new line.

✔ When you are working in the SQL*Plus Worksheet, the closing semicolon marks the end of the SQL command. If you are writing a series of queries, separate each one with a semicolon.

Using an Editor While Running SQL*Plus Worksheet

I call up my editor to beg for a deadline extension. You can call up an editor to save files, edit files, and start up files. In SQL*Plus Worksheet, simply click the File⇨Open menu selection to get text from a file and click the File⇨Save input as. . . menu selection to save your SQL commands into file. When you are in SQL*Plus, you can type the following editing commands right in the command line.

✔ EDIT: Opens a temporary file and starts the local text editor for the current SQL query. When you close the file, its contents are written into your current SQL*Plus session.

✔ EDIT filename: Opens a file with the name specified. This command lets you make permanent SQL scripts. You replace filename with the actual file name and, if you want, include the path and suffix.

✔ SAVE filename: Saves the current SQL query in a file. As with the EDIT command, replace filename with the actual file name and, if you want, include the path and suffix.

✔ GET filename: Retrieves a SQL query from the file that you name. The file must contain only one SQL statement: for example, a SELECT statement or an UPDATE statement. If the file contains more than one SQL statement, use the START command.

✔ START filename: Retrieves a file and runs it in the current SQL Worksheet session.

✔ LIST: Lists your current SQL command.

Pulling Out Data without Breaking Anything

"Don't touch that! I said *don't!* There — you broke it! Are you happy now?" Do these phrases sound familiar? If so, you may have a nagging hesitation about constructing a new query.

Don't worry. Data is never changed when you run a query — never. You may slow the entire company to a halt and black out the lights on a city block, but the data is okay.

I wander around in the park and lie awake nights worrying that you may break your fingers if you spend a great deal of time typing long, involved queries. When this insomnia occurs, I just slip on my handy little tinfoil hat to filter out evil thoughts. In an effort to save your fingers, I want to share with you the secret of the alias. An *alias* is an alternative name for a table or a column in a query. Using aliases in the FROM clause of a query saves typing.

A table alias is defined by placing it immediately after the table name and is separated from the table name by a space. In the following partial query, H is the alias for the HUMAN table:

```
SELECT H.HUMAN_ID, H.FIRST_NAME, P.LAND_DESC
FROM HUMAN H, PROPERTY_LIST P
WHERE H.HUMAN_ID = P.HUMAN_ID;
```

The HUMAN table's alias is the letter H. The PROPERTY_LIST table's alias is the letter P. The letters are used as a prefix in the SELECT and the WHERE clauses to save typing out the table names.

You can also define a column alias. This alias appears as the column heading when you execute the SQL. For example, the following query has a column alias for each of its columns:

```
SELECT HUMAN_ID "Human ID", PROPERTY_ID "Prop#",
       LAND_DESC Description
FROM PROPERTY_LIST
WHERE PROPERTY_ID > 'B';
```

Notice that I used double quotes around two of the aliases. Quotes are only needed if you use special characters such as the # sign or spaces, commas, and percent signs or if you want to preserve lowercase letters in the heading. Take careful note that I did not use the column alias in the WHERE clause. The WHERE clause must reference the actual column name. The results look like this:

```
Human ID   Prop#      DESCRIPTION
---------- ---------- -----------
NY-0000145 B-999      APARTMENT
1 row selected.
```

Now that you have determined the whereabouts of Human B-999, you turn over the coordinates to your general and continue into the next galaxy.

Combining Tables: The Meat and Potatoes of SQL

When a query combines data from two tables, the query is called a *join* (or *joining tables*). The key to joining tables is just that — the key! Know your tables, their keys, and how they connect. I've created examples for you in this section, beginning with simple ones and moving on to more complex ones.

Basic join query structure

The basic structure of a join is the same as that of any other query. The primary differences are that you list columns from several tables in the SELECT clause and that you list several tables and tell SQL how they fit together in the WHERE clause. Here's the basic layout:

```
SELECT ALIAS1.COLUMN, ALIAS2.COLUMN, ...
FROM TABLE ALIAS1, TABLE ALIAS2, ...
WHERE ALIAS1.COLUMN = ALIAS2.COLUMN
AND CLAUSE
GROUP BY CLAUSE
ORDER BY CLAUSE;
```

A table alias (indicated in the preceding query as ALIAS1 and ALIAS2) assigns each table in the FROM clause a shorthand nickname. Use the alias (followed by a period) as an identifier to show which table is the source of each column in the other parts of the query (the SELECT, WHERE, GROUP BY, and ORDER BY clauses). Although a table alias is not technically required unless two columns in different tables have identical names, I find it to be important for creating clear and easy-to-follow join queries.

The next section shows several examples of join queries in action. As a general rule, the more tables you add to a query, the more complex the WHERE clause becomes.

Build your query gradually by starting with one table in the query and getting it to run. Next, add one more table and get the query working with two tables. Build onto the query, always stopping to test your results to make sure that your query still works. This way, if you do run into problems, figuring out what part of the query caused the problem — most likely, where you made your most recent change — is much easier. This simple technique saves hours of guesswork, after you've constructed an entire query, in trying to figure out which part doesn't work.

Examples of join queries

Now for the fun part! Imagine that you are a mermaid. You have categorized and catalogued your fantastic collection of rare seaweed in your Oracle8i tables. You have two tables: one called TYPE_OF_SEAWEED for the kind of seaweed and one called SEAWEED_SAMPLE for each unique specimen in your collection. Figure 3-2 shows the two tables, their relationship, and sample data.

You want a simple report that lists the seaweed samples and shows whether they are edible. Here's the SQL code:

```
SELECT SS.SAMPLE_ID, SS.SELLING_PRICE,
SS.SAMPLE_DESCRIPTION, TS.EDIBLE
FROM SEAWEED_SAMPLE SS, TYPE_OF_SEAWEED TS
WHERE TS.TYPE_ID = SS.TYPE_ID
ORDER BY SS.SAMPLE_ID;
```

Here are the results:

SAMPLE_ID	SELLING_PRICE	SAMPLE_DESCRIPTION	EDIBLE
1	100	Leafy green	INEDIBLE
2	30	Purple delicate	EDIBLE
3	110	Green floater	EDIBLE
4	100	Leafy green	INEDIBLE
5	30	Purple delicate	EDIBLE
6	110	Green floater	EDIBLE

Your seaweed is in big demand because of the tidal wave that wiped out all the seaweed farms in the area. You begin selling your seaweed collection. You want to keep track of the people who buy from you in case you want to send them a flyer next year, so you add a table called CLIENT to your database. Now you have three tables, as shown in Figure 3-3. You add a new column to the SEAWEED_SAMPLE table, which is a foreign key to the CLIENT table. (If you don't know what a foreign key is, look it up in Chapter 6.)

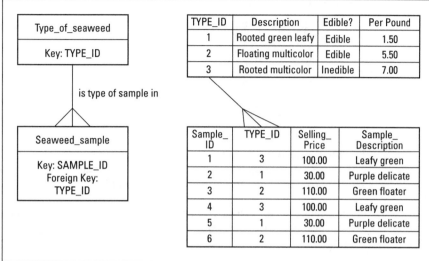

Figure 3-2:
The ultimate
mermaid
treasure —
and it's all
yours!

TYPE_ID	Description	Edible?	Per Pound
1	Rooted green leafy	Edible	1.50
2	Floating multicolor	Edible	5.50
3	Rooted multicolor	Inedible	7.00

Sample_ID	TYPE_ID	Selling_Price	Sample_Description
1	3	100.00	Leafy green
2	1	30.00	Purple delicate
3	2	110.00	Green floater
4	3	100.00	Leafy green
5	1	30.00	Purple delicate
6	2	110.00	Green floater

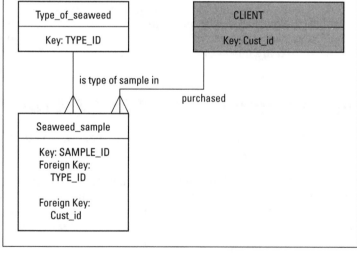

Figure 3-3:
The entre-
preneurial
mermaid
now tracks
clients who
buy her
seaweed
samples.

This query combines all three tables:

```
SELECT SAMPLE_ID, TS.EDIBLE, C.NAME
FROM SEAWEED_SAMPLE SS,
     TYPE_OF_SEAWEED TS,
     CLIENT C
WHERE TS.TYPE_ID = SS.TYPE_ID
AND SS.CUST_ID = C.CUST_ID;
```

The results look something like this:

```
SAMPLE_ID EDIBLE     NAME
---------------------------
1         INEDIBLE   Jane
4         INEDIBLE   Jane
3         EDIBLE     Joe
6         EDIBLE     Joe
2         EDIBLE     Harry
5         EDIBLE     Amy
```

The results show a list of the samples, which types of seaweed are edible, which are inedible, and which of your little mermaid friends bought the sample. You are such an enterprising mermaid!

In the preceding exercises you use SQL commands to get a basic report out of the database. The next section looks at some interesting extras that you get with SQL.

Using the Built-In Functions of Oracle8i

Oracle8i comes with many built-in functions. You can use some of these to manipulate the output of your query. In fact, you can use these functions in the WHERE clause to create truly unique queries. In the next two sections, I discuss two that are most commonly used: TO_CHAR and CONCATENATE.

Reformatting a date with TO_CHAR

One commonly used function is TO_CHAR, which allows you to reformat a date when it is displayed.

Swimming right along with my mermaid example, you determine that you want to send a few clients a birthday card. Query the CLIENT table to see each client's birth date. As a fun trick, you can also use the TO_CHAR function to find out what day of the week each client was born on. Here is the query:

```
SELECT CUST_ID, NAME,
       TO_CHAR(BIRTH_DATE,'MM/DD/YY') "BIRTHDATE",
       TO_CHAR(BIRTH_DATE,'DAY') "BIRTHDAY"
FROM CLIENT
ORDER BY BIRTH_DATE;
```

And the results look like this:

```
CUST_ID    NAME           Birthdate  Birthday
---------- -------------- ---------- ---------
1          Jane           06/11/59   Thursday
4          Amy            09/25/63   Wednesday
2          Joe            05/30/66   Monday
3          Harry          10/14/71   Thursday
5          Jimmy          01/07/74   Monday
```

The TO_CHAR function has a couple dozen parameters you can use to format the date any way you please.

The date datatype contains both time and date. If you do not specify a time, Oracle8i assigns the default time of midnight. Use the TO_CHAR function to view the time. For example TO_CHAR(birthdate,'mm/dd/yy hh:mi') displays the birth date and time.

Concatenating columns with CONCATENATE (||)

You can squeeze two columns together into a single display column just as easily as you put salami in a Kaiser roll. Here's how:

Place the CONCATENATE symbol (||) between two columns. If one of the columns is a date datatype column, add the TO_CHAR function around it to make it into a plain character column.

Here's another mermaid dream: You list your seaweed samples by name and put the edibility of each one in parentheses after its name. Here is the query:

```
SELECT SAMPLE_ID,
SAMPLE_DESCRIPTION || ' (' || EDIBLE || ')' DESCRIPTION
FROM SEAWEED_SAMPLE SS,
     TYPE_OF_SEAWEED TS
WHERE TS.TYPE_ID = SS.TYPE_ID;
```

Two columns, SAMPLE_DESCRIPTION and EDIBLE, were combined together. The parentheses are not in the data and were added as literal values enclosed in single quotes. The entire string was concatenated together with three sets of concatenation marks (each concatenation mark consists of a pair of vertical bars). The whole mess was named DESCRIPTION by using a column alias. Here are the results:

```
SAMPLE_ID  DESCRIPTION
---------- -----------------------
1          Leafy green (INEDIBLE)
2          Purple delicate (EDIBLE)
3          Green floater (EDIBLE)
4          Leafy green (INEDIBLE)
5          Purple delicate (EDIBLE)
6          Green Floater (EDIBLE)
6 rows selected.
```

In the following section, you can see another fine technique that can help you gain friends down at that new bar, The Database Connection.

Grouping and Summarizing Data

Here's a simple question: How do you find out the total number of rows in that massive table without waiting all day for your query results to scroll by?

The answer is: Summarize! In Oracle-speak, you use a group function. A *group function* is a function that performs a routine of some kind to a whole group of rows and displays the results. Group functions do not modify the underlying database.

A number of group functions exist. The most commonly used group functions are:

- ✔ SUM: Add up a column for the selected rows.
- ✔ MIN: Find the lowest value in a column for the selected rows.
- ✔ MAX: Find the highest value in a column for the selected rows.
- ✔ COUNT: Count the number of rows selected.

The basic syntax of the group function is:

```
SELECT groupfunction ( columnname )
FROM ....;
```

Replace *groupfunction* with the function name, and replace *columnname* with the column that requires the function. (In the case of COUNT, you can use * instead of a column name.)

The mermaid really needs to know exactly how many clients she has, so she issues the COUNT function on the CLIENT table like this:

```
SELECT COUNT(*)
FROM CLIENT;
```

The results are:

```
COUNT(*)
-----------------
                5
1 row selected.
```

Now, suppose that the mermaid (that's you, so start swishing your seashells, honey) wants to know how many seaweed samples each client has purchased. This calculation requires the use of a group function (COUNT) and the GROUP BY clause in the query. Here is what the query looks like:

```
SELECT NAME, COUNT(SAMPLE_ID)
FROM CLIENT C,
     SEAWEED_SAMPLE SS
WHERE SS.CUST_ID = C.CUST_ID
GROUP BY NAME
ORDER BY NAME;
```

The results are

```
NAME                                COUNT(SAMPLE_ID)
----------------------------------- ----------------
Amy                                                1
Harry                                              1
Jane                                               2
Joe                                                2
4 rows selected.
```

In the next section, you can look at the other really powerful feature of SQL: modifying your data.

Making Power Changes in the Data

The real power of SQL is evident in the way that it operates on many rows of data at one time. A single line of code can change every row in a table. You can use the same techniques that you use to gather rows together for a report to modify many rows at the same time. I break down the process for you in this section. The three basic commands are UPDATE, INSERT, and DELETE. Each command has some interesting subtleties.

Modifying data with the UPDATE command

Obviously, this overworked command allows you to modify data that you previously put in a table. Maybe you muffed it and put everyone's first name in the last-name field. Maybe you added a new column and need to plug in data. The UPDATE command can help you. The command has several forms. The next two sections cover the two basic forms of the UPDATE command.

Using literals

The most common form of the UPDATE command involves manipulating columns using data from the same row. The basic format of the statement looks like this:

```
UPDATE tablename SET columnname = expression,
columnname2 = expression2
WHERE where clause;
```

Replace tablename with your table's name, and replace columnname and columnname2 with the names of the columns that you want to modify. You can use expression (and expression2) to modify many things: a literal (such as today's date), another column, or some combination of both. Replace where clause with any valid where clause to tell Oracle8i which rows you want to include in the update. You can update all the rows in a table by leaving the WHERE clause off.

You head the ticket sales committee for an upcoming benefit dinner. Your job involves tracking every ticket sale, printing nametags for all the guests, and building a mailing list of all the guests. Naturally, you set up a table (TICKET) in your Oracle database to help you. You start with columns for FIRST_NAME and LAST_NAME. Later, you decide to combine those columns into a new column called FULL_NAME. Now you want to take every first and last name that you have put in the table, combine the names, and put the results in this new column. Here's the statement:

```
UPDATE TICKET
SET FULL_NAME =
FIRST_NAME || ' ' || LAST_NAME;
```

Oracle8i replies with this:

```
9 rows updated.
```

Simple yet effective. This statement updates every row in the table because no WHERE clause is on the end.

You now want to update all the rows of ticket holders who bought their tickets before October 10. You want to give these people an extra raffle ticket for the grand prize drawing because they were the early birds. You create a new column called EXTRA_TICKET that has YES in it for the early birds and NO in it for everyone else. I can think of several ways to update this column. The first method is straightforward and does the work in two separate statements: one for all the early birds and one for everyone else. Here is the UPDATE command for the early birds:

```
UPDATE TICKET
SET EXTRA_TICKET = 'YES'
WHERE PURCHASE_DATE < TO_DATE('10-OCT-97');
```

Oracle8i replies with this:

```
3 rows updated.
```

The UPDATE command for Johnny-come-latelys looks like this:

```
UPDATE TICKET
SET EXTRA_TICKET = 'NO'
WHERE PURCHASE_DATE >= TO_DATE('10-OCT-97');
```

Oracle8i replies with this:

```
6 rows updated.
```

Oracle's date format

Oracle has a standard default format for displaying dates. This standard also affects how you write literal dates in all SQL statements. The format is

DD-MON-YY

DD = day of the month, MON = month (first three letters of the month), and YY = year.

July 5, 1956, for example, is 05-JUL-56, and November 1, 1945, is 01-NOV-45, 01-nov-45, or 01-Nov-45.

The month can be in uppercase, lowercase, or any combination of uppercase and lowercase. April 13, 2005, is 13-Apr-2005.

When you leave the century off the year, Oracle assigns it either 19 or 20, depending on the current century. As I write these words, the current century is represented as 19. But we have only a few short months to go before the twenty-first century bowls us all over.

When you write a literal date in SQL, place it inside the TO_DATE function, which converts characters to a date. TO_DATE('01-OCT-96') converts October 10, 1996, to Oracle's date format.

If, for some reason, you have dates that are in a different format, you can tell Oracle what to expect. TO_DATE('10/15/87', 'mm/dd/yy') converts October 15, 1987, to the Oracle date format. You can use many variations of this format.

Using subqueries

The second variation on the UPDATE command has a great amount of flexibility because it uses a subquery — a query within the UPDATE command. The basic format goes like this:

```
UPDATE tablename SET (columnname, columnname2, ...) =
(SELECT columnname3, columnname4, ...
FROM tablename2
WHERE subquery where clause)
WHERE update where clause;
```

The placement of parentheses is very important.

Replace tablename with the table you are updating. Replace columnname, columnname2, ... with a list of columns you are updating. The subquery is everything inside the parentheses after the equal sign. Inside the subquery, you can place any query you want, so long as the columns in the subquery (columnname3, columnname4, ...) match the columns in the UPDATE command. *The subquery must return exactly one row.* Notice the two WHERE clauses. The first one (subquery where clause) corresponds to the subquery SELECT statement. The second one (update where clause) corresponds to the UPDATE command and tells Oracle8i which rows to update with the data retrieved in the subquery.

The subquery has incredible power! I love using subqueries! Subqueries save so much time and effort and show you how much you can do in SQL. Gush, gush. I put together a few examples to give you some ideas on how to use the subquery format. This format has so many variations that listing them all is impossible.

You run an art gallery. You have a table called MONTHLY_SALES. You update it at the end of the month with the sum of all sold art from the DAILY_SALES table. Here's your UPDATE command for January 1996:

```
UPDATE MONTHLY_SALES
SET (SALES_AMOUNT) =
 (SELECT SUM(SALES_AMOUNT)
  FROM DAILY_SALES
  WHERE SALES_DATE BETWEEN TO_DATE('01-JAN-99')
  AND TO_DATE('31-JAN-99'))
WHERE SALES_MONTH = TO_DATE('JAN-99','MON-YY');
```

Oracle8i tells you it's finished with this:

```
1 row updated.
```

I enclose the subquery in parentheses. The first WHERE clause in this statement relates to the subquery only. The second WHERE clause relates to the UPDATE statement, causing only one row in the TOTAL_SALES_PER_MONTH table to be updated (the one for January 1999).

Using correlated subqueries

The third variation on the UPDATE command is more difficult to understand, but it is also one of the most flexible of the UPDATE commands. This variation is similar to the preceding UPDATE command syntax, except that the subquery is slightly different. The basic format goes like this:

```
UPDATE tablename SET (columnname, columnname2, ...) =
(SELECT columnname3, columnname4, ...
FROM tablename2
WHERE tablename2.columnname5 = tablename.columnname6 and
        suquery where clause)
WHERE update where clause;
```

Replace tablename with the table to be updated. Replace columnname, columnname2, ... with a list of columns to be updated. The subquery is everything inside the parentheses after the equal sign. You can place any query you want inside the subquery. Columns in the subquery must correspond with the UPDATE command's list of columns. *The subquery must return exactly one row for each row updated.*

Notice the two WHERE clauses. The first one (beginning at the WHERE and ending with subquery where clause) corresponds to the correlated subquery SELECT statement. Replace tablename2.columnname5 = tablename.columnname6 with a join clause that connects (correlates) the table that you're updating with the table in the subquery. The second WHERE clause (update where clause) corresponds to the UPDATE command and tells Oracle8i which rows to update with the data retrieved in the subquery.

You are a mermaid — don't argue with me! You categorized and catalogued your seaweed collection beautifully in your Oracle tables. You have two tables: one called TYPE_OF_SEAWEED for the kind of seaweed and one called SEAWEED_SAMPLE for each unique specimen in your collection. One day, a tsunami of incredible force sweeps through your corner of the ocean, which makes certain types of seaweed suddenly very rare. You immediately increase the price per pound of all the edible seaweed. After you do that, you want to update the SELLING_PRICE of all the edible seaweed in your collection to reflect this new situation. All your samples are 20 pounds. You want to update the selling price in your SEAWEED_SAMPLE table so that every edible seaweed gets its price corrected.

Figure 3-4 shows a simple query of the TYPE_OF_SEAWEED table. Four rows include edible seaweed types that range in price from $1.50 to $5.50.

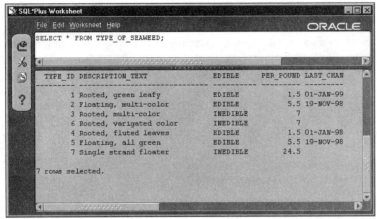

Figure 3-4:
The
sequestered
seaweed
selection of
the solitary
mermaid.

First, you double the price per pound of your edible seaweed. The price per pound is kept in the TYPE_OF_SEAWEED table. Here is the SQL code to double the price:

```
UPDATE TYPE_OF_SEAWEED
SET PER_POUND = 2 * PER_POUND,
LAST_CHANGE_DATE = SYSDATE
WHERE EDIBLE = 'EDIBLE';
```

Oracle8i tells you this:

```
4 rows processed.
```

The SQL code that updates the SEAWEED_SAMPLE table has a *correlated subquery* in it. A *correlated subquery* refers to a column outside the subquery.

Update the selling price of all your edible samples by recalculating the selling price using your updated TYPE_OF_SEAWEED table. The recalculation takes the PER_POUND column value for the correct type of seaweed and multiplies it by 20 (because all your samples are 20 pounds). Actually, many variations of SQL code give you the same results. The SQL code for changing the selling price of edible seaweed looks like this:

```
UPDATE SEAWEED_SAMPLE SS SET (SELLING_PRICE) =
   (SELECT TS.PER_POUND * 20
   FROM TYPE_OF_SEAWEED TS
   WHERE TS.TYPE_ID = SS.TYPE_ID
      AND EDIBLE = 'EDIBLE')
WHERE SS.TYPE_ID IN (SELECT TS1.TYPE_ID
         FROM TYPE_OF_SEAWEED TS1
         WHERE TS1.EDIBLE = 'EDIBLE');
```

Oracle8i complies and says

```
4 rows processed.
```

The alias `TS` tells you that the first `TYPE_ID` in the subquery refers to the `TYPE_OF_SEAWEED` table. The alias `SS` tells you that the second `TYPE_ID` comes from the `SEAWEED_SAMPLE` table, which is not in the subquery at all but in the outer part of the `UPDATE` command.

The last three lines are another `WHERE` clause that narrows down the rows to be updated by saying, "Update only those rows that have a `TYPE_ID` that is in a list of `TYPE_ID`s that are edible."

The correlated subquery is a powerful tool, and getting the hang of it may take some experimentation and study.

When you're trying an `UPDATE` command, remember that `ROLLBACK` can undo the updates.

Inserting new rows with grace and style

I'll be brief: The `INSERT` command has three forms that are similar to the `UPDATE` command.

Inserting a single row

Here's the way to insert a row where you know exactly what the row will look like:

```
INSERT INTO tablename (columnname1, columnname2, ...) values
(value1, value2, ...);
```

Replace `tablename` with the table into which you insert the row.

Replace `columnname1`, `columnname2`, and so on with the names of the columns you insert data into. You can omit the entire list of columns as long as your list of values matches the table's columns exactly.

Replace `value1`, `value2`, and so on with the actual data. You must enclose everything except numbers in single quotes. Dates must be in the standard Oracle format (`dd-mon-yy`) and in single quotes.

Make sure your list of values is in the same order as your list of columns. When you omit the list of columns, your list of values must be in the same order as the columns as they are defined in the table.

You, the enterprising mermaid, have discovered a new type of seaweed that has never before been identified. Your immediate response is, of course, to add it to the TYPE_OF_SEAWEED table in your fabulous underwater Oracle database. You currently have six types of seaweed in your table. Here's the code to add a seventh variety:

```
INSERT INTO TYPE_OF_SEAWEED
(TYPE_ID, DESCRIPTION_TEXT, EDIBLE, PER_POUND) VALUES
(4, 'Single strand floater','INEDIBLE',24.50);
```

Oracle replies:

```
1 row created.
```

Don't forget to COMMIT your changes to the database. Type:

```
COMMIT;
```

Oracle replies:

```
Commit complete.
```

Inserting with a subquery or correlated subquery

INSERT is similar to the subquery used in updates. Review the section on updates using subqueries for a detailed look at how to write a subquery. I will not repeat myself over and over again and again this time.

The basic format for this kind of INSERT command is:

```
INSERT INTO tablename (column1, column2, ... ) subquery;
```

The main difference between UPDATE and INSERT is that the INSERT command has no parentheses around the subquery. Again, you can leave the list of columns out if you are including every column in the table. You list the columns in the same order in which they appear in the table.

At the risk of getting hate mail from mermaids, I continue to play with this plausible example in which you are indeed a mermaid. Swish your tail and take a deep breath of water as you prepare to try this example.

Your neighbor, Millie Mermaid, gave you a disk with her mailing list on it. You want to insert all the merfolk into your CLIENT table. Here's the command:

```
INSERT INTO CLIENT
SELECT CUST_ID+125, NAME_OF_CLIENT,
STREET_ADDRESS || ' ' ||CITY_STATE_ZIP, NULL
FROM MILLIES_MAILING_LIST;
```

Oracle8i replies

```
4 rows processed.
```

Because you include every column in the right order, you do not have the column list in the command. Millie's table, called MILLIES_MAILING_LIST, has a CUST_ID, as yours does. You do have to accommodate some differences between her list and yours:

✔ Her address is broken into two columns, which you combine in your ADDRESS column by using the CONCATENATE function.

✔ You already have CUST_IDs from 1 to 125, so you add 125 to Millie's CUST_ID to make sure that you get a unique CUST_ID.

✔ Millie does not have a COUNTRY column, so you substitute NULL in this column for all the inserted rows.

Deleting rows with distinction

The DELETE command is simple and to the point:

```
DELETE FROM tablename
WHERE clause;
```

Replace tablename with the actual table name. Replace clause with any valid WHERE clause, like one that you would put in a query. The WHERE clause can include subqueries or correlated subqueries if you want.

You have changed your mind — not that this ever happens to you, I'm sure! You decide to throw out every inedible seaweed sample that you own because you're moving to a smaller sea cave. Here's the code:

```
DELETE FROM SEAWEED_SAMPLE
WHERE TYPE_ID IN (SELECT TYPE_ID FROM TYPE_OF_SEAWEED
        WHERE EDIBLE = 'INEDIBLE');
```

Oracle8i says

```
2 rows processed.
```

This code uses a subquery that creates a list of all the inedible seaweed types. Then the main WHERE clause uses that list to choose which rows to delete.

Test your DELETE statement by creating a SELECT statement that uses the same WHERE clause. This way, you can look at what rows are being selected for deletion before you delete them.

Fixing Mistakes, or Where's the Brake?!

When Oracle8i makes a change permanent, it calls this a *commit,* or *committing* the change, because you use the COMMIT command. After Oracle8i has committed something, you cannot undo it (unless, of course, you write some SQL that changes it back and then commit that change). Before the commit occurs, you can undo a command with the ROLLBACK command.

The COMMIT and ROLLBACK commands

When you use the COMMIT and ROLLBACK commands, here's what you tell Oracle8i to do:

- ✔ COMMIT: Save as permanent all changes made since the last commit was implemented in the database.
- ✔ ROLLBACK: Remove all changes since the last commit was implemented.

One interesting thing about the COMMIT command becomes evident when you look at data using SQL*Plus or SQL*Plus Worksheet. Suppose I update ten rows in a table. When I select the ten rows, I see my data with the changes. However, as in life, until you commit to change, others can't see the change. In other words, Joe can query **the same ten rows** before I commit my changes, and he sees them as unchanged even when I see them as changed. After I commit, Joe's next query shows the ten rows with the changes, just as I see them.

Another interesting point that only comes up when you share your database with others is the *locked row.* After I make a change to a row, Oracle8i *locks* that row to prevent others from changing the row. Others can still query the data, and they see the data as if it were not changed. If they attempt to change the data, they receive an error message. When I commit, the lock goes away. The lock prevents two people from overlaying each other's updates.

Commands that can't be undone, even with ROLLBACK

Some insidious commands have an automatic commit built in, which means that if you make changes that you have not yet committed to the database and you execute one of these commands, the changes get committed automatically. The most commonly used commands that automatically commit prior changes are

- ✔ ALTER: You can alter a table, index, tablespace, and more.
- ✔ CREATE: You can create tables, indexes, tablespaces, database links, synonyms, views, users, roles, and so on.
- ✔ DROP: You can drop just about anything you create.
- ✔ RENAME: You can change the name of a table, view, or index.

Now that you have gotten your feet wet with SQL for relational tables, batten down the hatches to launch into SQL for objects in the next chapter.

Chapter 4

Object SQL: The New Stuff

● ●

In This Chapter

▶ Having more fun than you dreamed possible

▶ Finding out what your objects look like

▶ Displaying object table data

▶ Fooling around with nested tables and varrays

▶ Putting more data into object tables

▶ Adding and removing data in nested tables

● ●

*T*here is more to the imagination than is dreamed of in your universe. How's that for a misquoted quote? Reading the Oracle8i documentation about objects and how to use them is a lot like reading the study guide for a Shakespearean play — the poetry gets lost in the translation.

This chapter gives you not only the facts but also the *feel* of objects (you'll know objects as if they were old familiar friends). After reading this chapter, you'll be just as comfortable querying object tables as you are querying good old relational tables.

In order to get the most out of this chapter, you need to understand the basic construction of a SQL query. If you want to brush up on this subject, page back to Chapter 3 and look it over.

All the examples in this chapter use a sample object schema called the BAKERY. You can create this schema by using the accompanying CD-ROM. Check out Appendix B and follow the instructions for creating the BAKERY schema.

The BAKERY schema contains two object tables:

▸ INGREDIENT_OBJECT_TABLE. This table contains a list of ingredients that the bakery has on hand for mixing up all the different kinds of bread.

▸ BREAD_OBJECT_TABLE. This table contains a nested table of ingredients and amounts that make up the RECIPE_NESTED_TABLE_COL column.

The BAKERY schema also contains a *hybrid table* — a table containing a combination of regular columns and object type columns — called the CUSTOMER_HYBRID_TABLE. This table has a varray containing a list of the breads that a particular customer has purchased. The varray column is named PURCHASE_VARRAY_COL. Chapter 2 has a good definition of *varray*.

I have deliberately named the objects, columns, types, and attributes with names that describe what kinds of objects they are. Table 4-1 shows all the pieces and parts that I use in this chapter.

Table 4-1 Sample Types, Objects, and Attributes for Chapter 4

Name	Kind of Item	Attribute	Attribute Datatype
INGREDIENT_ TYPE	OBJECT TYPE	INGREDIENT_NO	NUMBER
		INGREDIENT_ NAME	VARCHAR2
		PRICE_PER_ OUNCE	NUMBER
		OUNCES_IN_ STOCK	NUMBER
BREAD_TYPE	OBJECT TYPE	BREAD_NO	NUMBER
		BREAD_NAME	VARCHAR2
		SALE_PRICE	NUMBER
		IN_STOCK	NUMBER
		RECIPE_ NESTED_ TABLE_COL	
		RECIPE_NESTED_ TABLE_TYPE	
RECIPE_TYPE	OBJECT TYPE	INGREDIENT_ NO_REF	REF to INGREDIENT_TYPE
		AMOUNT_IN_ OUNCES	NUMBER
RECIPE_NESTED_ TABLE_TYPE	TABLE TYPE		Table of RECIPE_TYPE

Name	Kind of Item	Attribute	Attribute Datatype
PURCHASE_TYPE	OBJECT TYPE	BREAD_NO	NUMBER
PURCHASE VARRAY_TYPE	VARRAY TYPE		Varray (10) of PURCHASE_TYPE
BREAD_OBJECT_ TABLE	OBJECT TABLE		Row of BREAD_TYPE
INGREDIENT_ OBJECT_TYPE	OBJECT TABLE		Row of INGREDIENT_TYPE
ADDRESS_TYPE	OBJECT TYPE	STREET_ ADDRESS	VARCHAR2
		CITY	VARCHAR2
		STATE	VARCHAR2
		COUNTRY	VARCHAR2
CUSTOMER_ HYBRID_TABLE	HYBRID TABLE	CUSTOMER_ID	NUMBER
		FIRST_NAME	VARCHAR2
		LAST_NAME	VARCHAR2
		FULLADDRESS	ADDRESS_TYPE
		PHONENUMBER	VARCHAR2
		PURCHASE_ VARRAY_COL	PURCHASE_ VARRAY_TYPE

The SQL examples in this chapter use the items shown in Table 4-1. Notice that the item names have a distinct pattern. For example, an object table always has the suffix OBJECT_TABLE in its name. I named them this way so that you can easily distinguish when to use the type name and when to use the attribute name in the sample SQL. This distinction becomes clearer when you make your own objects and work with them.

Starting Up SQL Worksheet

To follow along with the examples in this chapter, use SQL*Plus Worksheet.

Start up SQL*Plus Worksheet by following these steps:

1. **If you have your LaunchPad open, choose Schema Manager from the DB: Administration menu. Otherwise, on Windows 95, 98, or NT, choose Start⇨Programs⇨Oracle HOME2⇨DBA Management Pack⇨ Schema Manager.**

   On UNIX, type the following command at the operating system prompt:

   ```
   oemapp worksheet
   ```

   If a login window appears, proceed to Step 2. Otherwise, you may have logged in with the incorrect user name. If you are sure you are logged in with the right user name, you are done. Otherwise, select File⇨ Change Database Connection and proceed to Step 2.

2. **Log in as the table owner and choose the radio button labeled Connect Directly to a Database.**

   If you want to follow the examples in this chapter, log in as BAKER, using the password BAKER. Leave the Service box blank to reach your PC's database or type in the instance name of the Oracle8i database on your network. Leave the Connect As box set to the default of Normal.

Follow along and type in the examples from this chapter to familiarize yourself with SQL for object tables. You're gonna love it.

To create and execute SQL in SQL*Plus Worksheet:

✔ **Click in the upper half of the screen and then type.** Press Enter to go to the next line and continue typing.

✔ **Use your mouse to highlight and make corrections as needed.**

✔ **Add a semicolon to the end of the command.**

✔ **Click the Execute button (the lightning bolt) to run the command.** The command is copied into the lower section and executed. The results appear in the lower half of the window.

✔ **When you're finished, highlight the old command in the upper half of the window, delete the whole thing, and start typing a new command.**

Querying Object Tables in SQL

Object tables, a fairly new Oracle invention, can seem tricky to use. Oracle8i adds some new twists on its SQL commands to handle many situations that arise with object tables. Find out how to create your own object tables in Chapter 11.

However, you still can't do some things with plain old SQL; for these opera-tions, you need to know PL/SQL, a subject that isn't covered in this book. A set of methods that are built-in for all object tables can be used only within PL/SQL blocks. These methods involve sorting, comparing, and adding null rows to nested tables and deleting rows from varrays. PL/SQL is not covered in this book because it is an advanced topic. If you want to learn about PL/SQL, check out another of my books, *Oracle8 Bible* (also published by IDG Books Worldwide, Inc.).

With SQL, you can do the basics — query, insert, update, and delete — and you find out how to do all those things in the next few sections. So, put on your favorite CD, grab your best brain-stimulating beverage, pull up a chair, and dive in.

The basic object-oriented SQL query

If your object table contains nothing but the usual datatypes in its object type attributes, you can proceed with a query that is just like a query you would use for a relational table.

For example, the INGREDIENT_OBJECT_TABLE contains rows made up of the INGREDIENT_TYPE. Looking at Table 4-1, you can see that INGREDIENT_TYPE is an object type with attributes that are either NUMBER or VARCHAR2. Because these attributes are standard to Oracle8i, you can create a simple query like this to display your ingredients:

```
SELECT * FROM INGREDIENT_OBJECT_TABLE;
```

SQL*Plus Worksheet displays the results:

```
INGREDIENT_NO INGREDIENT_NAME PRICE_PER_OUNCE OUNCES_IN_STOCK
------------- --------------- --------------- ---------------
          101 Cinnamon                      2             150
          102 Flour                       .04            3500
          103 Bananas                     .06             680
          104 Nuts                        .22             425
          105 Yeast                        .2             995
          106 Salt                        .03             245
6 rows selected.
```

You can add a WHERE clause to this query, just as you would do with a rela-tional table query. The following query lists any ingredients that have a price per ounce over .1:

```
SELECT * FROM INGREDIENT_OBJECT_TABLE
WHERE PRICE_PER_OUNCE > .1;
```

Oracle8i shows these results:

```
INGRED INGREDIENT_NAME PRICE_PER_OUNCE OUNCES_IN_STOCK
------ --------------- --------------- ---------------
   101 Cinnamon                     2              150
   104 Nuts                       .22              425
   105 Yeast                       .2              995
```

If you try this query on any table that contains another object type, a nested table, or a varray in one of its columns, the column that is an object type, nested table, or varray shows up with identifying data inside the record. Here is an example:

```
SELECT * FROM CUSTOMER_HYBRID_TABLE;
```

The table — CUSTOMER HYBRID TABLE — contains the FULLADDRESS column, which uses ADDRESS_TYPE as its datatype. The results of the query are shown in Figure 4-1.

Figure 4-1:
When you query a table with columns that contain objects, the results look different from when you query a relational table.

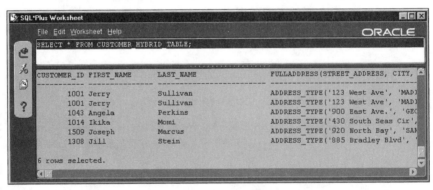

To remove the attributes from the column that contains the object type, use this format in the SELECT clause:

```
tablealias.columnname.attributename
```

The tablealias is the alias that you must specify in the FROM clause, the columnname is the column from the table, and the attributename is the attribute from the object type that defines the column. I define the concept of table aliases completely in Chapter 3.

For example, use this query to grab the first name and city of each of your customers:

```
SELECT FIRST_NAME,
C.FULLADDRESS.CITY
FROM CUSTOMER_HYBRID_TABLE C;
```

The table alias is the letter C, the column name is FULLADDRESS, and the attribute name is CITY. Here are the results of the query:

```
FIRST_NAME        FULLADDRESS.CITY
----------        ----------------
Jerry             MADISON
Angela            GEORGETOWN
Ikika             TOBAGO
Joseph            SAN FRANCISCO
Jill              BOSTON
6 rows selected.
```

The moment that you add anything related to objects to your SQL query, you must use a table alias. If you don't use an alias, you always get this error:

```
ORA-00904: invalid column name
```

Queries using a nested table

A *nested table* is a table embedded inside another table's column. By definition, you can get more than one row of data from the nested table for each row in the primary table. How do you do this?

Oracle8i has a new technique called *flattening* a nested table. In effect, you pretend that the nested table is a stand-alone table, but in the FROM clause, you don't name a table. Instead, you include an entire query (a subquery) that grabs the column containing the nested table. The basic format of the query is

```
SELECT alias1.ntattribute, ...
FROM TABLE (SELECT alias2.ntcolumn
            FROM tablename alias2
            WHERE clause) alias1;
```

Using the new technique of flattening a nested table, you replace

  ✔ alias1 with the alias that you create for the subquery

  ✔ ntattribute with the nested table attribute that you want to view

  ✔ tablename with the main table that contains the nested table

✔ `alias2` with an alias for the main table

✔ `clause` with a query criteria that makes the subquery return a single row of data from the main table (each main table row contains one complete nested table).

One fully flattened nested table is queried.

For example, the `BAKERY` schema contains a bread table that stores the bread names. One of the columns in the bread table contains a nested table that consists of a set of rows: one row for each ingredient that you need to make the bread. This column is named `RECIPE_NESTED_TABLE_COL`. Find `RECIPE_NESTED_TABLE_TYPE` in Table 4-1 to review the attributes in the nested table. Use the following query to return the ingredients needed to make a loaf of Cinnamon Swirl bread (bread number 1):

```
SELECT P.INGREDIENT_NO_REF.INGREDIENT_NAME,
       P.AMOUNT_IN_OUNCES
FROM TABLE (SELECT B.RECIPE_NESTED_TABLE_COL
            FROM BREAD_OBJECT_TABLE B
WHERE BREAD_NO = 1) P;
```

The query returns this list of ingredients:

```
INGREDIENT_NO_REF.INGREDIENT_NO AMOUNT_IN_OUNCES
------------------ -------------- ----------------
Cinnamon                                          2
Flour                                            64
Yeast                                             2
Salt                                             .3
```

Here's a cool trick: The following query shows you how to pull out all the rows from the bread table and list their recipe ingredients. The key is to use the `CURSOR` keyword in the `SELECT` clause and place a subquery inside the `SELECT` clause. Clever. Too clever to make sense, but you can definitely win some points for this kind of query. Here it is:

```
SELECT B.BREAD_NO, B.BREAD_NAME,
CURSOR (SELECT NT.INGREDIENT_NO_REF.INGREDIENT_NAME,
               NT.AMOUNT_IN_OUNCES
        FROM TABLE (B.RECIPE_NESTED_TABLE_COL) NT )
FROM BREAD_OBJECT_TABLE B;
```

Oracle displays this list of recipes:

```
  BREAD_NO BREAD_NAME            CURSOR(SELECTL.INGRE
---------- -----------          --------------------
         1 Cinnamon Swirl       CURSOR STATEMENT : 3
CURSOR STATEMENT : 3
INGREDIENT_NO_REF.INGREDIENT_NO AMOUNT_IN_OUNCES
------------------------------- ----------------
Cinnamon                                       2
Flour                                         64
Yeast                                          2
Salt                                          .3

         2 Nutty Banana        CURSOR STATEMENT : 3

CURSOR STATEMENT : 3

INGREDIENT_NO_REF.INGREDIENT_NO AMOUNT_IN_OUNCES
------------------------------- ----------------
Flour                                         72
Bananas                                        4
Yeast                                          2
Salt                                          .5

         3 Plain White         CURSOR STATEMENT : 3

CURSOR STATEMENT : 3

INGREDIENT_NO_REF.INGREDIENT_NO AMOUNT_IN_OUNCES
------------------------------- ----------------
Flour                                         72
Yeast                                          2
Salt                                          .5
```

Notice the attribute named NT.INGREDIENT_NO_REF.INGREDIENT_NAME in the previous query. This attribute is like an embedded join connecting to another table. Here's how it works:

- The NT table alias refers to the nested table column.

- The INGREDIENT_NO_REF column contains the Object ID (OID) of one row in the INGREDIENT_OBJECT_TABLE. This column is similar to a foreign key column, which contains the value of the primary key for one row of another table. The datatype of the OID attribute is always REF, which is a special datatype for object tables.

- The INGREDIENT_OBJECT_TABLE contains an attribute named INGREDIENT_NAME. Only object tables can be referenced with an OID. The OID is similar to a ROWID in a relational table.

- By stringing everything together, you get the ingredient name — for example, Cinnamon — for each row of the nested table.

Now, how about some fun with varrays?

Queries using a varray

As you know, a varray is like a nested table, except for two important differences:

- ✔ A varray can contain a maximum number of rows.
- ✔ A varray can't be flattened for simple queries.

These two differences limit the usefulness of a varray because it is more difficult to add and retrieve data from a varray without using PL/SQL.

I recommend that you use nested tables whenever you can so that you don't run into the limitations imposed on varrays.

One exception where you may use a varray is where you store a simple repeating value within a column, such as a list of ten favorite colors. In the example schema, the varray stores up to ten values that tell what bread a customer has purchased.

If you do use a varray, you can see the values stored in the varray by using two different kinds of query techniques. The first technique simply allows Oracle8i to display its interpretation of the varray in a long string. Just name the varray column in your SELECT clause.

For example, the CUSTOMER_HYBRID_TABLE contains a varray. You can query the CUSTOMER_ID column and the varray column as follows:

```
SELECT CUSTOMER_ID, PURCHASE_VARRAY_COL
FROM CUSTOMER_HYBRID_TABLE;
```

The results are messy but accurate, as shown in Figure 4-2.

Figure 4-2: A varray shows up with its parts dissected in this query.

```
SQL*Plus Worksheet                                                    _□×
   File  Edit  Worksheet  Help                                  ORACLE
  SELECT CUSTOMER_ID, PURCHASE_VARRAY_COL
  FROM CUSTOMER_HYBRID_TABLE;

  CUSTOMER_ID PURCHASE_VARRAY_COL(BREAD_NO)
  ----------- ----------------------------------------------------------
         1001 PURCHASE_VARRAY_TYPE(PURCHASE_TYPE(1), PURCHASE_TYPE(2))
         1001 PURCHASE_VARRAY_TYPE(PURCHASE_TYPE(1), PURCHASE_TYPE(2))
         1043 PURCHASE_VARRAY_TYPE(PURCHASE_TYPE(1), PURCHASE_TYPE(2), PURCHASE_TYPE(3))
         1014 PURCHASE_VARRAY_TYPE(PURCHASE_TYPE(1), PURCHASE_TYPE(3))
         1509 PURCHASE_VARRAY_TYPE(PURCHASE_TYPE(2), PURCHASE_TYPE(3))
         1308 PURCHASE_VARRAY_TYPE(PURCHASE_TYPE(2))

  6 rows selected.
```

The second technique yields results that are more like the query of a nested table, but this technique requires you to create a nested table type to use in the query. Because you can't name the attributes inside a varray in your query, you have to work around this by placing the entire varray in a nested table. You create this nested table inside the query, a technique called _casting_.

For example, create a nested table that matches the varray by using the following query:

```
CREATE TYPE PURCHASE_NESTED_TABLE_TYPE
AS TABLE OF PURCHASE_TYPE;
```

Next, use the CAST keyword to tell Oracle8i to interpret the varray as if it were a nested table. The query looks like this:

```
SELECT PURCHASES.BREAD_NO
FROM TABLE (SELECT CAST(CUST.PURCHASE_VARRAY_COL AS
          PURCHASE_NESTED_TABLE_TYPE)
FROM CUSTOMER_HYBRID_TABLE CUST
WHERE CUST.CUSTOMER_ID = 1001) PURCHASES;
```

These results show the data inside the varray:

```
BREAD_NO
----------
         1
         2
```

With the preceding information, you have a good start on varrays.

Making Changes to Object Table Data

When making changes to an object table, you use the UPDATE, INSERT, and DELETE commands, just as you do in relational SQL. The only difference is that with an object table, you must use an alias on the table. And of course, if you're dealing with a nested table, you must flatten it first. For more information on flattening a nested table, see the "Queries using a nested table" section earlier in this chapter. _Flattening_ allows you to make changes to a nested table in the same way that you make changes to a relational table or object table (depending on the characteristics of the nested table).

Updating an object

Say that you want to change the street address of one of your bakery customers. The street address is stored in a column with an object type as its datatype. How do you tell Oracle8i to update just one attribute within that column? Here's how:

```
UPDATE CUSTOMER_HYBRID_TABLE C
SET C.FULLADDRESS.STREET_ADDRESS = '987 West Side Ave.'
WHERE CUSTOMER_ID = 1001;
```

Updating one row in a nested table

To update one row in a nested table, you need to flatten the nested table and then update it as if it were a regular table.

Say that you've made a change to your famous Nutty Banana Bread (bread number 2) recipe by increasing the amount of bananas. Use this update command to change the amount of that one ingredient:

```
UPDATE TABLE (SELECT B.RECIPE_NESTED_TABLE_COL
              FROM BREAD_OBJECT_TABLE B
              WHERE BREAD_NO = 2) RECIPE_LIST
SET RECIPE_LIST.AMOUNT_IN_OUNCES = 100  WHERE
RECIPE_LIST.INGREDIENT_NO_REF.INGREDIENT_NAME =
 'Bananas';
```

SQL*Plus Worksheet replies

```
1 row updated.
```

Inserting rows into an object table

The accompanying CD-ROM includes lots of examples of inserting data into object tables. Take a look at the file named BAKERY.sql in the Make directory.

The trick to inserting rows into an object is to name the object type and follow it with a list of the values in parentheses.

Say that you just got another regular customer at your bakery to fill in your questionnaire. To add this person to the CUSTOMER_HYBRID_TABLE, enter this SQL command:

```
INSERT INTO CUSTOMER_HYBRID_TABLE VALUES
(1041, 'Joe','Smith',
ADDRESS_TYPE('123 West Ave','MADISON','WI','USA'),
'222-333-4444',
PURCHASE_VARRAY_TYPE());
```

The preceding SQL command shows you how to add data to an object type column. The object type column is called FULLADDRESS, but you don't see that name in the command. Instead, you see the object type name followed by a list of data in parentheses:

```
ADDRESS_TYPE('123 West Ave','MADISON','WI','USA')
```

Each field inside the parentheses is a value for one attribute in the ADDRESS_TYPE object.

Here's how you insert a row into an object table that contains a nested table, when you want no data in the nested table:

```
INSERT INTO BREAD_OBJECT_TABLE VALUES
 (4,'Sourdough',.95, 12,RECIPE_NESTED_TABLE_TYPE());
```

You list the nested table *type* (not the nested table *column*) and follow it with an empty pair of parentheses:

```
RECIPE_NESTED_TABLE_TYPE()
```

A later section shows you how to insert rows into the nested table.

Inserting rows into a varray

You can use SQL to insert data into a varray at the same time that you insert the whole row. Here's an example:

```
INSERT INTO CUSTOMER_HYBRID_TABLE VALUES
(1041, 'Joe','Smith',
ADDRESS_TYPE('123 West Ave','MADISON','WI','USA'),
'222-333-4444',
PURCHASE_VARRAY_TYPE(PURCHASE_TYPE(1),
                PURCHASE_TYPE(2)));
```

The varray column is named PURCHASE_VARRAY_COL, but it is *not used* in the preceding INSERT command. Instead, you see the varray *type* named, followed by a list of values inside parentheses:

```
PURCHASE_VARRAY_TYPE(PURCHASE_TYPE(1),PURCHASE_TYPE(2))
```

In this case, the PURCHASE_VARRAY_TYPE contains a varray of an object type, so you must also name this object type and follow it with data in parentheses.

If the varray were a varray of a NUMBER datatype rather than of an object type, you'd be able to simply list the values:

```
PURCHASE_VARRAY_TYPE(1,2)
```

"How do I add data to a nested table?" you ask, anticipating my very next move as if you were reading my mind.

Inserting rows into a nested table

Once again, the flattening technique comes to the rescue. The INSERT command looks clumsy, but hey! It works!

Here are the two basic syntaxes for inserting rows into a nested table:

```
INSERT INTO TABLE (subquery of nested table column )
VALUES (....)
```

or

```
INSERT INTO TABLE (subquery of nested table column )
SELECT ....
```

Remember that the subquery must return one row. And just as you can with a relational table, you can sometimes use a list of values or a SELECT statement to fill the data into a row in your nested table.

For example, add the first row into the recipe nested table for the new sourdough bread that you just added to the database. This row represents the first ingredient in the recipe for sourdough bread. Here is the SQL:

```
INSERT INTO TABLE (
  SELECT  B.RECIPE_NESTED_TABLE_COL
  FROM    BREAD_OBJECT_TABLE B
  WHERE   B.BREAD_NO = 4
  )
  SELECT  REF(I), 2
  FROM    INGREDIENT_OBJECT_TABLE I
  WHERE   I.INGREDIENT_NO = 102;
```

Notice that the subquery retrieves the nested table column for one row in the BREAD_OBJECT_TABLE. When the BREAD_OBJECT_TABLE was created, the column containing the nested table was named RECIPE_NESTED_TABLE_COL. The attributes of each row in the nested table are defined in the RECIPE_TYPE object type. Refer to Table 4-1 to review the attributes.

When using object types, you must prefix attributes with table aliases; otherwise, you receive syntax errors when you try to execute your SQL code.

The first attribute in the nested table is a reference to the INGREDIENT_TYPE object type. You know this because the first attribute is of the REF datatype and has been defined to reference the INGREDIENT_TYPE, which means that you must place an OID into this attribute. Use the REF function to grab the OID for you. The syntax is

```
SELECT  REF(tablealias)
```

Replace tablealias with the alias of the table that you're querying.

Deleting rows from an object table

Deleting rows from an object table is just like deleting rows from a relational table. Remember that if your object table has a nested table in one of its columns, Oracle8i also deletes the corresponding nested table.

Say that you're never going to use cinnamon (ingredient 101) in your bakery again, so you want to delete the row from your list of ingredients, which you store in the INGREDIENT_OBJECT_TABLE. Do it like so:

```
DELETE FROM INGREDIENT_OBJECT_TABLE I
WHERE INGREDIENT_NO = 101;
```

SQL*Plus Worksheet replies

```
1 row deleted.
```

Watch out for dangling refs! Those guys could fall on you as you leave the stadium. Seriously, you must avoid dangling refs in your object tables. A *dangling ref* is a condition in which a row references a row that has been deleted. Oracle8i lets you do this without warning.

The previous example actually creates a dangling ref because you have existing bread recipes that use cinnamon. You can find the dangling refs in the RECIPE_NESTED_TABLE_COL column of the BREAD_OBJECT_TABLE.

Deleting a row from a nested table

I bet that you've already guessed how to delete a row from a nested table. That's right, the great and powerful *flattened* nested table. When deleting a row from a nested table, your WHERE clause refers to attributes of the nested table.

Say that because you've stopped using cinnamon in your Cinnamon Swirl bread, you want to delete that ingredient from your recipe. The recipe is stored in a nested table, so you flatten the nested table by grabbing the nested table inside a single row of the object table. Then you use this flattened table and delete one row from it. Here is the SQL:

```
DELETE TABLE (SELECT B.RECIPE_NESTED_TABLE_COL
             FROM   BREAD_OBJECT_TABLE B
             WHERE  B.BREAD_NO = 1) RECIPE_LIST
WHERE
RECIPE_LIST.INGREDIENT_NO_REF.INGREDIENT_NO = 101;
```

SQL*Plus Worksheet replies:

```
1 row deleted.
```

You have passed through the gauntlet and deserve one cream-puff pie (or a great crab and chives salad if you live in California).

Chapter 5

Using the Enterprise Manager DBA Tools

● ●

In This Chapter

▶ Reviewing the major DBA components

▶ Discovering what's useful to an application designer

▶ Exploring all the miscellaneous parts and what they do

● ●

*T*his chapter is like going to a school prom and dancing with every girl or boy (choose one, the other, or both; who am I to judge?). When you're done, you're tired, but you know their names and their favorite color/pet/ sports team. As in life, you gotta kiss a lot of toads before you find your Prince/Princess Charming. This chapter introduces you to all the components that make up the Enterprise Manager so you can try each one out a little.

Managing the Enterprise Manager

You are about to go exploring where no nerd has gone before. Well, hardly any. You are about to enter into a bunch of individual software modules that together make up the Enterprise Manager. Make it easy on yourself by setting up some parameters that help speed up your connection to each of the modules. I show you how to put the DBA tools and the Enterprise Manager console onto your desktop if you're running NT. Then you can quickly open any of the modules, and the toolbar's settings tell the module how to connect you with the database.

A new tool called the Oracle LaunchPad gives you an easy pick-list of applications on your desktop. To start the LaunchPad on Windows 95, 98, NT, or UNIX, type this command from the operating system command prompt:

```
olp
```

To start LaunchPad each time you start NT, follow these steps:

1. **Click Start⇨Settings⇨Taskbar on the NT menu bar.**

   This action brings up a small window in which you handle taskbar properties.

2. **Click the Start Menu Programs tab.**

   This tab is where you can add or remove programs that start automatically when you start NT.

3. **Click Add and then click Browse.**

   You see the typical Browse window in which you choose a program file from your local hard drive.

4. **Locate the LaunchPad program and then double-click it.**

   The LaunchPad program is named olp.bat. The file is found in the Bin directory under the home directory for Oracle Enterprise Manager. For example, on my copy of NT, the full path and file name is

   ```
   D:\Oracle\OEM2\BIN\olp.bat
   ```

   Your file name must be the same, but the path may vary. Figure 5-1 shows the window at this point.

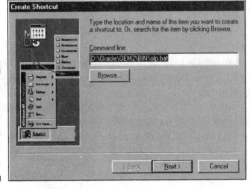

Figure 5-1: Locate the executable file in the BIN directory.

5. **Click Next and then double-click the StartUp folder.**

   In this folder, you tell the system you want it to start the program when NT starts up.

6. **Type some name that you will recognize in the text box.**

   For example, you may type

   ```
   Oracle Enterprise Manager LaunchPad
   ```

7. **Click Finish and then click OK.**

   Now you're ready to take off with the launchpad in place!

From this point forward, whenever you need to use SQL*Plus Worksheet, the Schema Manager, and so on, you simply click the appropriate menu choice in the LaunchPad. Figure 5-2 shows the LaunchPad.

To start LaunchPad without restarting NT, select Start⇨Run, type **olp**, and press OK.

Figure 5-2:
The LaunchPad has your DBA tools on it.

Now that you have streamlined the process of starting up and using the Enterprise Manager tools, you are ready to dive in! Put on your Speedos and get started. I begin with the top view and snorkel my way in from there.

Exploring Three Cornerstone Tools

This section covers three major tools within the Enterprise Manager DBA Management Pack: Storage Manager, Security Manager, and Schema Manager.

Storage Manager: The external viewpoint

The first stop on our round-the-world cruise of Enterprise Manager is the Storage Manager. Here you can get a good view floating above your Oracle world. This manager is concerned with the outermost layer of Oracle8i — where the rain meets the sea, you might say. Where logic meets physics.

Fire up the Storage Manager by following these simple instructions:

1. **Start up the Storage Manager on LaunchPad.**

   Click the DB: Administration menu bar. This action lists the tools on the right. Click the Storage Manager button on the menu. Storage Manager asks you to log in.

2. **Log in with a valid DBA Oracle8i user name and password.**

   One option is to log in with the user ID and password that is loaded into all Oracle8i databases: SYSTEM (password MANAGER). Leave the Service box empty if you are running your own personal copy of Oracle8i. Otherwise, fill in the name of the Oracle8i database (instance) on your network. Leave the Connect As box set to the default of Normal.

   Oracle8i fires up the Storage Manager for you.

3. **Double-click the Tablespaces folder in the left frame.**

   You see a graph showing you each tablespace and what portion is currently in use. This graph is handy for monitoring the storage space used (and unused) by the database. Figure 5-3 shows the Storage Manager window. Mainly, you see that the main focus of the Storage Manager is your files. The buttons and menus are the same as most of the Enterprise Manager tools. In Chapter 1, I describe these items in detail.

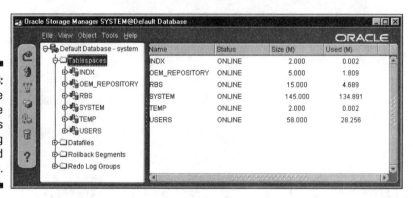

Figure 5-3: The space usage table shows remaining and used space.

4. Click any one of the tablespaces listed below the Tablespaces folder.

A two-tabbed window shows up in the right frame, as you see in Figure 5-4. Under the General tab, you can look at the datafiles that make up this tablespace. You can add a new datafile by clicking the Add button and filling in the next window that appears. You can take a tablespace offline, put it online, or change it to read-only using the buttons and checkboxes in the Status area.

5. Click the Extents tab.

Make a megabyte out of a kilobyte right here. Adjusting the size of a tablespace could not get any easier.

Moving along to the next stop on the tour, I want to direct your attention to the unassuming list on the left side of that coral reef. Look below your list of tablespaces and find the next folder, labeled Datafiles.

6. Double-click the Datafiles folder in the left frame.

A list of the same type as the one for the tablespaces shows up. This one lists each of your datafiles and tells you how much room is left in each one. Good data at a glance! Monitoring this list over a period of time can help you determine which of your datafiles is growing.

7. Click one of the datafiles listed in the left frame.

You have before you the inner secrets of the chosen datafile. Work with your datafiles here. Change a file name, adjust its size, take it offline, or take it out for a date!

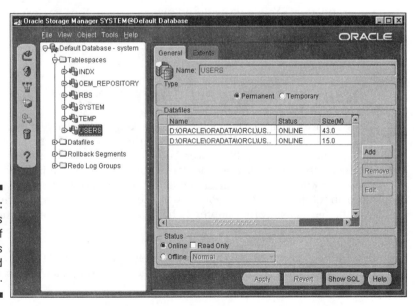

Figure 5-4:
Tablespaces have a lot of details connected with them.

The big green cube icon on the left side of your window creates something: It changes its meaning to match your area of focus. In other words, when you are here, looking at datafiles, the green cube creates a new datafile. When you are there, looking at tablespaces, the clever beast creates a new tablespace.

Next stop: rollback segments. This is the underbelly of the inner workings of Oracle8i. Scroll down until you see the folder labeled Rollback Segments in the left frame.

8. **Double-click the Rollback Segments folder.**

A list of your rollback segments appears below the folder on the left, and the same list, showing the current state of affairs, appears on the right. Here you can see at a glance if any of your rollback segments are filling up.

9. **Click any of the rollback segments listed on the left.**

The window on the right shows you the control panel for this rollback segment. Here you can take the rollback segment online or offline, shrink it, expand it, or copy it.

Rollback segments are happiest when left alone. The care and feeding of rollback segments is beyond the scope of this book. Read up on them in the *Oracle Server Administrator's Guide* before you make any changes to rollback segments.

10. **Close the Storage Manager by clicking the X box in the upper-right corner of the window.**

Congratulations! You have explored two parsecs of the Oracle8i galaxy and returned unharmed. You are ready to refuel and head into another domain: the Security Manager. Engage!

Security Manager: The keeper of the gate

Using Security Manager is like becoming a Klingon Security Officer. Nothing gets past you. You check IDs, ask "What's the password?", and boot aliens out if they don't have the right answer. You stamp everyone's passport with access rights to various areas on your Oracle8i ship. Sometimes you change a guy's password just so he has to come by and visit you. Chapter 9 tells much more about users. It shows you how to use Security Manager to create a user and change a password. Chapter 12 has hands-on instructions on how to create roles and privileges.

Rev up the Security Manager (affectionately known as "S&M" to the tinfoil hat crowd) and follow the instructions as I take you through a wild mouse ride into the realm of security.

1. **Start up the Security Manager on the LaunchPad.**

   Click the DB: Administration menu bar. This action lists the DBA tools on the right. Click the Security Manager button on the menu. If you have already logged into any LaunchPad application, you don't have to log in again, and you can skip to Step 3. Otherwise, Security Manager asks you to log in.

2. **Log in with a valid DBA Oracle8i user name and password.**

   One option is to log in with the user ID and password that is loaded into all Oracle8i databases: SYSTEM (password MANAGER). Leave the Service box empty if you are running your own personal copy of Oracle8i. Otherwise, fill in the name of the Oracle8i database (instance) on your network. Leave the Connect As box set to the default of Normal.

   Oracle8i fires up the Security Manager.

3. **Click the plus sign next to the Users folder in the left frame.**

   The left frame shows the gender of every user (just kidding!). Actually, Oracle8i appears to be non-gender-specific; all these users are wearing blue suits. Maybe they all work for IBM.

4. **Click any one of the users listed below the Users folder.**

   A tabbed window appears in the right frame, as you see in Figure 5-5. Under the General tab, you can look up a user's profile. You can change the password and assign default tablespaces. The default tablespaces tell Oracle8i where to put tables created by this user. The Quota tab lets you set limits on the amount of space available for this user's tables.

5. **Click the Role tab.**

   Here you can add a role, remove a role, or even add table access (Object Privileges). You see how to use these tools in Chapter 12. Speaking of roles, what if you want to see what kind of privileges have been assigned to a role? Funny you should ask! Look below your list of users on the left frame and find the next folder, labeled Roles.

6. **Click the plus sign next to the Roles folder on the left frame.**

   I love this. It's like going to a costume ball. The list of roles on the left has those cute happy masks. Someone on Oracle's development staff got really creative.

7. **Click one of the roles listed in the left frame.**

   The window on the right shows the details about this role and also displays a really ugly red mask. What were those Oracle designers up to, I wonder?

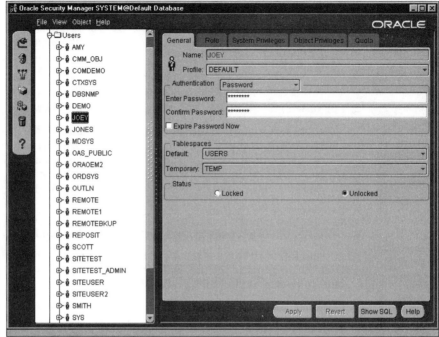

Figure 5-5:
Users have
names,
passwords,
privileges,
and profiles.

8. Click the Role tab.

Roles, like users, can be assigned. For example, you may create a single role called NEPTUNE and then give it all the roles you previously defined (SEASNAKE, MERMAID, WHALE) so that NEPTUNE has the privileges of all these roles combined.

If you remove the CONNECT role, Oracle8i will not allow the user to log in to the database. Also, SYS and SYSTEM are special users created to manage internal data dictionary tables and views. Do not change the roles or privileges of these two users.

9. Click the Object Privileges tab.

You see all the privileges that Oracle8i has given the role for tables, views, synonyms, and so on. This feature can be a handy diagnostic tool.

Our final stop in the Security Manager dive: Profiles.

10. Click the plus sign next to the Profiles folder below the list of roles in the left frame.

The Profiles folder appears below the Roles folder. After you expand the Profiles folder, you can see all the profiles that Oracle8i has set up for your database. Many times, all you see is the default profile. The right frame shows a summary of the profiles.

11. **Click any of the profiles listed on the left.**

The window that appears on the right lets you set parameters for this profile and limit users to a maximum amount of CPU time or storage space. There are other features here, but these are the primary ones. Figure 5-6 shows the profile property page.

12. **Close the Security Manager by clicking the X box in the upper-right corner of the window.**

If you happen to have more than one database to manage, you can switch from one database to another inside the Security Manager (and inside the other managers, too) by clicking File⇨Change Database Connections, which opens up a new login window. After logging in, you return to the windows of the Security Manager (or whatever manager had you involved).

When you are all safe and securely sound, you can turn the corner and cruise on down Main Street: the Schema Manager.

Schema Manager: The builder of tables

Finally, you're in the thick of things. The Schema Manager shows you all your tables, lets you add referential integrity (relationships between two tables), and gives you an easy way to copy tables.

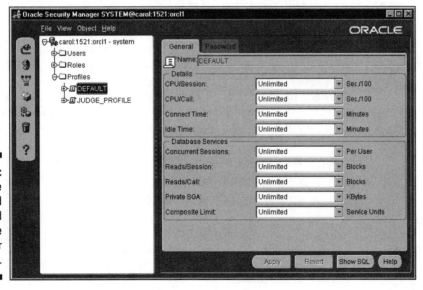

Figure 5-6:
A profile is defined once and can be re-used for many users.

You can even see and edit data here in Schema Manager! My guess is that the folks at Oracle Support got tired of explaining why the Schema Manager was unable to view data. Chapter 10 covers how to use the Schema Manager to create a new table.

Take Schema Manager for a spin. Just follow the instructions, relax, and adjust your helmet for a whirlwind tour.

1. **Start up the Schema Manager.**

   If you have your LaunchPad up, choose the Schema Manager from the DB: Administration menu. Otherwise, on Windows 95, 98, or NT, select Start⇨Programs⇨Oracle HOME2⇨DBA Management Pack⇨ Security Manager.

   On UNIX, type this on the command line:

   ```
   oemapp schema
   ```

   If you come to a login window, go to Step 2. Otherwise, skip to Step 3.

2. **Log in with a valid DBA Oracle8i user name and password.**

   One option is to log in with the user ID and password that is loaded into all Oracle8i databases: SYSTEM (password MANAGER). Leave the Service box empty if you are running your own personal copy of Oracle8i. Otherwise, fill in the name of the Oracle8i database (instance) on your network. Leave the Connect As box set to the default of Normal.

   Oracle8i fires up the Schema Manager for you.

   Schema Manager handles objects, including tables, views, synonyms, constraints on tables, relationships between tables, packages, and more. You can see a complete list of items tracked by the Schema Manager in the left frame when Schema Manager first opens. Pay no attention to the big purple ball on the right. I can only guess what kind of crazed, tinfoil-crowned lunatic dreamed up this bizarre graphic. (I would hate to be a mouse in the corner of his or her virtual bedroom!) I guess users just have to live with it. It disappears after another few mouse clicks, thank goodness.

3. **Choose View⇨By Schema from the menu bar.**

   You see a list of all the users that own tables or other objects. You can browse through the Schema Manager in either mode.

   A set of tables, views, and other objects that are all created by one user are collectively called a *schema.* You do not give a schema a name. It inherits the name of its creator. If the user's Oracle name is AMY, then the schema's name is AMY. This explains why you see user names listed in the Schema Manager.

4. **Choose View➪By Object from the menu bar.**

This action returns you to the default mode of the Schema Manager. Now you start moving through some of the more interesting features of the Schema Manager.

5. **Double-click the Synonyms folder in the left frame.**

You see a list of synonym owners in the left frame and a full list of synonyms in the right frame, as shown in Figure 5-7.

6. **Click the column heading labeled Synonym in the right frame.**

Oracle8i sorts the list of synonyms by name. You can sort by any column listed on the right side in Schema Manager, as in the other tools.

7. **Double-click the SYS schema in the left frame.**

Find this schema listed under the Synonyms folder. The left frame expands to show a list of the synonyms owned by SYS. The right frame only lists these synonyms rather than listing all of them. Don't you just adore the green sunglasses next to each synonym name?

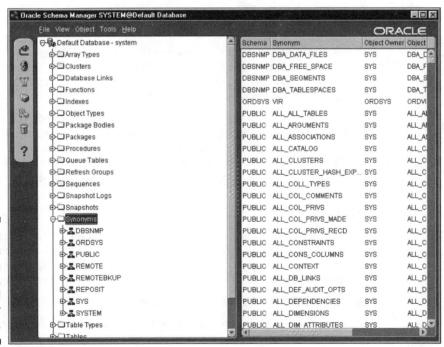

Figure 5-7:
Synonyms
have
schemas,
owners, and
other
attributes.

8. Click any one of the synonyms listed below the Synonyms folder on the left.

A property page shows up in the right frame. You can't do much more than look at this particular page because you can't dynamically change the features of synonyms. To change a synonym, you must remove it and re-create it.

Grayed-out text in a box means that you cannot change that feature.

9. Double-click the Tables folder in the left frame.

Just as with the synonyms, you get a complete list of all the tables in the database.

10. Double-click the SYS schema on the left below the Tables folder.

Just as you expected (it's becoming predictable), you see a list of all the tables created by SYS on the left and on the right.

11. Click one of the tables listed in the left frame.

The window on the right shows details about the table. This property page is more involved than most of the property pages you see in the Schema Manager.

12. Expand the Name column.

Click and drag the border between the Name and Schema column headings. Expand the Name column so you can read the full names listed below it. You can add new columns to a table by typing in the blank row in the Columns box.

You can modify some features (such as the datatype and size) right in this window. To add a new column at the end of the list of columns, simply type the new column name in the first empty row and continue to fill in the datatype, size, and so on. You cannot remove columns from an existing table. See Chapter 19 to find out about changing the columns in a table.

13. Click the Constraints tab.

This window is kind of confusing. It shows you all the constraints on the table. You can add or remove constraints here. This window is where you create primary keys and foreign keys. Chapter 18 takes you through the Constraints window to create primary keys and foreign keys.

14. Expand the list for the current table.

Just click the plus sign next to the table name in the left frame. Notice that you can list indexes, partitions, snapshot logs, and triggers for this table.

15. View and/or edit the table data.

Right-click the table icon next to the table name in the left window. The icon looks like a little bus schedule or a spreadsheet. The icon symbolizes the spreadsheet view of the table you want to work with.

A pop-up menu appears in which you can select Table Data Editor. You can find some really great new features here! Besides being able to edit the table, you can also do these tasks:

- **Create a query using SQL.** Click the SQL icon to create a query. You see a pre-formatted query that contains a list of all the columns. Add a WHERE clause (or whatever you want) and then view the results in the table.

- **Modify which columns you view.** Click the Graphical Select Mode. Here you can choose to hide or display columns, change the heading you see, add a WHERE clause, change the datatype of the display, and more. Schema Manager builds the query for you and displays both the SQL code and the results on the page.

Figure 5-8 shows the spreadsheet layout that you can use to view or edit data in your table.

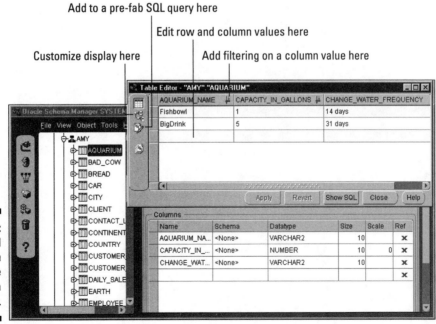

Add to a pre-fab SQL query here

Edit row and column values here

Customize display here

Add filtering on a column value here

Figure 5-8:
Fun and games with data inside Schema Manager.

16. **Close the edit window by clicking the X in the top right corner.**

17. **Expand the Views folder and then expand the SYS schema under the Views folder.**

    As predictable as Vulcan's brow, a list of SYS views appears on the left.

18. **Click any of the views listed on the left.**

    This feature is really cool. In the olden days, you had to wade your way through Martian mud to find the query that was behind a view (men are from Mars; women are from Venus; children are from Earth; programmers are from ?!). Now, it's a walk in the park. You can even make changes right in this text box and change the view by pressing the Apply button. Now, that's cool.

19. **Click the X box in the upper-right corner of the window to close the Schema Manager.**

What a joyride. You can see lots more of the Storage, Security, and Schema Managers in later chapters. I need a nap. Call me in the morning.

Part II
Getting Started

The 5th Wave   By Rich Tennant

"HERE ON ALTAIR-14, WE'VE IMPLEMENTED ANYTHING-TO-ANYTHING INTEGRATION."

In this part . . .

Databases don't grow on trees. They are carefully (or carelessly) grown from an idea hatched in the mind of some crazed genius, namely you. Perhaps you don't actually do the creating, but instead you're at the mercy of the whims of some other crazed genius. This part is your mini-lesson on database design and the inner workings of Oracle8i. It helps you answer these burning questions:

- ✔ If I put data into these tables, should I buy another hard drive?
- ✔ Who am I and what is my role in the world?
- ✔ What the heck did Joe Programmer/Analyst do six months ago?

After you discover that there is some method to the madness, I show you step by step how to create a new Oracle8i user. Enough theory—now get down to business and do something!

Chapter 6

The Relational Model and You

In This Chapter

▶ Discovering relational databases

▶ Playing with keys

▶ Actually using keys

▶ Examining the third normal form

▶ Stepping into the object-relational world

*T*his chapter gives you the information and the confidence that you need to create really terrific tables and join them into a relational database. While you're playing matchmaker and creating relationships among these tables, keep in mind how you're really going to use this stuff when you're on your own. The last sections in the chapter discuss what to do with those newfangled thingies — objects — and how Oracle8i works with objects.

Redundant Relational Database Redundancy

Imagine that you're at your doctor's office with a sprained wrist. The receptionist gives you a clipboard holding a long yellow form. You dutifully but sloppily begin to fill out the form, using your left hand because your right wrist is sprained. You fill in your name, last name first, and address; then you fill it in again in the next section of the form. By the time you reach the third section in which you read "Patient's name and address," your right wrist is throbbing and your left hand is cramped. You leap up and yell, "I hate repeating myself! I hate repeating myself! I hate repeating myself!" The receptionist calmly replies, "Perhaps you would like to file a complaint. Please fill in your name and address on this form in triplicate."

Most likely, the database that stores the information on that yellow form is not a relational database. Relational databases are famous for saving time, space, and wrists by minimizing repeated data. Data lives in one table and has a key. Other tables retrieve that data with the key. Here's how relational databases minimize repeated data.

The database has one table for both name and address. The operator types it in once, and the database assigns a *key* — a column or set of columns that identifies rows in a table. Another table tracks the doctor visit and contains a column for the key of the row with the patient's name and address. Another column gets the key for the billing name and address. A third column has the key for the insured's name and address. Relational databases have many advantages:

 ✔ The patient writes the name and address only once.

 ✔ The name and address are entered into the database only once.

 ✔ Any time the same patient returns, the same name and address can be used without any repeated typing.

 ✔ Changes in the name and address are entered once and affect all three tables automatically.

 ✔ If the names and addresses are different for the patient, billing party, or insured person, the database handles the differences without making special exceptions. Very simply, the second address is a new row in the PATIENT_NAME_&_ADDRESS table, and this new ID goes in the appropriate column of the DOCTOR_VISIT table.

Keys Rule

When you think of a key, you probably picture your house key or perhaps the key to your Jaguar. Without that key, you can admire your Jaguar like all the other poor schmucks on your block, but you can't drive it. If you lose your key, you have to get a new one made. If you get a totally new key, you may even have to change the locks so that the old key no longer works. Database keys have similar attributes:

 ✔ Keys are important in locating a particular row within a table.

 ✔ Keys get you inside a table quickly and directly.

 ✔ If you lose the key to a table, you must replace it. Losing the key to a table is unlikely, though possible.

Considering types of keys

Three kinds of keys are used in relational databases:

- ✔ **Primary key:** This key is the kingpin of all keys. The primary key may be one column or a set of columns. In all cases, the primary key contains a value that is unique across all the rows in that table. If you know the primary-key value, you can single out one row in a table, regardless of how many rows the table contains. A primary key for tables is like a Social Security number for U.S. citizens. A single column that contains an ID number is the best kind of primary key for fast retrieval of data.

- ✔ **Foreign key:** A key that resides in one table but is the key to a different table is called a *foreign key.* The primary key of the connected table is kept in the foreign-key column in the other table. Perfectly clear, right? See the "Importing foreign keys" section of this chapter for more details.

- ✔ **Alternate key:** The primary key identifies each row in a table. Sometimes you have a second way to identify a unique row. This second way is called an *alternate key,* and it is a column or set of columns, just like the primary key.

Importing foreign keys

A foreign key lives in a table for only one reason: to connect the table to another table. Like a foreign country's diplomat, a foreign key represents its entire country — that is, its entire table. By plugging a foreign key into a table, you make a link to all the information stored in the other table. Strategic and careful use of foreign keys requires logic and common sense — and sometimes experimentation. Be sure to declare all contraband when you pass through Customs. Search and detention can be unpleasant.

Imagine that you're a baker and you make ten kinds of bread. Each kind has a price and many different ingredients. Your database administrator (every baker has one) designed two tables for you: one for the bread and one for the ingredients. Each of these tables has a primary key. The BREAD table's primary key is BREAD_NO, and the INGREDIENT table's primary key is INGREDIENT_NO. To calculate the cost of a loaf of bread, you ask your database administrator to create a third table: the RECIPE table, where you have your head baker enter the ingredients and the amount of each ingredient for the bread. The three tables are diagrammed in Figure 6-1. The diagram shown in the figure is a classic type of diagram used in designing relational databases; it's called an Entity Relationship Diagram (or ERD).

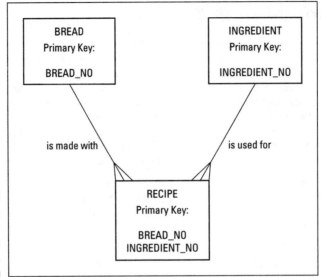

Figure 6-1:
Bakers
knead more
dough.

After dusting off the keyboard and the computer screen, you discover that your head baker left some data that you can use in the tables. Figure 6-2 shows you the three tables in Oracle8i.

Now you're probably wondering how to calculate the profit (selling price minus cost) of each kind of bread. By reading each table's foreign-key connections, you can determine that Nutty Banana Bread costs $3.54 to make. You're selling the bread for $3.25, so it must be your loss leader. Go ahead. Break out your calculator. Do the math. I show you the calculations here. Follow along with me by looking at Figure 6-2.

1. **Look at the BREAD table query results at the top of the figure.**

   You see that Nutty Banana Bread has a primary key of 2.

2. **Look at the RECIPE table query results at the bottom of the figure.**

   You see that the four rows have 2 as the foreign key in the BREAD_NO column.

3. **Read across the four rows.**

   You find numbers in the foreign-key column called INGREDIENT_NO.

4. **Go to the INGREDIENT table query results in the middle of the figure.**

   You see that the numbers are primary keys representing the following ingredients in Nutty Banana Bread:

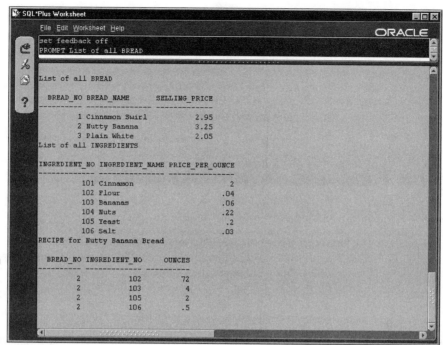

```
SQL*Plus Worksheet                                                    _ □ ×
 File  Edit  Worksheet  Help
                                                              ORACLE
 set feedback off
 PROMPT List of all BREAD

 List of all BREAD

   BREAD_NO BREAD_NAME      SELLING_PRICE
 ---------- --------------- -------------
          1 Cinnamon Swirl           2.95
          2 Nutty Banana             3.25
          3 Plain White              2.05
 List of all INGREDIENTS

 INGREDIENT_NO INGREDIENT_NAME PRICE_PER_OUNCE
 ------------- --------------- ---------------
           101 Cinnamon                      2
           102 Flour                       .04
           103 Bananas                     .06
           104 Nuts                        .22
           105 Yeast                        .2
           106 Salt                        .03
 RECIPE for Nutty Banana Bread

   BREAD_NO INGREDIENT_NO    OUNCES
 ---------- -------------    ------
          2           102        72
          2           103         4
          2           105         2
          2           106        .5
```

Figure 6-2:
Three great
tables show
their wares.

102 = Flour

103 = Bananas

105 = Yeast

106 = Salt

5. **Reading across the rows, find the cost of each ingredient.**

6. **Multiply the cost of each ingredient by the amount in the** RECIPE
   table.

   You can calculate the cost of a loaf of Nutty Banana Bread as follows:

72 oz. Flour	·	.04/oz.	=	2.88
4 oz. Bananas	·	.06/oz.	=	.24
2 oz. Yeast	·	.2/oz.	=	.40
.5 oz. Salt	·	.03/oz.	=	.015
Total Cost			=	3.535

For more foreign-key goodies, see Chapter 18, where you find out how to create foreign keys for yourself.

Giving the foreign-key columns the same names as the corresponding primary-key columns, which I illustrate in the baker example, clearly defines the relationships. In fact, many software tools generate SQL match tables by looking for identical column names. This is known as the "My other brother Darryl" convention, and you probably want to adhere to it.

The Key, the Whole Key, and Nothing but the Key

The heading of this section is the database designer's battle cry. The heading is also a cute summary of the most common style of relational databases — the so-called, much-maligned, often-imitated, never-duplicated *third normal form.*

The gurus who dreamed up relational database theory were strange. Their idea of normal does not fit in with the average guy's dream date. They have many definitions of normal, starting with the first normal form and ending somewhere around the 49th normal form. Even the nerds in the software-development department gave up after the third one. So that's how you get the third normal form. They never even touched my personal definition of normal, which is 98.6 degrees Fahrenheit.

Here's a breakdown of the third normal form (the normalization rules for primary keys):

- ✔ **First: The key.** Every column in a table and all the data in that column must relate to the key of the table.

- ✔ **Second: The whole key.** Each column and its data must apply to the entire key, not just part of it.

- ✔ **Third: Nothing but the key.** Every column and its data must relate to the key and not to any other columns in the table.

Here are some real-life database examples.

"Old MacDonald had a farm, E-I-E-I-O. And on that farm he had some cows, E-I-E-I-O."

The table that you see in Figure 6-3 breaks the first rule — the FARM_ADDRESS and OWNER columns do not directly relate to the BAD_COW primary key, which is COW_ID_NO. You can move FARM_ADDRESS and OWNER to a table called

FARM, as shown in Figure 6-4. This approach solves the problem that you run into when you have a change of address or owner for one of the farms in the FARM table. If you leave the address in this BAD_COW table, you have many rows to change. If you keep the address in a separate table, FARM, you have only one row to change.

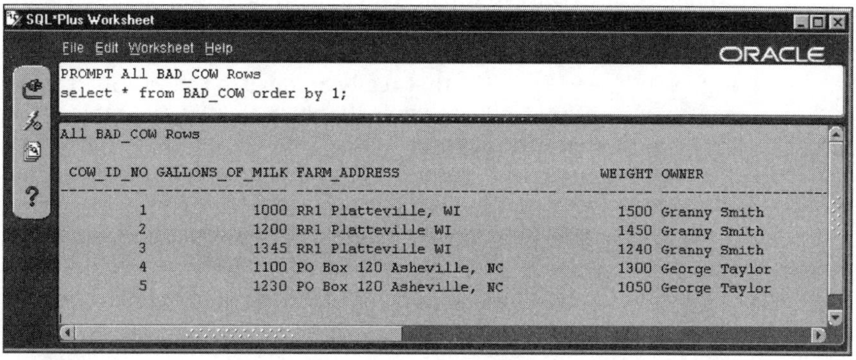

Figure 6-3:
The BAD_COW table violates the first normalization rule: the key.

Figure 6-4 shows you how to make BAD_COW into GOOD_COW and FARM, two relational tables connected by a key. The primary key in GOOD_COW meets the first rule of normalization — every column in the GOOD_COW table relates to a cow! Awesome. By the way, the FARM table also complies with the second normalization rule — every column in the FARM table relates to a farm. Plowing ahead, look at the second rule.

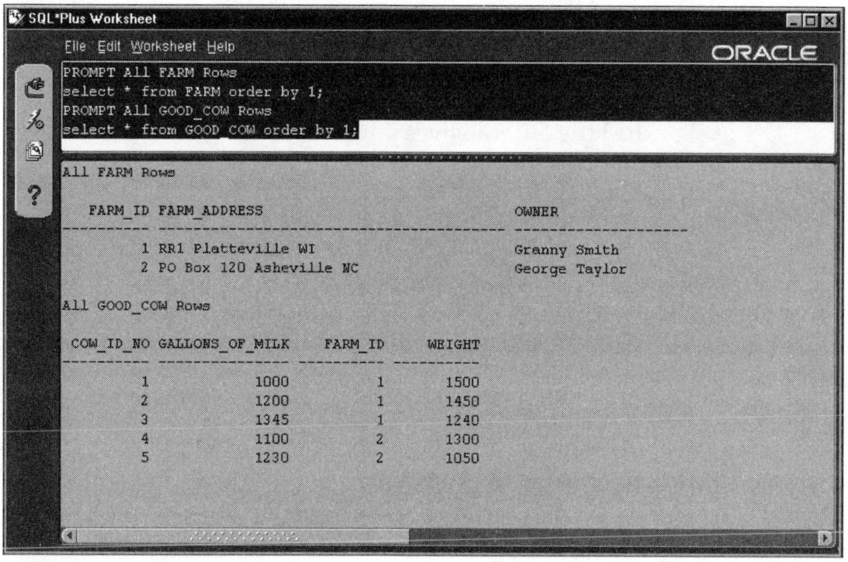

Figure 6-4:
The GOOD_COW and FARM tables comply with first normalization rule: the key.

"Pease porridge hot, pease porridge cold, pease porridge in the pot, nine days old."

The table in Figure 6-5 violates the second rule: the whole key. In this case, the key is two columns: FIRST_NAME and FOOD. The TEMPERATURE and FOOD_AGE columns relate to both columns in the key, but the PERSON_AGE column relates only to the first column in the key. Figure 6-6 shows you how to correct this problem. PERSON_AGE moves to a table called PERSON in which FIRST_NAME is the primary key. This prevents you from having to repeat data in the FOOD_PREFERENCE that really belongs in the PERSON table. If a person's age changes, you need to change it only in the PERSON table. Otherwise, you chase around in the FOOD_PREFERENCE table to update the data there, too.

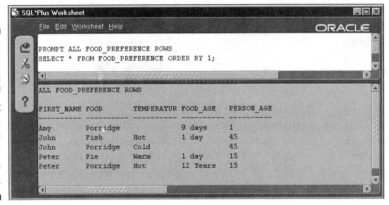

Figure 6-5: FOOD_PRE FERENCE is out of alignment with the second normaliza- tion rule: the whole key.

"Baa-baa, black sheep, have you any wool?"

"Yes, sir, yes, sir, three bags full. One for my master and one for my dame, and one for the little lad who lives down the lane."

The table in Figure 6-7 violates the third rule: nothing but the key. The OWNER column refers to the sheep's bags of wool rather than to the sheep. This column does not belong in the SHEEP table. Because you put the column in the wrong table, the data inside is confusing. The column contains three owners. Common sense says that a column called OWNER in a table called SHEEP has the owner of the sheep in it. To fix the problem, create a new table that relates to the SHEEP table but is especially for wool bags. Call the table WOOL_BAG, as I did in Figure 6-8, which shows a diagram of the two tables.

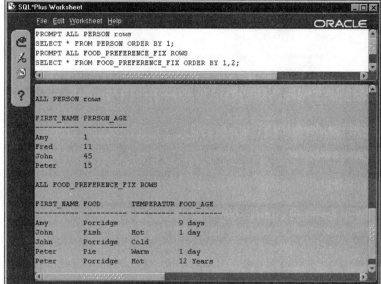

Figure 6-6:
FOOD_
PREFER-
ENCE_
FIX now
has no
out-of-place
columns.

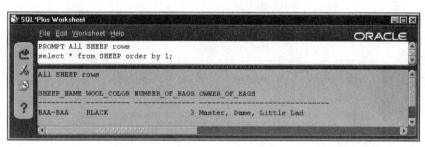

Figure 6-7:
The black
sheep of the
family
breaks the
third
normaliza-
tion rule:
nothing but
the key.

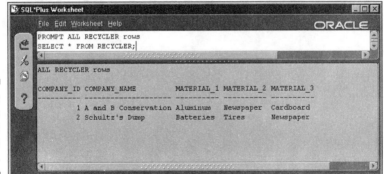

Figure 6-8:
The sheep
with three
wool bags in
perfect third
normal form.

One to Many: The Bread and Butter of Relational Databases

The concept is delightfully simple: Don't repeat the same column inside one row; move it to a new table. Or else.

You're tracking all the recycled materials collected in your community by two recycling companies. You create a table (see Figure 6-9) that has columns such as MATERIAL_1, MATERIAL_2, and MATERIAL_3.

Figure 6-9:
Recyclers
recycle
recyclable
materials.

You may already see a problem brewing. What if A and B Conservation starts recycling glass? You have to make big changes whenever the data changes. Maybe you can get extra pay for working overtime.

A better way to handle this problem is to use a single column for all the recycled material. This column moves to a separate table so that each new material gets a new row. Figure 6-10 shows the two tables that evolve from this revolutionary change.

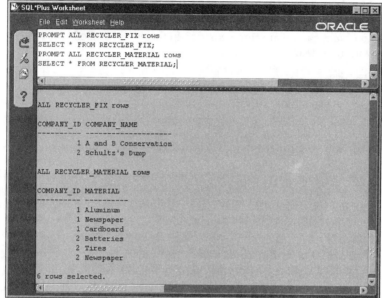

Figure 6-10:
Recyclers
and their
materials,
redesigned
for
flexibility.

This setup makes adding an endless list of recycled materials to either company's repertoire possible. Now you have many rows instead of many columns. You have moved repetitive columns out of one table and into their own table so that you have a constant, rather than an increasing, number of columns and an ever-increasing number of rows. This setup works much better because you are not required to make any changes in your table's design as new information is added. It's flexible. It's the backbone of every relational database. Maybe you can get extra pay for saving on overtime. If you are working as a civil servant, just ignore my last suggestion and continue what you were doing. Just kidding!

Objects and the Oracle8i Database

Are you ready? This section covers something that's new to Oracle: the object. Oracle8i technically can be called an *object-relational database.* This term means that Oracle8i contains all the features of a relational database combined with some of the features of an object-oriented database. The program is a *hybrid,* which means that you have some choices about how to set up your database design.

This section covers the basic definitions of Oracle8i's world of objects. Chapter 11 shows you how to create objects in your object-relational database if you choose to use them.

Defining an object

An object can be anything, sort of. In terms of Oracle8i, an *object* is a framework that defines

- ✔ How data is stored
- ✔ Where data is stored
- ✔ What kind of data is stored
- ✔ How to put data together into logical whole parts

That last item is the part that's really interesting and unique to objects. In fact, if you prefer, Oracle8i allows you to define the first three items in the traditional relational database style and then gives you a way to map these relational tables into objects.

Objects — a life of their own

Think of an *object* as a holistic set of concepts. Your object contains data about a real-world thing, such as a car part. In addition to the data, your object contains information about what can be done with the data. It's like having the car-parts data and the assembly instructions for the car. An object can contain other objects. You may define one object called PERSONAL_ADDRESS, which contains up to three lines of a person's address. Another object, called PERSONAL_INFO, contains a person's name, Social Security number, and the PERSONAL_ADDRESS object for that person.

The scoop on types

Types are Oracle8i's way of defining the format of an object column, an object table, a nested table, or a varray. Types are like wrappers around an object, the data, the methods, and even relational tables or views. The basic syntax for defining a type is similar to the syntax for defining a table. Table 6-1 shows a list of the types of types that you can define with Oracle8i.

I have mentioned the term *method* several times. The following section defines the term more clearly.

Table 6-1	Object-Relational Types
Name	*Purpose*
BODY	Contains definitions of the *methods* (or functions) that can be performed on an object.
OBJECT	A collection of data, tables, and methods defined and manipulated as a unit.
TABLE	Relational table mapped to an object.
VARRAY	Variable-length array, similar to a nested table but referenced and accessed as a set rather than as individual rows of data.
NESTED TABLE	A table within a table or within some object. Oracle8i stores this type as though it were a relational table, but it can be used only in the context of the object type.

Methods to their madness

Methods are self-contained bits of programming code that travel with an object, delivering parts or modifying data according to the method code. Methods are the heart of object-oriented technology.

Suppose that you are working with an object-relational database schema that contains information about making a model airplane. A model airplane has several subassemblies, such as the engine and the instrument panel, which are made up of individual parts. A change in any individual part may affect the assembly of the entire plane. If the fuel gauge in the cockpit is changed to a different diameter, for example, the hole drilled in the instrument panel must also be changed. You can use object *types* to define the individual parts, the subassemblies, and the entire airplane. Object *methods* define how these object types interact with one another. One program uses the object types and methods to handle changes in the data. Another program can use the objects and their associated methods to extract a complete instruction booklet for the plane.

Connecting relational tables with objects

Oracle8i is a hybrid of both relational and object-oriented databases. To allow you to combine the two to get the best of both worlds, Oracle8i provides two bridges between relational tables and objects:

✔ **Object view:** An *object view* maps relational tables into an object. Like relational views, the object view does not actually have data of its own; it is merely a way of looking at the underlying tables. The object view allows you to use existing relational tables in an object-oriented way.

✔ **Object table:** An *object table* is a table made up of rows that are themselves objects. An object table is a way to collect groups of like objects and manipulate them with more traditional relational table techniques. Object tables can have primary keys and indexes.

If you use object views, the underlying data resides in relational tables that can be updated with the usual SQL commands.

When you use object tables, the underlying data resides in objects. You must maintain data through those objects, usually by using a programming language such as Java or PL/SQL.

SQL has been extended to handle more object queries, inserts, updates, and deletions. Expect even more convenient extensions for objects in the future.

Chapter 7

Diagramming Your World

. . . .

In This Chapter

▶ Drawing a database diagram

▶ Adding tables and relationships to the diagram

▶ Making a diagram look great

▶ Determining the difference between monogamy and monotony

▶ Creating a diagram for objects using UML

. . . .

*T*his chapter gives you the basics on *tree diagrams,* the easiest and clearest method of depicting a database schema (set of related tables). You don't have to be an artist to create tree diagrams. The tree diagram is also called the Entity Relationship Diagram (ERD), which is an industry standard for the design of relational databases.

Confidentially, I'm not all that attached to pencil and paper. You can use your Microsoft Paint or PowerPoint program (or any similar kind of drawing software) to create diagrams easily. If you want to get fancier and faster, you can use diagramming software such as ERWin or Oracle Designer/2000. Any way you slice it, a diagram is the best way to describe your schema to others (and yourself) quickly.

Getting Something Down on Paper

The first step is always the hardest one. For starters, I suggest that you put a rough draft of your relational database tables (your schema) on paper. After you do that, you can tweak, erase, add, cut, paste, twiddle, and twaddle all day long. After all, you need to know where you are before you can get to where you're going. Figure 7-1 shows a typical first-cut diagram.

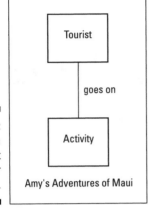

Figure 7-1:
Start with a
rough draft
of your
database.

Here are the simple basics for creating a database on paper:

✔ **A box with a label:** Symbolizes one piece or a set of pieces of information that you want to keep track of by using a database — an entity. You may want to use a noun or noun phrase to label the box. The entity (usually) becomes a table in your database.

✔ **A line with a label connecting two boxes:** Signifies a relationship between the two boxes. You may want to use a verb or verb phrase to describe the relationship.

Try not to worry about getting every detail down at first; just allow the diagramming process to evolve. Typically, the database design cycle, shown in Figure 7-2, starts with too few details (the "Duh!" phase in the figure), moves to the over-complicated phase (the "Sucker Doesn't Work!" phase), and then adjusts back to the simple but complete "Aaaaaaah!" phase.

A lot of tech weenies like to think that a relational database is a three-dimensional matrix that resembles a cube or a space-age Lego-block construction. (Some of these same tech weenies are the ones who wear tinfoil hats to filter out cosmic rays and confuse spy satellites.) You don't need to be an architect to design databases, and you don't need a degree in advanced geometry to understand relational diagrams. All you need is common sense and some pixie dust.

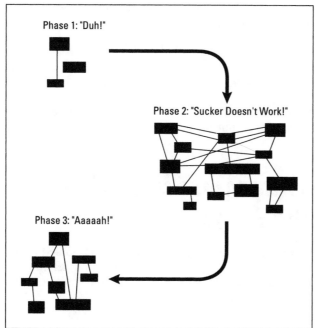

Phase 1: "Duh!"

Phase 2: "Sucker Doesn't Work!"

Figure 7-2:
The highly
technical
names for
database
design
phases.

Phase 3: "Aaaaah!"

As you set out to create a great relational database design, watch out for some of these common pitfalls:

✔ **Primary keys whose contents change.** These keys are primary keys (see the "Primary-key and foreign-key definitions" sidebar for a definition) that contain columns with "real" data in them instead of a simple identifying number.

✔ **Repeating columns in a table.** Repeating columns violate the third normal form, which is discussed in Chapter 6. Repeating columns appear in odd places, so be on the lookout for them.

Repeating columns can be converted into nested tables or varrays in an object table.

✔ **Incorrect relationships.** The most common error is identifying a relationship as one to many when it's actually many to many (see the next section for more on these relationships). To avoid this pitfall, be sure to ask yourself (or the person who is using your creations) these questions:

  • Does one row in Table A ever connect to more than one row in Table B?

- Does one row in Table A always connect to exactly zero or exactly one row in Table B?

- Can one row in Table A ever connect to more than one row in Table B?

These three questions ask nearly the same thing, but each one is phrased slightly differently to ferret out the hidden relationships.

Use diligence and careful thought while designing your database, just as you did when you designed your tax return last spring.

Using Tree Diagrams: Easy When You Know the Lingo

The relational database diagram that I recommend is called the *tree diagram* because it consists of boxes connected with lines and resembles an upside-down tree with branches going downward. The few basic components of the diagram are shown in Figure 7-3.

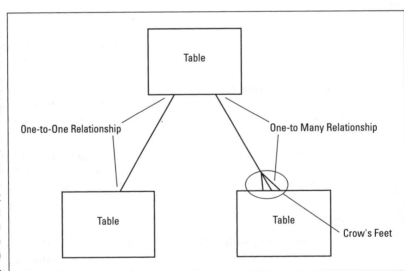

Figure 7-3:
I call this a tree diagram because it resembles a tree with branches or roots and square fruit. (Extra-credit question: Determine the square fruit of pie.)

Primary-key and foreign-key definitions

A *primary key* is the column or group of columns that uniquely identifies any row in a table. Every row in a table has a value in the primary key that is different when compared to the primary key in every other row in that table.

A *foreign key* is a copy of a primary key from one table that is placed in a second table. This type of key is a reference point that ties all the data from one row in the original table into the second table without copying any data except the primary key.

These components are

- **Table:** You draw this component as a box. Usually, the table name appears in the middle of the box. In more detailed diagrams, you may include the primary key, column names, or a sentence or two describing the table.

- **Relationship:** You draw this component as a line between two tables. Usually a short phrase written next to the line describes the relationship. You can describe different kinds of relationships by using several variations on the line.

Relationships, although they are about tables, are determined by looking at a row inside one table and seeing how that row relates to any of the rows in the other table. Here are the three relationship categories:

- **One to one:** One-to-one relationships are monogamous, not to be confused with monotonous. Monotony is a result of the universal law that only boring people get bored. To depict this relationship, draw a simple line between two tables on the diagram.

  Like an old married couple, one row in Table A is connected to one — and only one — row in Table B. Either place the primary key (see the "Primary-key and foreign-key definitions" sidebar or Chapter 5 for an explanation) of Table A in Table B or place the primary key of Table B in Table A to show the relationship (see Figure 7-4). When you copy the primary key of one table into another table, the copy is called a *foreign key.*

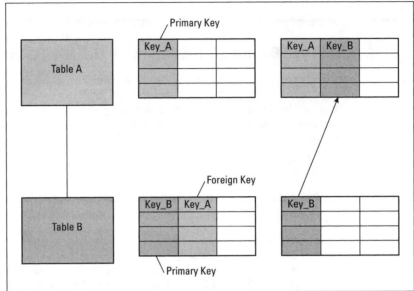

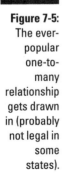

Figure 7-4:
Two ways to
resolve a
one-to-one
relationship
(may violate
some local
ordinances).

✔ **One to many:** Flower to petals — not a recommended cure for monotony. Draw this relationship as a line with branches on one end (called crow's feet because they resemble chicken feet).

A flower (row in Table A) has many little petals (rows in Table B). Each petal (row in Table B) grows on only one flower (row in Table A). Always place the primary key of Table A in Table B to show the relationship (see Figure 7-5).

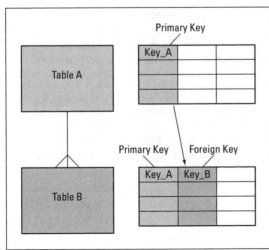

Figure 7-5:
The ever-
popular
one-to-
many
relationship
gets drawn
in (probably
not legal in
some
states).

✔ **Many to many:** Free-for-all; a permanent cure for monogamy. Like an amusement park, one cotton-candy-covered kid (row in Table A) goes on lots of rides (rows in Table B). Likewise, one ride (row in Table B) has lots of kids (rows in Table A) riding it. Create a new table and place the primary key of Table A and the primary key of Table B in this intersection table to show the relationship (see Figure 7-6).

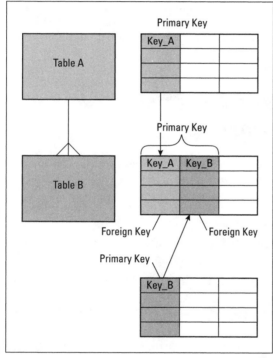

Figure 7-6:
A new table is born when a many-to-many relationship exists.

When you define a many-to-many relationship, you have to break it into the appropriate number of one-to-many relationships before actually creating the tables.

Hooking Up with Objects

Chapter 2 describes the basic concepts behind Oracle8i's objects and object-relational objects. As for your diagrams, you can add objects to the diagrams several ways, depending on what kinds of objects you want to portray.

Just as the Entity Relationship Diagram (ERD) is a standard for depicting relational databases, the Unified Modeling Language (UML) is a standard for describing object-oriented databases. The UML standard contains many different ways to describe, plot, diagram, and illustrate an object model. This chapter looks at a part of the standard that Oracle uses to diagram its objects in Designer/2000: the Static Structure Model (also known as a type model).

The Static Structure Model, affectionately known as S&M (just kidding), shows the relationship of objects to one another, the attributes they contain, and the functions (methods) you can perform on them. The diagrams can then be translated into object types, object tables, and object methods.

Understanding the Basic UML Type Model Diagram

Figure 7-7 shows an example of a type model with the various components labeled. The components are

- ✓ **Type:** A type defines what an object stores and the processes that can be performed on the object.

- ✓ **Method:** A method is some task that can be done with an object. A method is also called an operation.

- ✓ **Attribute:** An attribute, as in relational tables, is a definition of one piece of information that can be stored within the object. Attributes can be objects, so you can get a layering effect where one object contains another object.

- ✓ **Association:** Similar to a relationship in relational databases, the association tells you how two objects relate to one another. When you create an association in the Oracle8i database, you use a *reference* definition. Associations can be

    - **Required or optional:** Use a solid line for required associations; use a dotted line for optional associations.

    - **One to many or one to one:** Use a diamond at the *many* end of the relationship to symbolize that one instance of object A can relate to one or more instances of object B.

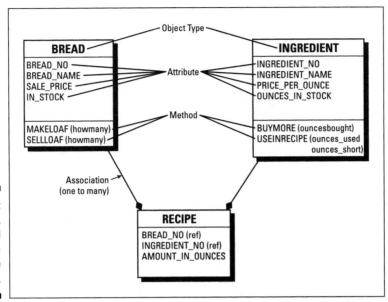

Figure 7-7:
A nice,
well-behaved
Static
Structure
Model.

When you create a table definition out of an object type definition, you have *instantiated* the object type. A row of an object table is called an *instance*.

After you've instantiated an object type (created an object table using the object type), you can't modify that object type. You must drop the object table that you created before you can modify or drop the object type. Check out Chapter 11 for the lowdown on how to create object types, object tables, and associations.

Now that you've seen the general concepts and drawn your logical diagrams, you're ready to look into the more specific details of how Oracle8i puts these concepts into action. Chapter 8 . . . engage!

Chapter 8

Getting Familiar with Oracle8i Data-Dictionary Views

In This Chapter

▶ Admiring data-dictionary views from afar

▶ Using data-dictionary views for your own advancement

▶ Using the SQL*Plus Worksheet to peek inside data-dictionary views

*W*hat are users in the Oracle8i database, and what have they created? How does Oracle8i know which tables a user can see and which tables a user can't touch? Where is the off switch?

You can find the answers to all these questions — except the last — with data-dictionary views.

Viewing Oracle8i's Data-Dictionary Views

Data-dictionary views are actually views based on underlying tables called system tables. *System tables* gather information about tables, rows, views, columns, security, users, and even the files allocated to store the Oracle8i database itself. System tables keep track of all the users, as well as what each user can and can't do. This chapter tells you how to access that information by looking at the data-dictionary views.

Oracle8i depends on the data-dictionary views and the underlying system tables, so don't mess with them. Look at the data-dictionary views as often as you want, but don't alter these views or the system tables in any way. Unless the database administrator (DBA) gives you special permission, you aren't able to make changes in either the data-dictionary views or the system tables. If, however, you have your own desktop version of Oracle8i, you're the DBA. You can, if a demon possesses you, add rows or alter the structure of these views or tables, but for now, you just have to exorcise that demon.

Using Data-Dictionary Views

Table 8-1 shows you the best-kept secrets in the Oracle8i database, including info about what resides in data-dictionary views. The views make it easy for you to interpret the internal workings of Oracle8i.

Table 8-1	The Ultimate Table of Views	
View	*Who Needs It*	*What the View Shows You*
ALL_CATALOG	DBA, table owner, user	Every table, view, and synonym that you can look at. You may or may not be allowed to update these items. This view helps you determine what resources the database has.
ALL_TAB_COMMENTS	Anyone	Comments, which usually contain a short description of the table's contents. You may occasionally find useful puns or one-liners here.
ALL_TAB_GRANTS	DBA, table owner	The privileges that you currently have in any table in the database. This includes grants to PUBLIC (Oracle's special user that is shared by all Oracle users; see the tip after this table for more about PUBLIC). See Chapter 12 for information about using PUBLIC with table privileges (grants).
ALL_TAB_GRANTS_RECD	DBA, table owner	The privileges that you receive from others for any table; includes grants to PUBLIC.
ALL_USERS	Anyone	The names and creation dates for all other users in the database.

View	Who Needs It	What the View Shows You
DBA_FREE_SPACE	DBA	The remaining free space in each tablespace.
PRODUCT_COMPONENT_ucts VERSION	Anyone	Shows all installed prod-(such as SQL*Plus and PL/SQL) and their complete version numbers, which is useful if you're reporting errors to Oracle.
USER_CATALOG	Anyone	All tables, views, and synonyms that you can see, even if you didn't create them.
USER_INDEXES	Table owner	All the indexes that you create.
USER_TABLES	Table owner	Your tables as well as statistics about them.
USER_TAB_COLUMNS	Table owner	All the columns that you create.
USER_TAB_GRANTS_	DBA, table owner	Privileges that you grant to others for your tables.
USER_VIEWS	Table owner	Your views, complete with the SQL code that you use to create them. Here's a great opportunity to share your views with a captive audience.
ALL_OBJECT_TABLES	DBA, object programmer	List of all object-oriented tables in the database.
ALL_TYPES	DBA, object programmer	List of all object types. See Chapter 2 for a definition of object-oriented types.
ALL_TYPE_METHODS	DBA, object programmer	All object types that are methods. See Chapter 2.

The Oracle8i PUBLIC user handles situations in which you want to allow all users to see your table. PUBLIC simplifies your life by allowing you to grant privileges to PUBLIC rather than to many individuals. Oracle8i automatically gives anything granted to PUBLIC to any newly created users. This arrangement may not seem to be fair to those who have more seniority. Tough. (See Chapter 12 for details on granting privileges for tables.)

In the data-dictionary views, you can find much of the information that's displayed graphically in the Enterprise Manager tools. You can use the data-dictionary views to write SQL queries to gather information about your database. You may want to create a report on the status of your database by using other report-writing tools. The data-dictionary views give you a great source of information on which to base reports. (Writing queries on data-dictionary views is no different than writing queries on any table or view in your database.)

*Looking at Data-Dictionary Views with the SQL*Plus Worksheet*

This section deals with two useful queries that you use to take a quick look around in the data-dictionary views. The first query is how you list all the data-dictionary views that are available for you to explore. The second query is how you list all the Oracle user names that are defined in the Oracle8i database you're using.

To query a data-dictionary view and show part of the results, follow these steps:

1. **Select the SQL*Plus Worksheet menu option.**

   If you're using Windows 95, 98, or NT, choose Start⇨Programs⇨ Oracle — HOME2⇨DBA Management Pack⇨SQL*Plus Worksheet. Note that the Oracle HOME2 label may have a different number, such as HOME0 or HOME1, on your NT.

   On UNIX, type **oemapp worksheet** at an operating system command line.

2. **Log in by filling in a valid Oracle8i DBA user name, password, and service in the security screen that pops up and choose the radio button labeled Connect Directly to a Database. Then click the OK button.**

   One option is to log in with the user ID and password that are loaded into all Oracle8i databases: SYSTEM (password MANAGER). Leave the Service box blank if you work on a local database on your PC. If you don't, check with your DBA and type in the name of the Oracle database to which you connect. Accept the Connect As box as Normal. The SQL*Plus Worksheet appears after you click the OK button.

3. **Type the following SQL command and then click the Execute button:**

```
desc ALL_SYNONYMS;
```

The results scroll into the bottom frame, as shown in Figure 8-1. Oracle8i lists all the columns contained in the ALL_SYNONYMS view.

Figure 8-1:
A slice of synonyms appears in the SQL*Plus Worksheet window.

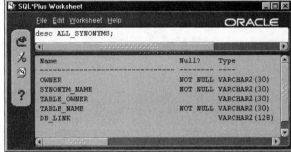

4. **Type the following SQL command and then click the Execute button:**

```
select TABLE_NAME from ALL_SYNONYMS
        where TABLE_NAME like 'USER%' or TABLE_NAME like
            'ALL%'
order by TABLE_NAME;
```

The query's WHERE clause (everything between where and order by in the preceding command) narrows the results by restricting the query to those data-dictionary views that begin with USER or ALL. These two groups of data-dictionary views (about 125) are very useful. Another 250 not-so-useful views are stored in the ALL_SYNONYMS data-dictionary view.

Oracle8i lists the results of your query. Figure 8-2 shows a partial listing of the type that you receive after running the query.

These views are just a few of the data-dictionary views that are available. The DBA restricts you to seeing only what you have privileges to see, so unless you're the DBA, you can probably see just a small slice of the whole database pie.

Page ahead to Chapter 12 if you're interested in the subject of privileges, grants, and how they fit together. Chapter 20 also has a section on security, which can also have practical uses at airport terminals.

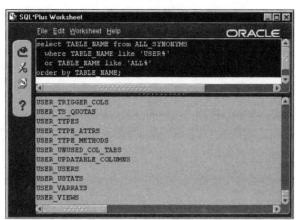

Figure 8-2:
Peruse these useful user synonyms for your use.

The data-dictionary views give you a great deal of useful information about your database. Use these views well. Use them often. Enjoy their companionship. Make them some little tinfoil hats, too, so that they feel like part of the group. Well, at least keep in mind that you can use them later without too much trouble.

Chapter 9

Oracle's User

· ·

In This Chapter

▶ Discovering the use of the users (see the Department of Redundancy Department)

▶ Observing your role in life

▶ Conjuring users

▶ Using Security Manager

▶ Changing your password

· ·

I'm not saying that this is true for you, but for me, having a strong sense of who I am really helps me get through life. This chapter is all about you and your identity. In Oracle8i, you log in with a user ID and a password — your Oracle8i identity. Your Oracle8i identity, specifically your Oracle8i user ID, gets assigned one or more roles (a collection of capabilities) by your database administrator (DBA). This chapter covers how you create your Oracle8i identity and how you can (if you're the DBA) create others. Even if you're not the DBA, you can use the information in this chapter to understand how you, as an Oracle8i user, fit into the picture.

Playing a Role

Here's a fun fact about Oracle8i: Every table in Oracle8i is created by an Oracle8i user ID. You call the Oracle8i user ID that creates the table (or object) the table's *owner*. The owner can do anything to the table, including dropping it from a (virtual) moving train. Every Oracle8i user has the potential to create tables, because the database administrator (DBA) can assign any user the *role* (group of capabilities) that allows the user to do so. The DBA stratifies users into roles that limit or expand their capabilities and, with infinite wisdom, decrees which users are also owners and which are merely tourists who can look around but cannot vote in a local election.

My point is that being an Oracle8i user is not bad, like being a drug user or something. In fact, being an Oracle8i user can be pretty cool. (This is your brain on databases.) Perhaps you work in an office, sharing accounting-database tables with 20 other staff members. You have your own Oracle8i user ID. Your co-workers have their own Oracle8i user IDs as well. One Oracle8i user ID (possibly not anyone in your group, but someone in the MIS department) creates all the tables that you use. This Oracle8i user ID (the one who creates the tables) owns all those tables and therefore is called, lo and behold, the *table owner.*

Oracle8i allows users like you to share tables with their owners, provided that the owner gives you permission to do various activities with the tables. The owner may allow you only to look at the data and not change anything in one table, for example. In a different table, the owner may allow your Oracle8i user ID to add new rows or modify the data in existing rows. Each of these actions has a specific privilege that the table owner grants to you. To understand how the kind of user you are affects what you can do with Oracle8i, you first have to understand what kinds of users Oracle8i has.

Note: When a user creates something in the database, the item can be a table, object table, object view, index, synonym, or a view. Throughout this chapter, I refer to *tables, table owners,* and *table privileges* for convenience. Fact is, the object can be any kind of database object that either stores or looks at data. The concepts I discuss in this chapter apply to these other kinds of database objects as well.

What kinds of users are there?

Asking, in a database context, the age-old question "Who am I, and what is my role in life?" brings us to Oracle8i roles. Oracle8i comes loaded with a set of roles. Five of these roles are important for you to know about. The others are pretty much behind-the-scenes roles. In addition to these basic roles, the DBA can create as many other roles as necessary. (Chapter 12 tells you all about how we programmer types use custom-made roles.) Roles become time-saving tools for the table owner because the table owner can assign a set of privileges once to a role instead of assigning the privileges to each individual Oracle8i user ID.

Here are the five basic roles that come as standard Oracle8i equipment:

- ✔ **DBA:** The Grand Poobah of all roles. In the Oracle8i world, more than one DBA can exist. Incredible, but true. The Oracle8i DBA can create new Oracle8i user IDs, add disk space to the database, start and stop the database, and create roles and synonyms for use by all other Oracle8i users. The DBA can export tables that belong to any user. The DBA can also create more DBAs. It's a form of cloning, but totally legal.

✔ **EXP_FULL_DATABASE and IMP_FULL_DATABASE:** The Romulus and Remus of the Oracle8i realm, these two can make a copy of the entire universe and duplicate it elsewhere. What power! Few are chosen for these honored positions. Usually, the DBA adds these roles to his or her own plate.

✔ **RESOURCE:** This role is the one that makes you an owner (that is, as soon as you create a table to own). All the movers and shakers in the database have this role, which allows you to make tables, indexes, views, and synonyms. You can export and import your own tables. You can drop, modify, re-create, adjust, bend, and create relationships for your own tables. You can assign (grant) privileges — such as the capability to read or modify your table — to other users. Even though you can do all this to your own tables, you cannot do anything to another user's tables unless that table's owner has given you privileges.

✔ **CONNECT:** The people who use the database for any reason whatsoever are in this role. The CONNECT role gets you in the door, nothing more. You are not allowed to create any tables. The only way that you can do anything after you connect to the database is by receiving additional privileges from owners. Owners can allow you to look at their tables and add, modify, and delete data from their tables by granting you the privileges.

The DBA can also give you more privileges by assigning additional roles to you. These roles are created for the purpose of giving a set of privileges to any user who is a member of that role.

What kind of user are you?

If you share Oracle8i at your workplace and you wear a pocket protector, you may have the authority to create tables. If you're not sure, ask the DBA this question: "I just created this table with 10 million rows. Now how do I get rid of the pesky thing?" Then see how fast the DBA runs over to your desk. If the DBA is at your desk in fewer than ten seconds, you have the power to create tables; otherwise, you probably don't.

If the DBA doesn't give you an indication of what your user role is, how can you find out? By using either SQL*Plus Worksheet or the Security Manager.

The SQL*Plus Worksheet method

To follow along with the examples that I am about to show you, start SQL*Plus Worksheet. To start SQL*Plus Worksheet, follow these steps:

1. **Start up your SQL*Plus Worksheet like this:**

   If you have your LaunchPad up, choose the Schema Manager from the DB: Administration menu. Otherwise, on Windows 95, 98, or NT, select Start⇨Programs⇨Oracle HOME2⇨DBA Management Pack⇨ SQL*Plus Worksheet.

   On UNIX, type this on the command line:

   ```
   oemapp worksheet
   ```

   If you come to a login window, go to Step 2. Otherwise, skip to Step 3.

2. **Log in with your own Oracle8i user name and password.**

   Choose the radio button labeled Connect Directly to a Database. If you installed the sample schema, log in as user name AMY and password AMY123. A third option is to log in with the user ID and password that are loaded into all Oracle8i databases: SCOTT and TIGER, respectively. Leave the Service box empty if you are running your own personal Oracle8i; otherwise, fill in the name of the Oracle8i database (instance) on your network. Leave the Connect As box set to Normal. The SQL*Plus Worksheet window appears.

   Here's how you find out your role in the great theater of life by using SQL*Plus Worksheet. Type this command:

   ```
   select GRANTED_ROLE, DEFAULT_ROLE from USER_ROLE_PRIVS;
   ```

   After you click the Execute button (the lightning bolt), Oracle8i gives you the results, which look something like the following:

   ```
   GRANTED_ROLE              DEF
   --------------------      ---
   CONNECT                   YES
   RESOURCE                  YES
   2 rows selected.
   ```

   Figure 9-1 shows what this query and its results look like within SQL*Plus Worksheet.

Figure 9-1:
Your
SQL*Plus
Worksheet
after
querying
for your
roles.

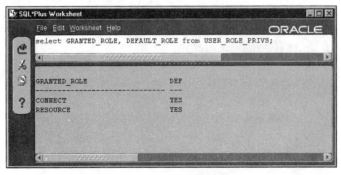

In this example, you have two roles: the CONNECT role and the RESOURCE role. Having these roles means that you can log in to Oracle8i and really have fun creating your own tables and doing other tasks. Refer to the list in the preceding section for more of an explanation about roles.

If you see other roles, they're probably associated with jobs you do that require you to log in to Oracle8i screens. As long as you have the RESOURCE role, which allows you to create tables, you're in business.

The Security Manager method

Here's how you can find out what your user role is by using the Security Manager:

1. **Start up your Security Manager like this:**

   If you have your LaunchPad up, choose the Security Manager from the DB: Administration menu. Otherwise, on Windows 95, 98, or NT, select Start⇨Programs⇨Oracle HOME2⇨DBA Management Pack⇨ Security Manager.

   On UNIX, type this on the command line:

   ```
   oemapp security
   ```

   If you come to a login window, go to Step 2. Otherwise, skip to Step 3.

2. **Log in with a valid DBA Oracle8i user name and password.**

   Choose the radio button labeled Connect Directly to a Database. One option is to log in with the user ID and password that are loaded into all Oracle8i databases: SYSTEM and MANAGER, respectively. Leave the Service box empty if you are running your own personal Oracle8i; otherwise, fill in the name of the Oracle8i database (instance) on your network. Leave the Connect As box set to Normal. The Security Manager window appears, as you can see in Figure 9-2.

3. **Double-click the Users folder in the left frame.**

   This action brings up a list of users on the right and on the left. The list on the right shows a few important details about all the users. The list on the left is used to zoom in on each user so that details are displayed on the right.

4. **Double-click the user name that interests you.**

   You get a property sheet on the right with page tabs across the top.

5. **Click the Role tab to see what roles this user does and does not have.**

   Oracle8i lists both the available roles and the granted (assigned) roles. As you can see in Figure 9-3, the roles that this user currently has appear at the bottom.

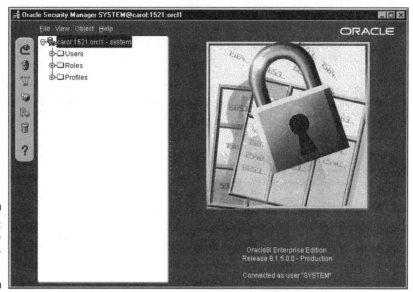

Figure 9-2:
The Security
Manager
awaits!

Assigned roles

Available roles

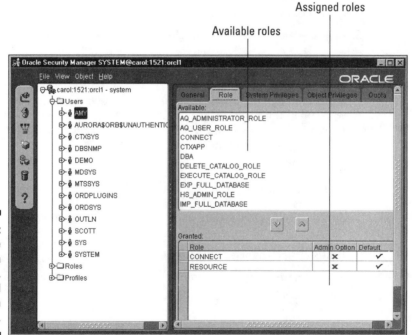

Figure 9-3:
Available
roles are on
the top.
Assigned
roles are on
the bottom.

The Role tab is where you can add or remove roles. See Chapter 12 for complete instructions. Because you logged in to the Security Manager as a DBA, you can click any of the user IDs, look at their roles, and even change them.

Creating a New User from Scratch

Creating a new life is a big responsibility — you have to feed it and change it every day for years. Creating a new user in Oracle8i, on the other hand, carries some responsibilities but generally won't get you up in the middle of the night stumbling for a bottle and a burp cloth.

The Security Manager makes quick work of creating a user and assigning it a few roles.

All right, then; here's an easy way to create a new user life in Oracle8i by using the Security Manager. If you have the Security Manager open already, skip to Step 4.

1. **Start the Enterprise Manager Toolbar.**

   If you have your LaunchPad open, choose the Security Manager from the DB: Administration menu. Otherwise, on Windows 95, 98, or NT, select Start⇨Programs⇨Oracle HOME2⇨DBA Management Pack⇨ Security Manager.

   On UNIX, type this on the command line:

   ```
   oemapp security
   ```

   If you come to a login window, go to Step 2. Otherwise, skip to Step 3.

2. **Log in with a valid DBA Oracle8i user name and password.**

   Choose the Connect Directly to a Database radio button. One option is to log in with the user ID and password that are loaded into all Oracle8i databases: SYSTEM and MANAGER, respectively. Leave the Service box empty if you are running your own personal copy of Oracle8i; otherwise, fill in the name of the Oracle8i database (instance) on your network. Leave the Connect As box set to Normal. The Security Manager window appears (refer to Figure 9-2).

3. **Choose Object⇨Create.**

   This command brings up the Create On pop-up window where you decide what kind of thing you are creating.

4. **Choose User and click Create.**

   This brings you to the Create User dialog box, which should resemble Figure 9-4. This window is not really a wizard, but it should be, because creating new life definitely is in the realm of wizards.

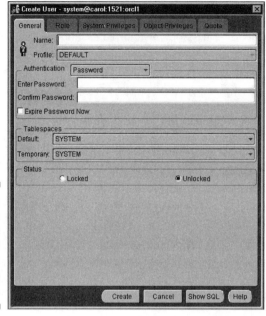

Figure 9-4:
Creating a
new user is
a snap with
the Create
User dialog
box.

5. **Type a name for the new user ID.**

   Oracle has rules about what you can name a user ID. See the "Choosing a name for your new baby" sidebar for details and advice on names for user IDs and passwords.

6. **Choose the type of authentication you desire.**

   Click the list arrow in the Authentication box to see your three choices:

   • **Password.** Probably the most common selection. This is the traditional method of authentication, which requires the user to type in a password to enter a database transaction.

   • **External.** This method of authentication allows the user to pass into the database using his or her identity from the operating system. For example, if you log in to your NT network as HOMER, the Oracle8i ID for you is OPS$HOMER. (OPS$ is the default value of the prefix assigned by the DBA for all externally authenticated users.) To log in to SQL*Plus or some application, you simply type a slash where you normally enter your Oracle8i user ID and password. This feature is convenient because the user doesn't need to know a second ID and password.

- **Global.** This method of authentication was new in Version 8 of Oracle. Intended for use across distributed database systems, this method requires authentication to take place outside the database using the Oracle Security Service (OSS). This method lets you use a common user ID and password to reach any database in your distributed network of databases.

For the sample, choose Password authentication.

7. **Type the password in both the Enter Password box and the Confirm Password box.**

The password appears on-screen as a line of asterisks (*).

8. **Turn on or leave off the Expire Password Now check box.**

If you check the box, the user must enter a new password the first time he or she logs in to the database.

9. **Select a default tablespace.**

Click the arrow in the Default box to see your choices. Normally, you select USERS as the default tablespace, which is the tablespace that Oracle8i puts the user's tables in if the user creates any tables and does not explicitly assign them to a different tablespace.

10. **Select a temporary tablespace.**

Click the arrow in the Temporary box to see your choices. Normally, you select TEMP as the temporary tablespace, which is the tablespace that Oracle8i puts data in while it is generating query results or preparing a view — temporarily grabbing some space and releasing it after the job is done.

11. **Select the status for the new user.**

The default setting is Unlocked. This setting means that the user may log in to the database as soon as you are done creating the user. If you want to wait and unlock the user ID at some other time, select Locked, which prevents the user from logging in to the database.

12. **Assign roles to the new user.**

Click the Role tab in the Create User window. The list of available roles appears, as shown in Figure 9-5. To allow the new user to create tables, you must double-click the RESOURCE role. By default, all users are assigned the CONNECT role, which is required for logging in to the database.

Figure 9-5:
While
creating a
user, you
can also
assign the
initial roles.

13. Click the Create button and your work is done.

Oracle8i creates the new user ID and returns you to the main window of
the Security Manager.

Remember to write down the name and password that you create and keep
them in a secure and hidden place (not taped to your monitor).

Choosing a name for your new baby

What's in a name? Don't ask me; I named my kid
Blue. But I got more conventional and gave him
the middle name Skyler. Then I got psychic and
gave him another middle name: Mercury.
Worked for me.

As the DBA, you have the responsibility of creating all the new user IDs for your Oracle8i
database. When setting up a name for a new

user, you have to follow the rules. You can use
up to 30 characters. A letter and single-digit
number each count as one character. The same
rules apply to setting up passwords. My advice
is to use a single word or acronym for a new
user name. You will appreciate this later when
you have to type the name as the identifier in
front of every table you create.

Changing Your Password

Whether you are a DBA or not, Oracle8i may require you to select a password for your Oracle8i user ID. The password, like the user name, can be up to 30 characters long. Here are my recommendations:

▸ Choose a password that you can easily remember *and* that has a number in it. Take your middle name (Skyler), for example, and then add a number or two (Skyler1). A password that contains both numbers and letters is hundreds of times more difficult for a hacker to crack!

▸ Change your password as often as your DBA tells you to. If no one tells you anything, tell yourself to change your password every two months.

The following section shows how to change your password by using SQL*Plus Worksheet. As the DBA, you can change anyone's password in the Security Manager. Go to the section after this next one to see how.

Changing your password in SQL*Plus Worksheet

You should check with your DBA before changing your password to see whether the DBA needs to know about it. After the DBA creates your user ID and password, you and Oracle8i keep the password secret, and no one can see it — not even the DBA. Both you and the DBA can change your password by following these steps. If SQL*Plus Worksheet is already open, skip to Step 4.

1. **Start the Enterprise Manager Toolbar.**

   If you have your LaunchPad up, choose the Schema Manager from the DB: Administration menu. Otherwise, on Windows 95, 98, or NT, select Start⇨Programs⇨Oracle HOME2⇨DBA Management Pack⇨ SQL*Plus Worksheet.

   On UNIX, type this on the command line:

   ```
   oemapp worksheet
   ```

   If you come to a login window, go to Step 2. Otherwise, skip to Step 3.

2. **Log in.**

   Choose the Connect Directly to a Database radio button. If you want to change your own password, log in with your own user ID and password. If you want to change another user's password, log in with the DBA's user ID and password. You can use the default user ID of SYSTEM and password of MANAGER if you installed a default database. Leave the Service box empty if you are running your own personal copy of Oracle8i; otherwise, fill in the name of the Oracle8i database (instance) on your network. Leave the Connect As box set to Normal.

3. **Type the following command:**

   ```
   ALTER USER username IDENTIFIED BY newpassword;
   ```

   Replace username with your user name and replace newpassword with your new password.

4. **Execute the command by clicking the Execute button (lightning bolt) on the left.**

   Oracle8i replies

   ```
   Statement processed.
   ```

5. **Close the SQL*Plus Worksheet by clicking the X in the top-right corner of the SQL*Plus Worksheet window.**

That's all there is to it.

Changing any user's password in Security Manager

If you are the DBA, you can change the password of any of the users created in the database. Here are the steps, which are similar to the steps for creating a new user. If you have the Security Manager open already, skip to Step 4.

1. **Start the Enterprise Manager Toolbar.**

   If you have your LaunchPad open, choose the Security Manager from the DB: Administration menu. Otherwise, on Windows 95, 98, or NT, select Start⇨Programs⇨Oracle HOME2⇨DBA Management Pack⇨ Security Manager.

   On UNIX, type this on the command line:

   ```
   oemapp security
   ```

   If you come to a login window, go to Step 2. Otherwise, skip to Step 3.

2. **Log in with a valid DBA Oracle8i user name and password.**

   Choose the Connect Directly to a Database radio button. One option is
   to log in with the user ID and password that are loaded into all Oracle8i
   databases: SYSTEM and MANAGER, respectively. Leave the Connect box
   empty if you are running your own personal copy of Oracle8i; otherwise,
   fill in the name of the Oracle8i database (instance) on your network.
   Leave the Connect As box set to Normal. The Security Manager window
   appears (refer to Figure 9-2).

3. **Double-click the User folder in the left window.**

   This action brings up a list of users on the left and on the right.

4. **Click the user whose password you are changing.**

   The user's profile window appears in the right frame.

5. **Type the new password in the Enter Password box and again in the
   Confirm Password box.**

   Write down the name and password you just changed and keep them in
   a secure and hidden place.

6. **Click the Apply button to complete the job.**

   Security Manager accepts the change and returns you to the main
   window.

You're finished. Easy, wasn't it? Chapter 12 covers another aspect of passwords: setting a time limit for a password so it expires automatically. In the
next section, you see how to change your identity. It's kind of like being Odo
on the space station.

Changing User Identity

You can adjust your identity, as far as Oracle8i is concerned. When you
change your identity, Oracle8i treats you as though you never were that
other user. You need to know how to do the quick change by using a menu
selection.

Connecting anew in Enterprise Manager tools

All the Enterprise Manager tools allow you to switch identities with the click
of a mouse. Here's how you do it in SQL*Plus Worksheet:

1. **Choose File⇨Change Database Connection.**

   If you have unsaved work in the worksheet, SQL*Plus Worksheet prompts you to either save it or dump it. After you handle the worksheet contents, you return to the login window.

2. **Type in the new user ID, password, and so on.**

3. **Click OK.**

   Oracle8i returns you to the SQL*Plus Worksheet, and you start fresh.

All the Enterprise Manager tools have Change Database Connection as a selection in the File menu. I find that I use this option most often when I'm in SQL*Plus Worksheet.

Now you are ready to face the world with a brand-new face. No one will ever know what silliness came before, for you have become . . . a different user! You are connected, baby.

Part III
Putting Oracle8i to Work

The 5th Wave   By Rich Tennant

"SOMEONE KEEPS GOING INTO MY PERSONAL FILE. I'D SURE AS HECK LIKE TO FIND OUT WHO USES THE PASSWORD 'PEANUT-BREATH'."

In this part . . .

This part is kind of like puberty. You have a brand-new body of knowledge, and now you're trying to put it all into practice.

You get revved up in the first chapter in this section by creating your very own tables. Find out how the experts do it!

Next, read about all of your choices for creating a secure working environment for your database tables. I give you some common-sense guidelines to help you make wise decisions about security using Oracle8i roles and privileges.

Have a grand tour of the newest toy in the Oracle8i playroom: WebDB. Try creating a Web page from your data.

Have you ever considered using your database from a distance, such as from across the Internet or across the room? Find out what you can do with Java and Oracle8i in Chapter 15.

All this work you've done deserves tender loving care and protection. How would you feel if you lost it all and had to start over? Don't get caught with your data showing. As Chapter 16 explains, back up now or lose sleep later.

Chapter 10

Defining Tables, Tablespaces, and Columns

● ●

In This Chapter

▶ Pondering the possibilities of tablespaces

▶ Talking the technical talk about columns

▶ Creating a table with SQL

▶ Discovering special SQL words for when you bang your thumb

▶ Wizarding a table with Schema Manager

● ●

*T*his chapter is full of good stuff, so fasten your seat belt. You're about to discover where to put tables, how to name your columns, and what datatypes to assign them. You also see how to make tables with SQL code or the Schema Manager. Get ready: You're flying now!

Tablespace: The Final Frontier

Tablespaces are the portions of the database that Oracle8i reserves for your tables. Your database administrator (DBA) may not have told you a thing about tablespaces. On the other hand, this same DBA may come whining to your desk, saying that you just brought the database to its knees by using all the space in the SYSTEM tablespace. Read on to find out what you actually did.

If the DBA allows you to create tables or other objects, he or she assigns a *default tablespace,* which is where all your objects go. This default tablespace is sort of like your own private science lab. If your DBA has done a good job, your default tablespace is tucked away in a safe corner. That way, your incredible genius can blossom without disturbing anyone. Here, you have the liberty to ponder endlessly such burning issues as which fork you should use first or what to do if the little umbrella is missing from your mai tai.

You may, however, have to lower yourself to paying attention to where your tables go. You can tell Oracle8i where to put the tables as you make them. You see how to do so in the sections on creating tables in this chapter.

How do you decide whether you need to pay attention to where your tables actually go? And how much structure (meaning the mapping of tables into tablespaces) do you need, anyway? You really need very little structure when you're working on a PC. Just take a look at your PC desktop and then take a look at someone else's; I bet that they both look rather chaotic. Anyway, if you're working on a PC, have Oracle8i take care of the structure for you. Oracle8i will place all the tables into the default tablespace and arrange them in the files you have assigned to that tablespace. The exact placement of tables in the files is up to Oracle8i and has no bearing on how you use the tables.

Suppose that you are responsible for planning the table structure for the database or your part of the database. You can create a single large tablespace for an entire set of tables rather than many small tablespaces. I recommend being conservative about the number of tablespaces that you create. Every tablespace you add increases the work that you have in managing the database. When you have many tablespaces, you may run into a problem: The overall database has enough space to hold all your data but cannot use all the space because you placed a table in a tablespace that is out of room. Tables cannot span multiple tablespaces. (One exception that allows a table to span multiple tablespaces is the partitioned table, which is appropriate only for large tables — tables that take up more than 1GB of space.) Remember — always consult your DBA about table placement.

A Word or Two about Columns

Oracle8i needs tables, and tables need columns. Even if a table contains no rows, it must have columns. When creating columns, you want to consider names, datatypes, and null values. This section goes into more detail about column datatypes and null values in your data. Chapter 2 covers the naming conventions used for columns, as well as for tables, indexes, and other database items.

Defining columns in Oracle8i

You define columns during the process of creating a new table in the database. You must name the column; then you tell Oracle8i what kind of data goes into the column by specifying the datatype of the column. In a nutshell, Table 10-1 shows all your choices when you define columns in Oracle8i. You may want to mark the table for later reference.

Table 10-1	The Complete Guide to Datatypes	
Datatype	*Parameters*	*Description*
VARCHAR2(n)	n=1 to 4,000	Text string with variable length. Specify the maximum length (n) when defining the column. This datatype holds letters, numbers, and symbols in the standard ASCII text set (or EBCDIC, or whatever set is standard for your database). If your data is shorter than the maximum size, Oracle8i adjusts the length of the column to the size of the data. If your data has trailing blanks, Oracle8i removes the trailing blanks. VARCHAR2 is the most commonly used datatype.
NUMBER(p,s)	p=1 to 38, s=-84 to 127	Number. Specify the precision (p), which is the number of digits, and the scale (s), which is the number of digits to the right of the decimal place. You define a number with a maximum of 999.99, for example, as NUMBER (5,2). Oracle8i truncates data that does not fit into the scale. You define the columns as NUMBER (5,2), for example, and then add a new row to the table, telling Oracle8i to put the number 575.316 in this column. The number that actually gets stored in the column is 575.32 because Oracle8i automatically truncates the decimals at the hundredths, which is the scale that Oracle8i defined for that column. If you define a column as NUMBER (3,0) and then add a row with data 575.316 in that column, the actual number stored is 575.
DATE	none	Valid dates range from January 1, 4712 B.C. to December 31, 4712 A.D. Oracle8i stores DATE internally as a 7-byte number and, by definition, also includes the time in hours, minutes, and seconds.

(continued)

Table 10-1 *(continued)*

Datatype	Parameters	Description
CHAR(n)	n=1 to 255	Text string with fixed length. The default length is 1. You can specify the maximum length (n) when defining the column. If you add data to this kind of column and the data is shorter than (n), Oracle8i adds blanks to the end of the data to make it a fixed length. Suppose that your column is datatype CHAR(10). You insert a row with HENRY in the column. HENRY is five characters long. Oracle8i takes HENRY, adds five blanks to the end of it, and then stores it in the database that way. The main difference between CHAR and VARCHAR2 is that CHAR pads the data with blank spaces and VARCHAR2 strips off blank spaces, making VARCHAR2 more compact and efficient for storing data than CHAR.
NCHAR(n)	n=1 to 2,000	See CHAR, which is the same except that the characters stored depend on a national character set (Chinese characters, for example). Oracle8i supports many languages this way.
NVARCHAR2(n)	n=1 to 4,000	See VARCHAR2. NVARCHAR2 has the same attributes, except that it stores characters for any language (national character set) supported by Oracle8i.
LONG	none	Maximum size is 2GB. Used for large chunks of data that do not need text searching done on them. Use VARCHAR2 when you need to do text searching. LONG is an older datatype that will eventually disappear in the wake of the large object datatypes: BLOB, CLOB, and NCLOB.

Datatype	Parameters	Description
RAW(n)	n=1 to 2000	Raw binary data of variable length. You must specify the maximum length (n) when defining the column. Oracle8i uses the RAW datatype for small graphics or formatted text files, such as Microsoft Word documents. RAW is an older datatype that will eventually disappear and be replaced by the large object datatypes: BLOB, CLOB, NCLOB, and BFILE.
LONG RAW	none	Raw binary data of variable length. The maximum length is 2GB. Oracle8i uses the LONG RAW datatype for larger graphics; formatted text files, such as Word documents; audio; video; and other nontext data. You cannot have both a LONG and a LONG RAW column in the same table. LONG RAW is an older datatype that will eventually disappear and be replaced by the large object datatypes: BLOB, CLOB, NCLOB, and BFILE.
BLOB, CLOB, NCLOB	none	Three kinds of large objects (LOBs); used for larger graphics; formatted text files, such as Word documents; audio; video; and other nontext data. Maximum size is 4GB. LOBs come in several flavors, depending on the kind of bytes that you use. Oracle8i actually stores these internal LOBs inside the database. (See also BFILE.) Special functions for reading, storing, and writing LOBs are available, but I do not cover them in this book. If you want to use this datatype, refer to your Oracle8i manual.

(continued)

Table 10-1 *(continued)*

Datatype	Parameters	Description
BFILE	none	Large binary object (LOB) stored outside the database. Maximum size is 4GB. This external LOB type gets tracked in the database but actually stores data in a datafile outside the database. Oracle8i can read and query BFILEs but cannot write to them. Special functions for reading, storing, and writing LOBs are available, but I don't cover them in this book. If you want to use this datatype, refer to your Oracle8i manual.
REF	schema.objectname	Reference object identifier. This type of column is used within object tables to define a "foreign key" to another object.
ROWID	none	Internal Oracle datatype that stores the physical locator string for a row of data. Generally speaking, you never create a column of this datatype. However, you can query the ROWID of any table's rows by adding ROWID to the SELECT clause.
UROWID	(n)	Hexidecimal string that shows the logical location of a row on an index-organized table. UROWID is an obscure datatype that is seldom used.

In the example at the end of the "What is a null?" sidebar, the word *null* represents a literal null value. (You may be comparing two columns that contain nulls, and the same logic holds.) Oracle8i gets around this problem (which is a standard SQL requirement) by giving you the IS NULL and IS NOT NULL operators. Rewrite the statement from the sidebar in one of two ways. Oracle8i evaluates the following statement as true:

```
SELLING_PRICE is null
```

Likewise, Oracle8i evaluates the following statement as false:

```
SELLING_PRICE is not null
```

The most commonly used datatypes are VARCHAR2, DATE, and NUMBER. You commonly use the CHAR datatype for coded data of a constant length, such as state abbreviations.

The other datatypes are rather specialized and infrequently used (unless you're creating a database with delivery-on-demand music-CD selections or something fun like that).

Allowing nulls or not

When designing columns, you need to consider whether to allow nulls in the columns. Here's the rule: Primary keys (the unique identifier for a table) cannot contain nulls. Otherwise, anything goes. I advise allowing nulls everywhere except primary keys. Even if your brain knows that the column will always contain data, exceptions to rules always exist. If you define the column to not allow nulls, you may be in a bind if you are adding a new row that really has no value for that column.

Suppose that you do choose to define the column so that you don't allow nulls. You can do so by adding the NOT NULL constraint to the column in the CREATE TABLE statement (see the next section).

See Chapter 19 for information on how to change a column's null value setting (from nulls allowed to nulls not allowed, and vice versa).

A Table of Your Own with SQL

So you want to create a table of your very own, eh? You've come to the right place. The simplified format of the command to create a table looks like this:

```
CREATE TABLE tablename
(column datatype (p[, s])[null/not null] [primary key],
 column datatype (p[, s])[null/not null] [primary key],
 column datatype (p[, s])[null/not null] [primary key],
 column datatype (p[, s])[null/not null])
[tablespace tablespacename];
```

Items in brackets are optional. If you don't specify NULL or NOT NULL, the default is NULL. If you don't specify the primary-key parameter, Oracle8i does not create a primary key for the table. The letter p stands for number or precision, and s stands for scale. (Refer to Table 10-1 for definitions.) If you omit the tablespace parameter, Oracle8i places the table in your default tablespace.

Now try a real example on for size.

What is a null?

When the column of a row has no data, Oracle8i describes the column as being *null* or having a *null value.* Use null when you do not know the value of the data. If I put together a table for the fish in my aquarium, for example, I may have a null value (no data) in the DEATH_DATE column of the row for Wesley. This value means either that Wesley is alive or that I don't know when he died.

Oracle8i allows null values in columns of all datatypes. Oracle8i doesn't allow null values in only two instances:

✔ Primary-key columns

✔ Any column defined with the NOT NULL constraint

As another example to show you the definition of a null value, imagine that you are filling out a questionnaire at the local pizza parlor. One question asks you "What is your favorite topping on pizza: cheese or mushrooms?" You like both so much, you cannot decide, and you leave the answer blank. The lack of data indicates that you have not selected your favorite topping. The pizza parlor's database has a null value in the FAVORITE_TOPPING column when your questionnaire is added to the table. In other words, your favorite topping is unknown.

Do not use null to represent zero. Zero is a known quantity. You can add, subtract, and generally use zero in calculations. You cannot add, subtract, or use null values in calculations. When you add a null to ten, the results equal null. Saying the same thing in a different way: Add some unknown quantity to ten, and you get another unknown quantity.

Nulls do not equal nulls or any other value. Oracle8i evaluates the following statement as false, for example, even when there is a null value in the SELLING_PRICE column:

SELLING_PRICE = NULL

The correct way to write this phrase is:

SELLING_PRICE IS NULL

This CREATE TABLE code creates a table for the fish in my aquarium. I can track all kinds of information about my fish with this table. The pieces of information that I want to track for each fish are

✔ The name of the fish

✔ The name of the aquarium that I have the fish in (just in case I get several aquariums)

✔ The birthday of my fish

✔ When the poor thing died (if it has died)

✔ Its color

✔ The breed of fish

✔ Male, female, or unknown gender

✔ A comment about why the fish died or any other comments, such as where I bought it or what its favorite color is

Each of these items becomes a column in the FISH_NEW table.

Here are the steps for using SQL*Plus Worksheet to create this table. Start SQL Worksheet so that you can follow along with the example.

1. **Start the SQL*Plus Worksheet.**

   If you have your LaunchPad up, choose the SQL*Plus Worksheet from the DB: Administration menu. Otherwise, on Windows 95, 98, or NT, select Start⇨Programs⇨Oracle HOME2⇨DBA Management Pack⇨ SQL*Plus Worksheet.

   On UNIX, type this on the command line:

   ```
   oemapp worksheet
   ```

   If you come to a login window, go to Step 2. Otherwise, skip to Step 3.

2. **Log in as the owner of the table that you're changing with a valid Oracle8i user name and password.**

   If you have installed the sample schema included on the CD-ROM, log in as AMY with password AMY123. Leave the Service box empty if you are running your own personal Oracle8i; otherwise, fill in the name of the Oracle8i database (instance) on your network. Leave the Connect As box set to Normal.

3. **Type the code to create the table in the top part of the window, as shown in Figure 10-1.**

   If you are using the sample schema, type the following code in the top part of the window:

   ```
   create table FISH_NEW
   (NAME_OF_FISH VARCHAR2(10) NOT NULL PRIMARY KEY,
   AQUARIUM_NAME VARCHAR2(10) NULL,
   BIRTH_DATE DATE NULL,
   DEATH_DATE DATE NULL,
   COLORS VARCHAR2(10) NULL,
   BREED VARCHAR2(10) NULL,
   SEX CHAR(1) NULL,
   COMMENT_TEXT VARCHAR2(100))
   TABLESPACE USERS;
   ```

4. Click the Execute button to run the command.

SQL*Plus Worksheet runs the command. After the command is run, SQL*Plus Worksheet replies in the top window:

```
Table created.
```

Now that you've created your own table, can you get it out of your life? No problem! Just drop it. This command works better on databases than it does with my dog ("Drop it, boy, drop it!"). Here's the SQL code to remove a table:

```
DROP TABLE tablename;
```

`tablename` is (naturally) the name of the table that you want to remove.

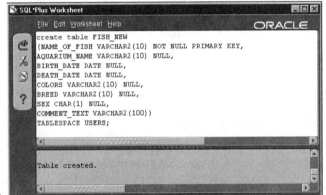

Figure 10-1:
Creating a fishy table in SQL*Plus Worksheet.

Use the `DROP` command only when you are certain that you can't fix the table and you don't need the data, because you can't restore the table by using `ROLLBACK` after you drop it. The only way to restore the table is from a backup copy. See Chapter 3 for a discussion of the `ROLLBACK` command.

`DROP` and `DELETE` are very different commands. `DROP` removes the table definition from your database, without a trace. `DELETE` removes the rows from a table but leaves the table itself intact. See Chapter 4 for instructions on how to delete rows by using SQL.

Schema Manager's Wizard for Tables

When you want to create a brand-new table, use the Schema Manager. This section shows you how.

To practice creating tables in general, follow the steps in this section and create a sample table — in this example a table for the fish in my aquarium. My aquarium has grown since my first edition of the book, and I still have my favorite fish, Wesley, who ate all the other fish that I had.

I can track all kinds of information about my fish with this table. The pieces of information that I want to track for each fish are

- ✔ My fish's given name
- ✔ The name of the aquarium I have the fish in (just in case I get several aquariums)
- ✔ The approximate date my fish was hatched
- ✔ The date of death on my fish's death certificate (if it has died)
- ✔ Its color
- ✔ The breed of fish
- ✔ The gender, if I can figure it out (male, female, or unknown)
- ✔ Any comment about my fish, such as where I bought it or what its favorite food is

Each of these items becomes a column in the FISH_NEW table.

Here are the steps for using Schema Manager to create this table:

1. **Start the Schema Manager.**

   If you have your LaunchPad up, choose the Schema Manager from the DB: Administration menu. Otherwise, on Windows 95, 98, or NT, select Start➪Programs➪Oracle HOME2➪DBA Management Pack➪ Schema Manager.

   On UNIX, type this on the command line:

   ```
   oemapp schema
   ```

   If you come to a login window, go to Step 2. Otherwise, skip to Step 3.

2. **Log in with a valid DBA Oracle8i user name and password.**

   One option is to log in with the user ID and password that are loaded into all Oracle8i databases: SYSTEM and MANAGER, respectively. Leave the Service box empty if you are running your own personal Oracle8i; otherwise, fill in the name of the Oracle8i database (instance) on your network. Leave the Connect As box set to Normal.

3. **Choose Object⇨Create.**

   A window called Create Object appears.

4. **Select Table, accept the default checkbox for Use Wizard, and then click OK.**

   The manual method is good when you are familiar with creating tables. For now, go ahead and use the wizard. This selection brings up the Table Wizard Object Creation Wizard. (I'm not kidding!)

5. **Click the first box and then type the name of the table.**

   Chapter 2 has a list of naming standards for tables. For the example, type **FISH_NEW**.

6. **Click the arrow in the second box and select one of the available schema.**

   The schema is the table owner. For the example, select AMY.

7. **Leave the tablespace as the default and click Next.**

   The wizard selects the default tablespace for the schema that you selected, which usually is the appropriate choice. Figure 10-2 shows the first page of the wizard filled in for the FISH_NEW table owned by AMY.

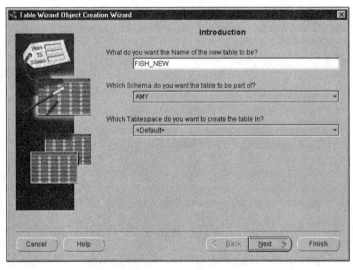

Figure 10-2: The FISH_NEW table begins to take shape before your eyes.

8. **Click the Next button to continue.**

9. **Type a column name in the Column Name text box.**

   Type a default value, if you want. Oracle8i places this value in the column if you insert a new row without specifying a value for this column. For our example, type in NAME_OF_FISH.

10. Choose a datatype from the Column Datatype drop-down list.

See the list of datatypes in Table 10-1 for descriptions of all the choices that you have. VARCHAR2 is the most commonly used datatype for text information. Type the first letter of the datatype to select it faster. Use VARCHAR2 for the first example column.

11. Adjust the size of the column, if necessary, by typing the maximum size you want in the Length and Precision boxes.

(Oracle8i grays out Length and Precision if you don't need them for the datatype that you select.) Oracle8i measures size in number of characters or digits. If your column holds a person's last name, for example, you may adjust the size to 30 because last names are never longer than 30 letters. For the first column in the FISH_NEW example, type in 10 for the length.

12. (Optional) Fill in the default value.

The default value is the data that goes in the column when you add any new rows to this table. You assign a default value of YES to the ADD_TO_MAILING_LIST column in your NAME_AND_ADDRESS table, for example. Unless you specifically put in a value of NO (or MAYBE, or something else) in the ADD_TO_MAILING_LIST column when you insert new rows, every new row gets a YES in the ADD_TO_MAILING_LIST column.

The default value can be a phrase, word, letter, number, date, or whatever fits the datatype of this column. Figure 10-3 shows the window filled in for the first column in the FISH_NEW table, called NAME_OF_FISH.

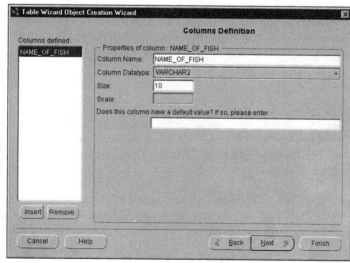

Figure 10-3:
The
FISH_NEW
table
receives its
first column.

13. Add more columns as needed.

Click the Insert button on the left side of the window to add a new column. As each column is defined, it is added to the box labeled Columns Defined. Select any column name from the Columns Defined box to back up and review any of your columns. Select a column and click Remove to delete the column. Repeat Steps 10 through 13 until you've defined all your columns to your satisfaction.

14. Continue to the next page by clicking the Next button.

This action brings up the Primary Key Definition page.

15. (Optional) Define a primary key.

If you want to create a primary key for the table at this time, click the Yes radio button. This opens the area where you define the key. Select each column in the primary key by clicking inside the Order heading of the row with the column name that you want to add. In the example, NAME_OF_FISH is the primary key. Clicking in the first row below the Order heading puts a number 1 in the box.

16. Go to the next page by clicking the Next button.

You see the page for defining Null and Unique constraints. Your first column appears in the window.

17. Answer the question Can the column value be null? **for the displayed column.**

If the column can have blanks (nulls), choose the Yes radio button below the question Can the column value be null? Remember, choose the No radio button for all columns in your primary key because these columns must not have nulls. Click the No radio button for columns that require data. In the FISH_NEW example, what good is your chart without each fish's name?

18. Answer the question Does the column value have to be unique? **for the displayed column.**

A primary key is always unique by definition. Choosing Yes as your primary key is actually redundant; in fact, it can cause trouble if your primary key contains multiple columns. The wizard is not very smart on this one. Use the Yes radio button only when you have a single column (other than your primary key) that must be unique for all rows.

19. Go to other columns as needed.

Click the blue arrow that points to the right to view the next column. Click the other arrow, which points to the left, to back up and review a column. Repeat Steps 18 and 19 for any columns that either do not allow nulls (NOT NULL) or must have a unique value in all rows.

20. Go to the Foreign Key page by clicking the Next button.

You can either define the Foreign Key box now, as you create your table, or later (just as easily) when you are ready. See Chapter 18 for full instructions on adding the foreign key to your table. (The instructions are good for both creating a new table and changing an existing one.)

21. Go to the Check Constraints page by clicking the Next button.

The Check Constraints box is an advanced, optional feature of Oracle8i and is not covered in this book. Just leave the No radio button checked and move on.

22. Go to the Storage Information page by clicking the Next button. Check the Override default storage parameters box and fill in the blanks for initial storage parameters.

The wizard calculates a good starting size for your table. For my FISH_NEW example, I filled in the boxes, saying that I initially need four rows. The table will have growth of one row per month, with low insert and update activity.

23. Go to the Review page by clicking the Next button.

Now you have a final chance to review and make adjustments.

24. (Optional) Rearrange columns.

Figure 10-4 shows the two arrows that you can use to move columns up or down in the matrix. Generally, I recommend that you make the primary-key columns the first columns of the table. This setup makes your table more compatible with other databases, such as Paradox, which require the primary key to be first. Otherwise, arrange the columns any way you please; it makes no difference to Oracle8i.

If you want to remove a column, use the Back button to get to the Column Definition page. Then select the column that you want to remove and click the Remove button. To add a column, use the same technique, except click the Insert button.

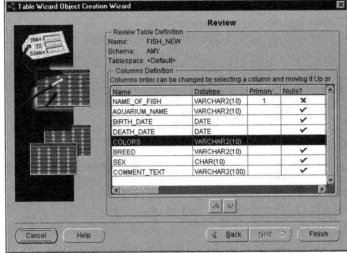

Figure 10-4:
Rearrange
the order of
your
columns
here, if
necessary.

Some designers like to arrange columns in alphabetical order; others like to arrange them in a "logical" order (name, address, city, state, and so on). Arranging columns the latter way is better if you use SQL*Forms or other tools that generate data-entry screens by using the order of your columns as a guide. These tools set up the data-entry screen so that the user enters each column in the order in which it appears in the database table. The closer your columns match the order in which you want people to enter the data, the easier modifying the data-entry screen created by your tool will be.

25. Click Finish when you're done.

Congratulations — you finished your table definition. Schema Manager generates the table and returns you to the main window.

26. Refresh your view by choosing View➪Refresh to refresh the Schema Manager's list of tables.

You see your new table in the list after you do so.

As in life, the only constant in Oracle8i is change. After you create a table, its structure can change. To see how to change columns or their attributes by using the Schema Manager, see Chapter 19. Also, Chapter 18 shows you how to add or change primary and foreign keys.

Chapter 11

Creating Object Types, Objects, and References

- -

In This Chapter

▶ Creating object types

▶ Getting ready for nested tables

▶ Preparing for varrays

▶ Cross-eyed referees, or cross-references in objects

- -

*T*his chapter provides some easy examples to help you get acquainted with your new best friend: the object. You create a simple set of objects that are related to one another. You also see where methods may be added to the set of objects, but you don't actually create them because you would need to use PL/SQL, a subject that is beyond the scope of this book. If you aren't clear on what an object is, you may want to head back to Chapter 6 and read the sections on objects before reading this chapter.

Enterprise Manager's Schema Manager now has wizards smart enough to handle object types, object tables, and other related items. These improved wizards make it so much easier to figure out what you're doing. No tinfoil hat required! Really!

To really get into this chapter, grab your baker's hat and a white apron. Okay, a baseball cap or Easter bonnet will do for the baker's hat. Then imagine that you are a bread baker and you want your Oracle8i database to keep track of your excellent recipes, the inventory of ingredients in your bakery, and a bit of information about your customers. Figure 11-1 shows a Static Type Diagram of the Perfect Bakery.

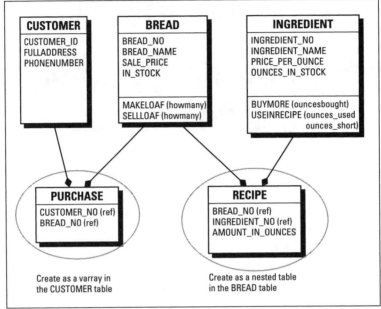

Figure 11-1:
You buy
ingredients,
use them to
bake bread,
and sell
the bread
to your
customers.

In a nutshell, here are the steps to create a set of related objects:

1. **Create an object type to define one row or part of a row for each object.**

2. **Create a table type for each nested table and varray.**

3. **Create object tables using the types created.**

4. **Create object-relational tables using the types created (if any).**

In the sample bakery schema, you create the following items, in this order:

- ✔ INGREDIENT object type
- ✔ BREAD object type
- ✔ RECIPE object type
- ✔ RECIPE_NEST table object
- ✔ Updated BREAD object type that includes RECIPE_NEST
- ✔ PURCHASE object type
- ✔ PURCHASE_ARRAY array type
- ✔ BREAD_OBJTAB object table
- ✔ INGREDIENT_OBJTAB object table
- ✔ CUSTOMER_HYBRID_TAB object-relational table

The order that I chose in this list is not arbitrary. Associations between object types cause them to be troublesome. I got into an endless loop several times before figuring out the perfect sequence of events. The main problem that I ran into was this: When an object — such as the BREAD object in the example — is associated as a parent object with two other objects, you must completely define the parent object before adding any new associated objects.

In other words, after you create an object type, you can't modify it if any other type references it. This is a real headache and is similar to saying, "You can't add any columns to a table that is referenced in any foreign keys of other tables." I must assume that the creators of the object-relational database engine will solve this problem in the future and enable you to disconnect associations the same way that you do with foreign key constraints.

For now, however, be aware that you may well run into the following error message during your forays into creating objects:

```
VBO-1003: data source could not be updated
ORA-02303: cannot drop or replace a type with type or table
dependencies
```

If you get these error messages, your only recourse is to drop all the related objects and start over. You must drop them in reverse order to avoid receiving the same errors when dropping the object type.

The first step toward creating the Perfect Bakery database schema is to design the object types for each of the objects that you need.

Types Need No Space

Unlike your new roommates, types need no space in your closet. That is, defining a type doesn't gobble up space in your database. Defining a type is more like defining a datatype than defining a table. In fact, Oracle sometimes refers to types as *user-defined datatypes.* The type itself never holds any data, whereas the table usually holds no data when defined, but grows in size as data is added to the table rows. Types are used while defining the kind of data that a table contains, which is the same way that datatypes are used in tables.

You can create these three kinds of types in Oracle8i:

- ✔ **Object type:** This type defines a row in an object table. An object type can also be used within another object type, so it may contain only part of an object table row. In fact, after it's defined, an object type can be used as the datatype of a column within a relational table.

- ✔ **Array type:** This type defines a limited set of repeating rows where each row is a single attribute. The attribute can be a regular datatype (such as a number or date) or can be defined as an object type.

> ✔ **Table type:** This type defines a nested table. A nested table can contain multiple attributes. Like the array type, an attribute in the table type can be a regular datatype (such as a number or date) or an object type.

In the bakery example, you define four object types, one array type, and one table type.

Defining an object type

Defining an object type is similar to defining a table, except that you don't define space requirements for an object type. (The space definition comes later in this chapter, when you define an object table that uses the object type.)

If you want to follow along with the bakery example, run the script named AMYOBJ_user.sql that creates the AMYOBJ schema. You can find this script on the accompanying CD-ROM under the Make directory.

Follow these steps to create an object type:

1. **Start the Schema Manager.**

   If you have your LaunchPad open, choose the Schema Manager from the DB: Administration menu. Otherwise, on Windows 95, 98, or NT, choose Start➪Programs➪Oracle HOME2➪DBA Management Pack➪ Schema Manager.

   On UNIX, type **oemapp schema** on the command line.

   If a login window appears, proceed to Step 2. Otherwise, skip to Step 3.

2. **Log in as a DBA and select the radio button labeled Connect Directly to a Database.**

   SYSTEM is another built-in user name that comes with every Oracle8i database. The default password for SYSTEM is MANAGER. Use this user name and password or type in the user name and password of any valid Oracle8i user with DBA privileges. Leave the Service box blank to reach your PC's database or type in the instance name of the Oracle8i database on your network. Leave the Connect As box set to Normal.

3. **Choose Object➪Create from the main menu.**

   A pop-up menu appears, listing all the possible objects that you can create.

4. **Select Object Type and click Create.**

   You see the Create Object Type window, where you define the object type.

5. Type in a name and select a schema for the object.

For the bakery example, you create the INGREDIENT object type first, so type **INGREDIENT** in the name box and select AMYOBJ as the schema. Figure 11-2 shows the Create Object Type window at this point.

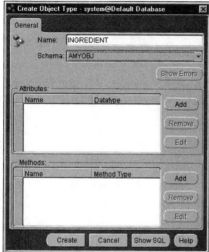

Figure 11-2:
Begin creating an object type by giving it a name and choosing the user (schema) that will own the object type.

6. Click the Add button in the Attributes box.

You see the Create Attribute window.

7. Define one attribute.

Here you add each attribute one at a time to this object type. For the example object type, the first attribute is named INGREDIENT_NO and is the NUMBER datatype. Figure 11-3 shows the filled-in fields for this attribute.

The Schema box inside the Datatype portion of this window is new. Because the datatype for the example is the usual Oracle8i datatype, leave the Schema window at the default setting, None. If, however, the attribute is defined by another object type, select the schema of that defining object type in the Schema box. When you do so, Oracle8i adds the object type to the list of datatypes from which you make your selection. Figure 11-4 shows the attribute window for an attribute with an object type datatype.

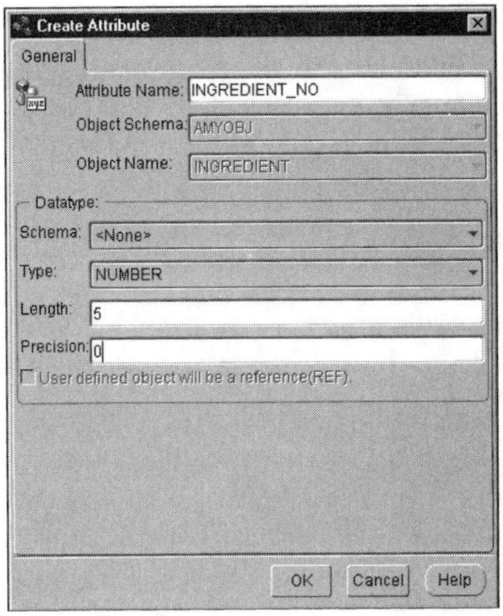

Figure 11-3:
You reach this attribute definition window by clicking the Add button.

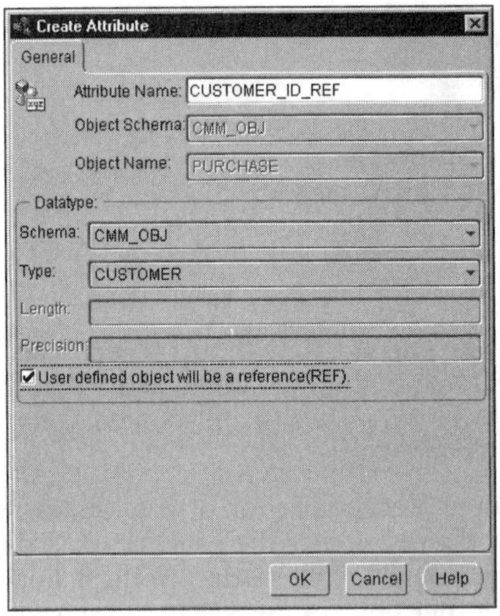

Figure 11-4:
If you select a datatype schema, Oracle8i adds that schema's object types to the list of datatypes.

To define a referenced object (similar to a foreign key), you must do two things: Select the schema and object type that defines the referenced object and then click the check box labeled User Defined Object Will Be a Reference (REF), which tells the Oracle8i database to create a column of the REF datatype. After an object table is created and a row is added, the REF column contains an Object ID (OID) belonging to one row of the referenced object.

After you select a datatype, fill in the proper length and precision if needed. The boxes for length and precision are white and editable if you've chosen a datatype that required their definition. Refer to Table 10-1 in Chapter 10 for all the gory details.

8. **Click OK to complete the attribute definition.**

   You return to the main Create Object Type window.

9. **Repeat Steps 6 through 8 for all attributes.**

10. **Click the Create button to save the object type to the database.**

    The database thinks for a moment and then gives you a pop-up window saying

    ```
    Object type created successfully.
    ```

    Oracle8i returns you to the main window of the Schema Manager.

For the example schema, create all the object types by following the preceding steps. Refer to Figure 11-1 to see the elements of each object type in the example. Create the objects that aren't dependent on other objects — CUSTOMER, BREAD, and INGREDIENT — first. Then create the RECIPE object type. Don't create the PURCHASE object type now; you create that later in this chapter, when you need to define the array type.

When you create an object type to become an array or a nested table, you can leave out the reference attribute of the object that carries the array or nested table.

For example, in the sample schema, omit the BREAD_NO (ref) attribute in the RECIPE object type. The RECIPE object type is used in a table type that is then embedded in a column of the BREAD object type and therefore does not require separate storage of the BREAD_NO.

If you prefer not to create the object types yourself, you can continue with the example by running the script named AMYOBJ_object_types.sql. This script creates all the object types for you. Sure, take the easy way out!

Making a table type

While most migratory birds use sticks, the rare Ootypee bird builds its nest with old Formica tables and always builds inside another bird's nest, taking up so much room that it sometimes falls off into space. And so, the story of the nested table begins.

A *nested table* stores a table of data in one column within another table. Sometimes the nested table takes up more room than the original table and must be moved to its own location in the database.

Creating a nested table within an object type requires that you first define a table type. A table type is almost exactly like an array type except that it has no limit on its repetitions.

I am too good to you! By running the script named `AMYOBJ_table_type.sql`, you create the `RECIPE_NEST` table type and add it to the `BREAD` object type.

Follow these steps to create a table type:

1. **Start the Schema Manager.**

   If you have your LaunchPad open, choose the Schema Manager from the DB: Administration menu. Otherwise, on Windows 95, 98, or NT, select Start⇨Programs⇨Oracle HOME2⇨DBA Management Pack⇨ Schema Manager.

   On UNIX platforms, type **oemapp schema** on the command line.

   If a login window appears, proceed to Step 2. Otherwise, skip to Step 3.

2. **Log in as a DBA and select the radio button labeled Connect Directly to a Database.**

   SYSTEM is another built-in user name that comes with every Oracle8i database. The default password for SYSTEM is MANAGER. Use this user name and password or type in the user name and password of any valid Oracle8i user with DBA privileges. Leave the Service box blank to reach your PC's database or type in the instance name of the Oracle8i database on your network. Leave the Connect As box set to the default, Normal.

3. **Choose Object⇨Create from the main menu.**

   A pop-up menu appears, listing all the possible objects that you can create.

4. **Select Table Type and click Create.**

   You see the Create Table Type window, where you define the table type.

5. **Type in a name and select a schema for the table type.**

   For the example, you create the `RECIPE_NEST` table type first, so type **RECIPE_NEST** in the name box and select `AMYOBJ` as the schema. See Figure 11-5.

6. **Select a schema (if needed) and a datatype.**

   If you're using a regular datatype, such as `NUMBER`, leave the schema set to the default, None. If you're using an object type, select the schema of the object type that you need.

   If you're diligently building the sample schema, select `AMYOBJ` as the schema and select `RECIPE` as the datatype. Leave the checkbox blank.

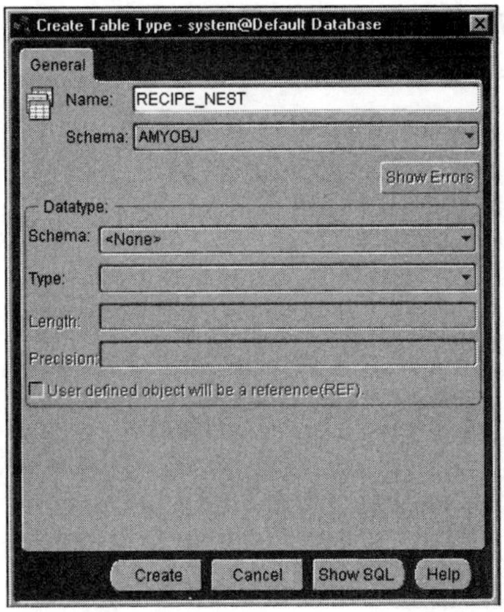

Figure 11-5:
A table type
eventually
becomes a
nested
table.

7. **Click the Create button.**

   The database ponders for a moment and then displays a pop-up window
   saying

   ```
   Table type created successfully.
   ```

   At this point, Oracle8i returns you to the main window of the Schema
   Manager.

   Now that you have a table type, you want to use it. The remaining steps
   show you how to add a nested table to an object type definition. In the
   example, you want to add the RECIPE_NEST table type to the BREAD
   object type as the RECIPE_NEST attribute. Follow the bouncing ball....

8. **Select the object type that you want to contain the nested table.**

   In the example, select the BREAD object type in the left frame of Schema
   Manager. The edit window for the object type opens.

9. **Click the Add button to create a new attribute.**

   You see the Create Attribute window in which you define the nested
   table attribute in this object.

10. **Type a name and then select the schema and the table type in the
    Datatype area.**

    In the example, you're adding the RECIPE_NEST table type to the BREAD
    object type, so name the attribute BREAD_RECIPE. Type in this attribute
    name, select AMYOBJ as the schema, and select RECIPE_NEST as the
    datatype. Your screen should look like Figure 11-6.

Figure 11-6:
Add a
nested table
to the object
type just as
you add
any other
attribute.

11. **Click OK to return to the main definition window.**

   You see the attribute added to your object type.

12. **Click Apply to save the object type to the database.**

   The database ponders for a moment and then displays a pop-up window
   saying

   ```
   Object type created successfully.
   ```

   The object type is re-created with the change included, and Oracle 8i
   returns you to the main window of the Schema Manager.

Even if you have your entire schema laid out in a diagram, determining which
object type to create first takes some planning. Just remember to start creating the objects with the fewest associations and work your way to the objects
with the most associations.

Creating an array type

A varray is a ray that swims only in very cold oceans, which is why it has the
v in the front of its name. Having been a professional fisherperson in
Antarctica prior to becoming an Oracle oracle, I know a fish tale when I
see one.

A *varray* consists of a single repeating attribute that can be repeated a finite number of times. It's like storing a miniature table inside your object. You create a varray by defining an array type and then using the array type as the attribute within an object type.

The first step toward creating a varray is to decide what kind of attribute will be repeated. The attribute can be either a regular datatype, such as NUMBER, or an object type.

If you choose to create a varray with a regular datatype, you can immediately define the array type.

Because you can't use an object type that doesn't exist, you absolutely must create the object type before using it as the datatype in an array type. In the example schema, create the object type named PURCHASE; its only attribute is a reference to the BREAD object type. Follow the instructions in the "Defining an object type" section to create this new object type. Then, use the PURCHASE object type to create an array type.

To create an array type, follow the steps in the preceding section, except select Array Type rather than Table Type in Step 4 and type in the maximum number of repetitions allowed for the array in Step 5. Also type in the name of the varray in Step 5. For this example, type in PURCHASE_ARRAY as the varray name. Figure 11-7 shows the Create Array Type window with the sample schema's table type defined.

Once again, I bail you out. You can opt out of creating the array type in the sample schema by running the script named AMYOBJ_array_type.sql. This script creates the array type for you.

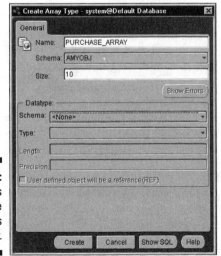

Figure 11-7:
Array types become varrays later.

You can add the array type as an attribute's datatype to any of your objects.

In the sample schema, the CUSTOMER hybrid table can use PURCHASE_ARRAY as one of its columns. You create the CUSTOMER hybrid table in the section "Making hybrid tables," later in this chapter after you create the framework for the schema. The next step is to instantiate some objects!

Objects Still Sit inside Tablespaces

After you have the complete set of object types, array types, and table types, you can create the object tables needed to actually store data. When defining object tables, as with relational tables, you must define the amount of space that is required as well as which tablespace the object table is stored in.

Another kind of table that uses object types is the object-relational table, or hybrid table. You define this table as if it were a relational table, except one or more of the columns has an object type, array type, or table type as its datatype. So you end up with a relational table with objects embedded inside a few of its columns. You create both kinds of tables in the following two sections of this chapter.

Making an object table

Using the Schema Manager to create an object table is easy. If you want to continue with the sample schema (refer to Figure 11-1), follow the steps in this section to create the object tables: BREAD and INGREDIENT.

In the previous sections of this chapter, you create an object type for each of these objects. Here you create the object tables.

You can create the two object tables for the sample schema by running the AMYOBJ_object_tables.sql script included on the accompanying CD. (Just remember that there is value in making your own mistakes.)

You may notice that the following steps for creating an object table are very much like creating a normal table (if you're already in the Schema Manager, skip to Step 3):

1. **Start the Schema Manager.**

   If you have your LaunchPad open, choose the Schema Manager from the DB: Administration menu. Otherwise, on Windows 95, 98, and NT, choose Start➪Programs➪Oracle HOME2➪DBA Management Pack➪ Schema Manager.

On UNIX, type **oemapp schema** on the command line.

If a login window appears, proceed to Step 2. Otherwise, skip to Step 3.

2. **Log in as a DBA and select the radio button labeled Connect Directly to a Database.**

SYSTEM is another built-in user name that comes with every Oracle8i database. The default password for SYSTEM is MANAGER. Use this user name and password or type in the user name and password of any valid Oracle8i user with DBA privileges. Leave the Service box blank to reach your PC's database or type in the instance name of the Oracle8i database on your network. Leave the Connect As box set to the default, Normal.

3. **Choose Object⇨Create from the main menu.**

A pop-up menu appears, listing all the possible objects that you can create.

4. **Select Table, remove the check from the Use Wizard checkbox, and click Create.**

The wizard isn't educated in the ways of object tables and only guides you in creating relational tables. Instead, you see the Create Table window in which you define the object table.

5. **Type a name and select a schema for the object table.**

For the example, create the INGREDIENT_OBJTAB object table first. Select AMYOBJ as the schema.

6. **Click the Object Table radio button.**

After you click the radio button, the lower part of the window changes its format to help you define the object table.

7. **Select the schema and object type that the object table uses.**

In the example, first select AMYOBJ as the schema and INGREDIENT as the object type. After you do this, the lower portion of the window displays all the attributes contained in the object type. Figure 11-8 shows the Create Table window at this point in the example.

8. **(Optional) Define default values, constraints, and storage if needed.**

Someday in the not-too-distant future, you may find that you need these options and that you're ready to explore. For now, leave these options in their default modes.

9. **Click Create to complete the definition and commit it to the database.**

The database evaluates your humble request and grants it, saying

```
Table created successfully.
```

That was so easy!

Figure 11-8:
After you
select an
object type,
the
attributes
automatically
appear.

Next, to continue with the example, follow the same steps to create the
`BREAD_OBJTAB` object table. When you create the `BREAD_OBJTAB` object
table, you see an additional window after you select the `BREAD` object type.
This window, shown in Figure 11-9, defines the storage table for the nested
table. In the example, I call the nested table `BREAD_RECIPE_TABLE`.

Making hybrid tables

A hybrid table cannot naturally reproduce; it must be created from hybrid
seeds. I know this because I used to be a hybrid table farmer in Iowa.

A *hybrid table* (or object column table) contains regular relational columns
and one or more columns that use an object type, array type, or table type as
the column's datatype.

What hybrid tables are becomes more clear when you try an example.

Go ahead and take a peek at the SQL for the hybrid table. You can find it in
the file called `AMYOBJ_hybrid_table.sql` in the Make directory of the CD.

Follow these steps to create a hybrid table (if you're already in the Schema
Manager, skip to Step 3):

Figure 11-9:
When the selected object type includes a nested table, you must define a unique table name for the nested table.

1. **Start the Schema Manager.**

   If you have your LaunchPad open, choose the Schema Manager from the DB: Administration menu. Otherwise, on Windows 95, 98, and NT, choose Start⇨Programs⇨Oracle HOME2⇨DBA Management Pack⇨ Schema Manager.

   On UNIX, type **oemapp schema** at the command prompt.

   If a login window appears, proceed to Step 2. Otherwise, skip to Step 3.

2. **Log in as a DBA and select the radio button labeled Connect Directly to a Database.**

   SYSTEM is another built-in user name that comes with every Oracle8i database. The default password for SYSTEM is MANAGER. Use this user name and password or type in the user name and password of any valid Oracle8i user with DBA privileges. Leave the Service box blank to reach your PC's database or type in the instance name of the Oracle8i database on your network. Leave the Connect As box set to the default, Normal.

3. **Choose Object⇨Create from the main menu.**

   A pop-up menu appears, listing all the possible objects that you can create.

4. **Select Table, remove the check from the Use Wizard checkbox, and click Create.**

   The wizard isn't educated in the ways of hybrid tables and only guides you in creating relational tables. Instead, you see the Create Table window in which you define the object table.

5. **Type in a name and select a schema for the hybrid table.**

For the example, create the CUSTOMER_HYBRID_TAB hybrid table and select AMYOBJ as the schema.

6. **Define the relational columns as usual.**

The sample table has three relational columns (refer to Figure 11-1): CUSTOMER_ID, FULLADDRESS, and PHONENUMBER. Define these columns as usual by typing the column names, datatypes, sizes, and so on in the appropriate boxes in the column definition window.

7. **Define the object column. Begin as if you're creating a normal column by typing the column name; then select a schema for the column and select the appropriate type as the datatype.**

For the example, select the AMYOBJ schema and the PURCHASE_ARRAY type. Figure 11-10 shows the Create Table window with all the columns defined.

8. **Click Create to complete the process.**

The Oracle8i engine grumbles and then says

```
Table created successfully.
```

You're finished with the entire sample schema. Fantastic! Did you find out a thing or two? I sure did.

Chapter 4 covers all kinds of interesting details on how to add data and query these kinds of object tables. Check it out. Chapter 12 looks into users, roles, and other mysteries of life.

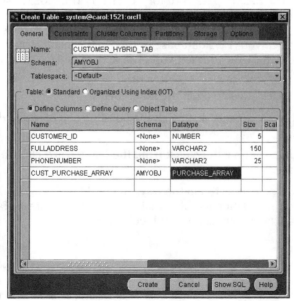

Figure 11-10:
This hybrid table contains three relational columns and one varray object column.

Chapter 12

Security Options: Roles, Profiles, and Grants

In This Chapter

▶ Finding your built-in security blankets (the Nankie Phenomenon)

▶ Playing roles

▶ Designing roles in Security Manager

▶ Creating and assigning roles with SQL (the Director's Office)

▶ Examining user profiles (is this my good side?)

Database designers can get bogged down in security. The concern about safety often starts innocently enough. Somebody in your office reads about a hacker in Australia who figured out the password to a protected file and ended up printing a love note in the newspaper. What you don't find out until much later is that the kid is the son of the office's vice president, who talks in his sleep.

Anyway, I devote this chapter to showing off the Oracle8i security features that are at your disposal. You can't control what the office vice president says in his sleep, unless he neglects to wear his little tinfoil nightcap. You can control what role he is assigned and the table privileges assigned to that role.

Security Blanket Included

Here's what you get as standard security in the Oracle8i database world:

✔ All tables and objects have an owner — the user who created the tables and objects.

✔ If you're the owner, the DBA and you are allowed to:

• View the data

- View and modify the table or object structure (column names and so on)

- Add and delete data rows

- Add, change, and remove data in any table or object row or column

- Modify the structure (add, change, and remove columns)

- Remove the entire table or object

- Create synonyms, views, indexes, primary keys, relationships, and references

- Grant and revoke permission to any user or role to perform the preceding tasks

The security measures that you have are kind of like the relationship Dr. Frankenstein had with his little creation — they can get out of hand. Here's an interesting fact about security: If you query a table that you don't have permission to see, you get this error message:

```
ORA-00942: table or view does not exist
```

This message has panicked many an innocent database user and designer. Just remember, if you're logged into the database as any user besides the table owner, the table is still there, and the cause of the misleading error message is that the table owner has not granted you the privilege needed to see the table.

You must prefix table names with the owner's name when querying or modifying data in a table not owned by you. For example, when logged in as HARRY, you must add the owner prefix to query the AQUARIUM table owned by AMY:

```
SELECT * FROM AMY.AQUARIUM;
```

The only exception to the owner-prefix rule is when a synonym that points to the table is created. See Chapter 13 for details.

Meanwhile, this chapter contains a wealth of information about creating a reasonable security scheme for your Oracle8i database and deciphering the meanings of terms such as *role* and *profile*.

Roles Meet the Real World

Roles help you keep track of who can do what in the database. To illustrate, I can show you how roles existed in the olden days — back when I was your age.

Suppose that you are in charge of an office that has 35 employees, 15 of whom are salaried and 20 of whom are hourly. Two of the office managers are hourly. The rest of the managers are salaried. You want all hourly employees to enter their time-card information in the TIMECARD table; then you want all the managers to review and adjust the pay rates in the PAY_RATE table. Figure 12-1 shows how you grant table permissions directly to each employee in the pre-role era of Oracle Version 6 and earlier.

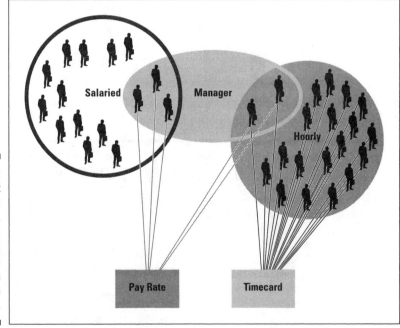

Figure 12-1:
Ancient Oracle practices, including granting table permissions directly to users.

Now that Oracle8i exists, you can create two roles:

  ✔ The manager role can view and change pay rates.
  ✔ The hourly employee role can enter time-card data.

The two roles overlap, as shown in Figure 12-2, because managers can also be hourly employees. Using Oracle8i, you can grant the table permissions to two roles instead of to each employee.

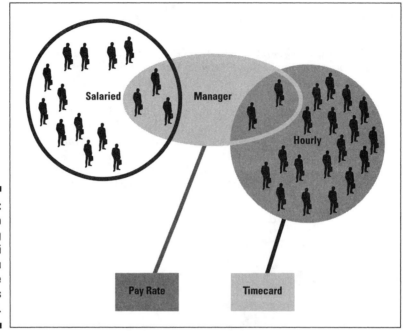

Figure 12-2:
The modern
streamlining
of Oracle8i
lets you
grant table
permissions
to roles.

Armed guards versus open arms

You may spend more time designing and implementing the security system than you do building the rest of the database system. A broad spectrum of security approaches exists. In the strictest approach, users have multiple passwords. In the most lackadaisical approach, every user logs on as the DBA, and you conveniently post the ID and the password in public.

Here's a typical security approach:

✔ One common login ID (and no additional password) is required for read-only access to the database.

✔ Roles for designers allow them to create and remove tables.

✔ Roles for users allow them to update certain tables or allow them access to groups of tables for each functional area.

Roles, grants, and profiles are for Oracle8i databases that many users share. You don't need roles if you work with your own private database, unless you have multiple personalities.

You can go totally overboard devising roles for every conceivable situation, mixing and matching the roles like my family's socks — which usually doesn't work. A little common sense and intuition go a long way when you're devising roles. Remember, simpler usually is better.

At first glance, a clever person may exclaim, "Wait just a darned minute! Oracle has increased my workload! Now I assign the employees roles and grant table permissions to roles." This observation is clever — but inaccurate in the long run. You may not notice the advantages of the role system until you start making changes. Without roles, when you add a new table that is used along with the TIMECARD table, you give table permissions to each of 20 individual employees. With roles, you need only one permission. You get the idea?

Roles and Privileges with Security Manager

If you have Personal Oracle8i or if you are the DBA, creating and assigning roles is so simple, it's scary! Only the DBA can create roles, unless the DBA grants this privilege to another user or role. Only the table owner can grant privileges (unless the table owner gives this right to another user or role, or unless someone bribes the headwaiter).

This section shows you how to create roles and assign the roles to users. To help illustrate the steps, imagine that you want to create two roles for your employees. One role, called HOURLY, gives employees access to the TIMECARD table, where they can log hours worked. Only hourly employees need this role. The other role, called MANAGER, lets a manager review and change the pay rate for an employee, which is stored in the PAY_RATE table.

Begin by creating the two new roles you have in mind.

Creating a role

Here are the steps for creating a role by using the Security Manager.

1. **Start up the Security Manager.**

   If you have your LaunchPad open, choose the Security Manager from the DB: Administration menu. Otherwise, on Windows 95, 98, or NT, choose Start➪Programs➪Oracle HOME2➪DBA Management Pack➪ Security Manager.

   On UNIX, type **oemapp security** on the command line.

   If you come to a login window, go to Step 2. Otherwise, skip to Step 3.

2. **Log in with a valid DBA Oracle8i user name and password.**

   One option is to log in with the user ID and password that are loaded into all Oracle8i databases: SYSTEM (password MANAGER). Leave the Service box empty if you are running your own personal Oracle8i. Otherwise, fill in the name of the Oracle8i database (instance) on your network. Leave the Connect As box set to the default of Normal.

3. **Choose Object⇨Create⇨Role from the top menu and click the Create button.**

   The Create Role dialog box appears, as shown in Figure 12-3.

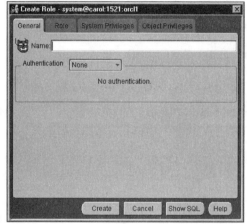

Figure 12-3:
Getting
ready to
make a new
mask, I
mean role.

4. **Type the new role name in the Name box.**

   Follow the Oracle8i naming rules listed in Chapter 2. Type **MANAGER** in the Name box to start creating roles for the example.

5. **Select the authentication that you prefer.**

   Usually, you select None, indicating that you need no role-specific authentication.

6. **Click the Role tab.**

   Select roles and assign them to the role by clicking the Add button. You can add general database roles in this tab. The MANAGER role has no roles assigned.

7. **Click the Create button.**

   This step creates the role and returns you to the main window.

8. **Repeat Steps 3 through 7 to create a second role.**

   Create another role called HOURLY, and in Step 4, type **HOURLY** as the role name.

9. **Close Security Manager by clicking the X box in the top right corner of the window.**

You have a new role, complete with privileges. Next, you assign the appropriate users to the new roles.

Assigning users to a role

After you create the role, you, as the DBA, can assign this new role to users. Table owners can add more table privileges to this role also.

Continuing with the example from the previous section, you created two new roles, HOURLY and MANAGER, to define two groups of employees. You now assign some users to their respective roles. One user, JONES, is both a manager and an hourly employee. Another user, SMITH, is an hourly employee. Here are the steps for assigning JONES his two roles. If you are already in the Security Manager, skip to Step 4.

1. **Start up the Security Manager.**

   If you have your LaunchPad open, choose the Security Manager from the DB: Administration menu. Otherwise, on Windows 95, 98, or NT, choose Start⇨Programs⇨Oracle HOME2⇨DBA Management Pack⇨ Security Manager.

   On UNIX, type **oemapp security** on the command line.

   If you come to a login window, go to Step 2. Otherwise, skip to Step 3.

2. **Log in with a valid DBA Oracle8i user name and password.**

   One option is to log in with the user ID and password that are loaded into all Oracle8i databases: SYSTEM (password MANAGER). Leave the Service box empty if you are running your own personal Oracle8i. Otherwise, fill in the name of the Oracle8i database (instance) on your network. Leave the Connect As box set to the default of Normal.

3. **Select the User folder by double-clicking it in the left frame.**

   This action brings up a list of all the user IDs in the database.

4. **Click the user ID that will receive the new role.**

   This action brings up the User Property page, as shown in Figure 12-4. For the example, click JONES.

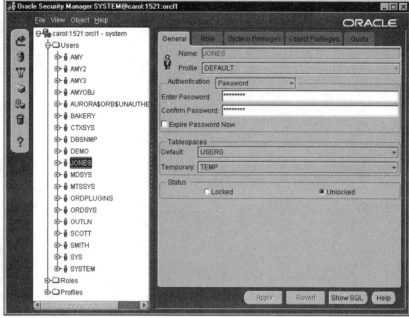

Figure 12-4:
Users are
listed on the
left, and
one user's
properties
are
displayed
on the right.

5. **View the Role properties by clicking the Role tab near the top of the property page.**

   The window displays the current list of roles for the user, as shown in Figure 12-5. The window lists all the granted roles on the bottom and all the remaining roles on the top.

6. **Select a new role and click the down arrow to grant the role.**

   To assign a role, select the role in the top window and then click the down arrow between the top and bottom windows. For this example, scroll through the available roles until you find the MANAGER role. Then select this role and click the down arrow.

   Oracle8i copies the chosen role (the MANAGER role in this case) into the lower list, indicating that the role is now assigned to the user (JONES).

7. **(Optional) Repeat Step 6 for the HOURLY role.**

   You have assigned both roles to JONES.

8. **(Optional) Click the Show SQL button.**

   This optional step shows you how to view the SQL command(s) generated by your actions. Oracle8i generates the SQL commands as you work. Then it executes them when you press the Apply (or Create) button. Once executed, the commands disappear from the SQL window.

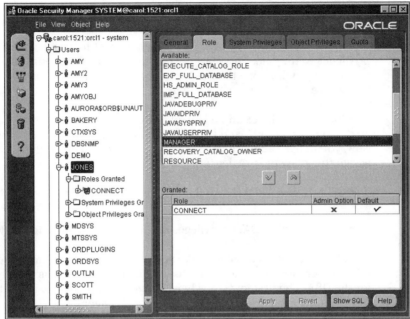

9. Click the Apply button to save your work to the database.

10. (Optional) Finish the example.

You can assign SMITH the role of HOURLY by following Steps 3 through 9 again, selecting SMITH in Step 3 and HOURLY in Step 6.

When you want to remove a role, simply go to the same place (the Role tab of the User property page) and move granted roles (found in the bottom window) up to the available roles (found in the top window).

A role can have an assigned password, which means that a user must enter an additional password to access the role. Use this password-protected role only for high-security areas, such as the recipe tables for your famous banana bread.

Roles can sometimes be confusing, but they are a great way to enforce security. After you set up the roles and get the appropriate table privileges granted, adding users to and removing users from the roles is easy. Using roles instead of granting table privileges directly to each user ID saves time in the long run.

Assigning privileges to roles

When you use roles for security, you usually want to assign specific table privileges to the role. This feature simplifies your job because you only assign the privilege one time — to the role — instead of assigning the privilege to every user that comes along.

Continuing with the example I introduce earlier in this chapter, you have created two roles, HOURLY and MANAGER, and assigned two users to those roles. Now, you assign table privileges to each role as needed. In this example, you assign the following privileges:

- ✔ SELECT and UPDATE privileges on the PAY_RATE table to the MANAGER role.
- ✔ SELECT and UPDATE privileges on the TIMECARD table to the HOURLY role.

The ability to assign privileges like SELECT and UPDATE belongs solely to the table owner. However, the ability to use Security Manager is usually reserved for the DBA. The first few steps here assign extra privileges to the table owner so the table owner can use Security Manager.

Here are the steps to assign table privileges to roles using Security Manager.

1. **Start the Security Manager.**

   If you have your LaunchPad open, choose the Security Manager from the DB: Administration menu. Otherwise, on Windows 95, 98, or NT, choose Start⇨Programs⇨Oracle HOME2⇨DBA Management Pack⇨ Security Manager.

   On UNIX, type **oemapp security** on the command line.

   If you come to a login window, go to Step 2. Otherwise, skip to Step 3.

2. **Log in with a valid DBA Oracle8i user name and password.**

   One option is to log in with the user ID and password that are loaded into all Oracle8i databases: SYSTEM (password MANAGER). Leave the Service box empty if you are running your own personal copy of Oracle8i. Otherwise, fill in the name of the Oracle8i database (instance) on your network. Leave the Connect As box set to the default of Normal.

3. **Double-click the folder labeled User in the left frame.**

4. **Click the table owner.**

   In the example, click AMY.

5. **Click the Role tab.**

   This displays current and available roles.

6. **Select** SELECT_CATALOG_ROLE **and click the down arrow.**

   The role appears in the top window. When you select the role and then click the down arrow, the role moves to the bottom of the window.

7. **Click the System Privileges tab.**

   Now you see the system privileges available.

8. **Select** SELECT ANY TABLE **and click the down arrow.**

   The privilege moves into the bottom part of the window.

9. **Click Apply.**

   Oracle8i saves the new role and the new privilege to AMY's database.

10. **Choose File⇨Change database connection.**

    A login window appears.

11. **Log in as the owner of the table.**

    In this case, log in as AMY, with password AMY123. Leave the Service box empty if you're running your own personal copy of Oracle8i. Otherwise, fill in the name of the Oracle8i database (instance) on your network. Leave the Connect As box set to the default of Normal.

12. **Double-click the Roles folder in the left frame.**

    A list of roles appears below the folder.

13. **Click the** MANAGER **role on the left to open the Role property page.**

14. **Click the Object Privileges tab.**

    Here you assign the privileges that allow this role some access to the tables. The top-left quarter of the property page labeled Object shows you a list of schemas.

15. **Double-click the schema that matches the table owner.**

    For the example, double-click AMY. A list of object types appears below AMY.

16. **Double-click the Tables folder.**

    A list of AMY's tables appears beneath the Tables folder.

17. **Click the table for which you will assign privileges.**

    A list of available privileges appears in the small window to the right of the table name. In the example, click the PAY_RATE table.

18. **Select the privilege that you want to add and click the down arrow.**

    For the example, choose SELECT in the Available Privileges window and click the down arrow. The window near the bottom of the screen shows the privilege that you added to the role. Figure 12-6 shows what your screen looks like.

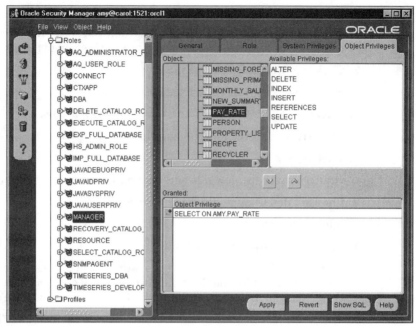

Figure 12-6:
A privilege
added to
the role.

19. **Repeat Steps 17 and 18 for more tables and privileges.**

    Add the UPDATE privilege for the PAY_RATE table.

20. **Click the Apply button.**

    You now have added the SELECT and UPDATE privileges for the PAY_RATE table to the MANAGER role.

21. **Repeat the preceding steps for any other roles you want to assign table privileges to.**

    For the example, repeat the steps for the HOURLY role, clicking the TIMECARD table in Step 17.

Your journey is over.

The next section briefly shows you how to accomplish the same death-defying feats using bare SQL.

Roles and Privileges with SQL

Creating and assigning roles is easy, even using raw SQL. Sometimes the DBA allows people who create tables to also create roles — check with your DBA to find out. As with most of the SQL commands shown in the book, you can use either SQL*Plus or SQL*Plus Worksheet to execute your commands.

To create a role in SQL, simply type

```
CREATE ROLE rolename;
```

where *rolename* is, obviously, the name of the role. The SQL*Plus Worksheet responds with

```
Statement processed.
```

To assign (or grant) someone a role, simply type

```
GRANT rolename TO username;
```

where `rolename` is the role and `username` is — you guessed it! — the Oracle user ID of the person to whom you are granting the role. Oracle8i responds with

```
Grant succeeded.
```

To assign table privileges, simply type

```
GRANT privilege1, privilege2, privilege3 ON tablename TO
rolename;
```

where each `privilege` is replaced by one table privilege. SELECT, INSERT, UPDATE, and DELETE are the most commonly used privileges, although others fall into the domain of the DBA and so are not covered by this book.

Only the DBA can create roles, unless the DBA has granted this privilege to another user or role. However, only the table owner can grant privileges (unless the table owner has given this right to another user or role, or someone has bribed the headwaiter).

Imagine that you want to create two roles for your employees. One role, called HOURLY, gives employees access to the TIMECARD table, where they can log hours worked. Only hourly employees need this role. The other role, called MANAGER, lets a manager review and change the pay rate for an employee, which is stored in the PAY_RATE table. Here are the steps to creating the roles, assigning the users, and assigning the table privileges.

1. **Start the SQL*Plus Worksheet.**

   If you have your LaunchPad open, choose the SQL*Plus Worksheet from the DB: Administration menu. Otherwise, on Windows 95, 98, or NT, choose Start⮞Programs⮞Oracle HOME2⮞DBA Management Pack⮞ SQL*Plus Manager.

On UNIX, type **oemapp worksheet** on the command line.

If you come to a login window, go to Step 2. Otherwise, skip to Step 3.

2. **Log in with a valid DBA Oracle8i user name and password.**

One option is to log in with the user ID and password that are loaded into all Oracle8i databases: SYSTEM (password MANAGER). Leave the Service box empty if you are running your own personal copy of Oracle8i. Otherwise, fill in the name of the Oracle8i database (instance) on your network. Leave the Connect As box set to the default of Normal.

3. **Create the HOURLY role by typing the following:**

```
create role HOURLY;
```

After you click the Execute button, SQL*Plus Worksheet replies

```
Statement processed.
```

4. **Create the MANAGER role by typing this SQL command:**

```
create role MANAGER;
```

Click the Execute button. SQL*Plus Worksheet replies

```
Statement processed.
```

5. **Assign your employees to each role.**

One user, JONES, is both a manager and an hourly employee. The first command for JONES is

```
grant HOURLY to JONES;
```

After you click the Execute button, SQL*Plus Worksheet replies

```
Statement processed.
```

The second command for JONES is

```
grant MANAGER to JONES;
```

SQL*Plus Worksheet replies

```
Statement processed.
```

6. **Connect as the table owner.**

You must switch over to the user ID of the table owner to assign table privileges. To connect to AMY, type this SQL command:

```
Connect AMY/AMY123@sid;
```

@sid is the database name preceded by the @ symbol. Leave the @sid out if you use a local database. Click the Execute button and SQL*Plus Worksheet replies

```
Statement processed.
```

7. **Assign the appropriate table privileges to each role.**

First, the TIMECARD table's privileges get assigned to the HOURLY role.

```
Grant SELECT. INSERT. UPDATE. DELETE
on TIMECARD to HOURLY;
```

SQL*Plus Worksheet replies

```
Statement processed.
```

Next, the PAY_RATE table's privileges get assigned to the MANAGER role.

```
Grant SELECT. INSERT. UPDATE. DELETE
on PAY_RATE to MANAGER;
```

SQL*Plus Worksheet replies

```
Statement processed.
```

8. **Exit SQL*Plus Worksheet.**

Click the X box in the top right corner of the window.

Profiles: The Power Players

Another way to control access to your database, besides assigning roles, is through the use of profiles. You may have a particularly paranoid boss. To relieve paranoia, first offer to check under your boss's bed and in the closets. If this tactic does not relieve the problem, offer to construct a tinfoil hat that blocks evil thought patterns and cosmic rays. I'm not kidding! Then assure your boss that even though he is paranoid, *they* still may be out to get him.

You or your boss may actually have a valid security concern about unauthorized people who may wreak havoc in your lovely tables. Perhaps you want to be certain that when people leave for lunch, they are logged off the database quickly. You may want to limit a user's total Central Processing Unit (CPU) time so that you can Darn That Query from Heck before it generates a results table ten times the size of the entire database.

You can assign profiles to users, roles, and groups of users to limit access to system resources. You can tell Oracle8i to limit

- ✔ Idle time
- ✔ CPU time
- ✔ Storage space
- ✔ Hang time in high surf (just kidding)
- ✔ Concurrent sessions per user
- ✔ Number of days until password expires
- ✔ Connect time
- ✔ Logical reads per session
- ✔ Other stuff

The next section shows how to create and assign profiles.

Creating a profile

A new feature in Oracle8i is the capability to set up restrictions on a user's password using a profile. For example, you can create a profile that keeps track of the last time each user changed his or her password and causes the password to expire after 30 days. You can even set a grace period of a few days so the user can still get in with his or her old password after getting a warning from the system. Good stuff. This one will save some DBA a lot of headaches and coding.

Have some fun — try out a profile. In this example, you are in charge of the Justice Department's archive database. You need a special profile for judges that gives them the ability to stay connected up to two hours. In addition, you want to prevent fraudulent use of a judge's user ID by restricting the user ID to a single concurrent login. A second login by the same user ID is rejected. You also add some special restrictions to the passwords so that judges must change their passwords and not reuse the ten previous passwords.

Here are the steps to create a special profile for your judges.

1. **Start the Enterprise Manager Toolbar.**

   If you have your LaunchPad open, choose the Security Manager from the DB: Administration menu. Otherwise, on Windows 95, 98, or NT, choose Start➪Programs➪Oracle HOME2➪DBA Management Pack➪ Security Manager.

   On UNIX, type **oemapp security** on the command line.

   If you come to a login window, go to Step 2. Otherwise, skip to Step 3.

2. **Log in with a valid DBA Oracle8i user name and password.**

   One option is to log in with the user ID and password that are loaded into all Oracle8i databases: SYSTEM and MANAGER, respectively. Leave the Service box empty if you are running your own personal copy of Oracle8i; otherwise, fill in the name of the Oracle8i database (instance) on your network. Leave the Connect As box set to Normal. The Security Manager window appears.

3. **Begin creating a new profile by choosing Object⇨Profile and then clicking the Create button on the top menu.**

   The Create Profile window, in which you define the profile, appears.

4. **Assign the name and the properties you want for the profile in the first window.**

   For the judge profile example, type **JUDGE_PROFILE** in the Name box and then select

   - Connect Time: 120 Minutes

   - Idle Time: 60 Minutes

   - Concurrent Sessions: 1 Per User

   Figure 12-7 shows the profile window after selecting these parameters.

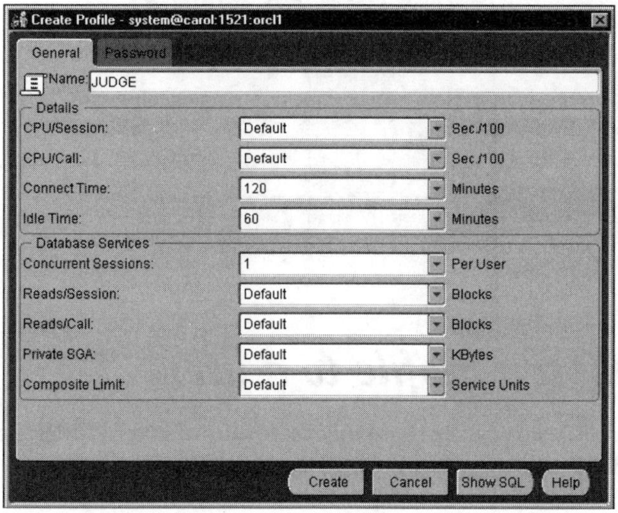

Figure 12-7: A profile can specify the number of concurrent sessions for a user.

5. **Click the Password tab.**

   This action brings up the next window of profile parameters, where you specify password-related values. For this example, choose:

- • Password expires in 30 days. This selection means that the pass word expires 30 days after it has been changed.

- • Password locks 21 days after expiration. This tells the database that if the user does not change the password within 21 days of the expiration date, he or she is not allowed to change the pass word without DBA intervention.

- • Keep password history for 10 previous passwords.

- • Lock the account for one day if three consecutive failed login attempts occur.

Figure 12-8 shows the Password tab of the Create Profile window.

6. Click Create to complete this profile.

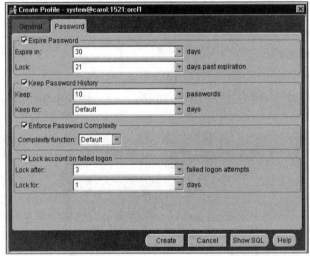

Figure 12-8:
This profile gives the user 21 days after expiration to change the password.

Assigning a profile to a user

Assigning profiles to a user that you create allows you to further customize each user's capabilities and limits within the database. Follow these simple steps to assign a profile to a user. If you are already in Security Manager, skip to Step 3.

1. Start the Security Manager.

If you have your LaunchPad open, choose the Security Manager from the DB: Administration menu. Otherwise, on Windows 95, 98, or NT, choose Start➪Programs➪Oracle HOME2➪DBA Management Pack➪ Security Manager.

On UNIX, type **oemapp security** on the command line.

If you come to a login window, go to Step 2. Otherwise, skip to Step 3.

2. Log in with a valid DBA Oracle8i user name and password.

One option is to log in with the user ID and password that are loaded into all Oracle8i databases: SYSTEM and MANAGER, respectively. Leave the Service box empty if you are running your own personal copy of Oracle8i; otherwise, fill in the name of the Oracle8i database (instance) on your network. Leave the Connect As box set to Normal. The Security Manager window appears.

3. Double-click the Users folder in the Navigator window of Security Manager.

You see a list of users appear below the folder.

4. Select the user that needs the profile.

For this example, you will assign the JUDGE_PROFILE profile created in the previous section to the user named AMY. When you select AMY, the right side of the screen displays the details about this user.

5. Click the Profile selection arrow and choose the profile.

When you click the arrow in the Profile box, you view all the available profiles. Select JUDGE_PROFILE for the example, as shown in Figure 12-9.

6. Click Apply to save your changes to the database.

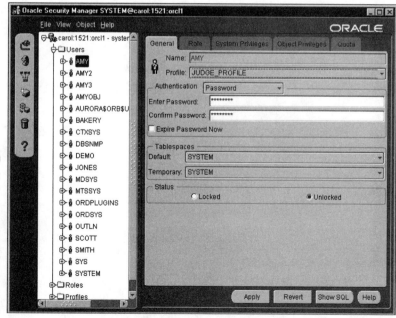

Figure 12-9: Each user has the DEFAULT profile unless you select a different profile here.

Creating customized profiles helps you, as DBA, to control the use of your database by various people who are assigned certain roles in your database. You may limit the role that you name VAMPIRES, for example, to ten CPU seconds per session so that the users don't suck the system dry. The role that you name MUTANT_CLONES probably should have a limit on concurrent sessions so that users don't start multiplying like rabbits.

Take a rest and then flip the page to see another aspect of security: synonyms and views.

Chapter 13

Views and Synonyms: Do You See What I See?

· ·

In This Chapter

▶ Narrowing your view

▶ Using views to tie everything together

▶ Creating views with SQL

▶ Creating object views with Schema Manager

▶ Using the grant command

▶ Sparring with synonyms

▶ Combining a grant and a synonym

· ·

*I*n this chapter, you find out about alternative ways to view tables in Oracle8i. You also discover how to make tables look as though they have different names or fewer columns and rows. You see how to combine tables into single larger tables without actually duplicating data. All these tricks make security easier to plan.

Schema Manager has improved its toolset by adding a window for creating object views. You'll love this fast and easy-to-use tool.

The features in this chapter are kind of like sunglasses at the beach: They're not essential, but using them makes viewing swimsuits (or the lack thereof) much easier. Sunglasses also allow you to block out the incredible glare from the white Maui sand (which keeps blowing onto your keyboard) and the glares from the people you're staring at.

The best way to create a view is to use SQL in the SQL*Plus Worksheet. After you install the sample schema that's on the CD-ROM, you can run all the SQL examples in this chapter in the SQL*Plus Worksheet. Appendix B contains instructions on how to install the CD-ROM samples in an Oracle8i database.

You'll find that creating views is really just like creating queries. Some views are based on very simple queries while others are based on very complex queries. Dive right in and give views a try.

Views: Like a Table — Almost

Views have one primary purpose: They rearrange the way you see a table, a portion of a table, or a group of tables without actually creating any copies of the underlying data.

A *view* is a window into the underlying table. A view changes the outward appearance of the table without actually changing the data in the table.

Imagine that you have a really great comprehensive table called NAME_AND_ADDRESS. This table contains the name and address of every customer you have ever done business with. The table also contains the name and address of every potential customer who filled out a questionnaire at your store.

Your sales department uses the NAME_AND_ADDRESS table to go after new leads and drum up new business. In fact, salespeople get frustrated because they have to weed through all the hundreds of current and past customers' names to find all the hundreds of prospects' names.

Your accounting department uses the NAME_AND_ADDRESS table as its master mailing list. People in accounting send Christmas cards to all your current and past clients. The accounting department also gets tired of having to continually separate the rows of current and past clients from the rows of potential clients.

Views help you solve the dilemma of having two different interest groups sharing one table. You can create two views of the NAME_AND_ADDRESS table. One of the views that you can create has only potential clients in it. You name it PROSPECT and instruct your sales department to use the new view instead of the NAME_AND_ADDRESS table. From the salespeople's points of view (pardon my pun), you have given them a customized table for their own special needs. Your salespeople decide that you really love them.

Next, you create another view called CLIENT, which you limit to current and past customers. You ask your accountants to use this view in lieu of the NAME_AND_ADDRESS table. The accountants buy you a new desktop pen set to show their appreciation.

The two views that you just created each contain a subset of the data in the underlying table. See the next section for a look at different ways to create views that contain subsets of a table's data. You can also create views that span several tables and make them appear to be a single table. You can explore these kinds of views in subsequent sections of this chapter.

You can use views just as you use tables in queries, reports, and online forms. Here are the restrictions that apply to using views:

✔ If the view combines multiple tables, you can view the table data, but sometimes you can't update the data.

✔ In general, the user who creates a view should own all the referenced tables. If some of the tables belong to other users, complex rules regarding updates through the view exist. Views that are for query only aren't a problem as long as you have permission (the SELECT privilege) to query the table.

Views that narrow

The basic command for creating a new view looks like this:

```
CREATE [or REPLACE] VIEW viewname as
SELECT columnname1, columnname2, etc.
FROM tablename
WHERE where-clause;
```

Replace viewname with the name of your view. Replace columnname1, columnname2, etc. with valid column names. Replace tablename with a valid table name. Replace where-clause with a valid WHERE clause. Actually, you can replace everything from the word SELECT through the end of the command with just about any valid query. Once created, Oracle8i replies with

```
View created.
```

You can change a view by revising the query and adding the or REPLACE phrase (in brackets in the preceding code) to the command. Oracle8i replaces the existing view or simply creates a new view if one doesn't already exist.

To remove a view, drop it, as follows:

```
drop view viewname;
```

Oracle8i tells you that it took care of it, as follows:

```
View dropped.
```

Sometimes, a view becomes invalid because you made changes in the underlying table. In these cases, the next time you use the view, you get an error message indicating that the view is invalid. If you dropped the underlying table, for example, Oracle8i says

```
ORA-04063: View "owner.viewname" has errors.
```

owner is the view owner, and viewname is the name of the view.

This chapter includes lots of examples to give you a good idea of the versatility of views. Enjoy yourself.

Your top-secret spy agency has a table called SPY_MASTER that contains counter-intelligence agents' names. You want your secretary to run a report that lists these agents and their code names, sorted by country. You also want to be the only person who is able to view or change the agents' actual names in the table.

You create a view called UNCLASSIFIED_AGENT that includes the agents' code names and the countries to which you have currently assigned them. You grant permission for your secretary to see this view. Figure 13-1 shows the table and the view. The view is like a window that allows you to see into one part of the table and contains only two of the three columns. You'd better be nice to your secretary!

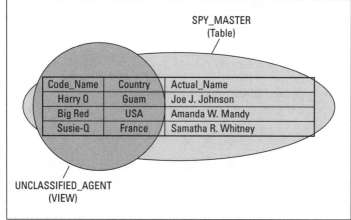

Figure 13-1:
The spy table must be protected.

The code for creating the UNCLASSIFIED_AGENT view goes like this:

```
create view UNCLASSIFIED_AGENT as
select CODE_NAME, COUNTRY
from SPY_MASTER;
```

Your company payroll table contains the pay rate for each employee. You want to give managers the capability to view and modify only their subordinates' pay rates. The table, EMPLOYEE_PAY_RATE, includes each employee's ID number and pay rate, and the manager's ID number. You set up a view that customizes the PAY_RATE table so that each manager sees only his or her own employees, as shown in Figure 13-2. You call the view PAY_RATE_BY_MANAGER and give the MANAGER role permission to see and change data in this view.

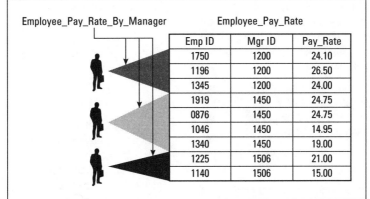

Figure 13-2: The view for your managers looks like this.

Employee_Pay_Rate_By_Manager   Employee_Pay_Rate

Emp ID	Mgr ID	Pay_Rate
1750	1200	24.10
1196	1200	26.50
1345	1200	24.00
1919	1450	24.75
0876	1450	24.75
1046	1450	14.95
1340	1450	19.00
1225	1506	21.00
1140	1506	15.00

You can set up the code for creating this view in two ways. The first way creates a set of views, one for each manager. The SQL code looks like this:

```
create view MGR_1450_PAY_RATE_VIEW as
select * from PAY_RATE
where MGR_ID = 1450;
```

The second way to set up the code requires a little more preparation. This way requires another table — the MANAGER table, which connects the manager's ID with the actual Oracle8i user ID. The SQL for the view looks like this:

```
create view PAY_RATE_BY_MANAGER_VIEW as
select * from PAY_RATE
where MGR_ID =  (select MGR_ID from MANAGER
                where USER = MANAGER.ORACLE_ID);
```

The preceding example code contains the *pseudocolumn* called USER in the last line. This column automatically contains the Oracle user name of the person running the query. For example, if the sales manager logs in as HARRYK, then the pseudocolumn USER equals HARRYK, and the row in the MANAGER table that contains HARRYK in the ORACLE_ID column matches the USER column. This way, each manager sees only his or her own underlings. See the sidebar "Pseudocolumns and the DUAL table" for more information about pseudocolumns.

On a similar note, Oracle8i has a small table called DUAL that the SYSTEM

Pseudocolumns and the DUAL table

The column named USER is a pseudocolumn — a column that Oracle8i defines for convenience. You can treat pseudocolumns just as you do any other column in queries, but you can't change pseudocolumn values.

DUAL is a real table in Oracle8i that you can use any time you want to retrieve a single row of pseudocolumns or a single row of literal values that require no table access.

Here's a list of some of the pseudocolumns that are available to you:

✔ **USER:** Oracle ID of current user logged on. USER is useful for security validation because if you forget what user ID you used, you can type

```
select USER from DUAL;
```

The results tell you the user ID:

```
USER
_____

AMY
```

✔ **SYSDATE:** Current date and time. SYSDATE is in the standard date format for Oracle8i. You can use SYSDATE to date-stamp rows or add today's date to a report. Here's how:

```
select
to_char(sysdate,'mm/dd/yyyy
hh:mi:ss') from dual;
```

The results show the current date and time in the specified format:

```
TO_CHAR(SYSDATE,'MM/DD/YYYY
HH24:MI:SS')
```
_____

```
09/09/1999 17:09:59
```

✔ **ROWID:** Unique location of a row. ROWID contains a hexadecimal number for the block, row, and file where the row is stored. ROWID is the fastest path for retrieving a row, but you can't use ROWID as the table's primary key because it can change if you relocate the table.

✔ **ROWNUM:** A number assigned sequentially to rows retrieved from a query. The first row returned is assigned ROWNUM 1, the second row is assigned ROWNUM 2, and so on. This pseudocolumn is useful for limiting the total rows returned in a query in which ROWNUM is less than 100.

✔ **NESTED_TABLE_ID:** A unique identifier assigned to each row in a nested table. This identifier is similar to a ROWID on a relational table.

user ID owns and that is accessible to all Oracle users. DUAL always has one row and one column. (Now that I think about it, I wonder why Oracle called the table DUAL — I would call it SINGLE!) See the sidebar "Pseudocolumns and the DUAL table" for a discussion on pseudocolumns and the proper use of the DUAL table.

Views that tie everything together

This section shows you how to use views to expand and combine multiple tables. You can use views to group common information from several tables in a single table without duplicating data. You retrieve the underlying data from the original tables when you use the view, which means that the views automatically use any changes made in the original tables.

The general syntax is this:

```
CREATE VIEW viewname AS
SELECT columnname1, columnname2, etc.
FROM tablename1, tablename2
WHERE tablename1.columnname3 = tablename2.columnname4;
```

Replace viewname with the name of your new view. Replace everything after SELECT with a valid query that joins multiple tables.

You have created a table called COUNTRY in which each country has a number ID assigned, called COUNTRY_ID. The COUNTRY_ID appears as a foreign key in other tables, such as your CUSTOMER_ACCOUNT table. A foreign key connects one table to another.

The CUSTOMER_ACCOUNT table uses the COUNTRY_ID from the COUNTRY table for the customer's location. Figure 13-3 diagrams the table layout.

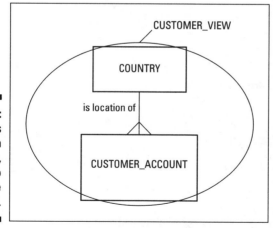

Figure 13-3: Customers live in countries, so the two tables are related.

You need a view that combines the COUNTRY_NAME and the CUSTOMER_ACCOUNT tables so that you have a simple and convenient way to create reports. This view allows you to create reports as though you had only one table with all the information in it. Writing a query on one table is easier and saves you time and effort. This view can be especially handy when other people need to write their own queries and are not experts like you on the subtleties of foreign keys. Figure 13-4 shows the data that appears in the tables and how it goes into the view.

COUNTRY

ID	COUNTRY NAME
01	United States
02	Great Britain
03	Japan

CUSTOMER_ACCOUNT

CUST_ID	NAME	ADDRESS	COUNTRY_ID
001	Jane Smith	120 West	01
002	Harry Winters		01
003	Harry Owens	RR3 W. Vir	02

CUSTOMER_VIEW

CUST_ID	NAME	ADDRESS	COUNTRY_ID
001	Jane Smith	120 West	United States
002	Harry Winters		United States
003	Harry Owens	RR3 W. Vir	Japan

Figure 13-4:
Stuffing data into a view allows easier access.

Here's the SQL code for creating this view:

```
create view CUSTOMER_VIEW as
  select CUST_ID, NAME, ADDRESS, COUNTRY_NAME
  from CUSTOMER_ACCOUNT,
     COUNTRY
  where COUNTRY.COUNTRY_ID = CUSTOMER_ACCOUNT.COUNTRY_ID;
```

Views with Schema Manager

Schema Manager has a great little window for looking at the SQL command used to create a view. The following two sections show you how to look at the query that you used when creating a view and how to make changes in a view.

You can also create a view with Schema Manager, although it doesn't save you much time. I recommend that you stick with the SQL method of creating views and then use Schema Manager to make small changes in the views. However, to create object views more easily, I recommend that you use Schema Manager. See the "Object views with Schema Manager" section later in this chapter.

Looking at views with Schema Manager

Follow these steps to start Schema Manager and start looking at views:

1. **Start the Schema Manager.**

   If you have your LaunchPad up, choose the Schema Manager from the DB: Administration menu. Otherwise, on Windows 95, 98, or NT, select Start⇨Programs⇨Oracle HOME2⇨DBA Management Pack⇨ Schema Manager.

   On UNIX, type **oemapp schema** on the command line.

   If you come to a login window, go to Step 2. Otherwise, skip to Step 3.

2. **Log in with a valid DBA Oracle8i user name and password.**

   One option is to log in with the user ID and password that are loaded into all Oracle8i databases: SYSTEM and MANAGER, respectively. Leave the Service box empty if you're running your own personal Oracle8i; otherwise, fill in the name of the Oracle8i database (instance) on your network. Leave the Connect As box set to Normal.

3. **Double-click the Views folder in the left frame.**

   A list of schemas appears below the Views folder in the left frame. A list of all the views in the database appears in the right frame. Notice the Status column in the right frame. Each view is either Valid or Invalid.

4. **Double-click a schema in the left frame.**

   If you're using the example query, double-click the schema named AMY. You now see only AMY's views in the right frame. You also get a list of AMY's views below the AMY schema in the right frame.

5. **Click a view in the left frame.**

   For the example, click the view named CUSTOMER_A_VIEW. The specifications for this view appear in the right frame, as shown in Figure 13-5.

At this point, you can look at the SQL query that your view uses to retrieve data. If the view is invalid, you may want to make a correction in the SQL query; see the next section to find out how.

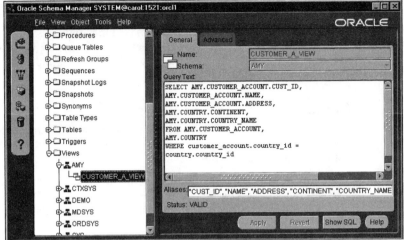

Figure 13-5:
Schema
Manager
reveals
AMY's view.

Changing a view with Schema Manager

If you followed the steps in the preceding section, you're ready to change a view with Schema Manager; otherwise, go back to the preceding section and follow all six steps. You should see a window showing the SQL code of the view that you want to change. If you're following the example from the preceding section, you see the SQL code of CUSTOMER_A_VIEW in the right frame (refer to Figure 13-5). Okay, go ahead and make a change in your view by following these steps:

1. **Change the SQL code by adding, changing, or removing text.**

   For the example, delete AMY.COUNTRY.CONTINENT, to remove the column CONTINENT from the query.

2. **Apply the change by clicking the Apply button near the bottom of the window in the right frame.**

   If your syntax is wrong, Oracle8i displays a pop-up window with an error message. In this case, review your changes and correct any syntax errors that you made. Then click the Apply button again. When your syntax is perfect, you receive no message from Oracle8i, but the Apply button is grayed out, meaning your changes have been applied.

3. **Click the schema.**

   Oracle8i removes the view window from the right frame.

   For the example, click the AMY schema. Notice that the status column for CUSTOMER_A_VIEW then shows that it's a valid view.

4. **Exit Schema Manager by clicking the X box in the top right corner of the window.**

Now you know how to look at a view and change your view. It's all a matter of your point of view, right?

Object views with Schema Manager

Object views — like the relational table views that are also covered in this chapter — are a method of transforming the way data appears to your end users while keeping the data stored the way you prefer.

With an object view, you can store data in relational tables and still be able to use the new features of Oracle8i. You can also interface with object-oriented programming languages more easily.

So how do you go about creating this thing called an object view? Follow these basic steps:

1. **Develop a query that reflects the data that you want to place into the object view.**

2. **Create an object type in Schema Manager that defines attributes corresponding to each column in the query.**

3. **Use the query and the object type to build the object view in Schema Manager.**

The following three sections show you how to complete these steps by using an example from the sample tables. Follow along!

First, creating a query

The first step toward creating an object view is to develop a query. If you want to follow the example from the sample tables, use the following query:

```
select CUST_ID, NAME, ADDRESS, COUNTRY_NAME
  from CUSTOMER_ACCOUNT,
     COUNTRY
where COUNTRY.COUNTRY_ID = CUSTOMER_ACCOUNT.COUNTRY_ID;
```

Check out Chapter 3 for all the basics of creating queries. It's there waiting for you anytime.

Second, creating an object type

The second step is to use Schema Manager to create an object type that contains an attribute for each column in the query. Follow these steps:

1. **Start the Schema Manager.**

   If you have your LaunchPad up, choose the Schema Manager from the DB: Administration menu. Otherwise, on Windows 95, 98, or NT, select Start⇨Programs⇨Oracle HOME2⇨DBA Management Pack⇨ Schema Manager.

   On UNIX, type **oemapp schema** on the command line:

   If you come to a login window, go to Step 2. Otherwise, skip to Step 3.

2. Log in with a valid DBA Oracle8i user name and password.

One option is to log in with the user ID and password that are loaded into all Oracle8i databases: SYSTEM and MANAGER, respectively. Leave the Service box empty if you're running your own personal Oracle8i; otherwise, fill in the name of the Oracle8i database (instance) on your network. Leave the Connect As box set to Normal.

3. Choose Objects⇨Create from the top menu.

A list of objects that you can create appears in a pop-up window.

4. Select Object Type and click Create.

You can see the Create Object Type window.

5. Type in the object type name.

If you're using the example query from the preceding section, type the name CUSTOMER_TYPE.

6. Select the schema that will own the object type.

Use the drop-down list in the Schema box to select the schema. Generally, the object view that you plan to create and the object type that you are creating belong in the same schema. For the example, use AMY.

The following steps create attributes that become part of the Attributes box. The other box, labeled Methods, is not used in this example. You must use PL/SQL to create a method, and this technique falls into advanced features that this book does not cover.

Figure 13-6 shows the Create Object Type window at this point in the definition process.

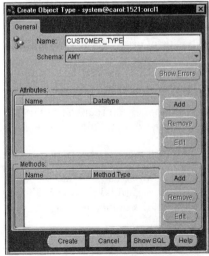

Figure 13-6: Schema Manager begins an object type definition here.

7. **Click the Add button to create an attribute.**

   The Create Attribute window appears. Here you fill in details about the attribute.

8. **Type an attribute name in the Attribute Name box.**

   For the example, the first attribute is named CUST_ID.

9. **Fill in details about the datatype for this attribute.**

   You can use other object types by selecting a schema. The list of datatypes will be expanded to include all the object types owned by that schema.

   For regular datatypes, leave <none> in the Schema field and then choose from the datatypes in the Type field. In the example, the first attribute is a NUMBER datatype with no length or precision defined, as shown in Figure 13-7.

   The idea is to make one attribute match each of the columns in the query. The attributes must be in the same order as the columns in the query and should use the same datatypes as the queried columns.

10. **Click OK and return to the Create Object Type window.**

    You can see the attribute listed in the Attributes box.

11. **Continue to add attributes as needed by repeating Steps 7 through 10.**

12. **After you define all the attributes, click the Create button.**

Success! You have created the object type. Time to wrap it all up in an object view.

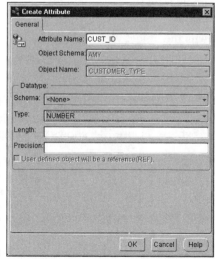

Figure 13-7:
An attribute
has a
datatype
that is either
another
object type
or a regular
datatype.

Third, creating the object view

The final step is to create the object view itself.

Oracle has enhanced Schema Manager's Create View window to support the creation of object views, making them quite easy to create. If you already have Schema Manager open, skip to Step 3; otherwise, start with Step 1 to create an object view:

1. **Start the Schema Manager.**

   If you have your LaunchPad up, choose the Schema Manager from the DB: Administration menu. Otherwise, on Windows 95, 98, or NT, select Start⇨Programs⇨Oracle HOME2⇨DBA Management Pack⇨ Schema Manager.

   On UNIX, type **oemapp schema** on the command line.

   If you come to a login window, go to Step 2. Otherwise, skip to Step 3.

2. **Log in with a valid DBA Oracle8i user name and password.**

   One option is to log in with the user ID and password that are loaded into all Oracle8i databases: SYSTEM and MANAGER, respectively. Leave the Service box empty if you're running your own personal Oracle8i; otherwise, fill in the name of the Oracle8i database (instance) on your network. Leave the Connect As box set to Normal.

3. **Choose Objects⇨Create from the top menu.**

   A list of objects that you can create appears in a pop-up window.

4. **Select View and click Create.**

   You see the Create View window.

5. **Type in the object view name.**

   If you're following the example from the preceding two sections, use the name CUSTOMER_OBJECT_VIEW.

6. **Select the schema that owns the object view.**

   Use the arrow to the right of the Schema box to pick and choose a schema.

7. **Type in a query in the Query Text box.**

   You can copy the query from a file opened in any text editor and paste the query into the Query Text box. Figure 13-8 shows the sample view up to this point.

8. **Click the Advanced tab.**

   This tab shows the extra parameters that you can specify for the view.

Figure 13-8:
Schema
Manager
starts off an
object view
as if it were
a regular old
boring view.

9. **Click the As Object check box.**

   The object definition section of the window is now editable.

10. **Select the schema that owns the object type you created.**

    Under normal circumstances, this schema will be the same as the view schema. For the example, select AMY.

11. **Select the object type you created that corresponds to the query of this view.**

    In the example from the preceding section, you created an object type with four attributes called CUSTOMER_TYPE; select this object type.

12. **Click the Object Name check box and choose Specify Attributes.**

    You can define the unique key field (Object ID, also known as OID) for the object view using attributes of the object type. An OID is essential when creating object views.

13. **Click the attribute or attributes that make up the unique key field(s) for the object view.**

    As you click each attribute, a sequence number appears in the Order column. This column shows you the order in which the unique key will be built. For the example, click CUST_ID. Figure 13-9 shows the Advanced tab after you fill it in for an object view.

14. **Click Create to commit this *object d'art* to your repertoire.**

    Well done!

The next section expands your mind with rose-colored glasses called synonyms.

Figure 13-9:
Schema
Manager's
Advanced
tab contains
all the
details
needed for
completing
an object
view.

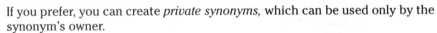

Synonyms: Nicknames for Tables and Views

No, it's not that spice on sticky buns — a *synonym* is an alternate name. You can make a synonym for a table, a view, or even another synonym. After you create a synonym, you can use it as though it were a table. Like views, synonyms don't duplicate data — they're only a different route to the same data. Darn! Now I'm getting hungry!

You can create *public synonyms* for everyone to use. Usually only the database administrator (DBA) can make a public synonym. As with any other privilege in the database, however, your DBA can bequeath the capability to create public synonyms to you or to a role to which you belong.

If you prefer, you can create *private synonyms,* which can be used only by the synonym's owner.

Here's how you create a synonym for an object using Schema Manager:

1. **Start the Schema Manager.**

    If you have your LaunchPad up, choose the Schema Manager from the DB: Administration menu. Otherwise, on Windows 95, 98, or NT, select Start➪Programs➪Oracle HOME2➪DBA Management Pack➪ Schema Manager.

On UNIX, type **oemapp schema** on the command line.

If you come to a login window, go to Step 2. Otherwise, skip to Step 3.

2. **Log in with a valid DBA Oracle8i user name and password.**

   One option is to log in with the user ID and password that are loaded into all Oracle8i databases: SYSTEM and MANAGER, respectively. Leave the Service box empty if you're running your own personal Oracle8i; otherwise, fill in the name of the Oracle8i database (instance) on your network. Leave the Connect As box set to Normal.

3. **Choose Objects⇨Create from the top menu.**

   A list of objects that you can create appears in a pop-up window.

4. **Select Synonym and click Create.**

   You see the Create Synonym window. Check out those cool sunglasses! Retro to the max.

5. **Type in the synonym name.**

   For this example, you want to create a public synonym for the CUSTOMER_ACCOUNT table, which is named CUSTOMER_ACCOUNT.

6. **Select either PUBLIC or a schema name in the Schema Box.**

   Select PUBLIC to create a public synonym. Select a schema name, such as AMY, to create a private synonym for that user. For the example, select PUBLIC.

7. **Select the object type.**

   For the example, select TABLE. As you can see from the pull-down menu, you can create synonyms for many kinds of objects.

8. **Select the schema and object name of the object underlying the synonym.**

   For the example, select AMY as the schema and CUSTOMER_ACCOUNT as the object. Figure 13-10 shows the completed synonym window for the example.

9. **Click Create to complete this action.**

The synonym name doesn't have to match the table's name. If you're creating public synonyms, they must be unique among all public synonyms.

When you create a *private synonym,* it has the same features as a public synonym, except that it's only for the use of the synonym creator and not for everyone else. I don't use private synonyms often, and you shouldn't either. Private synonyms can be confusing because they look as if they are really tables that you own yourself.

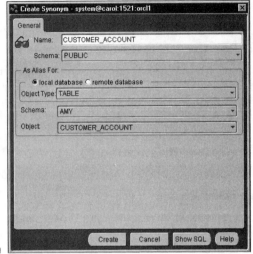

Figure 13-10:
Creating a
public
synonym is
a simple
task with
Schema
Manager.

One good use of the private synonym is to create a shorthand name for a table. Suppose that you give a table some long name, such as `CA_GRANT_STEP_ATTRIBUTE_TYPE`. Later, you're experimenting with a query in SQL*Plus that uses this table. Your fingers get into wrestling matches, trying to type the table name over and over.

Good uses for synonyms

Here are ways to use synonyms to your advantage:

- ✔ If you're tired of typing a long name for a table, create a synonym. For example, create a synonym named `EE` that points to the `EMPLOYEE_TRUST_FUND_ACCOUNT` table.

- ✔ Use public synonyms for centrally located lookup tables. After you create the public synonym, you also must allow others to view the data by granting privileges on the underlying table. For example:

```
GRANT SELECT ON STATE_CODE TO PUBLIC;
```

✔ Modify screen terminology, which gives two groups of users two different perspectives on the same information. People in the sales department call a customer a client, for example, and have a fit when they see a table called CUSTOMER in their database. Sales shares the table with the people in the accounting department, who would rather die than call a customer a client. You create a synonym called CLIENT and make sure that the sales department uses it. You're subsequently revered as being a wise and ancient sage, and promoted and worshipped accordingly. Little do these people know that the underlying table for the CLIENT synonym is still the same old CUSTOMER table! The accounting department folks (who are always right, or so they say) continue to use the CUSTOMER table.

✔ Make multiple sets of tables that mirror one another but have different owners. Larger companies that need both a test-phase database and a production-phase database use this method.

A grant and a synonym combined

A common mistake that Oracle8i users make in creating public synonyms is assuming that they can then share their tables with other Oracle8i users. Creating a public synonym for a table doesn't automatically allow other users to view or change the data in your table. You must assign the appropriate privileges, using the Security Manager described in Chapter 12. Generally speaking, you don't grant privileges on a synonym — you always grant privileges on the underlying table or view.

Chapter 14

WebDB: The Best New Tool for the Internet

● ●

In This Chapter:

▶ Discovering WebDB

▶ Looking at your data with WebDB

▶ Creating a report on the Web

▶ Mastering the details of master-detail forms

● ●

 *W*ebDB was born from a couple of different tools that originated several years ago when the people at Oracle started eyeing the Internet's potential. The Web site generator portion of WebDB grew from an in-house project Oracle used for its customer service staff. The database browser function is similar to the Discoverer tool available from Oracle. The template-based design tool for Web pages grew from the original Web Application Server that combined customized PL/SQL procedures with Web formatting functions.

Today, WebDB has grown into a full-fledged development tool that stands on its own very well. It's easier to use than Oracle's form design tool, Developer. You don't even need to know any HTML or SQL to use it, although knowledge of both makes it easier for you to understand and use WebDB to the fullest.

This chapter gives you a fly-by of all the features in WebDB and then demonstrates a few of the coolest features. When you're done, you'll be ready to crank out Web pages like a pro.

A free trial version of WebDB is available on Oracle's Web site at www.oracle.com. Just click on the Free Downloads link in the top menu on the Web site to find it.

Exploring WebDB

As its name implies, WebDB has something to do with putting a database together with a Web site. More precisely, WebDB is the middle part of a three-tier architectural sandwich that includes the Web browser on the top and the database on the bottom. The Web Server can be thrown in as a condiment, but you can also use the WebDB Listener to do the job if you prefer.

So, here's how all the layers fit together:

1. **You create a schema with tables and data.**

2. **You tell WebDB that this schema will be viewed or modified using WebDB pages.**

3. **You create Web pages, forms, and reports using the WebDB Build tools.**

4. **You tell WebDB who is allowed to look at your WebDB creations.**

5. **You and others use a Web browser to view the WebDB pages, forms, and reports.**

6. **The WebDB Listener serves the pages and sends data changes to the database.**

WebDB can do many things for you. I explore in detail just a few of these features. However, just so you are well informed, which I know you always aspire to be in this information age, here's a list of some easy-to-use features of WebDB:

- ✔ **Lets you design in your browser.** This is so cool! All the features of this tool work inside the Web browser.

- ✔ **Automatically opens selected tables for browsing on the Web.** Your end users don't need to know anything but how to move a mouse to use this feature.

- ✔ **Builds reports easily.** Enables you to create reports in HTML, Excel, or plain text formats from one design.

- ✔ **Automatically generates parameter entry forms for your reports.** Just add a parameter in your query and WebDB is smart enough to figure out that you need end-user input for it.

- ✔ **Gives you an easy test environment.** Bounce between test runs and the design tool without leaving your browser session.

- ✔ **Handles the security of your Web objects as if they were database objects.** You can define roles that are allowed to access the WebDB pages and then grant these roles to any Oracle user.

Some of the more advanced features take a bit more time to get comfortable with. Here's a list of some of these advanced features of WebDB:

✔ **Creates reusable lists of lookup tables and other reusable objects.**

✔ **Makes interconnected Web pages that pass parameters to each other.**

✔ **Generates a complete Web site that is stored in the database.** Among other things, this Web site lets you design a template for various types of pages and assign corners to groups of users who are allowed to post their own news articles from their browsers.

✔ **Monitors your Web pages.** You can look at which pages are used most often and least often. This feature even shows you performance statistics.

Figure 14-1 shows the initial Web page where you begin working with WebDB.

Next I offer some steps for building example Web pages using WebDB. The first step in creating WebDB components is to assign the schema involved to the WEBDB_DEVELOPER role.

I found that installing WebDB takes a long time, although doing so is easy. One word of caution if you're preparing to install WebDB: Be careful to install it in its own Oracle Home directory if you're using your own copy of Oracle8i! Otherwise, WebDB misbehaves.

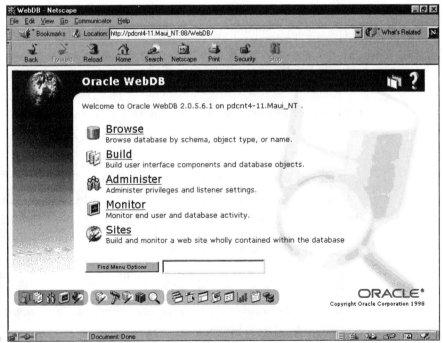

Figure 14-1:
WebDB
has many
features
to choose
from.

Assigning WebDB Developers

This part of WebDB contains bits and pieces that overlap with the Security Manager in Enterprise Manager's DBA Management Package. For example, you can create a brand-new user here. However, because you know how to do that (see Chapter 9 if you don't), I focus on new stuff here. I show you just the part you need to use to allow an existing schema to build its own Web page components. Follow along, if you dare:

1. **Start up the WebDB main page.**

   Start up your browser and then type the WebDB main page URL. The URL format is

   ```
   http://hostname:portnumber/WebDB/
   ```

   Replace hostname with the host that serves WebDB. For example, if you are using your own copy of WebDB and Oracle8i, your computer is the host. Replace portnumber with the port specified when WebDB was installed. For example, the actual URL on my home computer is

   ```
   http://carol:80/WebDB/
   ```

2. **Log in as the WebDB administrator.**

   The default administrator is named WEBDB and the password is WEBDB. The WebDB main page appears (refer to Figure 14-1).

3. **Click Administer in the list of links.**

   This action brings up the main administration page.

4. **Click User Manager in the list of links.**

   This action takes you to a create/search/history page, as shown in Figure 14-2. This kind of page is typical of most of the tools within WebDB. Here you have three choices: Create something, find something, or choose something you recently worked on.

5. **Type the schema name in the User Name box in the section labeled Find an Existing User and then click Find.**

   For this example, I use the AMY schema that you can install from the CD-ROM in the back of this book.

   The User Manager page appears with a property page for the user (schema) that you specified.

6. **Click the checkboxes for WebDB Developer and Component Building Schema and click Apply.**

   This action causes the schema to be assigned the WEBDB_DEVELOPER role, as shown in Figure 14-3. Notice the WEBDB_DEVELOPER role now appears in the list of roles.

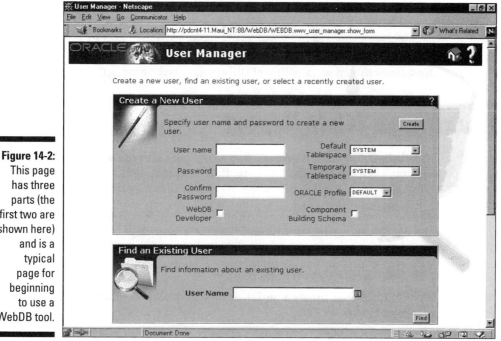

Figure 14-2:
This page has three parts (the first two are shown here) and is a typical page for beginning to use a WebDB tool.

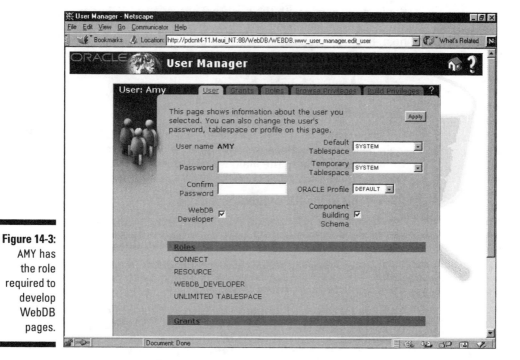

Figure 14-3:
AMY has the role required to develop WebDB pages.

7. **Click the home symbol in the top-right corner of the page to return to the main page.**

   This symbol returns you to the page shown in Figure 14-1.

Now that AMY can work with WebDB, she can make a report!

Creating a Web Report

The Web Report page is an easy way to get your feet wet with WebDB. In this section, I help you build a report on the SEAWEED_SAMPLE table in the AMY schema.

Follow these easy steps to create and run your report. If you are already in the WebDB main page as the WebDB administrator, exit your browser and then begin.

1. **Start up the WebDB main page.**

   Start up your browser and then type in the WebDB main page URL. The URL format is

   ```
   http://hostname:portnumber/WebDB/
   ```

   Replace hostname with the host that serves WebDB. For example, if you are using your own copy of WebDB and Oracle8i, your computer is the host. Replace portnumber with the port specified when WebDB was installed. For example, the actual URL on my home computer is

   ```
   http://carol:80/WebDB/
   ```

2. **Log in as the WebDB Developer.**

   For this example, log in as AMY with password AMY123. The WebDB main page appears. Because you logged in as a user, rather than the WebDB administrator, the main window does not contain all the selections in Figure 14-1.

3. **Click Build in the list of links.**

   This step brings up the main component building menu page.

4. **Click User Interface Components in the list of links.**

   This action takes you to another list of links.

5. **Click Reports in the list of links.**

   This link takes you to a create/find/history page where you must decide what to do. You want to create a new report, so keep going.

6. Begin a new report.

You can use either the Query Wizard or your own SQL query as the basis of your report. For this example, leave the radio button set to the default of Report from Query Wizard. Then click the Create button in the Create a New Report section of the page. Lo and behold, you see the unsinkable Query Wizard.

7. Select the schema and type a report name. Then click the Next arrow.

For the example, choose AMY as the schema and type **AMY_SEAWEED_REPORT** in the Report Name box. Figure 14-4 shows the first page of the wizard.

8. Choose the tables or views for the report and click the Next arrow.

Choose more than one table or view by holding the Control key down when you click on your selections. For this example, I selected two tables: SEAWEED_SAMPLE and TYPE_OF_SEAWEED, as shown in Figure 14-5.

9. Adjust the join criteria, if needed, and click the Next arrow.

The WebDB Report Wizard looks for a relationship between the two tables and uses it as the join conditions. For the example, the SEAWEED_SAMPLE table has a foreign key constraint stating that the TYPE_ID column is a foreign key referencing the TYPE_OF_SEAWEED table. The wizard uses this information to create a join between the two tables. Figure 14-6 shows the Join Conditions page.

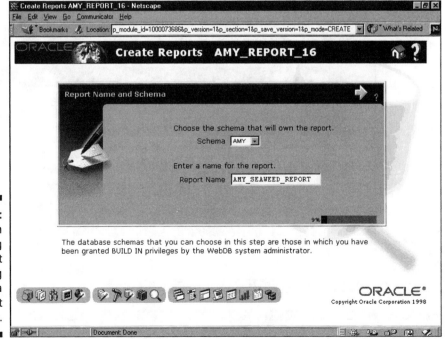

Figure 14-4:
Begin creating your report by choosing a schema and a report name.

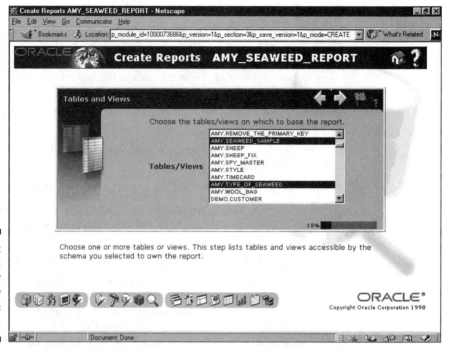

Figure 14-5:
Select a
table or
view by
clicking its
name here.

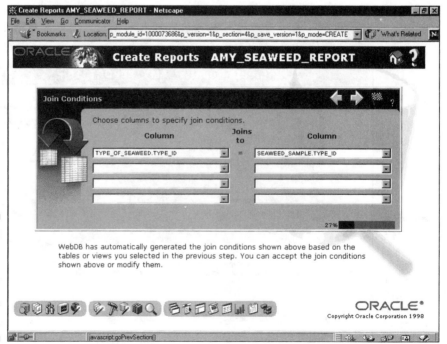

Figure 14-6:
The wizard
creates join
conditions,
which you
can revise if
needed.

10. **Choose which columns to display in the report by selecting and clicking the small right-pointing arrow; click the Next arrow when done.**

    The wizard provides a list of all possible columns on the left side of the Table/View Columns page. Select a column and then click the right-pointing arrow. The column moves into the Selected Column box. After selecting all the columns that you want, click the Next arrow to continue. For the example, choose the SAMPLE_ID, DESCRIPTION_TEXT, and SELLING_PRICE columns.

11. **Add column conditions as needed and click the Next arrow.**

    This page enables you to filter data by adding conditions to any of the columns in the tables that you selected for the report. Build the conditions by following these steps:

    1. **Click the arrow in the Column Name box and choose a column.**

    2. **Click the arrow in the Condition box and choose an operator, such as equal, greater than, and so on.**

    3. **Type a value in the Value box to complete the condition.**

    For the example, limit the query to rows that contain edible seaweed. To do this, choose the TYPE_OF_SEAWEED.EDIBLE column and the = condition and type **EDIBLE** in the Value box. Figure 14-7 shows the Column Conditions page for the example report.

12. **Either accept the default column formatting or adjust the column formatting; then click the Next arrow.**

    The wizard displays its choices for formatting the display columns of the report. If you want to modify the formatting, make adjustments in this page. Otherwise, accept the defaults. Click the Next arrow to continue. For the example, accept the default settings.

13. **Either accept the default display options or adjust the display options; then click the Next arrow.**

    You have many options to look over. Notice that you can change the output format from HTML (Web page format) to Excel (spreadsheet format) or ASCII (plain text format). You can add breaks so that the report displays data in a hierarchy. You can change the font, the background color, the sort order, and many other options.

    Figure 14-8 shows the Display Options page with the default settings. For the example report, accept the defaults and click the Next arrow.

14. **Either accept the default (no parameters) or define the parameters; then click the Next arrow.**

    Parameters enable your user to specify query criteria, such as a data range, department number, and so on. WebDB automatically builds a parameter form where users enter the data in text boxes. Parameters are optional, and for the example report, I have not specified any parameters.

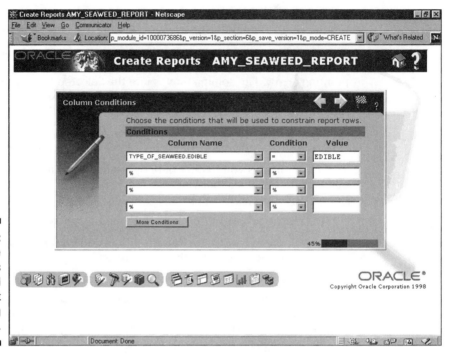

Figure 14-7:
Limit the
rows
displayed
in the report
by adding
conditions.

Figure 14-8:
The Display
Options
page has
settings for
breaks,
sorting,
font size,
and more.

15. **Specify additional text and a template; then click the Next arrow.**

    WebDB provides a set of templates that give your reports a similar look. Choose template number three (PUBLIC.TEMPLATE_3) for the example report. You can also type text that appears at the top or the bottom of your report pages or in a pop-up help page that is automatically displayed when the user clicks the help button.

16. **Either accept the default (no added PL/SQL) or type in special PL/SQL; then click the Next arrow.**

    This option enables advanced designers to create special reports with added features such as performing extra calculations or validations before displaying the report. For the example, leave all the PL/SQL boxes blank (the default) so that no extra PL/SQL is executed. Then click the Next arrow.

17. **Complete the report by clicking the OK button.**

    The last page verifies that you want to create the report. At this point, you can use the Back arrow to review all the pages of the wizard. When you're satisfied with your creation, click the OK button.

18. **Click Run to test the report.**

    Figure 14-9 shows what the report looks like when you use the default template. Not bad for a first try!

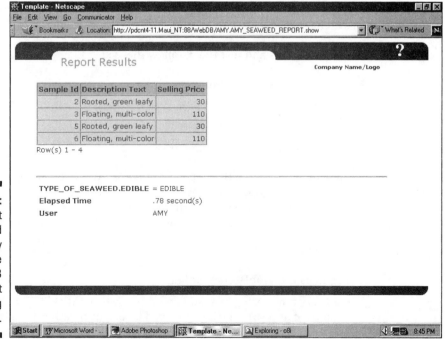

Figure 14-9: This report was created very quickly with the WebDB report building tool.

To run the report directly from the Web, use this URL:

```
http://hostname:portnumber/WebDB/owner.reportname.show
```

Replace `hostname` with the host that serves WebDB. For example, if you're using your own copy of WebDB and Oracle8i, your computer is the host. Replace `portnumber` with the port specified when WebDB was installed. Replace `owner` with the schema that created the report. Replace `reportname` with the actual report that you just created. For example, the actual URL on my home computer is

```
http://carol:80/WebDB/AMY.SEAWEED_SAMPLE_REPORT.show
```

There you have it!

Going for a Form

Now, create a set of Web pages that are interconnected and allow you to add and change data in the database.

I demonstrate the master-detail style of forms because for some reason, the WebDB designers put extra effort into making this structure easier to create and use than the other styles of forms that are available.

So, for this example, I use the same two tables I use to create the report earlier in this chapter: `SEAWEED_SAMPLE` and `TYPE_OF_SEAWEED` in the `AMY` schema.

To create the forms and test them, follow these steps:

1. **Start up the WebDB main page.**

   Start up your browser and then type the WebDB main page URL. The URL format is

   ```
   http://hostname:portnumber/WebDB/
   ```

   Replace `hostname` with the host that serves WebDB. For example, if you are using your own copy of WebDB and Oracle8i, your computer is the host. Replace `portnumber` with the port specified when WebDB was installed. For example, the actual URL on my home computer is

   ```
   http://carol:80/WebDB/
   ```

2. **Log in as the WebDB Developer.**

   For this example, log in as AMY with password AMY123. The WebDB main page appears. Since you logged in as a user rather than the WebDB administrator, the main window does not contain all the selections in Figure 14-1.

3. **Click Build in the list of links.**

This link brings up the main component building menu page.

4. **Click User Interface Components in the list of links.**

This choice gets you to another list of links.

5. **Click Forms in the list of links.**

This one gets you to a create/find/history page where you must decide what to do. You want to create a new form, so keep going.

6. **Begin a new form.**

For this example, choose the master-detail type of form. Then click the Create button.

7. **Select the schema and type a name. Then click the Next arrow.**

For the example, choose AMY as the schema and type **SEAWEED_FORM** in the Form Name box.

8. **Choose the master table for the form.**

For this example, TYPE_OF_SEAWEED, as shown in Figure 14-10, is the master table.

9. **Choose the detail table for the form.**

For this example, the SEAWEED_SAMPLE, as shown in Figure 14-10, is the detail table.

10. **Either accept the default join conditions or modify the join conditions; then click the Next button.**

The WebDB Report Wizard looks for a relationship between the two tables and uses it as the join conditions. For the example, the SEAWEED_SAMPLE table has a foreign key constraint stating that the TYPE_ID column is a foreign key referencing the TYPE_OF_SEAWEED table. The wizard uses this information to create a join between the two tables. Refer to Figure 14-6 to see the Join Conditions page.

11. **Either accept the default master row formatting or make changes; then click the Next arrow.**

The form displays one row of the master table, followed by multiple rows of the detail table. Figure 14-11 shows the Master Row formatting page. Here you can define the format of each column in the master table. The default settings display all the columns in the master table and enable the user to update the data in all the columns. If you want to hide a column, click the Disp checkbox next to the column. If you want to prevent the user from updating a column, click the Upd checkbox next to the column.

For the example form, hide the LAST_CHANGE column and do not allow update on the TYPE_ID column.

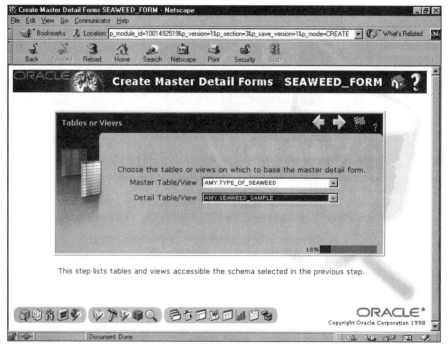

Figure 14-10:
Choose the
Master
Table and
Detail Table
for your
form.

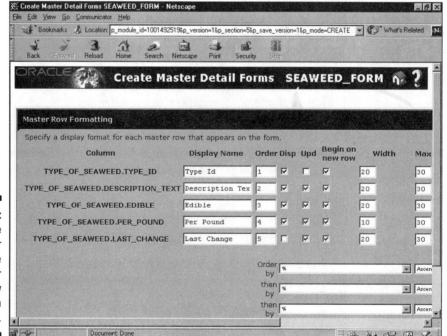

Figure 14-11:
Choose
formats for
the single
master
table row
displayed on
the form.

12. **Either accept the default detail row formatting or make changes; then click the Next arrow.**

    The form displays multiple rows of the detail table, and you can either accept the default settings or modify formatting here. Refer to Figure 14-11, because the Detail Row Formatting page looks very similar to the Format Master Row Formatting page.

    For the example form, accept the default formatting.

13. **Either accept the default Display Options or make changes; then click the Next arrow.**

    Refer to Figure 14-8, which shows a similar page. For the example, accept the default settings.

14. **Either accept the default Button Options or modify the options; then click the Next arrow.**

    This page enables you to display the Save and Delete buttons in the location that you specify. For the example form, accept the default settings.

15. **Either accept the default Master Row Finder page or add text; then click the Next button.**

    WebDB designs a query page for your users that enables them to quickly search for a master row. Add a heading to the query page if you want. This page is the starting point for the sample form, so type instructions in the Header box, such as **Click the Add button to insert a new row.** Figure 14-12 shows the text added for the example form.

16. **Either accept the default text and template options or make changes; then click the Next arrow.**

    For the example form, select PUBLIC.TEMPLATE_6 from the pull-down menu in the Template box.

17. **Skip over the Add PL/SQL page and click the Next arrow.**

    This page enables advanced designers to specify customized actions using PL/SQL. For the example, leave all the PL/SQL boxes blank (the default) so that no extra PL/SQL is executed. Then click the Next arrow.

18. **Complete the form by clicking the OK button.**

    The last page verifies that you want to create the form. At this point, you can use the Back arrow to review all the pages of the wizard. When you're satisfied with your creation, click the OK button.

19. **Click Parameters to test the form.**

    The Parameters form contains the query criteria for the master table and is the beginning point for running the master-detail form. Figure 14-13 shows the Parameter form.

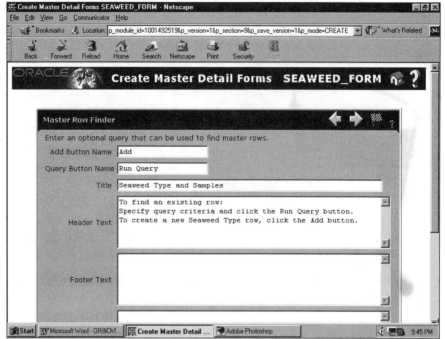

Figure 14-12:
Add
instructions
to help
users find
their way
around the
form.

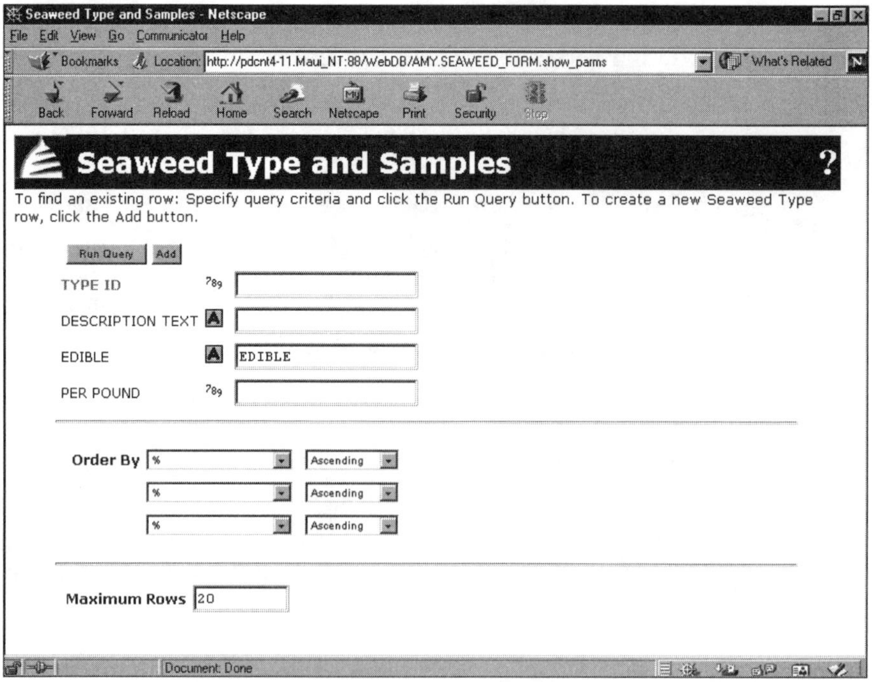

Figure 14-13:
Start the
master-
detail form
by running
the
Parameter
form.

To run the form directly from the Web, use the following URL format:

```
http://hostname:portnumber/WebDB/owner.formname.start
```

Replace `hostname` with the host that serves WebDB, such as your own computer if you're running your own copy of Oracle and WebDB. Replace `portnumber` with the port specified when WebDB was installed. Replace `formname` with the actual report you just created. For example, the actual URL on my home computer is

```
http://carol:80/AMY.SEAWEED_FORM.start
```

Figure 14-14 shows the Master Finder form, which you reach by clicking the Run Query button on the Parameter form (Figure 14-13).

To reach the detail list, click the Edit link in any row on the display page. Figure 14-15 shows the detail page.

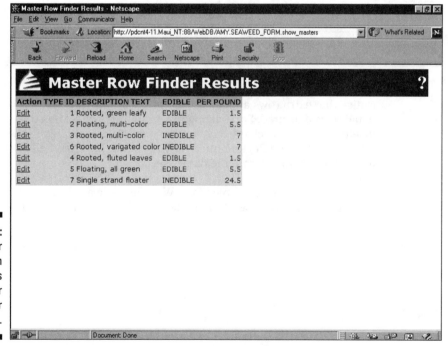

Figure 14-14:
The Master Finder form displays master rows for selection.

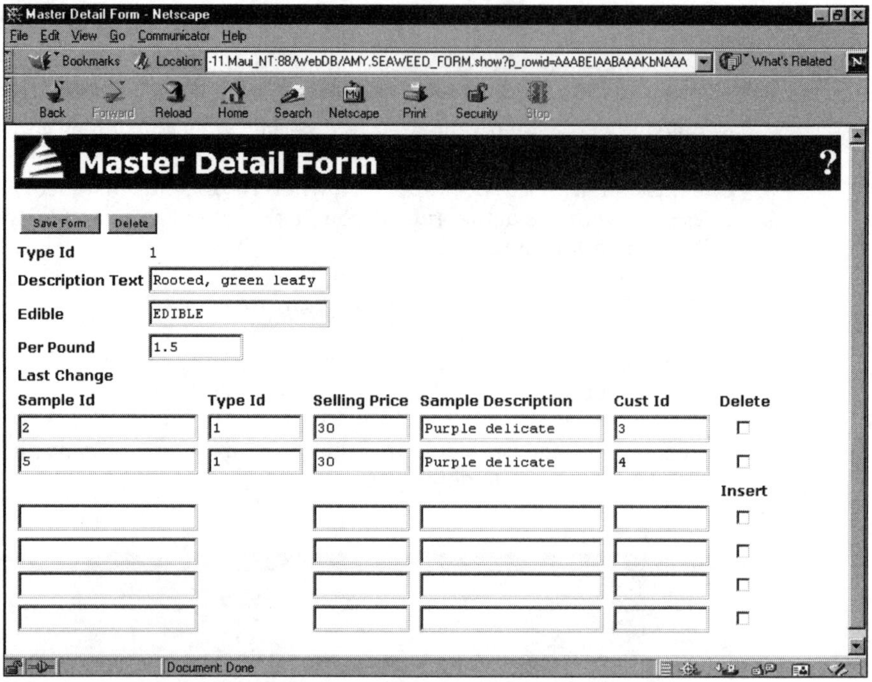

Figure 14-15:
The detail page shows one master row and all related detail rows.

Notice that extra rows appear at the bottom so you can easily add more detail rows if desired. For existing rows, you use a checkbox to select rows to delete. When you click the Save button, new rows are saved to the database. When you click the Delete button, any rows that have the Delete checkbox marked are removed from the database.

Your have a working example of the Web database application that will win you kudos from your friends, neighbors, and Furbys around the world.

Chapter 15

Java and the Internet Database

In This Chapter

▶ Taking a look at Oracle8i's Java Virtual Machine

▶ Adding a Java stored procedure into your database

▶ Running your Java from the Web

▶ Running your Java from an applet

This is so exciting! Even the beta release of Oracle8i didn't have this feature: a Java Virtual Machine (JVM) that comes installed inside your Oracle8i database. JVM enables you to create, interpret, and execute Java applications. This chapter gives you information about what a JVM is and how to use it. Along the way, you find out how to create a Java stored procedure and then run it inside the database. Finally, you discover how to run a Java stored procedure from the Web.

You don't have to know how to program in Java to follow along with the examples in this chapter. However, if you want to find out more about Java, check out *Java For Dummies,* 3rd Edition, by Aaron E. Walsh (IDG Books Worldwide, Inc.).

Discovering Java Virtual Machine (JVM)

A Java Virtual Machine (JVM) is like a miniature operating system. A Java Virtual Machine runs Java applications, which is why *Java* appears in its name. It's called a *virtual machine* because you can run programs inside it as if they were running on a separate computer. The great advantage of JVM is that it handles all operating-system-dependent commands for you. Commands that previously required special commands for each operating system can now be written exactly the same way, regardless of what kind of operating system the JVM interacts with. Java programs become totally portable, and Java programmers get big bucks.

Using Oracle8i's JVM — some benefits

If you've ever run Java applications on your computer, you have been using a Java Virtual Machine in your computer. For example, many Web sites use Java *applets* (mini-applications) for fun and interactive tasks, such as calculating a mortgage payment or playing tic-tac-toe. To run the applet, your Web browser contains a JVM of its own. Most developers who create Java applets and applications use the Java Virtual Machine from JavaSoft, which is called Java Run-time Environment (JRE). Oracle's JVM, which can do anything that JRE can do, runs within the framework of your Oracle8i database. In addition, you get these benefits from using Oracle8i's JVM:

- **Better scaleability.** Oracle8i's JVM is scaleable to support many concurrent users. Unlike Oracle8i's JVM, other JVM products cannot share resources among concurrent users; therefore, they use ever greater resources with each additional user.

- **Can be used in place of PL/SQL or in combination with PL/SQL.** This means that you Java fans can skip figuring out PL/SQL and move right to creating triggers, procedures, and functions that work with Oracle database objects.

- **Supports SQLJ.** SQLJ is an extension of JDBC (Java Database Connectivity) and simplifies your programming of database access within Java. JDBC is an industry standard protocol that describes how to access a database within a Java application. SQLJ lets you embed SQL commands within your Java and then creates the corresponding JDBC commands to support the SQL, saving you many lines of code for each SQL command. You use SQLJ in the next section of this chapter.

- **Better native connectivity to the database.** You can use JDBC on your computer's Java Virtual Machine to reach an Oracle8i database even if the JVM isn't embedded in the database. However, if you use Oracle8i's JVM, your JDBC connects extra fast to your database because Oracle8i uses its internal, proprietary connection to the database (native connectivity). JDBC commands that originate outside the Oracle8i database go through a translation stage where the generic JDBC is translated into Oracle-specific commands. Likewise, the data returned from the database is translated from Oracle-specific formats to generic JDBC formats before returning to the application. All this translating is eliminated when you use Oracle8i's JVM.

The idea is that if you're currently using PL/SQL procedures and functions, you can use them in any Java component that you want to create inside the Oracle8i database. On top of that, you can use Java and SQLJ instead of PL/SQL to create triggers, procedures, and even applications.

One of these days, Java and SQLJ will totally replace PL/SQL.

Introducing SQLJ

How do you do? I am your new partner, SQLJ. Just call me SJ for short. I can save you a lot of time by writing all your JDBC commands for you. Just give me your SQL statement, and I'll translate it into the proper JDBC commands, keeping your Java program clean and simple. Go ahead, make my day.

Yes, that's right, you're spared the toil of writing all those JDBC commands that open the database, open a cursor, fetch the data row, fetch the next row, close the cursor, close the database . . . you get the idea.

With SQLJ, you simply embed the SQL command inside your Java program. And because you run your Java program in Oracle8i's JVM, you have ultrafast access paths into your data. SQLJ may be the most compelling reason to use the Oracle8i JVM — especially if you aren't a coffee-crazed geek wearing a tin-foil hat and sitting in your grandma's basement hacking on your customized turbocharged dual-boot machinery.

Creating a Stored Database Procedure with Java and SQLJ

The best way to show you what you can do with Java and SQLJ is to give you a fun example. For this example, assume that you are a bread baker extraordinaire who wants to use the BAKERY schema — which contains a set of associated Oracle8i objects — to track your secret bread recipes.

If you want to follow along with the examples in this chapter and have not already created the BAKERY schema, execute the BAKERY.sql file, which you can find in the Make directory of the accompanying CD-ROM. Running this file creates the BAKERY user and all the types, objects, and data that you need.

How do you begin using Java in your database? The best way I know to begin is in the middle, but people who sing Broadway musicals (namely, the Von Trapp family), insist that you start at the very beginning. To appease this enormous component of my reading audience, I shall start at the beginning. Here are the steps to create a Java program, which returns a calculated value when used in an SQL query:

1. **Write Java code with embedded SQLJ.**

2. **Load the Java source code into the database.**

3. **Create a SQL wrapper for the Java code so that it can be called from SQL commands.**

4. **Call the SQL wrapper in a SQL query.**

The final two steps aren't necessary if you're going to run the Java code from another Java application. However, if you want to write functions or procedures that are referenced in either SQL or PL/SQL, you need to complete the last two steps.

Grab your apron and get ready to mix up a batch of Java.

Step 1: Writing Java code with embedded SQLJ

You can use any Java editor that you want to create your code. I am not partial to any particular product, but if you want to stick with Oracle products, you can purchase the JDeveloper, which contains a Java editor.

For your delight and wonderment, in this section you create a Java application that adds up the cost of any bread recipe found in the BAKERY schema. You use one incoming parameter: the name of the bread. And you send back one value: the cost of the bread recipe in dollars and cents.

The cost is calculated by running a SQL query that finds the nested table containing the ingredients for the specified bread, retrieves the cost from the INGREDIENTS object table, and calculates the cost of each recipe amount. These costs are then totaled using the SUM function in the query.

In the following example, I use SQL to sum up the rows retrieved from the nested table. However, you can use a Java loop to retrieve each row and do the calculation yourself if you like. I use the SUM function to simplify the example.

Now, on to the Java code lines. First, you import the class of tools that enables you to translate Java objects of various types into their corresponding SQL datatypes without losing any accuracy. Use this line to import the tools:

```
import java.sql.*;
```

Next, enter these two lines to declare the class called RecipeCost, define the getCost method, and define the method's text string parameter called breadName:

```
public class RecipeCost {
  public static Number getCost (String breadName) {
```

Next, begin your execution block by defining a variable named sumCost that grabs the output of the SQL query. Enter these lines:

```
try {
    Number sumCost;
```

Next, you need to write the query that calculates the cost of the bread. Notice that curly brackets surround the query and that the command line begins with #sql. The #sql tells the Java interpreter inside Oracle8i's JVM that this statement should be converted to JDBC database commands. Enter this query to calculate the cost of the bread:

```
#sql { SELECT ROUND(SUM(NT.AMOUNT_IN_OUNCES *
NT.INGREDIENT_NO_REF.PRICE_PER_OUNCE),2)
        INTO :sumCost
        FROM TABLE (SELECT BREAD.RECIPE_NESTED_TABLE_COL
                FROM BREAD_OBJECT_TABLE BREAD
                WHERE BREAD.BREAD_NAME = :breadName) NT};
```

In the preceding statement, you see two Java variables, which are preceded by colons. The variable sumCost receives the value retrieved by the query. The variable breadName is translated into a constant, which then gets used in the query.

After the query has been executed, the sumCost variable contains the cost of the recipe. Return this value by entering this line:

```
                return sumCost;
```

As usual, check for errors. In this case, look for errors that are returned by the execution of the query. SQLException is defined inside the java.sql class. Your application returns null if the SQL query fails. Type the following line to trap SQL errors:

```
                } catch (SQLException e) { return null; } } }
```

The entire Java application code looks like this:

```
import java.sql.*;
public class RecipeCost {
  public static Number getCost (String breadName) {
try {
            Number sumCost;
            #sql { SELECT ROUND(SUM(NT.AMOUNT_IN_OUNCES *

        NT.INGREDIENT_NO_REF.PRICE_PER_OUNCE),2)
                INTO :sumCost
                FROM TABLE (SELECT
        BREAD.RECIPE_NESTED_TABLE_COL
                        FROM BREAD_OBJECT_TABLE
```

```
BREAD                                           WHERE BREAD.BREAD_NAME =
        :breadName) NT};
        return sumCost;
    } catch (SQLException e) { return null; } } }
```

Step 2: Loading the Java into the database

You can load the Java into the database three ways:

- ✔ Load Java source code into the database by using the CREATE JAVA command.
- ✔ Load already compiled Java into the database as class files or Jar files by using the LOADJAVA command.
- ✔ Load Java resource files (files that contain Java images or other data) by using the LOADJAVA command.

You use the first method for the following sample Java program. To load the Java source code and have it compiled by the database's Java compiler, add this line to the top of your Java source code:

```
create or replace java source named "javaname" as
```

Replace javaname with the name of the Java application you are creating.

Add a final line that contains a forward slash on the end of the Java text:

```
/
```

Follow these steps to load your Java source code into the database:

1. **Start SQL*Plus Worksheet.**

   If you have your LaunchPad open, choose the SQL*Plus Worksheet from the DB: Administration menu. Otherwise, on Windows 95, 98, or NT, select Start⇨Programs⇨Oracle HOME2⇨DBA Management Pack⇨ SQL*Plus Worksheet.

   On UNIX, type **oemapp worksheet** on the command line.

   If you come to a login window, go to Step 2. Otherwise, skip to Step 3.

2. **Log in as the schema that will own the Java application.**

   If you have loaded the sample database schema from the CD, log in as the user named BAKERY with the password BAKERY. Leave the Service box empty if you're running your own personal Oracle8i; otherwise, fill in the name of the Oracle8i database (instance) on your network. Leave the Connect As box set to Normal.

The Schema Manager window appears.

3. **Open the Java source code file by choosing File⇨Open and selecting the file.**

The file is loaded into the top window of the SQL*Plus Worksheet.

4. **Execute the file by clicking the Execute button.**

The file's contents are executed in the bottom window of the SQL*Plus Worksheet. After they're completed, you see this message in the bottom window:

```
Java created.
```

You have loaded your Java program into the database Java library.

Java programs in the Oracle8i Java library have security features similar to database procedures: Each Java program is owned by the schema that created it and can be executed by the owner and other users who have been granted the EXECUTE privilege for the Java program.

Unlike database procedures that always run with the owner's privileges, you can choose to run with either the owner's privileges or the invoker's privileges. (The *invoker* is the Oracle user that executes the program.) By default, Java programs run with the owner's privileges. Use the AUTHID INVOKER keywords to tell the Java program to run with the invoker's privileges. These keywords work only when the Java program runs inside of SQL or PL/SQL. I demonstrate how in the next section.

Step 3: Creating a SQL wrapper for the Java code

A SQL wrapper is a container for a Java program that enables the Java program to be used as if it were a PL/SQL function or procedure. In the example, you create a function that accepts a parameter (the name of the bread) and returns a value (the cost of the bread). The syntax for a SQL wrapper that makes a function is

```
create or replace function fname(parm1 parmtype)
RETURN returntype AUTHID authtype
as LANGUAGE JAVA NAME
'javaclass.javamethod(java.lang.javatype)
return java.sql.datatype';
```

Replace these words with actual names:

- ✔ fname: Use the name of the SQL function that you create.

- ✔ parm1 parmtype: Put parameters (if any) inside the parenthesis. Replace parm1 with the name of the first parameter and replace parmtype with the Oracle8i datatype of the parameter.

- ✔ returntype: Specify the Oracle8i datatype of the value returned from the function.

- ✔ authtype: Type either **CURRENT_USER** (to use the privileges of the invoker) or **DEFINER** (to use the privileges of the Java program owner).

- ✔ javamethod: Replace with the name of the Java program that you created in the Java library.

- ✔ javatype: Specify the Java datatype (such as String or Number) of the parameter (if any).

- ✔ datatype: Specify the Java datatype of the returned value.

Use the following command to create a function named getCost that acts as a SQL wrapper for the Java program named RecipeCost that we created in the previous section:

```
create or replace function getCost(breadName VARCHAR2)
RETURN NUMBER AUTHID CURRENT_USER
as LANGUAGE JAVA NAME
'RecipeCost.getCost(java.lang.String)
return java.sql.Number';
```

Now you have completed the definition of the SQL wrapper so you can use the Java program within SQL commands.

Step 4: Using the SQL wrapper in a SQL query

After creating a SQL wrapper for a Java program, all that you have left to do is use the SQL wrapper in a SQL command. The SQL wrapper is either a procedure or a function. You can run procedures within other procedures or within triggers. You can use functions as part of a SQL query.

The example SQL wrapper that you create in the previous section is a function called getCost. Here is a query that uses the function to list the cost of each bread in the BREAD_TABLE_OBJECT:

```
select BREAD_NO, BREAD_NAME,
getCost(BREAD_NAME) Recipe_Cost
from BREAD_OBJECT_TABLE
ORDER BY 3;
```

Here are the results:

```
BREAD_NO  BREAD_NAME              RECIPE_COST
--------------------------------------------
3         Plain White             3.30
2         Nutty Banana            3.54
1         Cinnamon Swirl          6.97
```

Ta-daa!!! I hope you are proud of yourself.

Running a Java Stored Procedure from a Java Applet on the Web

To run a stored procedure from the Web, you need to create an *applet* (a small Java application). For the example, you use an applet that is similar to the sample applet that's created when you install Oracle8i.

You can find the source code for the sample applet in the applet directory of the accompanying CD-ROM.

The applet runs a query that calls the Java stored procedure that you created earlier in this chapter.

Your environment must include a working copy of the Oracle JDBC driver, SQLJ, and Java 1.1.5 or higher. Your classpath must include the directory that contains the following paths (replace *oraclehome* with the full path name for your main oracle directory):

- *oraclehome*/jdbc/lib/classes111.zip
- *oraclehome*/sqlj/lib/translator.zip
- the current directory (.)

Figure 15-1 shows you what the applet looks like when you run it.

Now you're in the big leagues. Your Java is stored in the database and can be accessed through an applet on the Web. Be sure to ask your boss for a raise.

Figure 15-1:
Running an
applet that
calls the
Java stored
procedure
that you
created in
the previous
section.

Chapter 16

The Five Ws of Safeguarding Your Data

• •

In This Chapter

▶ Why back up

▶ What to back up

▶ When to back up

▶ How to choose backup weapons

▶ Where to store backup disks

• •

*Y*ou've heard this story, I'm sure: A poor soul plans to back up his disk drive on Wednesday, but on Tuesday the system crashes, and recovery takes him a month. Another good one: A rookie drops her table instead of deleting a few rows. She has no way to recover because she has no backup.

No, the five Ws is not a singing group (and if it were, this chapter would not be about its backup band). This chapter covers the five Ws of backups: why, what, where, and when. I know, I know that's only four Ws. (Hold up a mirror to see the secret fifth W — who!) I also included a lot of how-to information. Some of the methods describe shortcuts that you can use to speed up the process.

In this chapter, I concentrate on backup strategies that use Oracle8i tools. More backup options exist, such as replication and hot backups, but they are complex and require much study to use properly. If you're interested in those options, you may want to take a class.

Why Back Up — Onward and Upward!

Back up to save face. Do you want to be caught with your pants down because you didn't back up? Worse yet, do you want to face getting caught backing up with your pants down?

When I refer to *backing up,* I'm referring to different methods that accomplish similar tasks. Backing up your database essentially means making a duplicate copy of all, or a portion of, your database — kind of like wearing a belt and suspenders.

Many good reasons to back up your database exist. The reason that motivates me the most is that backing up saves me a great deal of time in the long run. Losing data because you didn't back it up costs you time: time to figure out what's missing, time to get another copy, time to remember all the things that you did during the past month, time to re-create everything that you can't replace. Time to get real about backing up your data.

If you use a PC, periodically backing up your entire PC hard drive helps you recover quickly from hardware problems. How often is "periodically"? The answer depends on how much you use your computer. If you use your computer daily, I recommend backing up at the end of each week. On the other hand, if you're a casual PC user, sitting down once or twice a week to play, work, or perhaps surf the Internet, I recommend backing up once a month.

If you prefer to back up your database using your operating system's backup tools, be careful. One of the default initialization parameters for running your database is the NOARCHIVE setting. *The default,* NOARCHIVE, *database must be shut down before you begin backing up the database files.* If the database is running, your backup files are useless. You won't be able to restore the files because some of the log files are in a consistent, recoverable state only when the database is closed. Even if you change the setting to ARCHIVE, you must be very careful when restoring from backup copies. Refer to the backup and recovery chapters in my book *Oracle8 Bible* (IDG Books Worldwide, Inc.), for complete details.

Backing up an entire database allows you to keep a snapshot of the database structure and data. Backing up portions of the database allows you to shorten the amount of time invested in backups while safeguarding parts of the database.

What to Back Up

Here are my guidelines for a backup plan. Ultimately, you are the judge. I am the executioner. We can hang the jury (or at least both the attorneys).

- Back up the entire database on a regular basis. For critical database systems that support a business operation on a daily basis, back up nightly. For normal daily use, back up once a week. For occasional use, back up once a month.

✔ During database development, when you create and drop tables frequently, back up the table owner before making major changes.

✔ Use backups to transfer entire groups of tables from one database to
  another.

When to Back Up (Before You Go Off the Cliff)

Generally, you don't wait until you crash to fasten your seat belt, unless you
are a teenager and know everything. Planning a backup schedule and sticking
to it pays off in the long run. No system is immune to losing data. I've seen
systems with full backup capabilities get zapped by lightning, which burned
up crucial disk drives.

Exactly when to back up depends on what kind of system you're running. If
you use common sense and lean a bit to the conservative side, you'll have a
good strategy for timing backups.

This chapter covers the following two backup choices:

✔ **Data Manager:** Helps you export and import tables using a wizard. This
  utility is part of the Enterprise Manager. Data Manager can also load the
  data into the database using a flat file.

✔ EXP **and** IMP: These utilities are like the non-GUI versions of Data
  Manager, with line commands for exporting (EXP) and importing (IMP) a
  database, a user, or a specified set of objects. The file that's created is in
  a highly compressed file structure that can be ported to other platforms.
  You can restore a backup file created by EXP only by using the IMP command. You can import exports from older versions of Oracle into newer
  versions of Oracle.

Other backup strategies that I don't cover include the list below. All of these
are covered in my book, *Oracle8 Bible:*

✔ **Backup Manager:** Copies the entire database in a compressed format to
  disk or tape. You shut down the database to run a full database backup
  and then restore by using the Recovery Manager. If your database runs
  in ARCHIVELOG mode, you have more choices of what to back up. This
  utility works only if you have more than one database: one to store your
  repository and one to back up.

✔ **Tablespace backups:** Copies selected tablespaces while the database is
  running in ARCHIVELOG mode. This technique is exotic. You generally
  use the tablespace backup only for large organizations in which the

database is online 24 hours a day. Tablespace backups require careful study, and I just can't cover them adequately in a few paragraphs.

✔ **Recovery logs:** You can design your recovery logs so that the database recovers activities up to the minute when a failure occurs. You should get expert help before implementing this kind of recovery scheme.

✔ **Audit utility:** Not exactly a backup utility, this utility allows you to track all activity in tables. Auditing can be incredibly detailed. You really don't need the Audit utility unless you're wearing a tinfoil hat to ward off evil thought rays and cosmic debris. The audit trail can eat up disk space in a hurry. You can get a fairly good description of this utility in the Oracle8i manual.

Which plan should you use? Again, the answer depends on your situation. Imagine that you're a musician who just produced a CD of your music. You're setting up a cool Web site with promotional materials on your home PC, and you're using Oracle8i to keep track of the CD distribution and accounting. You work about an hour a day on the PC, between rehearsals, radio spots, and signing autographs. I recommend that you use Oracle's Backup Manager to back up the database daily. I also recommend that you back up your PC at the end of each week, using software that backs up only changed files to disk, Zip drive, or tape.

On the other hand, what if you work in a federal office and you decide to enhance a set of tables with new features? You plan to add new tables and modify the existing ones. I recommend that you use the Data Manager or EXP command to save all the tables before you start making changes. Checkered tablecloths and potted plants may be good changes.

The full database export

A full database export is an alternative way to back up your database. Oracle8i recommends that you use the Backup Manager to handle full database backups and that you perform a full database export every time you do a full system backup (such as a backup of all files to tape). On a practical note, you shouldn't always do this step because it takes extra time.

To restore from a full database export, use the Recovery Manager.

You should do a full database import only when a failure on the disk wipes out your database or when you actually want to create a new database on another computer. Consult an expert before attempting this task.

What if your hard disk crashes?

If your hard disk crashes and you're in the process of restoring all your software, first try to start Oracle8i, which has built-in recovery steps that handle many situations. Oracle8i is often capable of restoring your database. If you can't start Oracle8i, use the Recovery Manager to restore your database. Use the Automatic recovery selection in the Recovery Manager window, and Oracle8i recovers the database to your most recent backup made with the Backup Manager.

How to Back Up (Choosing Your Backup Weapon)

The two backup tools that I cover in this book work with Oracle8i platforms. These tools are the Data Manager and the EXP tool.

Data Manager

This utility, part of the Enterprise Manager, makes saving and retrieving tables from a file easier than it should be. (It should be hard, like the olden days.) Actually, easy is good. I can handle an easy method of backing up and restoring parts of my database.

Use the Data Manager when you want to save certain tables or all the tables owned by one or more users but don't want to back up the entire database. This kind of tool can be useful to the systems analyst who has been slaving away on 50 tables and wants to back them up to move them to the production database machine — that sort of thing.

Exporting tables with a wizard

To export several tables to an export file, follow these steps:

1. **Start the Enterprise Manager console.**

   If you have your LaunchPad up, choose the Management Console from the Enterprise Manager menu. Otherwise, on Windows 95, 98, or NT, select Start⇨Programs⇨Oracle HOME2⇨Enterprise Management⇨ Enterprise Manager Console.

   On UNIX, type this on the command line:

   ```
   oemapp console
   ```

If you come to a login window, go to Step 2. Otherwise, skip to Step 3.

2. **Log in as the Enterprise Management Administrator.**

The default administrator is named SYSMAN with password OEM_TEMP. Leave the Management Host box as the default of localhost if you're running your own personal Oracle8i; otherwise, fill in the name of the Enterprise Management Server on your network. The Enterprise Manager control console window appears, as shown in Figure 16-1.

3. **Choose System⇨Preferences and then select the Preferred Credentials tab to set the Data Manager login credentials.**

The Edit Administrator Preferences property window appears. The Preferred Credentials tab lists service names that are used when administering the database through the Enterprise Manager console.

4. **Set the login data for the database you wish to perform backups on.**

For example, to back up data from a database named mydb.world, edit the login information seen when you select mydb.world. You must use a DBA login. The default DBA login for Oracle8i has a user name of SYSTEM and password of MANAGER. Accept the default role of Normal. Figure 16-2 shows the completed window for the database service called mydb.world.

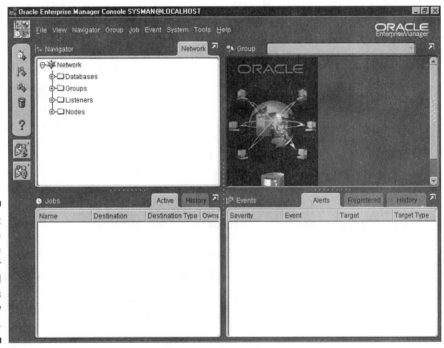

Figure 16-1:
The Enterprise Manager control console is now ready to use.

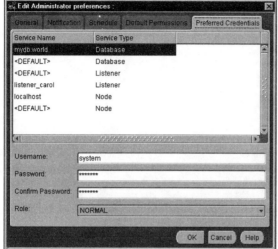

Figure 16-2:
You must
specify login
credentials
for the
database as
an Oracle8i
DBA.

5. **Set the login data for the node where the database resides.**

The login name for the node must be a user on the node's operating system who has the ability to submit a batch job. On NT, the user must also be an administrator.

For example, assume the database resides on the localhost node, which is an NT machine, and the user named Administrator has been set up as the administrator for the NT and has been granted the user rights to run a batch job. In this case, the localhost node login information contains Administrator in the Username box and Administrator's password in the Password box and in the Confirm password box. Figure 16-3 shows this example.

6. **Click OK to accept changes and return to the console.**

7. **Right-click the database node and choose Data Management⇨Export to start the Data Manager Export Wizard.**

The main Data Manager Export Wizard window appears, as shown in Figure 16-4.

8. **Click Next and then name the export file by either accepting the default name or typing your own file name; click Next when you're ready to continue.**

Be sure that you type the full path and file name if you are choosing your own name.

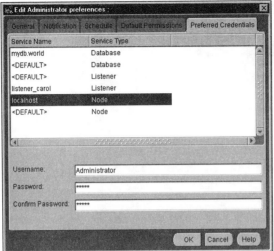

Figure 16-3:
You must
specify login
credentials
for the
node as an
operating
system
administrator.

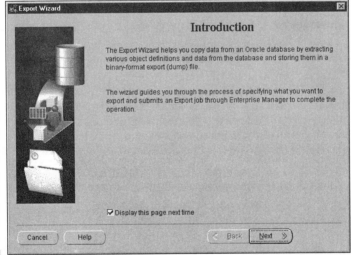

Figure 16-4:
The Data
Manager
Export
Wizard
introduces
itself on the
first screen.

9. **Choose an export type and click Next.**

   You have three choices:

   • **Database.** This is the default choice. Use this choice to export the entire database. After you export it, you can restore the entire database from the export file. If you choose this selection, skip to Step 10.

- **User.** Here you select one or more users and the wizard exports all the objects owned by each user. This selection is useful when you are moving an entire schema to another database, such as moving a schema from the test database to the production database.

- **Table.** You are able to choose individual tables with this choice. This choice is useful for saving a table just before making structural changes.

For this example, select User and click Next.

10. **Select Users or Tables in the left window.**

This page allows you to select one or more users if you chose User in the previous step. If you chose Table in the previous step, the page allows you to select one or more tables for export.

Choose a user or table by selecting it in the left window and clicking the arrow pointing to the right. The user or table moves into the right window, indicating that you have chosen the user or table for export.

Continue to choose more users or tables as needed until all the users or tables you need are listed in the right window. Figure 16-5 shows the Export Wizard window with two users, AMY and BAKERY, selected for export. Now you're ready to begin your export.

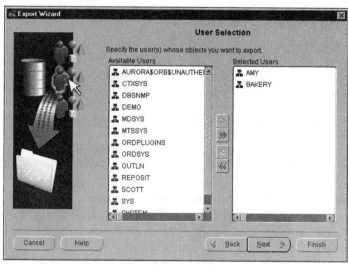

Figure 16-5:
Add or remove users to export by selecting and clicking the arrow buttons.

11. **Click the Finish button.**

You can go through the remaining pages of options if you have advanced knowledge of the database-export process. For now, you can accept Data Manager's default settings and skip directly to the finish line. Figure 16-6 shows the status window that now appears.

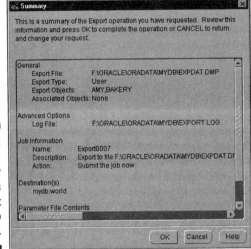

Figure 16-6:
The Data
Manager
Wizard lists
what it
plans to
export.

12. **Verify the list and then click the OK button.**

    The Data Manager begins its work. When the job is complete, you return to the main console window.

13. **Check the results of your export in the Jobs window by clicking the History tab.**

    The Jobs window is in the lower-left quarter of the console. Click the History tab and you see a list of jobs, including your export job. Figure 16-7 shows two export jobs. Double-click the job to view details including the success or failure of the job.

You have completed the steps for exporting tables with Data Manager. You can back up the file that you have created as you do any other file on your PC. Later, if you want to restore your tables to the state they were in when you created the exported file, you can use the Data Manager's Import Wizard.

Importing with Data Manager's Import Wizard

When is a good time to import? Well, unlike fine wine, which is good any time, you must reserve importing tables for special moments. Most commonly, importing restores tables that you have lost or damaged. The import re-creates the tables and then populates them with the data copied during the export. Use this backup method to restore tables that have been lost. You can also use the Import Wizard to create a copy of tables on a different Oracle8i database.

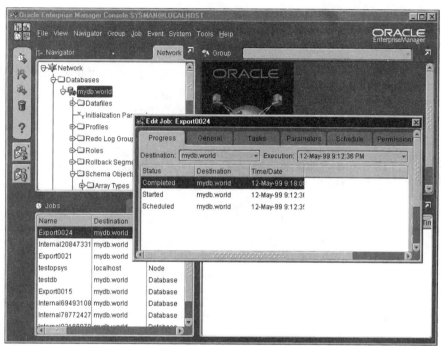

Figure 16-7:
Double-click
a job to view
its status.

Before importing with Data Manager, you must configure your preferred credentials for the target database and node. Follow Steps 1 to 6 in the "Exporting tables with a wizard" section earlier in this chapter.

To import objects contained in an export file, follow the next set of steps. If you're already in the Enterprise Manager's main window, skip to Step 3.

1. **Start the Enterprise Manager console.**

   If you have your LaunchPad up, choose the Management Console from the Enterprise Manager menu. Otherwise, on Windows 95, 98, or NT, select Start⇨Programs⇨Oracle HOME2⇨Enterprise Management⇨ Enterprise Manager Console.

   On UNIX, type this on the command line:

   ```
   oemapp console
   ```

   If you come to a login window, go to Step 2. Otherwise, skip to Step 3.

2. **Log in as the Enterprise Management Administrator.**

The default administrator is named SYSMAN with the password OEM_TEMP. Leave the Management Host box as the default of localhost if you're running your own personal Oracle8i; otherwise, fill in the name of the Enterprise Management Server on your network. The Enterprise Manager control console window appears. Refer to Figure 16-1.

3. **Right-click the database node and choose Data Management⇨Import to start the Data Management Wizard.**

The main Data Manager window appears. Refer to Figure 16-4.

4. **Click Next and then name the export file by either choosing a file from the list or typing your own file name; click Next when you're ready to continue.**

Remember to include the full path and file name if you are typing the file name. The file must be an export file created by the Data Manager.

The import file is processed using a batch job that's submitted and run while you watch the status of the job, as shown in Figure 16-8.

Don't worry! No data gets imported at this point. The wizard simply reads the file and prepares its next dialog screen for you.

Figure 16-8 shows the status window that appears.

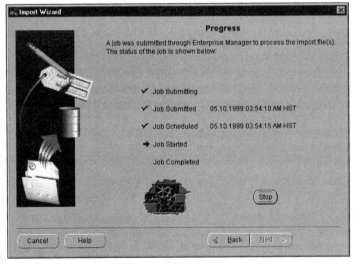

Figure 16-8: The Import Wizard reads the import file before continuing.

5. **Choose the type of import to do and click Next.**

The four possible choices are:

- **Database.** Import an entire database.

- **User.** Import a user and all its objects.

- **Table.** Import a table.

- **File.** Import the entire contents of the export file.

The available choices vary depending on what kind of export was done. For example, if a User export was selected, then the Database selection is not available during the import, but User, Table, and File are available.

For this example, choose Table and click Next.

6. **Specify tables to import and click Finish.**

Use the plus sign to view each user's tables. Select the desired table and click the arrow pointing to the right to move it to the Selected Tables box. Add as many tables as needed.

For the example, choose the CAR and CITY tables from the AMY schema, as shown in Figure 16-9.

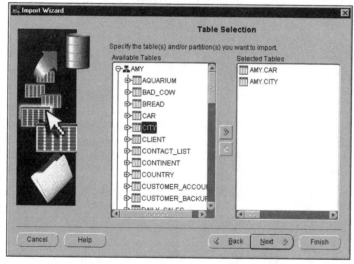

Figure 16-9:
Use the arrow buttons to move tables into or out of the Selected Tables box.

7. **Review the Summary window and click OK.**

Refer to Figure 16-6 for an example of the summary window, which tells you exactly what the wizard plans to do. After you click OK, the wizard submits a job and you return to the main console window.

8. **Check the results of your export in the Jobs window by clicking the History tab.**

The Jobs window is in the lower-left quarter of the console. Click the History tab and you see a list of jobs, including your import job. Double-click the job to view details including the success or failure of the job. Refer to Figure 16-7 to see the job status window.

You made it! You can reuse the same export file as many times as you want, if necessary. The Data Manager makes exporting and importing a whiz of a Wiz. Right, Toto?

EXP *and* IMP *commands*

The EXP and IMP commands, like my old Maui Cruiser, have been around since the Dark Ages and still run like champs. You can run the EXP and IMP commands from the command line in any operating system, so you don't need Enterprise Manager to use them.

EXP pulls tables or entire schemas (all tables, indexes, and other database objects owned by one Oracle8i user ID) out of the database in a compressed file format that is readable only by Oracle's IMP command.

IMP reads a file created by EXP and restores to the database the tables, indexes, or whatever database objects are in the file. Oracle8i prompts you for choices and can restore all or only specified objects, depending on what you want.

Exporting with the EXP *command*

Follow these steps to export tables using the EXP command:

1. **Start the EXP utility.**

   In Windows 95, 98, or NT, choose Start⇨Run. Then type

   ```
   EXP
   ```

   If you're running UNIX, type **EXP** at the command-line prompt.

2. **Type in your user ID and then press Enter to log on to the database.**

   EXP prompts you to enter a user name by displaying

   ```
   Username:
   ```

Do not use the INTERNAL or SYS user names with EXP. If you plan to do a full database export, use SYSTEM. (The default password for SYSTEM is MANAGER.)

3. **Type your password and press Enter.**

   Oracle8i asks you to enter a password by displaying

   ```
   Password:
   ```

   Notice that the insertion point moves, but Oracle8i doesn't display the letters on-screen. This feature protects your password from being seen by all those people who keep looking over your shoulder.

   Oracle8i checks your user name and password and tells you that you're connected to the database.

4. **If you want to accept the default buffer size (4096), press Enter; otherwise, type in a number and then press Enter.**

   Oracle8i prompts you for a buffer size by saying

   ```
   Enter array fetch buffer size: 4096 >
   ```

   The buffer size tells Oracle8i how much data to pull out of the database at a time. The default usually is acceptable unless you're exporting a large table (more than 10,000 rows). In the case of a large table, set the buffer size to the maximum value, which makes the fetching process run faster. (Sometimes I tell my dog, "Fetch, Buffer," but he ignores me.) In cases other than large tables, use the default.

5. **If you want to accept the default export-file location, press Enter; otherwise, type a file name of your own and then press Enter.**

   Oracle8i prompts you for a file name and suggests a default name by saying

   ```
   Export file: EXPDAT.DMP >
   ```

   Remember, Oracle8i creates the file in the current directory unless your file name includes the directory path.

6. **Choose the type of export that you want to do. You can accept the default by pressing Enter, or you can type in your choice and then press Enter.**

   You have three choices:

   - **Entire database:** You see this choice only if you are the DBA. Refer to the sidebar "The full database export" for a description of the full database export.

   - **Users:** This option allows you to export all the database objects (tables, indexes, views, grants, and so on) that belong to one user. If you are the DBA, you can export several users. If you aren't the DBA, you can export only your own user ID.

- **Tables:** This option allows you to export one or more tables that you own. A table export also exports database objects that belong to the table (indexes, grants, primary-key and other constraints, and of course the data).

Oracle8i asks you to choose an export type and suggests a default of tables (3) by saying

```
(1) E(ntire Database), (2)U(sers), or (3)T(ables): (2)U > 3
```

The remaining steps assume that you choose 3 (Table export). The prompts for User and Entire Database vary slightly from these prompts.

7. **If you want to export data with your tables, accept the default by pressing Enter. If you don't want to export data, type** no **in lowercase and press Enter.**

Oracle8i asks whether you want to export data and suggests that you do by saying

```
Export table data (yes/no): yes >
```

Normally, you want the table data. Sometimes, however, you want only the structure with no rows, which can be useful if you intend to use the export file for creating a new table in a separate database.

8. **If you want to compress your table data, accept the default by pressing Enter. If you don't want to compress the data, type** no **and then press Enter.**

Once again, you normally want to compress the table data. Compressing extents means that the table takes up less room and you free some wasted space in the table's structure. I can think of only one reason not to compress the extents: when you have deliberately created a table with a great deal of empty space in anticipation of a large number of rows that you may want to insert later. This situation is like calling ahead to a busy restaurant and making reservations. Oracle8i asks you about compression and sets the default to yes (yes, compress the table's extents into a single extent):

```
Compress extents (yes/no): yes >
```

9. **Type the name of the table or partition that you're exporting and then press Enter. If you're entering a partition name, first type the table name and then type a colon, followed by the partition name.**

Oracle8i asks you for a table name or partition by displaying

```
Table(T) or Partition(T:P) to be exported: (RETURN to
         quit) >
```

If you're exporting the CUSTOMER_ACCOUNT table, for example, type

```
CUSTOMER_ACCOUNT
```

If you log on as SYSTEM and want to export another user's tables, add the OWNER name to the table. For example, type the following:

```
AMY.CUSTOMER_ACCOUNT
```

Partition export is new for Oracle8i. This feature allows you to export one or more pieces of a table that is in several partitions. For example, if the CUSTOMER_ACCOUNT table has a partition named DENVER, export the partition like this:

```
AMY.CUSTOMER_ACCOUNT:DENVER
```

After you complete this step, Oracle8i responds by exporting a copy of the table and placing it in the export file. The program informs you of the deed and tells you how many rows it exported. In the example of the CUSTOMER_ACCOUNT table, here is what Oracle8i says:

```
. . exporting table CUSTOMER_ACCOUNT 4 rows exported
```

Then Oracle8i immediately asks for another table name by saying

```
Table(T) or Partition(T:P) to be exported: (RETURN to
        quit) >
```

10. **Repeat Step 8 until you've exported all the tables; then press Enter (without typing a table name) to stop the export.**

    Oracle8i completes the export and sends this message:

    ```
    Export terminated successfully.
    ```

    In Windows 95, 98, or NT, the preceding message flashes on-screen briefly; then the window closes. The message flashes quickly, so reading it is difficult.

After Oracle8i finishes the export, you can use the file to retrieve individual tables, or all the tables, by running the IMP utility.

Importing with the IMP command

The IMP command allows you to bring into your database any item (table, index, user, and so on) that you saved in an export created by EXP. You may import a table if you have made changes in the data that you don't like and want to revert to the older, unchanged data. Another time to import is when you've lost data because of some errors or a database failure.

1. **Start the** `IMP` **utility.**

   In Windows 95, 98, or NT, choose Start⇨Run and then type **IMP**. On UNIX, type **IMP** at the command line.

2. **Log on to the database, entering your user name and password when prompted.**

3. **If the displayed file name is the export file that you want to use, press Enter; otherwise, type the file name — including the full path if the file isn't in the current directory — and then press Enter.**

   Oracle8i prompts you as follows:

   ```
   Import file: EXPDAT.DMP >
   ```

4. **If you want to accept the default buffer size (30720), press Enter; otherwise, type in your own number and press Enter.**

   Oracle8i asks

   ```
   Enter insert buffer size(minimum is 4096) 30720 >
   ```

5. **If you want to import a file, press Enter to accept the default. If you simply want to review an export file, type** yes **and then press Enter.**

   Oracle8i asks

   ```
   List contents of import file only (yes/no): no >
   ```

   On rare occasions, you may want to review the contents of the export file without actually doing any importing.

6. **Choose how to handle possible errors caused by tables that already exist.**

   Oracle8i asks

   ```
   Ignore create error due to object existence (yes/no): no >
   ```

   `IMP` always tries to create the table before importing the rows. If the table already exists, `IMP` gets an error. Sometimes, you want `IMP` to add rows to an existing table. To do this, you must tell `IMP` to continue, even if it gets an error when it tries to create the table. If you know that the table exists and you want to add rows to it by using the import feature, type **yes**. If you want the import to stop with an error message if the feature can't create the table, type **no**. Then press Enter.

7. **If you want to import grants, accept the default (yes) by pressing Enter; otherwise, type** no **and then press Enter.**

   Oracle8i asks

   ```
   Import grants (yes/no): yes >
   ```

8. **If you want to import the data from the table, press Enter; otherwise, type** no **to import an empty table.**

   Oracle8i asks

   ```
   Import table data (yes/no): yes >
   ```

   Accepting the default *yes* brings in the data. Answering *no* imports only an empty table.

9. **To import everything in the file, accept the default by pressing Enter. To import parts that you specify, type** no **and press Enter.**

   Oracle8i asks

   ```
   Import entire export file (yes/no): yes >
   ```

   If you type **no**, Oracle8i prompts you for a user name and for table/partition names that you want to import and then imports them one at a time, prompting along the way. When you've imported all you want, leave the prompt line blank. Then press Enter to complete the import session.

   If you accept the default , Oracle8i completes the import session by informing you of its progress as it imports all the tables and other items (indexes, grants, and so on) from the export file.

   In either case, after Oracle8i completes the import, it displays

   ```
   Import terminated successfully.
   ```

Where to Hide Your Backup Files

Asking you where you hide your backup files is a truly personal question. It's like asking a lady where she keeps that spare hundred-dollar bill when she goes on a date.

Zip drives, Jaz drives, and removable hard drives have pretty much overshadowed tapes as the preferred storage medium for backups. I keep my backup files on a Zip disk in a locked drawer.

Now that CD-ROM writers are becoming more economical, I anticipate that in the future more people will choose to back up on CD-ROM. The new rewriteable CD-ROM technology is catching on.

Regardless of which cool hardware you use to store your backups, be sure that you move your backups to a physical location separate from the computer you're backing up. I know that leaving backup files on the same hard drive as the original data is temptingly convenient. Resist that lazy urge! One of the most common causes of database failure is hardware failure. So move those backup files to some kind of portable unit and then stash it somewhere, even if you just move it into the next room or a foot away into your storage cabinet.

Part IV

Tuning Up and Turbocharging

The 5th Wave   By Rich Tennant

"WE SORT OF HAVE OUR OWN WAY OF PREDICTING NETWORK PROBLEMS."

In this part . . .

You're running like a Cadillac—cruising with your Oracle8i schema (set of related tables) with all its related queries, scripts, and online screens in perfect harmony. Then, out of the blue, the engine starts to sputter. Now your cruising machine gets sluggish and sometimes won't even get out of first gear. What went wrong?

This section covers things that go wrong in Oracle8i and how to fix them. Oracle8i has a handful of little bugaboos that haunt every database after a while. A little tuning up here and there can get your database engine back into racing form.

Chapter 17

What's Slowing Your Query Down?

In This Chapter

▶ Looking into tune-ups, timing, and performance

▶ Analyzing your table for the Optimizer

▶ Taking little bites versus wolfing down your data

*P*erhaps you write SQL code in your spare time. If so, you probably have no spare time; I suggest that you get a life. On the other hand, you may use some additional software programs that generate all your queries for you. Everything goes well until one day you create a query that runs so slowly you consider taking it out and shooting it. The database administrator (DBA) starts yelling in your face. You take three aspirin and grab your manuals.

This chapter is all about performance tuning, or speeding up your query. I cover the bases with useful information for tuning up your SQL code. This chapter and the others in Part IV will have your code flying as never before.

Helping the Optimizer Do Its Job

Oracle8i has a brain called the *Optimizer*. The Optimizer has the unenviable job of figuring out the best way to execute your SQL code, no matter how garbled. If you help the Optimizer, it rewards you with good performance (meaning low costs and fast response times) on your SQL code. The best way to aid this overworked bit of software is to give it the information that it needs to do its job.

SQL, being a fourth-generation language, leaves many things open to interpretation. Basically, SQL outlines the ingredients and how they fit together as well as what the results should contain. SQL does not, however, clearly define the exact instructions for getting from point A to point B — which is where the Optimizer comes into play. The Optimizer looks over your SQL code and figures out a half-dozen different angles of attack to get the data that you want out of the database. Each of these angles is called a *plan*.

The Optimizer looks at the tables or objects involved in your query (or `INSERT`, `UPDATE`, and so on). It compares the size of the tables, the size of their rows, the indexes available to use, and other statistics it has on hand, and then makes its calculations. It figures out the amount of I/O (disk reading and writing) and the amount of CPU (computer brainpower) needed for all the various plans. The plan with the lowest overall cost wins.

The Optimizer makes decisions based on information that it has in the data-dictionary views. The information that it needs is updated only when you (or the DBA) update it by using the `ANALYZE` command. Each table that you don't analyze suffers because the Optimizer doesn't have important decision-making information for that table.

Keep your data-dictionary views current by regularly running the `ANALYZE` command on all your tables.

If you still have a query or other SQL code that seems to be running slowly, read on. I have some great hints for adjusting your code to speed up your query.

Moods and modes of the Optimizer

Which is the root word for Optimizer: *optimist* or *miser?*

Your Oracle8i database comes equipped with the most up-to-date Optimizer. However, it won't use any of its new features unless you give it statistics on at least some of your tables and objects.

Your Oracle8i Optimizer functions in two modes:

- **Cost-based.** This mode is the default mode, and it chooses the plan that delivers your data at the lowest cost in terms of system resources. System resources include Central Processing Unit (CPU) time, Input and Output (I/O) traffic, and volume of data.

- **Rule-based.** This was the only mode available in Oracle6. It remains in Oracle8i primarily to allow backward compatibility. If you have legacy SQL that was explicitly tuned for rule-based optimization, you can instruct the Optimizer to continue to use this mode. Be forewarned, however, that rule-based optimization is being phased out in future releases.

If you have a new database and you've never gathered statistics for any of its tables or objects, then the Oracle8i Optimizer will always use its older, less-efficient mode: rule-based optimization. So get with it!

If you're working with an older database (one that has been upgraded from earlier releases), you should verify that the database has the OPTIMIZER_MODE initialization parameter set to its default value of CHOOSE. This setting allows the Optimizer to use cost-based optimization whenever it can.

Follow the steps in the next section to gain access to the best Oracle8i Optimizer: cost-based optimization.

One command to analyze your entire schema

The GATHER_SCHEMA_STATS command is a great feature! It helps you be lazy and efficient all at once (that's actually the definition of "smart"). Either the schema owner or the DBA can run this command in SQL*Plus Worksheet or SQL*Plus. The general syntax is:

```
EXECUTE DBMS_STATS.GATHER_SCHEMA_STATS('schema_name');
```

Replace schema_name with the Oracle user name that owns the tables and objects.

To gather statistics for a schema, follow these steps:

1. **Start SQL*Plus Worksheet.**

   If you have your LaunchPad up, choose SQL*Plus Worksheet from the DB: Administration menu. Otherwise, on Windows 95, 98, or NT, select Start⇨Programs⇨Oracle HOME2⇨DBA Management Pack⇨ SQL*Plus Worksheet.

   On UNIX, type this on the command line:

   ```
   oemapp worksheet
   ```

   If you come to a login window, go to Step 2. Otherwise, skip to Step 3.

2. **Log in with your user name and password.**

   Choose the Connect Directly to a Database radio button. If you installed the sample schema, log in with user name AMY and password AMY123. A third option is to log in with the user ID and password that are loaded into all Oracle8i databases: SCOTT and TIGER, respectively. Leave the Service box empty if you are running your own personal Oracle8i; otherwise, fill in the name of the Oracle8i database (instance) on your network. Leave the Connect As box set to Normal. The SQL*Plus Worksheet window appears.

3. **Type the following command and replace** `schema_name` **with the Oracle user name that owns the tables and objects:**

```
EXECUTE DBMS_STATS.GATHER_SCHEMA_STATS('schema_name');
```

For the example, replace `schema_name` with `AMY`. This command gathers statistics on all the tables, columns, and indexes owned by `AMY`.

4. **Click the Execute button (the lightning bolt) to execute the command.**

After working for a while, SQL*Plus Worksheet displays

```
Statement processed.
```

Completing the `GATHER_SCHEMA_STATS` command makes sure that you have statistics on your tables, columns, objects, and indexes, which in turn ensures that you can use cost-based optimization. The next section shows you how to gather statistics for one table.

Personal attention: Analyzing one table at a time

Say you have a new table or a table that has a new index. You want to refresh the statistics for the table so that the Optimizer knows about your changes. In the old days, you had to run the `ANALYZE` command for the table, the columns, and the index. Now you can take care of all three at once with the `GATHER_TABLE_STATS` command. Here is the general syntax for this trick:

```
EXECUTE DBMS_STATS.GATHER_TABLE_STATS('sname','tname');
```

Replace `sname` with the Oracle user name that owns the table and `tname` with the table's actual name.

Because you're using the `EXECUTE` command, you must list all the parameters on a single line. Otherwise, you get syntax errors when you execute the command.

For example, the syntax for gathering statistics on the `AMY.CAR` table is:

```
EXECUTE DBMS_STATS.GATHER_TABLE_STATS('AMY', 'CAR');
```

The table owner or the DBA can run this command in SQL*Plus Worksheet or in SQL*Plus.

Another way to gather table statistics is to use the `ANALYZE` command, which is the underlying task that the `GATHER_TABLE_STATS` package handles. The basic syntax is:

```
ANALYZE TABLE table_name COMPUTE STATISTICS;
```

Replace `table_name` with the actual table name. The owner of the table can run this command in SQL*Plus Worksheet or SQL*Plus.

Whenever you add a new table, use the `GATHER_TABLE_STATS` command to update your data dictionary's statistics. Another time to gather statistics is when you add (or remove) columns or indexes to (or from) the table.

Sometimes you want to change the cost-based Optimizer's tuning to accomplish a different goal. The next section discusses how to do that.

A hint . . . you're getting warmer

When using the default settings, the Oracle8i Optimizer, in its infinite wisdom, knows that you usually want it to choose the most efficient plan that it can. But there are exceptions to every rule, and we mere mortals are graced with the following choices in optimization modes:

- ✔ ALL_ROWS. This mode tells the Optimizer that you want the most cost-effective plan it can devise using the cost-based Optimizer. The Optimizer uses default statistics for tables that are in the SQL statement and do not have statistics available.

- ✔ FIRST_ROWS. Fastest response time. This mode is best for interactive applications, such as Web pages, that display data. Because the objective of this kind of optimization is to deliver the first row of the query in as little time as possible, this goal is called FIRST_ROWS.

- ✔ CHOOSE. This is the default mode for Oracle8i databases. The Optimizer looks at the SQL statement and uses the ALL_ROWS (cost-effective) plan if at least one table in the statement has statistics available. If none of the tables has statistics available, the Optimizer uses the RULE plan (backward compatible).

- ✔ RULE. Uses rule-based optimization. Rule-based optimization determines the most cost-effective plan without considering the table statistics, such as distribution of data and volume of data. Even if statistics have been gathered, the Optimizer ignores them. This mode is equivalent to the Optimizer found in older versions of the Oracle database. If you have legacy SQL code that is well-tuned for the rule-based Optimizer, you can rest assured that the Oracle8i Optimizer will carry on the proud tradition by specifying this Optimizer mode. You can impose any of these modes on the entire database by specifying the mode in the OPTIMIZER_MODE initialization parameter.

If you prefer to impose a mode other than the one set up for the whole database, you can set the mode for a single SQL command by using the hint feature. A *hint* is an instruction to the Optimizer that changes which plan it chooses for the SQL statement.

You can use a great many hints, but they require careful study of the Optimizer plans. I cover only those hints that change the overall Optimizer mode. The remaining hints are more obscure and seldom used.

The general syntax of the Optimizer mode hint is

```
SELECT ... /* mode_name */
FROM ...
WHERE ...;
```

Replace mode_name with the actual Optimizer mode that you want to use.

You've created a lovely report for the manager of your bread company to use. The report is executed from her desktop and delivers the data to her Web browser. Naturally, you want to impress her with how incredibly quickly and efficiently your report can run. So you add the FIRST_ROWS hint to the query. The query looks like this:

```
SELECT B.BREAD_NAME, /* FIRST_ROWS */
B.SELLING_PRICE,
INGREDIENT_NAME, R.OUNCES*I.PRICE_PER_OUNCE
FROM INGREDIENT I,
     BREAD B,
     RECIPE R
WHERE R.BREAD_NO = B.BREAD_NO
AND R.INGREDIENT_NO =  I.INGREDIENT_NO
ORDER BY BREAD_NAME, INGREDIENT_NAME;
```

The first line contains the hint, FIRST_ROWS, enclosed inside a comment:

```
SELECT B.BREAD_NAME, /* FIRST_ROWS */
```

This type of hint must always appear in the first line of the query.

Getting Ahead While Testing and Tuning

You can extract data from your relational database a hundred different ways. The following two sections cover a few of the simpler techniques that help you create efficient, well-tuned queries and avoid common mistakes.

Baby steps versus giant leaps

A SQL query or command can run slowly for many reasons. To discover important performance clues, ask yourself a couple of questions: "When did the problem start?" and "What did I change just before I started having trouble?"

When you create a complex SQL statement, you may be wise to create it in small bites and then test each one as you go along. These steps can help you develop good habits for creating tricky SQL statements:

1. **Build the statement one table at a time.**

   Choose the main table and build the beginning statement, using only the main table.

2. **Test your beginning statement and make corrections.**

3. **Add another table, test the statement, and make corrections.**

4. **Continue adding tables, testing your statements, and making corrections until the SQL statement is complete.**

Often you can catch trouble spots in your code when you build the code gradually. Taking baby steps gives you steady, forward progress. Giant steps, in which you create an entire SQL command at one time, tend to fall short.

SQL*Plus Worksheet has a command to help you figure out whether you've improved the response time for your query. The next section discusses this command, which is called TIMING.

The SQL*Plus Worksheet's timing

The TIMING command in SQL*Plus Worksheet (or SQL*Plus) gives you great feedback on the performance speed of your SQL command. To turn the timing on, type

```
SET TIMING ON
```

This command is an environment command in SQL*Plus Worksheet, meaning that it changes the way SQL*Plus Worksheet displays the results of your queries and other commands. An environment command stays on until you reset it or leave SQL*Plus Worksheet. Wouldn't it be great if we could just set an environment command on the ozone layer or the Amazon rain forest?

To use Enterprise Manager to turn the TIMING setting on in SQL*Plus Worksheet, follow these steps:

1. **Start the SQL*Plus Worksheet.**

   If you have your LaunchPad up, choose the SQL*Plus Worksheet from the DB: Administration menu. Otherwise, on Windows 95, 98, or NT, select Start⇔Programs⇔Oracle HOME2⇔DBA Management Pack⇔ SQL*Plus Worksheet.

   On UNIX, type this on the command line:

   ```
   oemapp worksheet
   ```

   If you come to a login window, go to Step 2. Otherwise, skip to Step 3.

2. **Log in with a valid Oracle8i user name and password.**

   Choose the Connect Directly to a Database radio button. If you installed the sample schema, log in with user name AMY and password AMY123. A third option is to log in with the user ID and password that are loaded into all Oracle8i databases: SCOTT and TIGER, respectively. Leave the Service box empty if you are running your own personal Oracle8i; otherwise, fill in the name of the Oracle8i database (instance) on your network. Leave the Connect As box set to Normal. The SQL*Plus Worksheet window appears.

3. **Type the following code at the top of the window (as shown in Figure 17-1):**

   ```
   SET TIMING ON;
   ```

Figure 7-7: You can handle the SQL*Plus Worksheet setting by executing it (which is no t the same as taking it out and having it shot).

4. **Click the Execute button to run the command.**

   You see no feedback from Oracle8i when you click the Execute button. Statistics follow every SQL command that you execute. Whenever you run a SQL command, you see statistics similar to those shown in Figure 17-2.

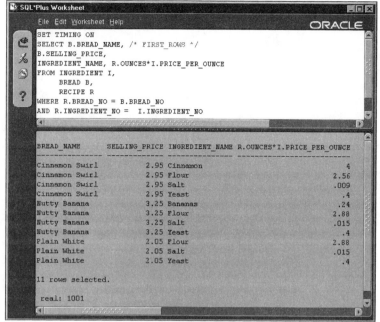

```
SQL*Plus Worksheet                                          _ □ ×
 File  Edit  Worksheet  Help                          ORACLE
SET TIMING ON
SELECT B.BREAD_NAME, /* FIRST_ROWS */
B.SELLING_PRICE,
INGREDIENT_NAME, R.OUNCES*I.PRICE_PER_OUNCE
FROM INGREDIENT I,
     BREAD B,
     RECIPE R
WHERE R.BREAD_NO = B.BREAD_NO
AND R.INGREDIENT_NO =  I.INGREDIENT_NO


BREAD_NAME       SELLING_PRICE INGREDIENT_NAME R.OUNCES*I.PRICE_PER_OUNCE
---------------  ------------- --------------- --------------------------
Cinnamon Swirl          2.95 Cinnamon                                 4
Cinnamon Swirl          2.95 Flour                                 2.56
Cinnamon Swirl          2.95 Salt                                  .009
Cinnamon Swirl          2.95 Yeast                                   .4
Nutty Banana            3.25 Bananas                                .24
Nutty Banana            3.25 Flour                                 2.88
Nutty Banana            3.25 Salt                                  .015
Nutty Banana            3.25 Yeast                                   .4
Plain White             2.05 Flour                                 2.88
Plain White             2.05 Salt                                  .015
Plain White             2.05 Yeast                                   .4

11 rows selected.

 real: 1001
```

Figure 17-2:
TIMING
shows you
the time that
it takes to
run a SQL
command.

The statistics are shown in real time, in thousandths of a second. Other operating systems show different statistics, such as the CPU time or buffers used.

The first time you run a SQL command, Oracle8i reads new data into its buffers. The data stays in the buffers until the end of the session or until Oracle8i runs out of buffers and reuses the one with this data. Consequently, when you use the timing statistics to compare variations on similar queries, make sure that you run each of them a second time. By doing so, you get timing statistics that don't include the initial loading of the buffers.

Now you have a method of testing the changes that you make in your query in an attempt to speed it up. You can look at the slow query's timing statistics, make changes in the query, and compare this changed query's timing statistics to the original query's. The next chapter describes how to add an index and discusses more about how to write a query that takes advantage of an index.

Chapter 18

Speeding Up Queries with Keys and Indexes

. . . .

In This Chapter

▶ Discovering why indexes are your friends

▶ Creating your own primary key

▶ Getting rid of the primary key

▶ Making the most of a foreign key

▶ Inventing your own index

▶ Dropping an index without breaking it

▶ Using Schema Manager to make indexes and keys

▶ Looking at how indexes are used

. . . .

*E*very table should have a primary key, as a general rule. In this chapter, you discover how to create a primary key with Enterprise Manager's Schema Manager. Primary keys are primarily keyed to speed because they have a built-in index. Get faster response from your queries by creating primary keys on all your tables. Add extra indexes on columns that are used for query criteria, and you have yourself a revved-up system.

Speeding up a slow query is a dilemma faced by almost anyone who works with Oracle8i. Oracle8i has a brain called an Optimizer that has the job of deciding how to go after the data that's requested in your query. In most cases, you can transform a slow tortoise query into a speedy rabbit query by adding an index to an important column in the query. In this chapter, you find out how to create the keys and the indexes. You also find out about loopholes that prevent the Optimizer from using the fresh new index.

Why Create an Index?

Speed, speed, and speed are the main reasons to create an index. When you run a query, you tell Oracle8i which parts of which tables you want to see. Oracle8i looks at its own resources and decides the most efficient way to get the data to you. An index helps Oracle8i get the data faster.

Oracle8i doesn't sift or sort your table's rows based on any index (unless you're working with complex, parallel table structures). As you add rows to a table, Oracle8i always adds them to the end of the current rows. Sometimes, Oracle8i moves a row from its original position to the end of the current rows. This happens if a row gets updated with a great deal of data at one time — data that doesn't fit into its current space in the table. Therefore, the table rows become jumbled up in sequence, even if you originally entered them in order.

Oracle8i keeps indexes as independent objects in the database. An index looks much like a table when you look at its internal structure, and it consists of rows of data. The columns in the index include a copy of the indexed column(s) and the row ID of the corresponding row in the table that you indexed.

Unlike tables, indexes are kept in perfect sorted order by the index columns. Every new row added to a table creates a row in the index. Oracle8i automatically adds the row into the index in its sorted order, which allows Oracle8i to use fast search algorithms on the index. After Oracle8i finds the row in the index, it uses the row ID to retrieve the table row.

What are a row ID and an OID?

A row ID contains the physical location of the row in a table and is the fastest retrieval method that Oracle8i uses. If Oracle8i knows a row ID, it knows the location of that row and can go directly to it without any delay. The row ID consists of several hexadecimal numbers that identify the storage space used for a single row from a single table. Every row has a row ID. You can query a row ID as you can any column, but you can't modify the ID. When a table is reorganized, such as during export and import of the entire table or database, the row ID changes.

Every row in an object table contains an Object ID, or OID. An OID is the equivalent of a row ID. It is a unique identifier that describes the location of the row's data to the Oracle8i database engine. Unlike the row ID, however, the OID is needed to relate two objects together. It works as a foreign key. The structure of the OID is similar to the row ID, but unlike a row ID, you can't directly query an OID. The only time that you can retrieve an OID is when you put it into the REF datatype (often within a PL/SQL procedure).

If you create a primary key constraint on your table, Oracle8i automatically creates an index on the primary key column or columns. A primary key constraint is a feature of Oracle8i that defines the table's primary key as a rule (constraint) enforced by the database.

Oracle8i doesn't require indexes or primary keys on any table. If you have neither one, then Oracle8i uses its only option, a *full table scan,* when you query the table. A full table scan is similar to starting at the 100s on the library shelf and reading every book label until you find the book you want. Likewise, using an index is like going to the card catalog, looking up your book's Dewey decimal number and then walking right to the appropriate aisle and finding the exact location of the book.

What can you use an index for? Lots of stuff:

- ✔ **Faster queries.** You can make an index on columns that you use for searches. If you have an online screen that allows searches by last name, for example, add an index on the LAST_NAME column of the table. This kind of index doesn't require unique values.

- ✔ **Unique values.** A primary key always requires unique values, meaning that the value of the primary key column (or columns) in one row of the table is unique when compared to the values of the primary key column (or columns) in all the other rows in the table. Oracle8i automatically generates an index to enforce unique values in the primary key of a table. You can also use this feature for any other column (or set of columns) that requires unique values in your table.

- ✔ **Foreign keys.** Foreign keys are used frequently in queries. You can speed up the performance of queries using foreign keys by adding an index on them.

In the next section, you find out how to create primary and foreign keys and their indexes.

Adding and Removing a Primary Key

When you name a column or set of columns as the primary key, Oracle8i automatically creates an index on that primary key, resulting in two positive effects.

The first positive effect is that the primary key, by definition, must have a unique value for every row added to the table. The unique index on the primary key enforces this rule. Every row added must pass the test and must have a unique primary key.

The second positive effect is that you often use the primary key to find a row in the table. An index on the primary key makes finding a row faster and more efficient.

The index that Oracle8i creates assumes the original name of the primary key. If you didn't name the primary key, Oracle8i names the index, using the following naming convention:

```
SYS_nnnn
```

Oracle8i replaces nnnn with a sequential number.

You can define the primary key for a table when you create it or after you create it. Refer to Chapter 10 to find out how to define the primary key for a table when you create it.

When you add a primary key to an existing table, Oracle8i verifies that all the table's rows have unique primary keys before it allows you to successfully add the primary key. If rows have duplicate primary keys, you must find them and either change the keys or eliminate the duplicate rows.

Install the sample tables included on the CD-ROM if you want to follow along with the examples in this chapter. Appendix B includes instructions on how to install the tables.

Enterprise Manager's Schema Manager has a nice dialog box for creating and changing tables. You can also use this dialog box to add or remove a table's primary key. (You can't modify a primary key; you can only add or remove it.) The next two sections include step-by-step instructions for each process.

Adding a primary key

Follow these steps to add a primary key. The process is quite easy. By the way, you can use the same process when you first create the table, if you prefer.

1. **Start the Schema Manager.**

   If you have your LaunchPad up, choose the Schema Manager from the DB: Administration menu. Otherwise, on Windows 95, 98, or NT, select Start⇨Programs⇨Oracle HOME2⇨DBA Management Pack⇨ SQL*Plus Worksheet.

   On UNIX, type this on the command line:

   ```
   oemapp worksheet
   ```

   If you come to a login window, go to Step 2. Otherwise, skip to Step 3.

2. **Log in with a valid DBA Oracle8i user name and password.**

   One option is to log in with the user ID and password that are loaded into all Oracle8i databases: SYSTEM and MANAGER, respectively. Leave the Service box empty if you're running your own personal Oracle8i; otherwise, fill in the name of the Oracle8i database (instance) on your network. Leave the Connect As box set to Normal. The Schema Manager window appears, as shown in Figure 18-1.

3. **Double-click the Tables icon in the left frame.**

   A list of schemas appears below the icon in the left frame, and a list of all the tables appears in the right window.

4. **Double-click the schema that owns the table you want to change.**

   Both the right and left frames show you a list of tables owned by that schema.

5. **Click the table that needs a primary key.**

   A properties window for the table appears in the right frame. In Figure 18-2, I selected the AMY schema and the MISSING_PRIMARY_KEY table.

6. **Click the Constraints tab.**

   You see a list of any constraints that already exist for this table, as shown in Figure 18-3.

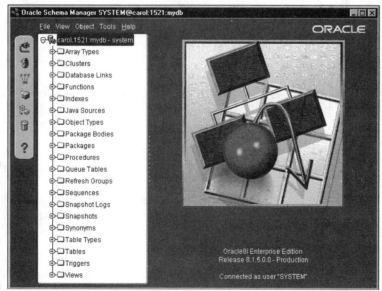

Figure 18-1:
The Schema
Manager
is again
tirelessly
at your
service.

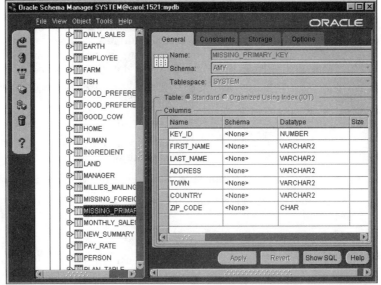

Figure 18-2:
Table
properties
show up in
the right half
of the
Schema
Manager.

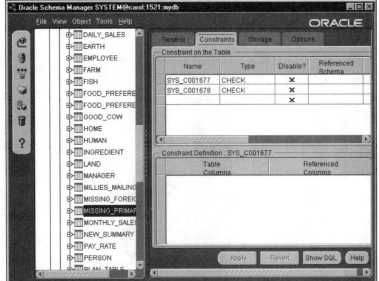

Figure 18-3:
Table
constraint
properties
show up in
the right half
of the
Schema
Manager.

7. **In the box labeled Constraints on the Table, type a constraint name in the Name column.**

I suggest that you use some standard method of naming primary keys. (I like to add PK to the table name.) Remember that Oracle8i uses this constraint name in error messages. So, a name that tells you what the constraint does and what table the constraint is on may help you debug errors later.

8. **Select** PRIMARY **in the Type column.**

9. **Leave the red X in the Disable column.**

10. **In the Table Columns column in the box labeled Constraint Definition, select the column or columns in the primary key.**

    The first column is labeled Table Columns. Click the down-pointing arrow to see a list of available columns. Select the one that you want to add to your primary key. If your primary key contains more than one column, select each one in order so that you see all of them listed.

11. **(Optional) Click the Show SQL button to see the actual SQL code generated to create your new primary key.**

    Figure 18-4 shows the constraint parameters and the SQL for adding a new primary key to AMY's MISSING_PRIMARY_KEY table.

12 **Click Apply when you're done.**

    Oracle8i executes the SQL that it generated for you. The index required to enforce your primary key is built as part of the primary-key constraint. Oracle8i checks every row in the table. If any of the rows have duplicate values in the primary key, a pop-up window appears with this message in it:

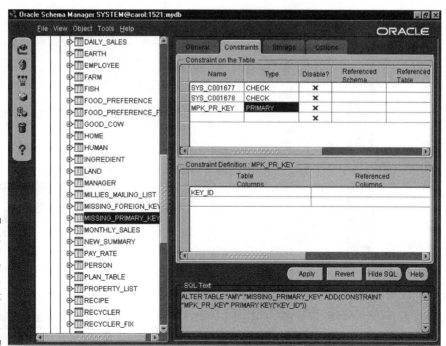

Figure 18-4: You can add a primary key as an afterthought in Schema Manager.

```
ORA-02437: cannot enable (tablename, keyname) - primary
           key violated
```

You need to fix the data so that every row has a unique primary key.

Removing a primary key

Every once in a while, you may make a mistake. I've heard that some people who are below the status of Oracle8i Priestess make mistakes. I know that you didn't mean to.

When you remove a primary key by choosing Drop With Cascade in Schema Manager, you may affect other tables. The Schema Manager automatically removes all foreign keys that refer to this primary key. Remember that you get neither a warning nor a list of what you changed.

Here's how to remove a primary key:

1. **Follow Steps 1 through 7 in the preceding section.**

   You see the constraints defined for the table that you want to work on. Figure 18-5 shows the constraints properties for the REMOVE_THE_PRIMARY_KEY table in the AMY schema.

Figure 18-5: You can easily remove this primary key with a right click.

2. **Select the Primary Key column and then right-click and select Drop.**

   A pop-up menu appears with only one choice: Drop. This removes the primary key and also removes all foreign keys from other tables where the foreign key references this primary key.

3. **(Optional) Click the Show SQL button.**

   You may want to find out the SQL code that removes a primary key. You see that code at the bottom of the right frame after you click the button.

   If you change your mind after removing the primary key, you can restore it by clicking the Revert button. *This works only before you click the Apply button.*

4. **Click the Apply button.**

   Oracle8i removes the primary-key constraint, the index, and all foreign keys that reference this primary key.

Creating and Dropping Foreign Keys

When you name a column or set of columns as a foreign key, Oracle8i creates a constraint but does not require an index. Remember, a foreign key tells the database that the column (or columns) represent the values of the primary key of a related table. (See Chapter 2 for more about foreign keys.) I recommend that you create an index for every foreign key that you create. This section shows you how to create a foreign-key constraint. The "Creating Your Own Indexes" section, later in this chapter, shows you how to create an index. An index on a foreign key is just another regular index.

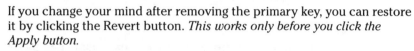

When you add a foreign key to an existing table, Oracle8i goes to the table referenced by the foreign key and then makes sure that each row in your table has either a null or a valid key in the columns that are foreign keys. If Oracle8i finds any foreign keys that don't match, you can't create the foreign key. In that case, you have to sniff out those bad foreign keys. Be on the alert for Limburger, garlic, or Roquefort; they may be signs of a foreign key gone very bad. Sometimes keys are missing in the reference table. Other times you need to change the foreign-key table data.

To add a foreign key, use the same Schema Manager dialog box that you use to create and change a table. You can also use the dialog box to remove the foreign key. The steps are similar to those for adding a primary key.

Adding a foreign key

The Schema Manager uses a series of menus to guide you through the creation of a foreign key. Follow these steps to create a foreign key using the Schema Manager:

1. **Start the Schema Manager.**

   If you have your LaunchPad up, choose the Schema Manager from the DB: Administration menu. Otherwise, on Windows 95, 98, or NT, select Start⇨Programs⇨Oracle HOME2⇨DBA Management Pack⇨ SQL*Plus Worksheet.

   On UNIX, type this on the command line:

   ```
   oemapp worksheet
   ```

   If you come to a login window, go to Step 2. Otherwise, skip to Step 3.

2. **Log in with a valid DBA Oracle8i user name and password.**

   One option is to log in with the user ID and password that are loaded into all Oracle8i databases: SYSTEM and MANAGER, respectively. Leave the Service box empty if you're running your own personal Oracle8i; otherwise, fill in the name of the Oracle8i database (instance) on your network. Leave the Connect As box set to Normal. The Schema Manager window appears.

3. **Double-click the Table icon in the left frame.**

   A list of schemas appears below the icon in the left frame, and a list of all the tables appears in the right window.

4. **Double-click the schema that owns the table that you want to change.**

   Both the right and left frames show you a list of tables owned by that schema.

5. **Click the table that needs a foreign key.**

   A properties window for the table appears in the right frame. In Figure 18-6, I selected the AMY schema and the MISSING_FOREIGN_KEY table.

6. **Click the Constraints tab.**

   You see a list of any constraints that already exist for this table.

7. **In the box labeled Constraints on the Table, type a constraint name in the Name column.**

   I suggest that you use some kind of standard method of naming foreign keys. (I like to add FK to the table name to create the constraint name.) Remember that Oracle8i uses this constraint name in error messages. A name that tells you what the constraint does and what table the constraint is on may help you debug errors later.

8. **Select FOREIGN in the Type column.**

9. **Leave the red X in the Disable column.**

10. **In the next column, select the referenced schema.**

    Click the down-pointing arrow in the Referenced Schema column to see a selection list. Select the owner of the table that this foreign key references.

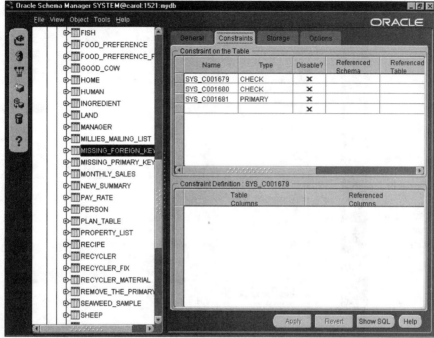

Figure 18-6:
Table
properties
show up
in the right
half of the
Schema
Manager.

11. Scroll to the next column and select the referenced table.

Click and drag the scroll bar to bring into view the columns off to the right in this section. Click the arrow in the Referenced Table column to reveal a list of tables and then choose one by clicking it.

12. In the Table Columns column in the box labeled Constraint Definition, select the table column or columns in the foreign key.

This first column is labeled Table Columns. Click the arrow, and you see a list of available columns; select the one that you want to add to your foreign key. If your foreign key contains more than one column, select each one in order so that you see all of them listed.

13. In the next column, select the corresponding column or columns in the referenced table.

This second column is called Referenced Columns. Click the arrow to get a list of columns in the referenced table. Click the column that corresponds with the column in this table. Do this for each column in the foreign key.

14. (Optional) Click the Show SQL button to see the actual SQL code generated to create your new foreign key.

Figure 18-7 shows the constraint parameters and the SQL for adding a new foreign key to AMY's MISSING_FOREIGN_KEY table.

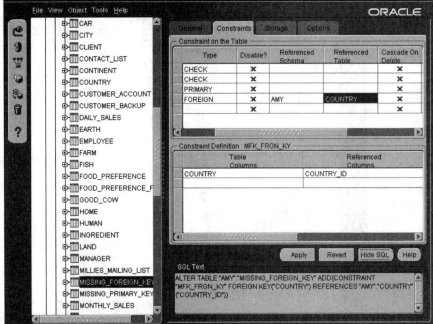

Figure 18-7:
This foreign
key has one
column that
corresponds
with one
column
in the
referenced
table.

15. Click Apply when you're done.

Oracle8i executes the SQL that it generated for you and checks the for-eign-key constraint against every row of data. If Oracle8i finds any invalid foreign-key values — other than nulls, which it ignores — you get the error message shown in Figure 18-8. You must fix the data so that every row has either nulls or a valid key in the Foreign Key column.

Figure 18-8:
The error
message
you get
when a
foreign key
doesn't fit.

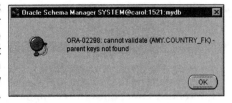

Removing a foreign key

You may need to remove a foreign key if you change or drop the referenced table. In fact, if you try to drop a table that is referenced in a foreign key of another table, you get an error message, like this:

```
ORA-02266: unique/primary keys in table referenced by
enabled foreign keys
```

To avoid this error, either remove the primary key (as I describe in the section "Removing a primary key" earlier in this chapter) or remove the offending foreign key by following these steps:

1. **Follow Steps 1 through 7 of the preceding section.**

   A list of constraints appears.

2. **Find the constraint that you want to remove and select it.**

3. **Right-click the foreign key and select Drop.**

   The foreign key disappears from the window.

4. **(Optional) Click the Show SQL button to see the SQL code that removes a foreign key.**

   After you click the button, you see the code at the bottom of the right frame.

   If you change your mind after removing the foreign key, you can restore it by clicking the Revert button. *This action works only before you click the Apply button.*

5. **Click the Apply button.**

   Oracle8i removes the foreign-key constraint.

Naming a foreign key

Make sure that you follow the naming rules and suggestions that I list in Chapter 2. In addition to these guidelines, I suggest that you name your foreign keys like this:

    FK_table_column

Replace `table` with the table name or a shortened version of the table name.

Replace `column` with the column in the foreign key. If more than one column exists in the foreign key, name all the columns in shortened versions.

Read on to find out how to add an index that helps Oracle8i use your foreign-key constraints more quickly and efficiently. Otherwise, you can just lie down and take a nap. I'm going to do that right now.

Creating Your Own Indexes

Oracle8i has few restrictions on what you can do when you create indexes. The main rules are these:

- ✔ You can't make two indexes that include the same columns.
- ✔ You can't index columns that have the LONG, BCLOB, NCLOB, or BFILE datatypes. These kinds of columns can contain huge amounts of data, and indexing them makes no sense anyway. The folks at Oracle made a logical choice on this one.

Make a rule of creating an index on a foreign key. This practice speeds up your queries because Oracle8i efficiently stores and maintains indexes for fast matching and lookups. Queries that join two tables always use the foreign key and the primary key in the WHERE clause. Having an index on the foreign key allows Oracle8i to quickly match the two indexes — the foreign-key index and the primary-key index — before going after the data.

Indexes can also speed up response time in a popular online screen. If you create a screen in which users search for phone numbers based on a person's last name, for example, you can create an index for the LAST_NAME column.

Avoid adding an index on a column that includes many of the same values in many rows. A column called SEX, for example, has three possible values: MALE, FEMALE, and NULL. In a table with 10,000 rows, an index that narrows down the number of rows to 3,333 may not speed up the performance much.

When you want to create an index, you can use the Schema Manager to help you. You can easily remove and modify an index as well.

An index can be either unique or nonunique. A *unique* index validates every new or changed row in a table for a unique value in the column or set of columns in the index. A *nonunique* index allows duplicate values in rows. You add a nonunique index to speed up the query.

The 20 percent rule

The fastest way to retrieve rows from a table is to access the row with the exact row ID. An index is the second-fastest way, but it decreases in performance as the proportion of rows retrieved increases. If you're retrieving approximately 20 percent of the rows in a table, using an index is just as fast. But beyond that magic 20 percent, *not* using an index is faster.

Keep this rule in mind when you create indexes intended to help speed up a query. Queries vary in the rows that they select from a table. If you have a query that you use often, determine the number of rows that it selects from the table. If this number is more than 20 percent of the total number of rows in the table, an index on the table may not improve the performance of the query. You may just want to try both methods. If the number of rows is less than 20 percent, an index will almost certainly help performance.

Adding an index

Start Schema Manager and follow these steps:

1. **Start the Schema Manager.**

   If you have your LaunchPad up, choose the Schema Manager from the DB: Administration menu. Otherwise, on Windows 95, 98, or NT, select Start⇨Programs⇨Oracle HOME2⇨DBA Management Pack⇨ Schema Manager.

   On UNIX, type this on the command line:

   ```
   oemapp schema
   ```

   If you come to a login window, go to Step 2. Otherwise, skip to Step 3.

2. **Log in with a valid DBA Oracle8i user name and password.**

   One option is to log in with the user ID and password that are loaded into all Oracle8i databases: SYSTEM and MANAGER, respectively. Leave the Service box empty if you're running your own personal Oracle8i; otherwise, fill in the name of the Oracle8i database (instance) on your network. Leave the Connect As box set to Normal. The Schema Manager window appears.

3. **Double-click the Table icon in the left frame.**

   A list of schemas appears below the icon in the left frame, and a list of all the tables appears in the right window.

4. **Double-click the schema that owns the table that you want to index.**

   Both the right and left frames show you a list of tables owned by that schema.

5. **Click the table that needs an index.**

   The table properties window appear magically on the right side of the window.

6. **Choose Object⇨Create Index on.**

   A window opens in which you complete the definition of the index.

7. **Fill in the index name.**

   Type the index name in the box labeled Name. Follow the usual naming standards for Oracle objects, as you do for tables and columns.

8. **Select the schema on which to create the index.**

   Click the selection arrow for the schema and choose the correct name. In the example database, choose AMY.

9. **Select the indexed columns by clicking them in order.**

   Select the first column in the index first, the second one next, and so on until you've numbered all the columns in the index. Figure 18-9 shows you what my sample index looks like.

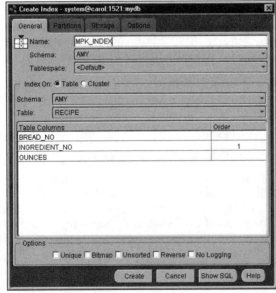

Figure 18-9:
Choose the columns by clicking them in order so that they are assigned numbers.

10. **Choose the appropriate options (Unique, Recoverable, Sorted, Bitmap) for your index.**

    Leave the Sorted box checked (default). If your index is unique, check the Unique box. The Bitmap box is for an alternative method of sorting, which I don't cover. Leave the Bitmap box blank. The Recoverable box tells Oracle8i to write this event (creation of the index) into its redo logs for later recovery, if necessary. Leave this box blank unless your DBA says otherwise.

11. **Click the Create button to finish.**

    Oracle8i executes the SQL it generated and returns you to the main window.

The index creator in Schema Manager can create as many indexes as you need in a flash.

Removing an index

Removing an index by using Schema Manager is easier than creating one. Follow these quick and easy steps:

1. **Start the Schema Manager.**

   If you have your LaunchPad up, choose the Schema Manager from the DB: Administration menu. Otherwise, on Windows 95, 98, or NT, select Start⇨Programs⇨Oracle HOME2⇨DBA Management Pack⇨ Schema Manager.

   On UNIX, type this on the command line:

   ```
   oemapp schema
   ```

   If you come to a login window, go to Step 2. Otherwise, skip to Step 3.

2. **Log in with a valid DBA Oracle8i user name and password.**

   One option is to log in with the user ID and password that are loaded into all Oracle8i databases: SYSTEM and MANAGER, respectively. Leave the Service box empty if you're running your own personal Oracle8i; otherwise, fill in the name of the Oracle8i database (instance) on your network. Leave the Connect As box set to Normal. The Schema Manager window appears.

3. **Double-click the Table icon in the left frame.**

   A list of schemas appears below the icon in the left frame, and a list of all the indexes appears in the right window.

4. **Double-click the schema that owns the table and index that you want to remove.**

   Both the right and left frames show you a list of tables owned by that schema.

5. **Click the plus sign next to the table with the index that you want to remove.**

   A list of folders, including the Index folder, appears below the table name in the right window.

6. **Click the plus sign next to the index folder.**

   The folder expands to show a list of indexes.

7. **Select the index that you want to remove.**

   Figure 18-10 shows the window just before you remove an index.

8. **Choose Object⇨Remove.**

   Schema Manager asks you if you're sure that you want to remove the index.

9. **Click Yes.**

   The Schema Manager removes the index and returns you to the main window. You see that Oracle8i has removed the index from the list of indexes.

The index is gone, just like that.

Index versus primary-key constraints

You probably already know that you can create your own unique index for a table's primary key if you do not define a primary-key constraint.

If you're working with a legacy system, you may face a situation in which you have many of these indexes attached to the older tables. Why go through all the trouble of removing those indexes and adding the primary-key constraints? Do you get royalties every time the primary key is used?

The best reason for replacing unique indexes with primary-key constraints is that you can't create any foreign-key constraints that refer to a table that has no primary key. You may start with the older tables and then build on new tables that fit in and enhance these older ones. Foreign keys define all the connections between the old and new tables. If you don't create a primary-key constraint, you are handicapped. Ultimately, you can't create the foreign-key constraints that make your schema (set of database tables) have integrity with good values in all the foreign keys. You don't have to be a Boy Scout to know that good values and integrity are desirable traits.

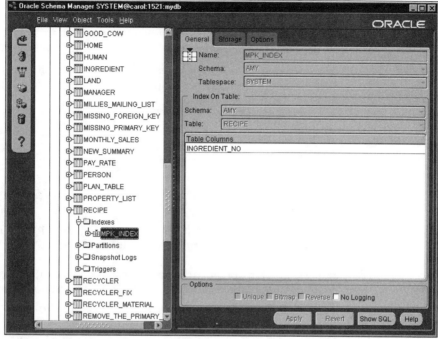

Figure 18-10: The properties page displays the index that gets deleted.

Using Indexes with Object Tables and Nested Tables

Object tables and nested tables store data, as do relational tables. Therefore, you can experience better performance when retrieving data from object tables and nested tables by adding an index.

The next sections cover the how-to's of index creation with object tables and nested tables. If you don't like objects, I object! Skip these sections. Otherwise, read on.

Creating an index on an object table

As you find out in Chapter 2, there are two kinds of object tables: tables of objects and tables with columns of objects.

You can create an index on various objects in the following cases:

✔ **You can create an index on the relational columns within a table, just as you do on a relational table.** This applies to tables that use a combination of relational columns and object columns. In this case, follow the instructions in the "Adding an index" section earlier in this chapter.

✔ **You can create an index on a nested table.** This requires using SQL, which I describe in the next section, "Creating an index on a nested table."

✔ **In special circumstances, you can create an index on a column that has the REF datatype.** I don't discuss this aspect of indexing objects because it is too complex to cover within the scope of this book.

Creating an index on a nested table

To create this kind of index, you need a nested table. See Chapter 11 for plenty of information on the exciting job of nesting tables.

For now, I assume that you already have a nested table somewhere, and you want to add an index. The general syntax of the command to use is

```
CREATE INDEX indexname ON
nestedtablename (columnname, columnname...);
```

Replace `indexname` with the name of your new index. Replace `nestedtablename` with the name of the nested table's physical storage table. Replace `columnname` with one or more columns that are to be indexed.

Use the following variation on the syntax when you want to create a unique index on a nested table (this enforces uniqueness, similar to a primary key):

```
CREATE INDEX indexname ON
nestedtablename (NESTED_TABLE_ID, columnname,columnname...);
```

In this format, the pseudocolumn called `NESTED_TABLE_ID` is included. `NESTED_TABLE_ID` is the unique ID that Oracle8i assigns to each row of a nested table. Including the unique ID in the indexed columns assures that the unique values of other columns are included in the index.

Say you have a table called `BREAD_RECIPE`, which contains a nested table of ingredients for your bread. The nested table is stored in the `RECIPE_NEST_TABLE` table. The SQL to create the index is

```
CREATE INDEX RECIPE_NEST_INGRED_IX ON
RECIPE_NEST_TABLE (NESTED_TABLE_ID, INGREDIENT_ID);
```

Use SQL*Plus Worksheet to execute the command.

Removing an index on an object table or a nested table

If you have a table that contains column objects, you may have created an index on one of the relational columns. In this case, remove the index by following the instructions in the "Removing an index" section earlier in this chapter.

If you've created an index on a nested table, use SQL to remove it. The syntax is

```
DROP INDEX indexname;
```

Execute the command in SQL*Plus Worksheet.

For example, to drop the RECIPE_NEST_INGRED_IX index, you use the following command:

```
DROP INDEX RECIPE_NEST_INGRED_IX;
```

Now that you know how to create indexes, you're ready to dig into the theory behind the practice.

Oracle's Brain on Indexes

Oracle8i uses indexes to get at your data faster. Oracle8i has a special part of its brain called the Optimizer. The Optimizer looks over any SQL command and decides the fastest, most efficient way to deliver the results.

The Optimizer uses a set of rules to determine the best way to go after your data. Its job is to scrutinize your WHERE clause in the same manner in which an IRS auditor pores over your books. The Optimizer weighs all the options, compares, contrasts, combines, unravels, and finally comes up with a plan that it uses to execute the SQL command.

Under most circumstances, the Optimizer obtains great results. Indexes speed up your queries, right? Sure they do — when the Optimizer decides to use them.

Here's the catch: Sometimes, you inadvertently write something in your WHERE clause that makes the Optimizer say, "Okay, if you want that, I'll do it, but I'll have to do it the hard way: without the index." Rules are rules!

Just to prepare you and to keep the Optimizer on your side, the following sections describe a list of conditions under which the Optimizer can't use an index, even when one is available.

Do you have an index?

Whenever a query is slow, make sure that the indexes you expect to exist actually exist. You can look at your indexes in the Schema Manager.

All your indexes are listed under the Indexes folder in the Schema Manager. To sort the list by table, simply click the Table column in the right frame after you see your list of indexes.

After you verify that the indexes exist, your next step is to verify that the query actually uses the indexes. The following sections explore the ways in which a WHERE clause can be your downfall, starting with the most common situation first.

The infamous null value and the index

When you create an index, the null value is not indexed (except when you're using the bitmap type of index). Any row in which the indexed column contains a null value is not included in the index. Even in cases in which the index has multiple columns, the row is not included in the index if all those columns contain a null value. The bitmap type of index does include rows with null values in the index. But this type of index is quite unusual, and I don't cover it here.

In Figure 18-11, for example, I built an index on the DEATH_DATE column of the FISH table. The five rows containing nulls in the DEATH_DATE column can't be indexed. The other rows that contain data are indexed.

What does this mean to you? *When you write a query that checks for nulls in a column, an index on the column does not increase your performance.*

Figure 18-11:
Two of these
rows are
indexed, and
five are not.

NAME_OF_	AQUARIUM_	BIRTH_DATE	DEATH_DATE	COLORS	BREED
Fish Two	Fishtank	01-Jan-99 12:00:00 AM	15-Mar-99 12:00:00 AM	black and tan	guppy
Fish Three	Fishtank	01-Jan-99 12:00:00 AM	08-Apr-99 12:00:00 AM	red and white	guppy
Fish Four	Fishtank	01-Mar-99 12:00:00 AM		transparent	guppy
Wesley	Fishtank	01-Jan-98 12:00:00 AM		gold	shark
Jerryskids	BigDrink	01-Jan-98 12:00:00 AM		multicolor	clownfish
Zoe	BigDrink	14-Feb-99 12:00:00 AM		black	molly
Ginger	BigDrink	12-Mar-99 12:00:00 AM		white and black	damselfi

Table Editor - "AMY"."FISH"

Apply   Revert   Show SQL   Close   Help

Wildcards can throw everything off

When a query contains a wildcard (%) that appears at the beginning of the word that you're searching for, the Optimizer can't use the index. The Optimizer goes through the table one row at a time.

Looking at the PERSON table with an index on LAST_NAME, you have to look for any person whose last name has SMITH in it. To find hyphenated last names like ADAM-SMITH, you use a wildcard (%). Your query may look like this:

```
SELECT * FROM PERSON
WHERE LAST_NAME LIKE '%SMITH';
```

The Optimizer will not use the index because the index does not help speed up the query. The Optimizer reads each row's LAST_NAME column. It checks for SMITH anywhere inside the column. Then it either chooses or eliminates that row and proceeds to the next one that is physically adjacent to it.

Sometimes, you can't avoid this kind of query. Just remember that the wild-card can slow the query.

When the wildcard appears elsewhere in the string, the Optimizer can some-times use the index. The index is available if the Optimizer needs it in this example query:

```
SELECT * FROM PERSON
WHERE LAST_NAME LIKE 'J%';
```

The logically illogical order of data

Imagine that you store all the records for your pet store's fish in your data-base table. As you purchase new fish, you enter them in the table called FISH. Each fish is identified by a unique name. Oracle8i stores rows sequen-tially as you enter them. One day, you put in three fish named Jerryskids, Ginger, and Zoe. You know that Oracle8i always indexes the primary key (the fish name), so you assume that Oracle8i always displays data in primary key order unless told otherwise. You write and run this SQL query, which lists everything in your FISH table:

```
SELECT * FROM FISH;
```

To your surprise, when you query the table, the events come out in the order in which you entered them, not in alphabetical order, as you see here:

```
NAME_OF_FISH BREED
------------ -----
Fish Two     guppy
Fish Three   guppy
Fish Four    guppy
Wesley       guppy
Jerryskids   Clownfish
Zoe          Molly
Ginger       Damselfish
7 rows selected.
```

What went wrong? You know that an index exists on the NAME_OF_FISH
column, but the Oracle8i Optimizer doesn't use it because it has no reference
to the NAME_OF_FISH column in the WHERE clause. In fact, no WHERE clause
exists at all. For alphabetical results, add an ORDER BY clause to your SQL
query, telling Oracle8i to sort all the data by NAME_OF_FISH. The ORDER BY
clause, like the WHERE clause, is evaluated by the Optimizer. The Optimizer
looks in the ORDER BY clause for indexed columns that the Optimizer can use
to speed up the query. Your fast-running, tuned, and in-order query looks like
this:

```
SELECT NAME_OF_FISH, BREED
FROM FISH
ORDER BY NAME_OF_FISH;
```

Oracle8i returns this response:

```
NAME_OF_FISH BREED
------------ -----
Fish Four    guppy
Fish Three   guppy
Fish Two     guppy
Ginger       Damselfish
Jerryskids   Clownfish
Wesley       guppy
Zoe          Molly
7 rows selected.
```

Adding an index to a table does not actually reorder the data in the table
(except when you've created an index-organized table). Oracle8i saves a
great deal of time by leaving the data alone and building an index that contains only indexed columns and row IDs. Oracle8i sorts the index for fast
retrieval. When the Optimizer finds part of the WHERE clause or the ORDER BY
clause in a query that refers to an indexed column, the Optimizer uses the
index to get data faster. The Optimizer narrows down the number of rows to
retrieve from the actual table by using the indexed data to eliminate rows.
For example, if the index contains the column FIRST_NAME, and the WHERE
clause contains the phrase WHERE FIRST_NAME = 'Joe', then the Optimizer
finds rows in the index that contain 'Joe' in the FIRST_NAME column and then
continues to execute the query using only this subset of rows.

Chapter 19

Correcting Flaws

● ●

In This Chapter

▶ Making changes in columns

▶ Saving data before a change

▶ Restoring data after a change

▶ Adding and rearranging columns

▶ Cleaning out your closets

● ●

*O*ften, you create tables as you develop your plans, which is called the prototype (or "wing it!") method. You may want to read this chapter when you notice an error — such as a column that has the wrong datatype — just after you finish creating a table. Another time that you may scurry to these pages is when you have a table or *schema* (set of tables) that you want to update with more tables and additions. As the old swami sez: "Whatever the reason, now is the time to change things!"

Categories of Column Changes

You can *attempt* to make two kinds of changes in a table: the kind that you can make and the kind that you can't make. Oracle8i has rules about what parts of a table you can change. So if you need to change part of a table and Oracle8i says "Not!", you can get around the rule only by dropping the table and then re-creating it.

You can make three types of changes to your table structure:

▸ **Easy.** Some changes require a single step, using the Schema Manager.

▸ **Medium.** Other changes are possible only if you save all your original column data, empty out the original table's column data, make the change to the table, and then restore the data.

▸ **Hard.** Some kinds of table structure changes require you to completely rebuild your table and all the relationships it has.

Table 19-1 shows the breakdown of table changes by category. Each of these categories has its own section in the chapter, so look here for the change that you want to make and then head to the appropriate section for the details on how to do it.

Table 19-1	Categories of Changes to Table Structure	
Easy	*Medium*	*Hard*
Shorten column (column has nulls in all rows)	Shorten column (column has data in some rows)	Remove a column
Lengthen column		Reorder columns
Add column at end of table		Add column in middle of table
Change NOT NULL to NULL (column can't be primary key)		Rename a column
Change NULL to NOT NULL (column has data in all rows)	Change NULL to NOT NULL (column has nulls in some rows)	
Change datatype of column (column has nulls in all rows)	Change datatype of column (column has data in some rows)	

This chapter covers all these kinds of changes. Enjoy! On top of that, at the end of the chapter, you find out how to change object tables. As they always say, "Nothing is constant in this world except change." Anyone who can accurately prove to me just who "they" are gets a free copy of my next book, *Godlike Alterations of the Time/Space Continuum For Dummies.*

To make the easiest changes, which have no restrictions (the first column in Table 19-1), requires a single step using the Schema Manager or SQL. To make the more difficult changes, which have some restrictions (the second column in Table 19-1), requires using a combination of SQL and the Schema Manager. To make the most difficult changes (the third column in Table 19-1) requires undoing and redoing your entire table. These kinds of changes take many steps, especially after you've added foreign keys, indexes, and data to your table.

Baby Bear: Easy as Porridge

This section shows you how to make the easiest changes in your existing tables. You can make these changes any time, regardless of what data is in the column that you plan to change. You can freely make these kinds of changes:

 ✔ Lengthening the size of a column

 ✔ Changing a column to allow nulls

 ✔ Adding a new column at the end of the table

You can also make the following changes, in certain circumstances, without any additional steps:

 ✔ Shortening the size of a column, if the column contains no data

 ✔ Changing the datatype of a column, if the column contains no data

 ✔ Changing the column from allowing nulls to not allowing nulls, if data appears in every row in this column

In these cases, you must review the data in your table. How many rows of data you have doesn't matter; nor does what all the other columns of data contain. Focus on the column that you want to change. Look at the data in that column in every row of your table. If every single row has nulls in that column, you can go ahead and shorten the size or change the datatype of the column. If even one row contains data, you can't make the change without first doing something to that row of data. See the section "Mama Bear: A Few Medium Steps," later in this chapter, for information on how to fix the data so that you can make the change.

Everything that you change in the table structure is changed in the table property page. To get to the table property page and start making changes, follow these steps:

1. **Start the Schema Manager.**

   If you have your LaunchPad open, choose the Schema Manager from the DB: Administration menu. Otherwise, on Windows 95, 98, or NT, choose Start⇨Programs⇨Oracle HOME2⇨DBA Management Pack⇨ Schema Manager.

   On UNIX, type **oemapp schema** on the command line.

   If you come to a login window, proceed to Step 2. Otherwise, skip to Step 3.

2. **Log in as a DBA and select the radio button labeled Connect Directly to a Database.**

   SYSTEM is a built-in user name that comes with every Oracle8i database; the default password for SYSTEM is MANAGER. Use this user name and password or type in the user name and password of any valid Oracle8i user with DBA privileges. Leave the Service box blank to reach your PC's database or type in the instance name of the Oracle8i database on your network. Leave the Connect As box set to the default of Normal.

3. **Click the plus sign next to the Table folder in the left frame.**

   A list of schemas appears below the folder.

4. **Open the schema's list of tables by clicking the plus sign next to the schema that owns the table you want to change.**

   A list of tables owned by that schema appears.

5. **Select the table that needs fixing.**

   A properties page for the table appears in the right frame. In Figure 19-1, I selected the AMY schema and the SEAWEED_SAMPLE table.

6. **Type in any changes that you want to make to the table.**

   To change a column length, for example, type in the length that you want.

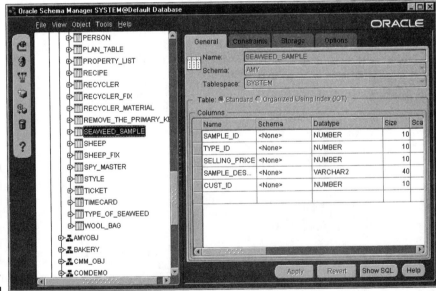

Figure 19-1: Getting ready to modify a table in Schema Manager.

7. **Click the Apply button when you're done.**

   Schema Manager makes the change. As long as you don't see an error message, you can be sure that the change took place. (No news is good news.)

   If you get an error message after you click the Apply button, you probably tried to change a column in a way that has other restrictions, as noted in Table 19-1. For example, you may have tried to change the size of a column from 20 characters to 10 characters. If the table has data in the column that you tried to change, you get an error message. Read the error message carefully to determine what's wrong. You may have to resort to the Mama Bear approach, discussed in the next section.

Mama Bear: A Few Medium Steps

Don't ask me why. Oh, go ahead and ask. *Reply hazy; ask again later.* Whatever the reason, Oracle8i has nitpicky rules about making changes in the column attributes. My own theory is that these rules came about because of the space-saving conventions that Oracle8i uses when it stores table definitions and data. Shuffling the order of columns is more difficult when they're arranged in compact, abbreviated forms. Just a theory, really.

You can make some changes only when no data exists in the column. In other words, for every row in the table, that column's data is null. These changes are

✔ Making a column shorter

✔ Changing the datatype

One type of change is just the opposite. Every row *must have data* in the column for changing to NOT NULL.

The next two sections show you how to handle cases in which your data just doesn't fit into the restrictions.

If the column must be null . . .

Changes that require every row in the table to have a null value include

✔ Making a column shorter

✔ Changing the datatype

If any row of your table has data in the column that you're about to change, you can't make the change right away. You must first eliminate the data in this column for all the rows in your table. If you use Schema Manager to try to make the change without fixing the data, you get an error message, stating the problem. This error message may be similar to these messages:

```
ORA-01439: column to be modified must be empty
to change datatype
ORA-01441: column to be modified must be empty
to decrease column length
```

Your two choices for fixing the data are

- ✔ **Get rid of it.** Think about it. Do you really need that data? Maybe the data is just test data anyway and isn't worth the hassle of saving. Maybe just retyping it later is faster.
- ✔ **Preserve it.** Often, your data is actually valuable, and you should preserve it. In the "Saving the data" section later in this chapter, I show you how to preserve your data and still make the change that you want to make.

Throwing out the data

Congratulations — you've decided that you don't need the data in your column after all. In this case, you can run the SQL command that removes the data quickly.

Before running the following SQL command, make sure that you don't need the data in the column you're updating.

The general format for removing all data from a column is

```
UPDATE tablename SET columnname = NULL;
```

Replace `tablename` and `columnname` with the actual table and column that you're working on.

For example, this SQL command changes all the data in the `SELLING_PRICE` column of the `SEAWEED_SAMPLE` table:

```
UPDATE SEAWEED_SAMPLE SET SELLING_PRICE = NULL;
```

By the way, if you change your mind after running this command, issue a `ROLLBACK` command:

```
ROLLBACK;
```

The ROLLBACK command restores the data. But remember that it works only during your current SQL session and only if you haven't issued any DDL commands. A DDL (Data Definition Language) command is any command that creates, modifies, or removes a database object such as a table or index. For example, the ALTER TABLE command is a DDL command.

Saving the data

Many times, you may want to keep your data. In these cases, you can use SQL*Plus Worksheet to save your data in a table that you create just for that purpose. Then you make your change and put the data back in the table. Start SQL*Plus Worksheet and follow along with this example.

1. **Start the SQL*Plus Worksheet.**

   If you have your LaunchPad open, choose the SQL*Plus Worksheet from the DB: Administration menu. Otherwise, on Windows 95, 98, or NT, select Start⇨Programs⇨Oracle HOME2⇨DBA Management Pack⇨ SQL*Plus Worksheet.

   On UNIX, type **oemapp worksheet** on the command line.

   If you come to a login window, go to Step 2. Otherwise, you're ready to go.

2. **Log in as the owner of the table that you're changing with a valid Oracle8i user name and password.**

   If you have installed the sample schema included on the CD-ROM, log in as AMY with password AMY123. Leave the Service box empty if you are running your own personal Oracle8i; otherwise, fill in the name of the Oracle8i database (instance) on your network. Leave the Connect As box set to Normal.

You use a table called DAILY_SALES to track your total sales each day. You decide to shorten the maximum size of the SALES_AMOUNT column from 10 digits to 8 digits. Because you have good data in the table, you definitely want to save the data. Before you adjust the column size, you use SQL*Plus Worksheet to create a holding table for the data. The holding table contains only two things: the primary-key column (or columns) and the column that you want to change.

You create the holding table by using this SQL code:

```
CREATE TABLE HOLD_SALES AS
SELECT SALES_DATE, SALES_AMOUNT
FROM DAILY_SALES;
```

Oracle8i responds

```
Table created.
```

Next, you remove the data from the original table's SALES_AMOUNT column, as follows:

```
UPDATE DAILY_SALES SET SALES_AMOUNT = NULL;
```

Oracle8i complies and says

```
10 rows updated.
```

Now you can modify the column size. Here is the SQL code for making the change:

```
ALTER TABLE STORE_STOCK MODIFY (SALE_PRICE NUMBER(8,2));
```

If you prefer, you can return to Schema Manager and make the table change by following the Baby Bear steps in the section "Baby Bear: Easy as Porridge," earlier in this chapter.

Finally, you copy the data back into the newly modified column, as follows:

```
UPDATE DAILY_SALES  DS_NEW
SET SALES_AMOUNT =
 (SELECT SALES_AMOUNT FROM HOLD_STORE_STOCK DS_OLD
  WHERE  DS_OLD.SALES_DATE = DS_NEW.SALES_DATE);
```

Oracle8i matches up the SALES_DATE primary-key columns and then copies the data back to the correct row in the original table.

The last task to complete is minor but important: Remove the holding table that you created. Here's the SQL command:

```
DROP TABLE HOLD_STORE_STOCK;
```

You've completed the task. Congratulations! Well done.

Before you go to all this trouble, make sure that the data is worth saving. This project is like cleaning out your closet. As you remove all the stuff from your closet, you notice how much of it you don't really want or can't squeeze into anyway. Don't waste time saving data that is old or incomplete or that you haven't been able to fit into since high school; send it off to the Salvation Army thrift store for someone else to enjoy.

Column must not have nulls

The second kind of restricted column change requires that every row have some data in the column that you want to change. Only one change falls into this category: changing a column constraint from null values allowed to null values not allowed. Every row in the table must comply with this new constraint. In other words, all the rows need data in the column that you want to change. If any of the column's rows include nulls, you get an error message like the one shown here, which informs you that you can't change the column:

```
ORA-02296: cannot enable ... null values found.
```

What do you do if you have null values in this column? Decide what to put in each row that contains nulls and then update the rows with the value. You must use SQL*Plus Worksheet or SQL*Plus to run the SQL statement that plugs in a default value for every null value.

A simple option that may work for you is plugging a standard default value into every row that has null in the column. Here is an example:

```
UPDATE MONTHLY_SALES
SET MANAGER_NAME = 'HARRY'
WHERE MANAGER_NAME IS NULL;
```

You can update your column any way that you want. You can use any valid update command, including those update commands with subqueries and correlated subqueries. Use your head.

After you fill in the default data, you can go back to the "Baby Bear: Easy as Porridge" section and make your table changes. Easy as porridge.

Papa Bear: A Lotta Steps

These changes are the hardest kind to do. Changes in which you must restructure your table include

- Removing a column
- Renaming a column
- Adding a column in the middle
- Reordering columns

Oracle8i's great storage efficiency and retrieval speed come at a cost: Changing certain parts of a table structure can be laborious. Here's what you do when you actually need to make these kinds of changes:

1. **Copy the table, including the data, to a new table. (Skip this step if the table contains no data or if you can throw out the data permanently.)**

2. **Remove the table.**

3. **Rebuild the table, incorporating the changes.**

4. Copy the data from the copied table that you created in Step 1 to the rebuilt table. (Skip this step if you skipped Step 1.)

5. Re-create all the indexes, foreign-key constraints, and table privileges.

How do you perform the preceding tasks? Glad you asked. Watch closely as I perform magical feats with Schema Manager. Unfortunately, you can't perform all the steps inside Schema Manager — you have to use plain SQL (in SQL*Plus Worksheet) to copy data from the old table to the new table.

Whenever you work in Schema Manager, click the Show SQL button and look at the SQL code that is generated; doing this is the easy way to familiarize yourself with SQL. Plus, you can cut and paste the code into a file that can be used to do the same task in SQL. You can also use the File⇨Save Input As menu selection to save your work.

Now you're ready to embark on a multistep journey to restructure all the known intergalactic time-space continuum. Well, you restructure a table for starters.

Danger, Will Robinson! One of the numbered steps later in this section removes a table from the database. When you remove a table, you also remove three other important database elements:

✔ Any indexes that you created for the table; they must be re-created.

✔ Any foreign keys in other tables that refer to this table's primary key.

✔ Any privileges that you gave for the table; they must be redone.

Be certain that you have either SQL scripts or some written record of these items so that you can re-create them with either SQL or Security and Schema Managers. If you're certain that you know what you need to restore afterward, proceed with the following steps. Otherwise, go do your homework and return to this page when you're ready.

To restructure a table by using Schema Manager, follow these steps:

1. Start the Schema Manager.

If you have your LaunchPad open, choose the Schema Manager from the DB: Administration menu. Otherwise, on Windows 95, 98, or NT, select Start⇨Programs⇨Oracle HOME2⇨DBA Management Pack⇨ Schema Manager.

On UNIX, type **oemapp schema** on the command line:

If you come to a login window, proceed to Step 2. Otherwise, skip to Step 3.

2. Log in as a DBA and select the radio button labeled Connect Directly to a Database.

SYSTEM is another built-in user name that comes with every Oracle8i database; the default password for SYSTEM is MANAGER. Use this user name and password or type in the user name and password of any valid Oracle8i user with DBA privileges. Leave the Service box blank to reach your PC's database or type in the instance name of the Oracle8i database on your network. Leave the Connect As box set to Normal.

3. Click the plus sign next to the Table folder in the left frame.

A list of schemas appears below the folder.

4. Click the plus sign next to the schema that owns the table that you want to change.

You see a list of tables owned by that schema.

5. Click the table that needs restructuring.

A properties window for the table appears in the right frame. If you want to follow the example, select the CONTACT_LIST table in the AMY schema. Figure 19-2 shows the table property page.

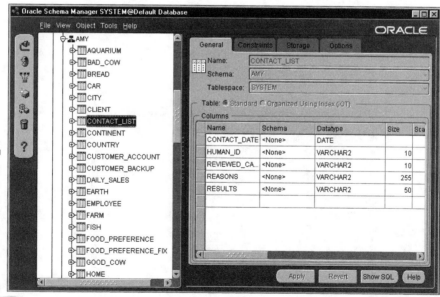

Figure 19-2: Prepare to modify a table by displaying the table property page.

6. Click the Create Like button.

This button is located between the green cube and the garbage can icons. It looks like a wire-frame box behind a green cube. If you place your mouse on this icon without clicking, a little box pops up and displays Create Like. After clicking this button, the Create Table properties box, shown in Figure 19-3, appears.

7. Fill in a valid Oracle8i name in the Name box.

Select a valid Oracle8i name, preferably with the word `HOLD` in it. For the example, call your copy of the `CONTACT_LIST` table `CONTACT_LIST_HOLD`. The Schema and Tablespace boxes should already have valid choices.

8. Click the Constraints tab.

Schema Manager automatically creates the constraints but replaces their original names with `<System Assigned>`. This setting means that when you create the table, Oracle8i automatically assigns a unique name to each constraint.

9. Click the Create button.

Schema Manager automatically creates the table and the constraints and says

```
Table created successfully.
```

New table name

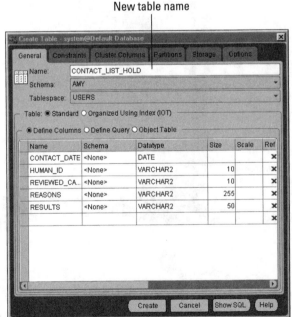

Figure 19-3:
The Create Table properties box is ready.

Then the Schema Manager returns you to the original window where the table is on the left and the property window is on the right.

If your table is empty (no rows) or if the data is expendable, skip to Step 11. Otherwise, continue to Step 10 to preserve your data.

10. **Log in to SQL*Plus Worksheet and copy the data into the new table.**

    For example, use this SQL to copy the CONTACT_LIST data into the CONTACT_LIST_HOLD table:

    ```
    INSERT INTO CONTACT LIST HOLD
    SELECT * FROM CONTACT_LIST;
    ```

    Save your changes by issuing the COMMIT command:

    ```
    COMMIT;
    ```

11. **Back in Schema Manager, select the original table and then click the Remove button to remove the old table.**

    Be sure that you're looking at the original table that you want to remove. For the example, click the CONTACT_LIST table and then choose Object⇨Remove from the main menu. Schema Manager opens a window, double-checking whether you really want to remove the table.

12. **Verify the table name to be removed and click Yes.**

    Make sure that the table you drop is the one that you intend to drop. *You can't undo this action.* After you remove the table, Schema Manager returns to its main window.

13. **Click the new table's name in the left frame to select it.**

    In the example, you just finished creating CONTACT_LIST_HOLD, so click CONTACT_LIST_HOLD. The familiar table properties window appears again in the right frame.

14. **Click the Create Like button.**

    Clicking this button begins the process of rebuilding your original table. The Create Table property page appears.

15. **Type the old table name in the Name box.**

    You're about to create the table that you removed, so first type the old table's name. For the example, type CONTACT_LIST because that table is the one that you removed in Steps 11 and 12.

16. **In the Create Table box, make adjustments in the columns, as needed. You can add new columns, change or move the columns that you see, and remove columns.**

    To remove a column:

1. **Click the gray box just to the left of the name of the column that you want to remove.**

   The entire column's attributes are highlighted.

2. **Right-click.**

   A shortcut menu appears.

3. **Select Delete.**

   The column disappears.

To add a column between two existing columns:

1. **Click the gray box just to the left of the name of the column that's sitting where you want to add a column.**

   The entire column's attributes are highlighted.

2. **Right-click.**

   A shortcut menu appears.

3. **Select Insert Above or Insert Below to open a new row, in which you can specify the new column's attributes.**

To change a column, simply type over the existing attributes.

To add a column at the end, simply begin typing in the open row below the last column.

For the example, add a new column called `REVIEWED_BY` after the column `REVIEWED_CASE`. Also change the length of the `RESULTS` column to 250 characters. Figure 19-4 shows the final appearance of the revised `CONTACT_LIST` table.

17. **Click the Constraints tab.**

    The list of constraints that you copied from your original table appear. The names are standard names that Oracle8i uses.

18. **Make adjustments in the constraints, as needed. If you made changes in any of the columns involved in the constraints, verify that the constraints are still valid.**

    You may want to rename the constraints to conform with your own naming standards. If not, just allow the system to create the names for you.

19. **Click the Create button.**

    Schema Manager whirs away and creates your new table, returning you this message:

```
Table successfully created.
```

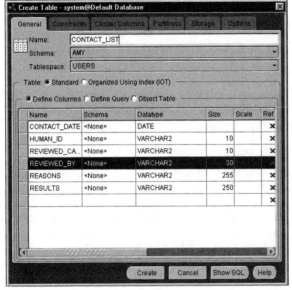

Figure 19-4:
Changes are
relatively
easy at this
point in
the table
creation
process.

Now you have a new table. If your old table contained data that you
need to put back in the new table, continue to the next step. If your table
was empty, or if you prefer to eliminate all the data that you had in your
old table, skip to Step 21.

20. Go back to the SQL*Plus Worksheet and copy the data from the holding table to the new table.

The SQL*Plus Worksheet command is an insert command with a subquery. The actual command that you use depends on what you changed.
If you added a new column, for example, you either exclude the new
column from the insert command or include it by adding a default literal
value in the query. You can use any valid query here as your subquery.
An example of an insert command is

```
INSERT INTO CONTACT_LIST
SELECT CONTACT_DATE, HUMAN_ID, REVIEWED_CASE,
'AMY'. REASONS. RESULTS
FROM CONTACT_LIST_HOLD;
```

In the preceding example, notice two things. First, I have no column list
of new columns, which is allowed when you can match the entire list of
columns exactly and in order in your subquery. Second, I added a literal,
'AMY', in place of a column name in the subquery; this means that every
row that is inserted has 'AMY' in the new REVIEWED_BY column. Run
your command by clicking the Execute button.

Save your changes by issuing the COMMIT command:

```
COMMIT;
```

Close the SQL*Plus Worksheet by clicking the X in the top-right corner.

21. Return to the Schema Manager.

22. Re-create any foreign-key references in other tables.

23. Re-create any additional indexes.

24. Remove the holding table by clicking the table that you created in Step 9 and then choosing Object⇨Remove from the main menu.

Schema Manager displays a window to verify your choice.

25. Verify the table name and click Yes.

You've completed the final steps of restructuring your table.

Finished! You've restructured your table just as you like it. This kind of change is difficult to do and requires careful attention to detail. Good job!

Now, for a real treat, read on to take a look at object tables.

Modification of Object Tables in Schema Manager

Here you have an interesting problem. When you make an object table, you identify what object type is to be used for each row in the object table. The attributes that you see when you look at the table in Schema Manager are actually the attributes of the object type.

The only changes to the attributes that you can make to the object table are

- Changing from NULL to NOT NULL
- Adding a default value
- Adding constraints, such as primary-key or check constraints

You handle these changes exactly the same way that you do with relational tables, so you can follow the directions in the previous sections of this chapter. Refer to Chapter 18 for details on how to create a primary key.

To add insult to injury, you can't modify an object type if it's being used by an object table. In fact, if the object type is used in another object type or in a table type or array type, you can't modify the object type. Oracle8i apparently has very high expectations for those of you who venture into the object side of this object-relational database. If you attempt to change the object type, you get this error message:

```
ORA-02303: cannot drop or replace a type with type or table
           dependents
```

For now, just be aware that all you can do is play your entire creation script
in reverse, make the changes to the object types as needed, and then fast forward to restore.

Seriously, you're going to work really hard if you need to modify an object
type after you've used it and entered data in the object table. You can get
some help from the table properties window in the Schema Manager. Here
you can see the object type used to create the object table. To view this
window, follow these steps:

1. **Start the Schema Manager.**

   If you have your LaunchPad open, choose the Schema Manager from the
   DB: Administration menu. Otherwise, on Windows 95, 98, or NT, select
   Start⇨Programs⇨Oracle HOME2⇨DBA Management Pack⇨
   Schema Manager.

   On UNIX, type **oemapp schema** on the command line.

   If you come to a login window, proceed to Step 2. Otherwise, skip to Step 3.

2. **Log in as a DBA and choose the radio button labeled Connect Directly
   to a Database.**

   SYSTEM is a built-in user name that comes with every Oracle8i database, and its default password is MANAGER. Use this user name and
   password or type in the user name and password of any valid Oracle8i
   user with DBA privileges. Leave the Service box blank to reach your PC's
   database or type in the instance name of the Oracle8i database on your
   network. Leave the Connect As box set to the default of Normal.

3. **Click the plus sign next to the Tables folder in the left frame.**

   A list of schemas appears below the folder.

4. **Click the plus sign next to the schema that owns the table that you
   want to change.**

   You see a list of tables owned by that schema.

5. **Click the table that you're interested in.**

   A properties window for the table appears in the right frame. For my
   example, I selected the BREAD_OBJECT_TABLE table in the BAKERY
   schema. Figure 19-5 shows the properties window. Notice that if you
   peer intently at the window, you can just make out the object type that
   defines the object table rows.

Object type

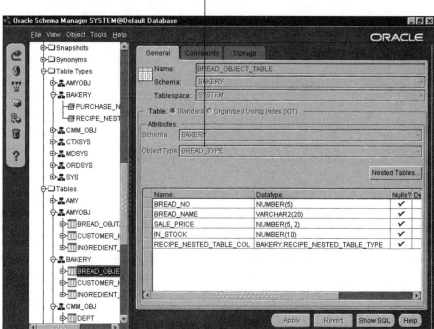

As for actually modifying an object type, after you remove all the dependencies, you can modify the object type in its properties window in Schema Manager. See Chapter 11 for details because you follow nearly the same process that you do when you create a new object type.

I'm sure that the Oracle8i development team is toiling through their weekends to fix this problem and allow some sort of change management for objects. You should see it in the next release or two. Maybe. I wouldn't bet the farm, but anything's possible, right?

Part V
The Part of Tens

The 5th Wave   By Rich Tennant

"THIS SECURITY PROGRAM WILL RESPOND TO THREE THINGS: AN INCORRECT ACCESS CODE, AN INAPPROPRIATE FILE REQUEST, OR SOMETIMES A CRAZY HUNCH THAT MAYBE YOU'RE JUST ANOTHER SLIME-BALL WITH MISAPPROPRIATION OF SECURED DATA ON HIS MIND."

In this part . . .

This is my favorite part. Here are a couple of short and sweet chapters, each containing ten gold-encrusted jewels for your treasure chest of Oracle8i know-how. You'll leave this section with a trick up your sleeve for every occasion. Have fun! I did!

Chapter 20

Ten Tips for Good Design

In This Chapter

▶ Naming tables with a flair

▶ Jumping to conclusions with prototypes

▶ Throwing caution to the wind and building a prototype

▶ Exchanging information with other Oracle users

▶ Maintaining and changing keys

▶ Exercising caution in changing table structures

▶ Exploring derived data columns

▶ Perusing the security options

▶ Using test data

▶ Talking with other humans

*I*n this chapter, I share some useful ideas that may lighten your load when you sit down to create an Oracle8i database schema of your own. Then again, I guess that sitting down already sort of lightens your load, huh? These ideas save you time and make the task of convincing your boss that you know what you're doing easier. If you tear out this chapter of the book, you look even smarter.

Name Tables and Columns Creatively and Clearly

What kind of silly person made up the rules about naming Oracle8i tables, columns, and so on? Probably Scott and his cat, Tiger, who prowl the bowels of every Oracle8i database from here to Mars, had something to do with the rules. Refer to Chapter 2 to see the naming rules spelled out in detail. When you know the rules, you can create names as you see fit.

The best way to annoy your own brain is to name tables and columns incon-
sistently. Imagine that you own a real estate business. Figure 20-1 shows two
of the tables that you use. One of the tables, called HOME, has a column in
which you enter a short description of the house. You call the column
HOME_DESC. Another table, called LAND, has a column in which you enter a
description of the land, which you call LAND_DESCR. You have abbreviated
description two different ways: DESC and DESCR.

Figure 20-1:
The pitfall of
naming
columns
inconsis-
tently is that
you must
memorize
everything.

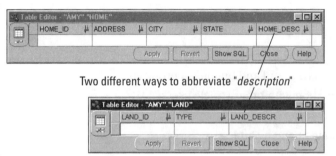

Two different ways to abbreviate "*description*"

A month later, you write a query using the LAND table and type LAND_DESC by
mistake. Because you weren't consistent in the way you abbreviated *description,* you need to look up the exact column name.

You multiply this problem each time you add another table designer to your
company's team of designers. Each person has a personal style for naming
columns, tables, indexes, and so on. Soon, you have to keep a list by your
side that contains every table and every column, just to keep all the names
straight.

Make sure that you establish a naming standard to share with the group.
Establish clear and concise naming standards for tables, columns, indexes,
primary keys, foreign keys, synonyms, views, and roles so that others can
quickly understand your table design. Decide ahead of time what abbreviations and acronyms you plan to use; then be consistent. Don't hesitate to use
force, threats, bribes, or name-calling to make your team members see things
your way.

Get creative in your names so that they truly describe their real-life counter-
parts. Your LAND table, for example, has a column called TYPE, as shown in
Figure 20-2. What does that name mean? Type of what? Land? Soil?
Vegetation? Perhaps it means the type of selling contract or type of parcel.

A table and its columns are much like a filing drawer. Have you ever tried
valiantly to find a letter that you know you filed but can't recall which folder
you filed it in? Perhaps you asked your spouse to get a paper from your desk

Figure 20-2:
What type
of type is
this type?
Not my type,
anyway.

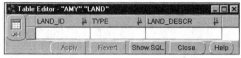

drawer or file drawer at home, but you had a hard time describing exactly where you wanted your spouse to look, even though you could clearly visualize the place. The more intuitively you name your tables and columns, the better.

Here's another example of how not to name columns. This problem crops up even in commercial databases; it appears when a table evolves to handle a more diverse amount of data than you originally designed it to hold. Often, one column becomes obsolete, and you need a new column. Rather than create a new column, you recycle the old column, using it for new data. What you get is a single column containing a mixture of data. A column named MANUFACTURER, for example, initially stored only manufacturers' names, but now it also stores distributors' names. You have no way of telling whether you're looking at the name of a manufacturer or a distributor.

Look Before You Leap (Design Before You Build)

I find that a little planning goes a long way. Grasping the big picture of your database project may seem overwhelming. Even so, no matter how big the project appears to be, when you have a vision for it and can see that vision as a whole in your mind, you're better equipped to create the product. I don't mean that you have to know how you'll build the database; you can figure out the details as you go along. I mean that you need to picture the final product. What will it look like on the computer screen? Who will use it and how? How good will getting it done right feel? Who on your team is helping you? Would you like French fries with that?

Envisioning the final product this way may seem silly, but from my own personal experience gained from years of designing and leading database projects, doing so really works. Fixing a vision of the result in some tangible way (how it feels, looks, and sounds) can smooth out the process tremendously. Vision is critical. Conveying your vision to others is also critical.

Go Ahead, Leap! (Build a Prototype)

Building a prototype has become standard operating procedure these days for projects large and small. A *prototype* is a small working model of the product. The prototype may actually work on a small scale, or it may be a simulation. With an Oracle8i database, you can easily build the actual tables that you plan to use. By adding only 10 or 20 rows to your tables, you can experiment with queries, relationships, reports, or online screens built with Oracle Forms or other software.

If you're on your own using Oracle8i, not much stands in the way of experimenting. In a larger organization, you may have some ground rules to follow. Plan your prototype and include these critical portions of your project in the prototype:

- **Bottlenecks.** Bottlenecks are the parts that can slow you, such as converting data from an old database.

- **Popular features.** Include the features that you know people are excited about. People have heard so much about Oracle8i and all of its cool special features. One feature that many projects include is a table, or group of tables, for creating mailing labels.

- **A little of everything.** Add a small portion of your entire plan. Incorporating small parts of your plan helps you refine the prototype so that when you're ready to create the real thing, you have valuable experience under your belt.

Don't be afraid to throw out the entire prototype. The beauty of a prototype is its disposability. Put a small amount of time and effort into a prototype so that if you go down the wrong road, you don't lose too much time and energy. You can create another prototype. You can create two more prototypes. Ideally, you're paid by the hour.

Share — Don't Reinvent the Wheel

Share information, share ideas, share your fears, and share your new red bike. Tell others that you'll even share your *Oracle8i For Dummies* book with them and then go buy several copies of the book to share. Remember that others have gone down the same path that you're travelling, unless you're really on the cutting edge. People usually are proud to share with you what they know. Don't be afraid to ask for help.

Meeting with your co-workers can bring you a fresh perspective that helps speed up your design and development time.

A great resource is the International Oracle Users Group. The International Oracle Users Group – Americas (IOUG-A) is an independent, not-for-profit organization of users of Oracle products and services. The group's goal is to help you, the Oracle8i user, create great databases with Oracle8i. The IOUG-A publishes a newsletter and holds meetings across the country. A European branch of the group also exists.

Remember that Primary Keys Are Your Friends

Primary keys form a core for your tables. Foreign keys contain primary keys from other tables. Primary keys are among the few pieces of data that you must carry in multiple tables. You can retrieve all the other data in a row from a table when you know the primary key.

The size and intelligence of primary keys help you streamline tables. The primary key should be small and stupid (not intelligent), which sounds really strange, especially to my single friends. "Small and stupid?" they ask. "That was my last date!" Allow me to explain why primary keys should be small and stupid.

Small keys take up less room

Any column that holds a four-digit number takes up less space than a column that holds 20 characters. This obvious fact is magnified when the column is a primary key. People almost always copy primary keys to other tables as foreign keys. The more rows that you have in the second table (the one with the foreign key), the more space that you use. Saving 16 characters in several thousand rows may seem insignificant at first, but it does make a difference.

Nonintelligent keys are easy to maintain

An _intelligent key_ (as opposed to a nonintelligent key) is a column or set of columns that you use as the primary key for a table and at the same time use to store meaningful data. (My musician husband suggests B-flat minor.)

A nonintelligent key is a column, or set of columns, whose sole purpose is to be the primary key for the table. (Definitely C major.) The advantage of using a nonintelligent key as the primary key in your table lies in its stability. No matter what happens to the data in that row, the data in the primary key remains the same. This advantage is magnified as soon as you duplicate the primary key in the foreign key of another table.

Two important arguments exist against using an intelligent key as the primary key for your table:

✔ The data that you place in this type of key can and does change over time. You must always change any foreign key that uses this primary key to match. This can change a simple single row update into a cascading update involving several rows in many tables.

✔ If you define a primary-key constraint (which you should do) on your primary-key column(s), Oracle8i's rules don't allow an update to the primary-key column(s). An intelligent key tends to need updates, so you're out of luck. You must go through some major hoop-jumping to update that key.

What is an intelligent key, anyway? An *intelligent key* is a primary key that has meaning for the row of data.

You, as self-proclaimed ruler of the universe, have a table called HUMAN that tracks this tiny corner of your domain. This table helps you locate your subjects and call them on your cellular phone. The primary key, HUMAN_ID, is a unique identifier that you create for your subjects. This key is an intelligent key because it contains information about the person rather than a simple sequential number. HUMAN_ID has two parts: a code number that identifies the town that a person lives in and a sequential number assigned when you hand out the person's ID card. The sequential number is not unique by itself but is unique within the town.

Figure 20-3 shows the table with example rows. The figure also shows how two other tables, CONTACT_LIST and PROPERTY_LIST, connect with the HUMAN table. These tables have foreign keys that reference the HUMAN table's primary key. Now you have an intelligent key replicated as a foreign key in two tables. This setup seems fine until something happens that causes you to reconsider your choice of the intelligent key. Read on — the suspense thickens.

One day, a subject moves to another town. You forgot to impose a law preventing this sort of nonconformist act. Now the primary key (the intelligent key) contains the wrong town code, so you need to change the key to keep the data in your table accurate. You assign the person a brand-new HUMAN_ID with the correct town code and a new sequential number. You print a new ID card for your loyal but mobile subject and then go about modifying your data.

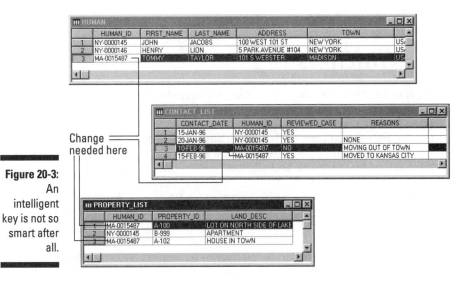

Change needed here

Figure 20-3:
An intelligent key is not so smart after all.

First, you update the HUMAN table with the change in the primary-key column for this person. Next, you change all the rows of data in the CONTACT_LIST and PROPERTY_LIST tables that are connected to this person so that they reflect the new correction in the primary key. Finally, just to be sure that you remember what you did, you create a new table called ID_HISTORY, which tracks the changes in HUMAN_ID as people move from town to town. What a lot of work!

The problem with intelligent keys crops up when all or part of the information in a key changes. Updating a primary key causes a ripple effect that requires more work, time, and effort to maintain. There must be a better way! There is: nonintelligent keys. Nonintelligent keys are much easier to manage.

Imagine the same scenario, but this time, you generate unique sequential numbers for subjects as you sign them up. The number that you assign to a person has no significance to that subject. If he or she moves to a new town, the primary key (nonintelligent key) stays the same. If the subject gets married and changes his or her name, the key stays the same. If the subject gets a promotion for all that incredible work designing databases, the key stays the same. This means that you don't need to change any of the related tables, such as CONTACT_LIST and PROPERTY_LIST.

Presto and voilà — small and nonintelligent make a great combination for primary keys.

Use Caution When Modifying Table Definitions

Remember last Christmas Eve when you were determined to peek at your presents under the tree? You sneaked down the stairs and cleverly pried open the corner of the wrapping paper on your biggest present. Having seen the big secret, you went off to bed feeling smug. The next morning, however, the excitement of the day seemed to be spoiled. The climax of opening that big box had lost its thrill. You can never undo the knowledge once you have it.

Similarly, you can't easily undo changes that you make in a table's structure. Changing a column name requires a series of tedious and time-consuming steps.

When you make table structure changes that require you to remove and re-create the table, you need to remove and re-create all the foreign keys in every table that relates to the table that you change. You may need to run a report first to be sure that you catch all the foreign keys.

Handle Derived Data Efficiently

Derived data is any data that exists as an extrapolation from other data. A column contains derived data, just as it contains any other data. The difference is simply that the source of the data in the column is some kind of manipulation of the data in other columns. If you add the subtotal and the tax, for example, you derive the total sale. The easiest way for me to explain derived data is to show you an example.

You track daily sales totals in your DAILY_SALES table. You create a new table called MONTHLY_SALES so that you can compare monthly totals quickly. I show the two tables in Figure 20-4.

The SALES_AMOUNT column in the MONTHLY_SALES table is derived data. Oracle8i arrives at the figure in the MONTHLY_SALES table by using the data in the SALES_AMOUNT column of the DAILY_SALES table. Here's the SQL code that calculates SALES_AMOUNT for the month of February 1996 and places the amount in the MONTHLY_SALES table:

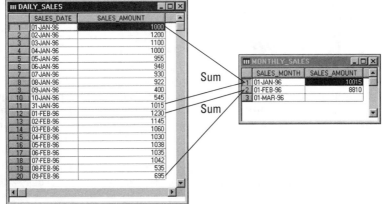

Figure 20-4:
Derived
data can
derive you
crazy.

```
UPDATE MONTHLY_SALES SET SALES_AMOUNT =
(SELECT SUM(SALES_AMOUNT)
 FROM DAILY_SALES
 WHERE SALES_DATE BETWEEN '01-FEB-96' AND '28-FEB-96')
WHERE SALES_MONTH = '01-FEB-96';
```

This example illustrates data that you derive by summarizing data in many rows of a table. Derived data can also be calculated within a row; one example is a person's age, which you calculate from a birth date. Another form of derived data results from comparing data in two columns. An example is a column that indicates when a bank account is below its established minimum balance. In all these cases, you can always re-create the value that you store in a column of derived data by redoing the calculation or comparison.

Derived data has a tendency to become outdated quickly. In the preceding example, the monthly total for the current month changes daily. Should you recalculate the monthly total every day? Once a week? Only at the end of the month? You decide and then delegate the task, because it's a pain in the you-know-where.

I recommend that you avoid storing derived data unless you find it necessary to improve performance. You can always use SQL code to calculate the total sales for a month. You don't need to store the results in a table to have them readily available. You can create a view that does the calculation, or you can do the calculation whenever you print a report.

Approach Security Roles in Practical Ways

A million opinions exist on how to handle security for databases. I have the million-and-first opinion. I developed my practical method on the job over many years, and I offer it for your consideration. I hope that my method helps you sort out a good strategy to use for your unique situation. Security concerns vary greatly, depending on these factors:

- **The number of people who use your database.** The more people who use the database, the more likely that someone will try accessing data that he or she isn't authorized to access.

- **The kinds of people who are allowed in your database.** If you allow every Tom, Dick, and Harry who's surfing the Net to drop in for a visit to your database, you definitely want to protect your data. If, on the other hand, your database is for employees only, your security risk is much smaller.

- **The location of people who use your database.** With the huge growth of the Internet, distributed work forces are using databases across the Internet. You may need secure connections across the Internet.

- **The kind of data in your database.** Data that you must keep private needs tight security. Bank and government information, for example, may need this kind of high security.

Low security

If you run Oracle8i on your PC, you need not worry about security. The roles that Oracle8i automatically sets up for you are adequate.

Medium security

The medium-security approach works well for the average internal corporate database, and it even works if the public has limited access to the database. The following breakdown of roles makes a practical, easy-to-manage security plan:

- **Shared Read-Only role.** This role can see all the tables but can't modify any data. Every Oracle8i user ID is assigned this role when the user ID is created. In some cases, a simple Oracle8i name (such as READONLY) and an easy-to-remember password (such as PASSGO) are set up for everyone who doesn't have his or her own private Oracle8i user ID.

✔ **General roles.** These roles correspond with a broad area of the database, such as an entire schema. For example, a schema and a set of online data-entry screens are created to support the personnel department. A general role called PERSONNEL has update privileges on all the tables in the schema. Each person in the accounting department gets assigned to this role. Another department, such as sales, may have its own schema and its own role.

High security

I describe some forms of high security in this section, but they are not, by any means, the limit of high security. This section just gives you an idea of how you can use the same basic techniques and achieve a higher level of security.

Here are two typical ways to add more security to your database system.

✔ **Theme-based roles.** These roles mirror job responsibilities in the real world. The roles have authority to change tables according to the duties of the people in each role. For example, you may call one role ACTUARY. A person given this role can review insurance claims and assign risk factors to the claimants. The ACTUARY role has update authority on tables that relate to these tasks.

✔ **Unique IDs for everyone.** Another feature of high security involves assigning a unique Oracle8i user ID to every person, which allows for better auditing trails in the data. For example, you might add columns to tables that record who changed the row last or who created the row. Using unique IDs goes hand in hand with the theme-based roles. You assign each user ID the appropriate role or roles for the user's job. The roles limit each user's ability to modify data, and the unique IDs let you trace who is modifying the data.

When you assign unique Oracle8i user IDs, you hand your database administrator (DBA) a great deal of work. If the DBA is unable to add or revoke roles quickly, you may find yourself with a security issue. I recommend creating SQL routines that can help automate adding and revoking roles in an accurate and timely manner.

Be Smart about Test Data

Test data is a set of fake rows of data. The purpose of test data is to verify the schema that you designed and any queries, screens, or other fancy finagling that you intend to use with your data. Most people fail to use test data because it is boring and seems like a waste of time. First, you have to create all the test data yourself; then you have to use it for a while. The final step is getting rid of the test data so that it doesn't get confused with real data.

Why would anyone ever want to use test data? Some good reasons to take the time and care to create and use test data exist. Test data allows you to create a controlled environment for experimenting and exercising your queries and SQL commands. The benefits of using test data are as follows:

- ✔ You control the data and, therefore, can predict and verify the results of queries and other SQL commands.

- ✔ You work with a smaller set of data compared with real-life data. I limit test data to a small number of rows (10 or 20 usually are enough) in each table.

- ✔ You don't have to worry about destroying actual data when trying new SQL commands, screens, or other changes.

If you choose to create and use test data, remember these pointers about Oracle8i:

- ✔ Oracle8i's ROLLBACK command in SQL*Plus Worksheet can speed up testing because the command gives you a fast way to restore data to its original state. The ROLLBACK command undoes inserts, updates, and deletions to all tables as far back as the last time you used the COMMIT command or when you logged on.

- ✔ Another fast way to get back to your starting point with test data is to use EXP and IMP. After you create the test data, use EXP to make a copy of all the tables. After you run SQL commands or use online screens to experiment with changes in the data, you may want to restore everything to its original state. Use IMP to bring back all your original data. Refer to Chapter 16 for a description of the EXP and IMP commands.

Talk to Non-Techie-Type Humans

Ricky Ricardo, talking about a neighbor's dog, says, "Oh, she doesn't mind sleeping in the yard. She's used to it."

Lucy, talking about the neighbor's wife, says, "Well, if that's the way he treats her, I don't blame her for going home to mother!"

A misunderstanding like this one can sometimes creep into an otherwise solid design. I once worked on a project in which everyone misinterpreted the word *grantee* for months. I was halfway through the project, after hundreds of hours of work, before an outsider made an offhand comment about *grantee.* Upon hearing the comment, I realized that I had designed part of the system incorrectly.

Make sure that you take your design for a walk to meet the people in your neighborhood. Sometimes, getting feedback from other people helps you improve your design and saves you a great deal of time and trouble down the road. At other times, you wind up scooping up a lot of you-know-what.

Chapter 21

Ten Handy Oracle8i Features

In This Chapter

▶ Awesome assistants

▶ Nifty network tools

▶ A swell SQL script

*O*kay, folks, here's what you've been waiting for: ten fun features that you may want to explore with Oracle8i. The last item is actually my own contribution: a SQL script to make your scripting life more interesting. All but a few of these tools come as standard features with your Oracle8i Enterprise Server.

ConText Cartridge

Cartridges are like mini-applications; they plug into your Oracle8i database and provide additional functionality that you can incorporate into your own applications. Watch for many more cartridges on the market, especially in the area of Internet connectivity and network computing. Cartridges that you add to your basic Oracle8i Enterprise Server usually cost a little (and sometimes cost a lot); they range from $200 to $10,000.

The ConText cartridge adds special search capabilities to the database. With ConText, you can set up intelligent searching based on themes. Themes help you search for words that are *related* to the keyword instead of that exact word. If you set up a theme called REAL ESTATE, for example, your database knows how to search for any text containing words related to REAL ESTATE, such as *house, home, realtor, realty, escrow, rental, land*, and *property*.

After ConText is set up, you can use SQL to query your database with ConText's special commands.

ConText has a linguistics attachment that can interpret forms of English words, such as plurals, verb structures, and so on. The ConText cartridge is one of the more expensive cartridges, running about $10,000.

Network Computer Architecture

The concept of the network computer has sprouted from a seed to a full flower in the past year. Oracle has partnered with other heavyweight companies to deliver software and hardware that supports the network-computer concept. A *network computer* (NC) is an inexpensive computer that connects with the Internet and has built-in features for browsing the World Wide Web and transacting business in a secure, private format. Some NCs hook up to your television set; others have their own small display screens.

The concept of the small, portable, yet personalized computer that you can use to browse the Internet has extended into the realm of software with Oracle's Network Computer Architecture (NCA). The NCA provides an environment for developing software applications especially for the Internet and the network computer. Some of the software that Oracle and its development partners have created for the network computer include the following:

- ✔ **Data Warehousing Tool:** Delivers data in its native format, such as Microsoft Word documents or Excel spreadsheets.
- ✔ **Internet Commerce Server:** A software suite that helps businesses build a complete Internet-based shopping service. Using templates, a business sets up its storefront, which is available on the Internet. Look online at `http://ntsolutions.oracle.com/products/ics/index.htm` for more on this product.
- ✔ **Media Server:** Image analysis and comparison tools that can plug into other applications.
- ✔ **Online Training:** Online training system based on the Internet and NC.
- ✔ **Virtual Worlds:** VRML (Virtual Reality Modeling Language) combined with a database to create all kinds of interesting business applications.

Web Assistant

The Web Assistant is a nice little wizard that sets up reports in HTML format. You give the wizard information such as this:

- ✔ The table that you want to display or a query that you want to use.
- ✔ A template for the Web page (background color, text color, headings, and so on).
- ✔ The frequency with which to refresh the Web page. If you want, you can refresh the Web page every few minutes.

To use the wizard, start it and follow along with its easy-to-use screens. If you're using Windows NT, start the program by choosing Start⇔Programs⇔ Oracle for Windows NT⇔Oracle Web Publishing Assistant; then follow along. Producing an actual Web page with data from your database takes only a few minutes. The wizard generates reports only, so you can't change your data-base's data from the Web with this assistant.

Migration Assistant for Access

This nifty tool comes with your Oracle8i application. This assistant helps you gather up your Access database and move it into Oracle8i. You can migrate just the database structure, or you can include all your data as well. Migration Assistant can even set up your old Access forms so that they run using the new Oracle8i tables instead of Access tables. During the migration process, you can make changes in column names and other structures, if you want.

To start the assistant from Windows NT, choose Start⇔Programs⇔ Oracle for Windows NT⇔Oracle Migration Assistant for MS Access. Then follow along with the little butterfly that guides you through the process.

Data Migration Assistant

The Data Migration Assistant helps you migrate Oracle7 or Oracle8 data into your new Oracle8i database. This program is especially built for migrating Oracle7 databases of Version 7.1 and later into the production release of Oracle8i. To start the assistant, follow these steps:

1. **Make sure that SQL*Net Version 2.0 or later is installed on your system.**

2. **Make sure that the Oracle7 or Oracle8 database is seen by SQL*Net.**

3. **Start the assistant.**

   If you're running Windows 95, 98, or NT, choose Start⇔Programs⇔ Oracle Home⇔Migration Utilities⇔Oracle Data Migration Assistant.

4. **Follow the prompts to migrate your database.**

That's all there is to it. Time to relax and enjoy the weekend.

File Packager

Now here's an interesting toy. The File Packager starts up a wizard, called the Product Wizard. The Product Wizard guides you through the process of transforming your database application into an installable package that the Oracle Installer can then use to install your application on other machines. Use this wizard if you want to create something to use on many distributed Oracle systems.

To run File Packager in Windows 95, 98, and NT, choose Start⇨Programs⇨ Oracle for Windows NT⇨Oracle File Packager.

Database Configuration Assistant

This wizard helps you create or delete an entire Oracle database. Database Assistant gives you a choice of which version of the database to create and allows you to customize your initial database parameters as well.

To run the wizard from Windows 95, 98, or NT, choose Start⇨Programs⇨ Oracle HOME⇨Database Administration⇨Oracle Database Assistant.

Net8

Net8, which is the newest version of SQL*Net, comes with its own assistant — the Oracle Net8 Assistant — to help you set up your configuration. The older SQL*Net had a utility called Easy Configuration. Net8 has its own version, called Net8 Easy Config. If you use the Net8 Assistant, however, you don't really need the Net8 Easy Config tool. The assistant has a built-in utility that goes hunting on your network for installations of Oracle — it sniffs them out for you.

Another feature that is new for Net8 is the Oracle Security Server. It adds special security features to all your network traffic — everything that is transmitted between two Net8 nodes. The Security Server uses cryptography across your network and requires users to enter a valid user name and password. The Server keeps track of which users are allowed to access which Oracle8i databases.

Oracle even has its own version of a firewall for protection across the Internet. The software is called the Connection Manager. You tell Connection Manager what IP addresses are allowed to access your database. Pretty cool stuff.

To start the Net8 Assistant in Windows 95, 98, or NT, choose Start⇨
Programs⇨Oracle HOME⇨Network Administration⇨Oracle Net8 Assistant.

Performance Monitor

The Performance Monitor watches activity on your database system. You can
see whether CPU usage reaches a peak during the day, for example, and
watch the I/O activity on database files. This monitor is best used by experi-
enced systems managers because it has graphs, line charts, histograms, and
other interesting (if indecipherable) tools.

To run Performance Monitor from Windows NT, choose Start⇨Programs⇨
Oracle HOME⇨Database Administration⇨Oracle for Windows NT
Performance Monitor.

Sniffing Out and Mending
Broken Relationships

Most relationships wither away from sheer neglect. Perhaps you didn't tell
your lover "I love you" often enough. Sniff, sniff. Perhaps you never got
around to implementing the foreign-key constraints in the database. Now
your tables have plenty of new data added, and you want to verify that the
foreign-key relationships are valid. You also want to find any records in which
problems lie. You must find any rows that contain invalid foreign-key values.

In general terms, the following SQL query finds all the rows in a table that
have an invalid value in the foreign-key column. Here's the generic SQL code:

```
SELECT key_column, fk_column
FROM fk_tablename
WHERE NOT EXISTS (SELECT 'X' FROM pk_tablename
WHERE fk_tablename.fk_column = pk_tablename.pk_column);
```

In the preceding SQL code, the column and table names mean the following:

  ✔ key_column: The primary-key column of the table that you're validating
    (the one with the foreign key)

  ✔ fk_column: The foreign-key column that you are validating

  ✔ fk_tablename: The name of the table that you are validating

✔ pk_tablename: The name of the table that is the parent of the foreign key you're checking

✔ pk_column: The primary key that matches the foreign key in the fk_tablename table

If your foreign key contains two columns, here is the general pattern (the same pattern applies for foreign keys that have three or more columns):

```
SELECT key_column1, key_column2, fk_column1, fk_column2
FROM fk_tablename
WHERE NOT EXISTS (SELECT 'X' FROM pk_tablename
WHERE fk_tablename.fk_column1 = pk_tablename.pk_column1
 AND fk_tablename.fk_column2 = pk_tablename.pk_column2);
```

You can make two choices to correct your data when a foreign key is invalid:

✔ Change the data in the foreign key.

✔ Add a new row in the referenced table.

Here's the SQL code for the first choice, which changes the data in the foreign key. This UPDATE command changes all the mismatched foreign-key data to one valid value. You type the valid value in the command in place of 'valid fk value'.

```
UPDATE fk_tablename SET fk_column = 'valid fk value'
WHERE NOT EXISTS (SELECT 'X' FROM pk_tablename
WHERE fk_tablename.fk_column = pk_tablename.pk_column);
```

You may instead want to update the foreign key to be a null value. In this case, you use NULL after the equal sign. The second choice is to add a new row to the referenced table. You do this with the INSERT command, which inserts a row into the referenced parent table. Refer to Chapter 3 for step-by-step instructions on inserting rows into tables by using SQL*Plus Worksheet or Schema Manager.

Part VI
Appendixes

The 5th Wave   By Rich Tennant

In this part . . .

No book, not even this fantastic book in your hands, can cover everything!

Appendix A has a very helpful glossary that explains database related jargon.

Appendix B helps you get up and running with the CD-ROM that comes with this book.

Appendix A

Glossary

• •

alias: A nickname or alternative name for a table or column that is used in SQL.

attribute: A feature or characteristic. For example, the datatype and size of a column are two of the column's attributes.

authentication, external: This form of authentication allows the user to pass into the database using his or her identity from the operating system. To log in to SQL*Plus or some application, you simply type a slash where you normally enter your Oracle8i user ID and password.

authentication, global: This form of authentication was new in Version 8 of Oracle. Intended for use across distributed database systems, this method requires authentication to be done outside the database using the Oracle Security Service (OSS). It lets you use a common user ID and password to reach any database in your distributed network of databases.

authentication, password: This is the traditional method of authentication where the user must type in a password to enter a database transaction.

block: A unit of storage for data and other information in the database.

Cartesian join: An unconditional join between two tables that results in a match between every row in one table and every row in another table.

column: A component of a database table. A column contains the definition of what kinds of data are to be collected and stored in the rows of the table.

comma-delimited file: A format for extracting data out of a database and placing it into a plain text file. Each line in the file contains one row and each column is separated from the following column by a comma.

commit: To permanently save all changes since the last commit was done to the database.

constraint: A rule applied to a table or a column that restricts the data that is allowed in any row in the table. For example, a primary key constraint defines the primary key for a table. All rows must have unique values in the columns included in the primary key constraint.

correlated sub-query: A sub-query that has references to the outer query.

DBA: The database administrator.

database engine: The set of programs that runs the database, keeping track of all the information, monitoring usage, checking security, checking for errors, and so on.

datatype: Defines the type of information that can be stored, such as dates, numbers, or characters.

derived data: Data that can be calculated, summarized, or otherwise extracted entirely from other data in the database.

entity: A table or group of tables. Used interchangeably with *table* in this book.

Entity Relationship Diagram: A style of drawing a relational database model that uses boxes, text, lines, and a few simple symbols to represent the entities and relationships in the model.

explicit data conversion: The user controls conversion of a column or expression from one datatype into another. The data conversion thus happens in a predictable manner. See also *implicit data conversion*.

export: Oracle8i utility to pull data out of the database into a file. The file is in a special format for use only with the Oracle8i import utility. Also used to refer to the act of using the export utility.

expression: A column, a literal, or a column with some function applied to it, such as addition. In SQL queries, expressions can be used almost anywhere a column can be used.

field: See *column*.

foreign key: The primary key of a reference table that is stored inside another table. The foreign key connects the two tables. It allows access to all the information stored in both tables without repeating data from either table, other than the key column.

fragmented table: A table that contains wasted space in the form of empty blocks and chained blocks.

full table scan: One of several choices of table access that the Oracle8i optimizer uses. This type of access requires the optimizer to read each row in the entire table. A full table scan is similar to starting at the 100s on the library shelf and reading every book label until you find the book you want.

GB: Gigabyte. Approximately one million bytes.

GRANT: SQL command for adding security privileges on a table, view, or synonym.

hierarchy: A relationship of tables where a parent table has a child table and that child table has its own child table and so on.

HTML: HyperText Markup Language. The primary language used to create Web pages. HTML consists of normal text and special codes, called *tags,* which tell a Web browser how to display the text. Tags determine the size of the font, color of the background, and other formatting details.

implicit data conversion: Oracle8i converts a column or expression from one datatype into another using its own internal logic. This function is unpredictable and subject to change with new releases. See also ***explicit data conversion***.

import: Oracle8i utility to bring data into the database from a file. The file must be in a special format created by using the export utility. Also used to refer to the act of using the import utility.

incremental space: In a table definition, the amount of space reserved if the table runs out of room and needs more space. The same amount of space is reserved again if the table again needs more space until the table hits the maximum space limitation.

initial space: In a table definition, this parameter sets the starting size of the table.

INSERT: A command to add a new row into a table.

instance: A single complete Oracle database. Each instance has its own name, number, and initialization parameters. Multiple instances can run on one computer.

intelligent key: An intelligent key is a primary key that has meaning for the row of data.

interactive: Any process where the computer asks for information from the user and then acts on it.

Internet: A global, public network of computers linked together with telephone lines and network software. See also ***World Wide Web***.

intranet: A network of computers connected via phone or cable lines that is inside one organization for internal use only.

join: A type of query in which two or more tables are connected, or *joined,* together.

key: A column or set of columns in a table that identifies a unique row of data. See also *primary key* and *foreign key.*

legacy system: A set of tables (schema) that have been brought into your Oracle8i system from an older source, such as Oracle7, or another database system.

literal: A word or phrase, number, or letter that is used at its face value (exactly as it is written) in a query or in a SQL*Plus command. A literal is always surrounded by single quotes.

local database: A database that resides on the computer the user is logged in to.

logical operator: A connection between two columns or expressions in a WHERE clause. Examples are: = (equal), <> (not equal), like, between, < (less than), > (greater than).

Management Pack: The Management Pack is a new term used for add-on components for the Enterprise Manager. The DBA Management Pack is simply a rebundling of the primary database tools that were included in prior versions of Enterprise Manager.

method: A self-contained bit of programming code that travels with an object, delivering parts or modifying data according to the method code.

non-intelligent key: A key that is unique and does not change, even when information in the row changes. A sequential ID number is an example of a non-intelligent key.

Null: Unknown or missing. A row can be created in a table without all the columns filled in. Columns where no data has been entered are defined as containing a *null value.*

object-relational database: A database that combines features of a relational database with features of an object-oriented database. Oracle8i is an object-relational database.

object table: A table whose rows are defined by an object type rather than explicit columns. The elements within the object type define what data is stored in the object table.

object type: Enables you to extend the definition of datatypes (classes of data) into customized *user-defined datatypes.* Oracle calls these special datatypes *object types.*

object view: An *object view* maps relational tables into an object table. Like relational views, the object view doesn't actually have data of its own; it's merely a way of looking at the underlying tables. The object view allows you to use existing relational tables in an object-oriented way.

objects: Things in a database or groups of things that stand on their own. For example, a table is an object but a row is not an object.

optimizer: An internal part of the Oracle8i database engine that determines the fastest access path for any given SQL command.

overhead: Information about tables, columns, rows, indexes, and other structures in the database.

owner: The user who creates a table.

package: A database program consisting of one or more procedures. A package executes when called using SQL or a programming language interface.

primary key: A column or set of columns in one table that uniquely identifies each row in the table. Every row in a table has a value in the primary key that is different from that of every other row in that table.

private synonym: A synonym that can only be used by the synonym creator, unless the creator grants privileges to others.

procedure: A database program that contains PL/SQL commands. A procedure can be contained within a package or can stand alone. A procedure executes when called using SQL or a programming language interface.

pseudocolumn: A column defined by Oracle8i that you can use in a query. For example, USER is a pseudocolumn that always contains the Oracle8i user ID of the current user.

public synonym: A synonym created by a database administrator (DBA) that can be used by anyone.

query: A question posed in SQL to look at data in the database.

record: See *row*.

relational database: A collection of tables connected together in a series of relationships so that they model some small part of the real world.

remote database: A database that does not reside on the computer the user is logged in to.

reorganize: To rebuild the internal physical structure of a table by dropping it and re-creating it. Data must be removed and restored using export and import.

REVOKE: A SQL command for removing security privileges.

role: A set of privileges that can be assigned to or removed from a user.

ROLLBACK: A command that removes all changes since the last commit was done.

row: A component of a database table. It contains the actual data, compartmentalized in columns.

row ID: A pseudocolumn that contains the exact physical address of a row. Retrieving a table row using its row ID is the fastest method available.

schema: Everything created by a single user ID in Oracle8i (tables, grants, roles, indexes, relationships, and objects).

script: A file that contains more than just a single SQL or SQL*Plus command.

SQL: Structured Query Language (SQL) is an English-like set of commands for defining database objects and querying and modifying data in those objects.

synonym: An alternate name for a table or view. Synonyms can be private (for use only by their creator) or public (for use by any user).

table: A set of related columns and rows in a relational database.

tablespace: A portion of the database that Oracle8i reserves for your tables. One database can have many tablespaces and each tablespace may contain many tables, indexes, procedures, or other objects. Each tablespace is mapped to one or more physical files.

third normal form: A set of rules specifying how tables and columns in a relational database relate to one another.

tree diagram: See *Entity Relationship Diagram*.

user: A unique login name in Oracle8i. A user's capabilities inside the database are determined by the user's role assignments.

user ID: See *user*.

view: A query that is named in the database so that it can be used as if it were a table. Views can be used anywhere tables can be used, except there are some restrictions on adding, removing, or changing rows from views that join tables.

Web page: A screen of data, graphics, music, and so on, that appears on the World Wide Web (Internet) or on an intranet. This is a general term referring to any document on the Web. It may be an order entry form, a database report, a video, a text document, or any number of other possibilities. The length of one page is totally flexible, and the document contains HTML tags.

World Wide Web: A portion of the Internet dedicated to documents in the HTML format. The Web, as it is often known, is a versatile, colorful, and highly interactive area.

Appendix B

About the CD

● ●

*T*he CD-ROM contains several sets of sample schemas and SQL examples from the book. It also contains some useful shareware and trial software that you may want to try.

Sample Schemas

The three schemas used in the book for examples are:

- ✔ AMY. This schema contains typical relational database tables, indexes, primary keys, and foreign keys. I use the AMY schema tables in many chapters of the book. Mermaid seaweed collections, bread recipes, farms, omnipotent rulers, and more are in these tables.

- ✔ AMYOBJ. This schema has a set of CREATE statements that incrementally build a set of object types and object tables. AMYOBJ is featured in Chapter 11, where you build the schema piece by piece. You are creating a set of object tables to save your secret bread recipes and data about your customers.

- ✔ BAKERY. The Perfect Bakery is your home business where you use object tables that include a varray, a nested table, and other interesting object types to save information about recipes, ingredients, and your precious clientele. This schema is featured in Chapter 4. It is very similar to the AMYOBJ schema but is completed by running a single SQL script instead of being built up from several scripts.

All the schemas are built with SQL scripts contained in the Make directory of the CD-ROM. Here are instructions for building each schema.

Build the AMY schema

To create the AMY user and install all the tables and data into the schema, follow these steps:

1. **Start up SQL*Plus Worksheet.**

   If you are running on NT or Windows 95 or Windows 98, select Start⇨Programs⇨Oracle HOME2⇨DBA Management Tools⇨ SQL*Plus Worksheet. A login window appears.

   On UNIX, type this command at the operating system prompt:

   ```
   oemapp worksheet
   ```

2. **Log in as a valid Oracle DBA.**

   The default user name and password of the Oracle8i DBA are SYSTEM and MANAGER. Leave the Connect box empty if you are running your own personal copy of Oracle8i. Otherwise, fill in the name of the Oracle8i instance on your network. Leave the Connect As box defaulted to Normal. The SQL*Plus Worksheet window appears.

3. **Open the AMY.sql SQL script.**

   The script is in the Make directory on the CD-ROM. Place the CD-ROM in your CD-ROM drive. To open the file in SQL*Plus Worksheet, click File⇨Open in the menu. A window opens in which you can locate your CD-ROM drive and then open the Make directory and select the file named AMY.sql. Click Open, and you will see the script in the upper window of SQL*Plus Worksheet.

4. **Adjust the `CONNECT` command if needed.**

   A few lines into the script is the following line:

   ```
   CONNECT AMY/AMY123;
   ```

   This line only works if you run Oracle8i on your own computer. If you are running on a networked database, modify the line to include your network node name for the Oracle8i database. For example, if my network node was named "sharpies," the command would be

   ```
   CONNECT AMY/AMY123@sharpies;
   ```

5. **Run the script.**

   Click the Execute button (the lightning bolt). The script runs in the lower window of SQL*Plus Worksheet and sends feedback frequently:

   ```
   Statement completed.
   ```

6. **Exit SQL*Plus Worksheet by clicking the X in the top right corner.**

Done! You now have lots of sample data to play with.

Create the AMYOBJ schema

You create this schema and all its objects step by step if you follow the
instructions in Chapter 11. If you want to create the schema yourself without
going through Chapter 11, follow these steps:

1. **Start up SQL*Plus Worksheet.**

   If you are running on NT or Windows 95 or Windows 98, select
   Start➪Programs➪Oracle HOME2➪DBA Management Tools➪
   SQL*Plus Worksheet. A login window appears.

   On UNIX, type this command at the operating system prompt:

   ```
   oemapp worksheet
   ```

2. **Log in as a valid Oracle DBA.**

   The default user name and password of the Oracle8i DBA are SYSTEM
   and MANAGER. Leave the Connect box empty if you are running your
   own personal copy of Oracle8i. Otherwise, fill in the name of the
   Oracle8i instance on your network. Leave the Connect As box defaulted
   to Normal. The SQL*Plus Worksheet window appears.

3. **Open the AMYOBJ_user.sql SQL script.**

   The script is in the Make directory on the CD-ROM. Place the CD-ROM in
   your CD-ROM drive. To open the file in SQL*Plus Worksheet, click
   File➪Open in the menu. A window opens in which you can locate your
   CD-ROM drive and then open the Make directory and select the file
   named AMYOBJ_user.sql. Click Open, and the script appears in the
   upper window of SQL*Plus Worksheet.

4. **Run the script.**

   Click the Execute button (the lightning bolt). The script runs in the
   lower window of SQL*Plus Worksheet and sends feedback:

   ```
   Statement completed.
   ```

5. **Connect to the AMYOBJ user.**

   Type the following line into the top window of SQL*Plus Worksheet:

   ```
   CONNECT AMYOBJ/AMYOBJ;
   ```

   This line only works if you run Oracle8i on your own computer. If you
   are running on a networked database, modify the line to include your
   network node name for the Oracle8i database. For example, if my network node was named "sharpies", the command would be

   ```
   CONNECT AMYOBJ/AMYOBJ@sharpies;
   ```

6. **Run these scripts in order.**

Make sure the CD-ROM is in your CD-ROM drive.

For each of the scripts listed here, click the Worksheet⇨Run script selection from the menu. Then locate the script file name in the Make directory of the CD-ROM. This selection automatically reads and executes the SQL script in the each file. The file names are:

- **AMYOBJ_object_types.sql**
- **AMYOBJ_table_type.sql**
- **AMYOBJ_array_type.sql**
- **AMYOBJ_object_tables.sql**
- **AMYOBJ_hybrid_table.sql**

Each script runs in the lower window of SQL*Plus Worksheet and sends feedback frequently:

```
Statement completed.
```

7. **Exit SQL*Plus Worksheet by clicking the X in the top right corner.**

Done! You have witnessed the creation of object types and object tables.

Create the BAKERY schema

This schema is very similar to the AMYOBJ schema in the previous section, except that it also loads data into the final object tables, varray, nested table, and hybrid table. Follow these steps to create everything in the BAKERY schema.

1. **Start up SQL*Plus Worksheet.**

If you are running on NT or Windows 95 or Windows 98, select Start⇨Programs⇨Oracle HOME2⇨DBA Management Tools⇨ SQL*Plus Worksheet. A login window appears.

On UNIX, type this command at the operating system prompt:

```
oemapp worksheet
```

2. **Log in as a valid Oracle DBA.**

The default user name and password of the Oracle8i DBA are SYSTEM and MANAGER. Leave the Connect box empty if you are running your own personal copy of Oracle8i. Otherwise, fill in the name of the Oracle8i instance on your network. Leave the Connect As box set to the default of Normal. The SQL*Plus Worksheet window appears.

3. **Open the BAKERY.sql SQL script.**

The script is in the Make directory on the CD-ROM. Place the CD-ROM in your CD-ROM drive. To open the file in SQL*Plus Worksheet, click File⇨Open in the menu. A window opens in which you can locate your CD-ROM drive and then open the Make directory and select the file named BAKERY.sql. Click Open, and the script appears in the upper window of SQL*Plus Worksheet.

4. **Adjust the `CONNECT` command if needed.**

A few lines into the script is the following line:

```
CONNECT BAKERY/BAKERY;
```

This line only works if you run Oracle8i on your own computer. If you are running on a networked database, modify the line to include your network node name for the Oracle8i database. For example, if my network node was named "sharpies", the command would be

```
CONNECT BAKERY/BAKERY@sharpies;
```

5. **Run the script.**

Click the Execute button (the lightning bolt). The script runs in the lower window of SQL*Plus Worksheet and sends feedback frequently:

```
Statement completed.
```

6. **Exit SQL*Plus Worksheet by clicking the X in the top right corner.**

Now you can play with a complete set of object tables!

Sample SQL Scripts

Many of the chapters contain short SQL statements as examples. You can run these yourself if you have installed the AMY and the BAKERY schemas, as I describe in the "Sample Schemas" section earlier in this appendix. The CD-ROM contains example SQL statements for some of the chapters. I have included the SQL statements that are kind of long to type out. Table B-1 lists all the scripts in the CD-ROM and where to find them.

Table B-1		Sample SQL Statements	
Chapter	*Directory*	*File*	*Description*
4	Chapter04	bakeryselect nestedtable.sql	Query a nested table
4	Chapter04	BAKERYDELETE NESTEDTABLE.SQL	Delete one row from a nested table
4	Chapter04	BAKERYSELECT VARRAY.SQL	Query a varray
4	Chapter04	bakeryupdate nestedtable.sql	Update a nested table
15	Chapter15	javarecipe costfunction.sql	Create Java stored procedure
17	Chapter17	mode.sql	SQL query with optimizer hint
17	Chapter17	table_stats.sql	Gather statistics for one table
18	Chapter18	create_plan _table.sql	Create table for explain plan command
18	Chapter18	explain_query_w_ mixed_datatypes.sql	Sample of explain plan; query uses mixture of datatypes
18	Chapter18	explain_query_with_ function.sql	Sample of explain plan; query has a function
18	Chapter18	explain_query_with_ nulls.sql	Sample of explain plan; query has nulls
18	Chapter18	query_with_nulls.sql	Query where indexed data contains nulls

Additional Software

The CD-ROM contains some bonus software that I selected from the hundreds of sample and trial programs available on the Web. Try some of these out!

SQL tools from Quest Software

✔ **TOAD:** Despite its lowly name, TOAD is the editing tool of choice for many Oracle developers. TOAD stands for Tool for Oracle Application Developers. It may be a prince in disguise. This is a 30-day trial copy.

To find out more about TOAD, check out the product's Web site: `http://www.quests.com/toad/toad_info.html`.

✔ **SQLNavigator:** Here's a good-looking development tool for writing SQL and PL/SQL. It has built-in syntax help, color-coded keywords, a new reporting tool, and sample code to use. This is a trial version.

To find out more about SQLNavigator, check out Quest's Web site: `http://www.quests.com`.

✔ **SQLab Xpert:** This tool is especially for the DBA in you. Use it to help you tune SQL statements like a pro.

To find out more about SQLab Xpert, check out Quest's Web site at `http://www.quests.com`.

There is an install routine in the QUEST folder that gives you a choice of programs. Double-click SETUP.BAT to start this routine. In this little interface, there's also a link to check on product updates with Quest and a link to Quest's home page.

Web design tools from Allaire Corporation

✔ **HomeSite 4.0:** This evaluation version of the award-winning Web page designer is yours to try. I, for one, am always looking for a better HTML editor. Try this one on me.

To find out more about HomeSite, check out the Web site at `http://www.allaire.com/Products/HomeSite/`.

✔ **ColdFusion Studio 4.0 for Windows:** If you want to see other options in the database-to-Web genre, try this evaluation copy. The Studio is the design suite for ColdFusion. You need the application server to serve your creation to the Web. ColdFusion has been around for quite a while and is very popular. It costs a lot less than many of its competitors.

To find out more about ColdFusion Studio, check out the Web site at `http://commerce.allaire.com/`.

Miscellaneous tools from 4Developers LLC

✔ **Registry Crawler 2.0:** Released in May 1999, this is a cool search tool that looks through your Windows registry to help you find all the hidden variables that the registry stores about your programs. It even has a new feature for bookmarking locations in the registry for easy, direct access from your desktop. This tool is shareware.

To find out more about Registry Crawler, check out the Web site at `http://www.4developers.com/news/index.htm#`.

I have a Web site of my own, and I've created a section for questions and answers especially for *Oracle8i For Dummies*. Drop in and visit at

`http://www.maui.net/~mcculc/o8ifordum/Welcome.html`

You can e-mail me at `mcculc@maui.net`.

Aloha!

Index

• Symbols •

|| (CONCATENATE symbol), 77–78
/ (forward slash)
  at end of SQL*Plus Worksheet commands, 26
  with SQL*Plus commands, 29
; (semicolon)
  at end of SQL*Plus Worksheet commands, 26
  with SQL*Plus commands, 29

• A •

about this book, 1–6
  assumptions about readers, 2
  icons, 5–6
  organization of book, 2–4
  overview, 1–2
  using the mouse, 4–5
  what Oracle8i lacks, 6
Agent, 36
alias, 72–73, 367
ALL_ROWS optimization mode, 295
Allaire Corporation Web design tools, 381
ALTER command, automatic commit built into, 89
alternate key, 125
AMY schema
  building, 375–376
  overview of, 375
AMYOBJ schema (on the CD), 191
  creating, 377–378
  developing array type with script, 195
  making table type with script, 192
  running, 188
ANALYZE command, 292
analyzing
  performance of individual tables, 294–295
  schemas, 293–294

applet, creating Java, 267–268
Apply button, 22, 23
ARCHIVE setting, 270
array type
  creating, 194–196
  defined, 187
assigning
  profiles to users, 218–220
  roles to new users, 161–162
assistants, 10, 12
association, 144, 145
attributes
  changing for object types, 340–342
  as component of type model diagram, 144, 145
  creating, 190, 194, 233
  defined, 367
  modifying for column, 329–333
  object SQL sample, 92–93
  prefixing with table aliases, 105
audit utility, backing up with, 272
authentication
  choosing user, 160–161
  defined, 367
  selecting for roles, 206

• B •

backing up data, 269–288. See also exporting; importing
  with Data Manager, 273–282
  defined, 270
  with EXP command, 282–285
  with full database export, 272
  importing with IMP command, 285–287
  NOARCHIVE setting, 270
  reasons for, 269–270
  restoring data after hard disk crashes, 273
  storing backup files, 287–288
  what to back up, 270–271
  when to back up, 271–272

Backup Manager, 271, 272, 273
BAKERY schema (on CD-ROM), 91–92, 261, 378–379
block, 367
bottlenecks, 348
BREAD_OBJECT_TABLE object table, 91
buffer size for exporting data, 283
buttons
  control-menu, 21
  on Schema Manager, 22–23

• C •

Cartesian join, 367
cartridges, 359
case sensitivity
  months in date format, 81
  of names, 51
CD-ROM, 375–382
  AMY schema, 375–376
  AMYOBJ schema, 188, 377–378
  BAKERY schema, 91–92, 261, 378–379
  ColdFusion Studio 4.0 for Windows, 381
  creating view with sample schema on, 221
  HomeSite 4.0, 381
  Registry Crawler 2.0, 382
  running AMYOBJ_object_types.sql script, 191, 192
  sample schemas on, 375
  sample SQL scripts on, 379–380
  SQLab Xpert, 381
  SQLNavigator, 381
  TOAD, 381
character restrictions for names, 50
checking space on tablespaces, 110
CHOOSE optimization mode, 295
clauses in queries, 67–68
Click Execute button (SQL*Plus Worksheet), 25
clicking with mouse, 4
ColdFusion Studio 4.0 for Windows (on CD-ROM), 381
collection, 59
columns
  adding between existing, 338, 339
  adding with Table Wizard Object Creation Wizard, 180–182

adjusting length, datatype, and allowing of nulls in, 327–329
avoiding repeating, 139
changing column constraint to restrict null values, 332–333
components of, 53–54
concatenating, 77–78
creating index on relational, 320
defined, 52, 367
deleting, 338
editing, hiding, and displaying in Schema Manager, 119
illustrated, 53
modifying attributes for, 329–333
naming consistently, 345–347
object types and, 57
rearranging in Table Wizard Object Creation Wizard, 183
removing data from, 330
restructuring, 325–326
selecting datatypes for, 170–174
specifying for WebDB Report Wizard, 249
column titles (Object contents window), 20
comma-delimited file, 367
commands. *See also specific commands listed by name*
  for creating view, 223
  executing with SQL*Plus or SQL*Plus Worksheet, 24
  EXP, 10, 11, 271, 282–285
  IMP, 10, 11, 271, 285–287
  reformatting date with TO_CHAR, 76–77
  SQL*Plus editing, 71
  symbols ending SQL*Plus, 29
  symbols ending SQL*Plus Worksheet, 26
  that cannot be undone, 89
commit, 89, 367
COMMIT command, 88
compressing table data on export, 284
CONCATENATE (||) symbol, 77–78
Concurrent Sessions option (Create Profile dialog box), 217
Configuration Assistant, 31–32
CONNECT role, 48, 49, 155
Connect Time option (Create Profile dialog box), 217

constraints
    adding to object tables, 340
    changing to restrict null values for
        existing columns, 332–333
    creating for foreign key, 310
    defined, 367
    index versus primary-key, 318
    setting up for primary keys, 305–307
Constraints tab (Schema Manager
        window), 305, 306, 310
Constraints window, 118
ConText cartridges, 359
control-menu button, 21
core utilities of Oracle8i, 10–12
correlated query, 86–87
correlated subqueries
    defined, 368
    inserting, 86–87
    with UPDATE command, 83–85
cost-based mode, 292–293
Create Array Type dialog box, 195
Create Attribute dialog box, 190, 194, 233
CREATE command, 89
Create Index dialog box, 316
Create Master Detail Forms wizard,
        254, 256
Create Object Type dialog box, 189, 232
Create Role dialog box, 206
Create Shortcut dialog box, 108
Create Synonym dialog box, 238
CREATE TABLE code, 176–177
Create Table properties box, 336
Create Table Type dialog box, 193
Create User dialog box, 160
Create View dialog box, 235
custom profiles, 220

● *D* ●

dangling refs, 105
data
    copying from holding table to new
        table, 339
    Data Migration Assistant, 361
    exporting with tables, 284
    grouping and summarizing, 78–79
    handling derived, 352–353
    manipulating with SQL*Plus and
        SQL*Plus Worksheet, 24

migrating, 361
Migration Assistant for Microsoft
        Access, 361
modifying with UPDATE command, 80–85
reasons for backing up, 269–270
removing from column, 330
running test, 355–356
saving in holding tables, 330, 331–332
database administrator
    logging in before importing objects,
        279–280
    logging in prior to backing up database,
        274–276
Database Configuration Assistant, 362
database engine, 368
database keys
    defined, 124
    normalization rules for, 128–132
    types of, 125
databases, 43–63. *See also* backing up
        data; redesigning columns and tables
    changing processes parameter when
        storing repository in, 31
    choosing Optimizer modes for, 292–293
    Database Configuration Assistant, 362
    defined, 44
    designing before building, 347
    examples of, 60–63
    exporting, 272, 276, 283
    functions of, 46
    loading Java source code into, 264–265
    logging in for database to be backed up,
        274–275
    logical and physical system of, 47–48
    object-oriented, 44
    object-relational, 44–45, 55–60
    prototyping, 348
    relational database concepts, 44, 46–55
    restoring data, 273
    security for, 204, 354–355
    selecting for repository, 33
    sharing design ideas with others,
        348–349
    soliciting user feedback on, 356–357
    terms used about, 43–45
    viewing traffic light in Instance
        Manager, 16
    what to back up, 270–271
data dictionaries, 294–295

Data Manager, 273–282
  exporting entire databases, 276
  exporting tables, 273–278
  exporting users and tables, 277
  logging in for database to be backed up, 274–276
  overview of, 271
Data Manager Wizard, 275–278
  importing with Import Wizard, 278–282
  summary of requested export operation, 278
Data Migration Assistant, 361
Data Warehousing Tool, 360
data-dictionary views, 147–152
  defined, 147
  looking at with SQL*Plus Worksheet, 150–152
  running ANALYZE command on, 292
  system tables and, 147
  using, 148–150
datafiles, 111
datatypes. See also redesigning columns and tables
  changing in columns, 327–329
  as component of column, 54
  date, 77
  defined, 368
  defining for varrays, 195
  listing of, 170–174
  null values and, 174–175
  object types, 57
date
  format of in statements, 81
  reformatting with TO_CHAR, 76–77
date datatype, 77
DBA (database administrator) role, 48, 154, 368
DBA Management Pack
  calling up, 37
  contents of, 13–14
  defined, 370
DBA tools. See Enterprise Manager DBA tools
default database, 44
default tablespace, 169

DELETE command, 87–88, 178
deleting
  row from nested table, 105–106
  rows from object table, 105
derived data, 352–353, 368
designing, 345–357. See also redesigning columns and tables
  before building database, 347
  building prototype databases, 348
  with feedback from users, 356–357
  handling derived data efficiently, 352–353
  naming tables and columns consistently, 345–347
  restructuring tables, 333–340, 352
  security, 204, 354–355
  sharing ideas with others, 348–349
  with test data, 355–356
  using primary keys, 349–351
desktop
  shutting down Oracle8i from, 39–42
  starting and stopping SQL*Plus on, 27–28
Detail Row Formatting page (WebDB), 255
double-clicking with mouse, 4
downloading WebDB, 241
DROP command
  automatic commit built into, 89
  removing tables with, 178
  when to use, 178
DUAL table, 225–226

• E •

Edit Administrator Preferences window, 274, 275
Edit Job window (Data Manager), 279
editor with SQL*Plus Worksheet, 71
Ellison, Larry, 9–10
Enforce Password Complexity option (Create Profile dialog box), 218
Enterprise Manager. See also Enterprise Manager DBA tools
  components of, 22, 23
  initializing Console, 30–38
  overview of, 11
  Schema Manager box, 185
  starting and stopping SQL*Plus Worksheet, 24–27

switching identities with tools in,
165–166
ways of using, 13
Enterprise Manager Console, 30–38
creating repository for, 31–34
logging in as administrator, 274, 279–280
starting and looking at, 36–38
starting Enterprise Manager Server, 35
starting the Agent, 36
Enterprise Manager Console window, 37
Enterprise Manager DBA tools, 107–120.
See also Schema Manager; Security
Manager
Schema Manager, 115–120
Security Manager, 112–115
starting LaunchPad, 108–109
Storage Manager, 110–112
Enterprise Manager Server, 10, 11, 13, 35
entity, 368. *See also* tables
Entity Relationship Diagram (ERD). *See
also* tree diagrams
defined, 368
tree diagrams as, 137, 372
UML and, 144
error message for invalid foreign key, 312
Event Log, 37
EXP command
backing up with, 271
copy tables of test data with, 356
overview of, 10, 11
EXP_FULL_DATABASE role, 155
Expire Password option (Create Profile
dialog box), 218
explicit data conversion, 368
exporting
as alternative to backing up, 272
choosing type of export, 283–284
compressing table data when, 284
data with tables, 284
defined, 368
entire database, 276, 283
with EXP command, 282–285
summary of requested export
operation, 278
users, tables, and schemas, 277

Export Wizard
adding and removing users to
export, 277
exporting tables with, 273–278
summary of requested export
operation, 278
expression, 368
external method of authentication,
160, 367

 • **F** •

File Packager, 362
FIRST_ROWS optimization mode, 295
fixing mistakes with COMMIT and ROLLBACK
commands, 88
flattening nested tables, 97–98, 101
folder titles (Object window), 20
foreign keys
about, 309
adding, 309–312
defined, 125, 141, 368
error message for invalid, 312
finding and correcting invalid values for,
363–364
importing, 125–128
naming, 313
query performance with index on, 303
removing, 313–314, 334
setting up in Table Wizard Object
Creation Wizard, 183
forms, WebDB, 252–258
forward slash (/)
with SQL*Plus commands, 29
with SQL*Plus Worksheet commands, 26
4Developers LLC, 382
fragmented table, 368
FROM clause, 68
full table scan, 303, 368
functions of databases, 46

 • **G** •

GATHER_SCHEMA_STATS command,
293–294
GATHER_TABLE_STATS command, 294–295

GB (gigabyte), 369
general roles for security, 355
global method of authentication, 161, 367
GRANT command, 369
granting privileges
   with Oracle8i, 203–204
   to table access, 213
green cube icon, 112
GROUP clause, 68
group function, 78
grouping and summarizing data, 78–79

• *H* •

help
   online training with Network Computer
      Architecture, 360
   Oracle online, 38–39
Help button, 22, 23
Help Navigator dialog box, 38
hint, 296
HomeSite 4.0 (on CD-ROM), 381
HTML (HyperText Markup Language), 369
hybrid tables, 92, 198–200

• *I* •

icons in this book, 5–6
Idle Time option (Create Profile dialog
      box), 217
IMP command
   backing up with, 271
   importing original data after running test
      data, 356
   importing with, 285–287
   overview of, 10, 11
IMP_FULL_DATABASE role, 155
implicit data conversion, 369
Import Wizard, 278–282
importing
   defined, 369
   foreign keys, 125–128
   with IMP command, 285–287
   with Import Wizard, 278–282
   logging in as system administrator
      before, 279–280
   specifying tables for, 281

incremental space, 52, 369
indexes
   adding, 315–317
   creating, 314
   enforcing unique values for primary key
      with, 303
   functions of, 302–303
   on nested table, 320
   on object table, 319–320
   Optimizer rules for using, 321–324
   performance response time with, 314
   primary-key constraints versus, 318
   removing, 317–318, 321, 334
   20 percent rule, 315
   viewing and sorting list of, 322
Indexes folder, 322
INGREDIENT_OBJECT_TABLE object
      table, 91
initial space, 52, 369
initialization parameters, 40, 41
INSERT command, 85–87
   defined, 369
   inserting single row with, 85–86
   inserting subquery or correlated query,
      86–87
inserting
   rows into nested table, 104–105
   rows into object table, 102–103
   rows into varray, 103–104
installing WebDB, 243
instance, 145, 369
Instance Manager
   overview of, 14
   shutting down Oracle on desktop, 39–42
   starting Oracle8i with, 15–16
   viewing traffic light in, 16
intelligent key, 349, 350, 369
interactive, 369
International Oracle Users Group–
      Americas (IOUG-A), 349
Internet, 369
Internet Commerce Server, 360
intranet, 369
invoker, 265

• J •

Java, 259–268
  creating SQL wrapper for Java code,
      265–266
  creating stored database procedure with
      SQLJ and, 261–267
  about Java Virtual Machine, 259–261
  loading source code into database,
      264–265
  overview, 259
  running stored procedure from applet on
      Web, 267–268
  about SQLJ, 260, 261
  using SQL wrapper in SQL query, 266–267
  writing Java code with embedded SQLJ,
      262–264
Java Database Connectivity (JDBC),
      defined, 260
Java Run-time Environment (JRE), 260
Java Virtual Machine. *See* JVM
JDBC (Java Database Connectivity), 260
joins
  basic query structure of, 73–74
  defined, 370
  examples of join queries, 74–76
  specifying in WebDB Report Wizard, 247,
      248, 253
  table alias and, 73
JRE (Java Run-time Environment), 260
JVM (Java Virtual Machine)
  about, 259–261
  benefits of Oracle's, 260
  support for SQLJ, 260

• K •

Keep Password History option (Create
      Profile dialog box), 218
keys. *See also* foreign keys; primary keys
  defined, 124, 370
  intelligent, 349, 350, 369
  nonintelligent, 349–350, 370

• L •

LaunchPad, 108–109
legacy system, 370
length, column, 54, 327–329
literals
  defined, 370
  using, 80–81
local database, 370
Lock account on failed logon option
      (Create Profile dialog box), 218
logging in
  for databases to be backed up, 274–276
  with Instance Manager, 15
  repository login information, 33
  for Schema Manager, 19
  on SQL*Plus Worksheet, 66
logical databases
  defined, 48
  roles in, 48–49
logical operator, 370

• M •

main menu bar, 20, 21
mainframe
  shutting down Oracle8i from, 42
  starting and stopping SQL*Plus on, 29
Management Pack
  calling up, 37
  contents of, 13–14
  defined, 370
MANAGER default password, 188
many-to-many relationships, 143
Map, 37
Master Detail Form page (WebDB), 258
master row, 255, 256
Master Row Finder page (WebDB),
      255, 256
Master Row Finder Results page
      (WebDB), 257
Master Row Formatting page (WebDB),
      253, 254
maximum table space, 52
Media Server, 360

menus
  main Schema Manager, 22–23
  for Schema Manager, 20
  for SQL*Plus Worksheet, 25–26
method
  as component of type model diagram, 144, 145
  defined, 370
migrating data
  Data Migration Assistant, 361
  Migration Assistant for Microsoft Access, 361
mouse activities, 4–5

• *N* •

naming
  conventions for in Oracle, 50–51
  foreign keys, 313
  new tables, 50–51, 180
  tables and columns consistently, 345–347
  user ID, 160, 162
navigating in Schema Manager window, 20
Navigator, 37
nested tables, 59
  creating index on, 320
  creating table type for, 191–194
  deleting row from, 105–106
  inserting rows into, 104–105
  removing index on, 321
  summing rows retrieved from, 262
  updating row in, 102
  varrays versus, 100
  writing queries using, 97–99
Nested Tables dialog box, 199
NESTED_TABLE_ID pseudocolumn, 226
Net8, 10, 12, 362–363
network
  shutting down Oracle8i from, 42
  starting and stopping SQL*Plus on, 29
Network Computer Architecture, 360
new users. *See* users, creating
NOARCHIVE setting, 270
nonintelligent key, 349–350, 370

nonunique index, 314
normalization rules
  avoiding repeating columns, 139
  for database keys, 128–132
null, defined, 370
null values
  allowing in tables or not, 175
  allowing in tables with Table Wizard Object Creation Wizard, 182
  changing columns containing, 329–332
  editing to not null attribute in object table, 340
  indexes and, 322
  modifying column constraint to restrict, 332–333
  null/not null as column component, 54
  using, 176
  using IS NULL and IS NOT NULL operators, 174

• *O* •

object column, 57, 58
object column tables, 198–200
Object contents window, 20
object methods, 59
object references, 58–59
object-oriented databases, 44
object-relational databases, 44–45, 55–60, 133–136
  about, 133–134
  connecting relational tables with objects, 58, 135–136
  defined, 370
  defining objects, 134–135
  nested tables, 59
  object methods, 59
  object references, 58–59
  object types, 57, 135
  objects in, 56
  Oracle as, 55–56
  varrays, 60
object-relational tables, 198–200
objects
  adding to tree diagrams, 143–144
  associations between object types, 187

connecting relational tables with, 58, 135–136
creating set of related, 186–187
creating synonyms for, 236–238
defined, 19, 56, 134–135, 371
defining referenced, 190
naming, 51
object SQL sample, 92–93
OID, 302
object SQL, 91–106
BAKERY object schema, 91–92
making changes to object table data, 101–106
querying object tables in SQL, 94–101
sample types, objects, and attributes, 92–93
starting SQL*Plus Worksheet, 93–94
object tables, 58, 101–106, 136
creating index on, 319–320
defined, 370
deleting rows from, 105
inserting rows into, 102–103
making, 196–198
querying in SQL, 94–101
removing index on, 321
updating objects in, 102
updating row in nested table, 102
object types, 57, 185–200
changing attributes for, 340–342
as component of type model diagram, 144–145
creating as array or nested table, 191
creating hybrid tables, 198–200
creating for object views, 231–236
defined, 59, 134, 187, 370
defining, 188–191
developing array types, 194–196
listing of object-relational, 135
making object tables, 196–198
making table types, 191–194
making types, 187–188
prefixing attributes with table aliases, 105
object views, 58, 136, 231–236
creating, 231, 234–236
creating synonyms, 236–238

defined, 371
designing queries, 231
developing object type, 231–233
using SQL or Schema Manager to create, 229
Object window, 19–21
OID (Object ID), 302
one-to-many relationships, 132–133, 142
one-to-one relationships, 141–142
optimization modes for tuning queries, 295–296
Optimizer, 291–292. *See also* performance
defined, 371
hints, 296
ignoring index for queries with wildcards, 323
modes for, 295
null value and index, 322
ordering of query events, 323–324
rule-based and cost-based modes for, 292–293
rules for using index, 321–324
Oracle Enterprise Manager Login dialog box, 15, 19
Oracle LaunchPad, 108–109
Oracle Storage Manager window, 110
Oracle8i, 9–42, 359–364
benefits of JVM, 260
contents of DBA Management Pack, 13–14
ConText cartridges, 359
core utilities of, 10–12
Data Migration Assistant, 361
Database Configuration Assistant, 362
development of, 9–10
File Packager, 362
finding and correcting invalid foreign-key values, 363–364
function and features of WebDB, 242–243
getting acquainted with SQL, 23–31
getting help, 38–39
granting permissions with, 203–204
initializing the Enterprise Manager Console, 30–38
limitations and strengths of, 6
main menu and buttons on Schema Manager, 22–23

Oracle8i *(continued)*
  Migration Assistant for Microsoft
    Access, 361
  naming conventions in, 50–51
  Net8 Assistant, 362–363
  Network Computer Architecture, 360
  Performance Monitor, 363
  restoring databases after hard disk
    crashes, 273
  Scott and Tiger, 30
  shutting down, 39–42
  standard security options for, 201–202
  starting, 14–18
  starting Schema Manager, 18–23
  using Enterprise Manager, 13
  Web Assistant wizard, 360–361
  WebDB, 12
ORDER BY clause, 68
overhead, 371
owners, 153–154, 371

● *P* ●

package, 371
Parameter form, 255, 256, 257
Password tab (Create Profile dialog
  box), 218
passwords. *See also* Security Manager
  assigning to roles, 209
  changing in SQL*Plus Worksheet,
    163–164
  creating authentication for users with,
    160, 367
  editing in Security Manager, 164–165
  logging in for Storage Manager, 110
  MANAGER, 188
  setting up parameters for profile, 218
  setting up temporary, 161
performance. *See also* indexes; Optimizer
  analyzing table, 294–295
  ignoring index for queries with
    wildcards, 323
  improving query, 297
  indexing queries with nulls in
    column, 322

  ordering of query events in order of
    entry, 323–324
  of queries with foreign key index, 303
  speeding up response time with
    indexes, 314
Performance Monitor, 363
physical databases, 47–48
plan, defined, 292
precompilers, 10, 11
primary keys
  about, 303–304
  adding, 304–308
  advantages of small, 349
  creating in Table Wizard Object Creation
    Wizard, 182
  defined, 52, 125, 141, 371
  designing, 349–351
  enforcing unique values for with
    index, 303
  index versus primary-key
    constraints, 318
  intelligent or nonintelligent, 349–351
  need for with tables, 301
  nulls and, 175
  removing, 308–309
  restoring, 309
  table constraint properties added to,
    305–307
  whose contents change, 139
private synonyms, 236, 237, 371
privileges
  assigning for tables in SQL, 212–215
  assigning to roles, 210–212
  granting table permissions to roles,
    203–205
  invoker, 265
  limiting access with profiles, 216
  public synonyms and assignment of, 239
  removing during table restructuring, 334
  with Security Manager, 205–212
  with SQL, 212–215
procedure
  creating SQLJ and Java database,
    261–267
  defined, 371
  running from applet on Web, 267–268
Product Wizard, 362

profiles, 215–220
  assigning to user, 218–220
  creating, 216–218
  default and custom, 219, 220
  limiting access with, 216
Profiles folder, 114–115
prototyping databases, 348
pseudocolumns
  defined, 371
  in example pay rate tables, 225
  list of Oracle, 226
public synonyms
  assignment of privileges and, 239
  defined, 371
  private and, 236, 237

• *Q* •

queries, 67–71, 94–101, 291–299. *See also*
    performance
  adding owner prefix to table
    names in, 202
  basic clauses in, 67–68
  building, 74
  correlated subqueries, 83–85, 86–87
  creating for object views, 231
  creating in Schema Manager, 119
  in data-dictionary view, 150–152
  improving performance for, 297
  improving speed of with indexes and
    keys, 301–303
  joining tables, 73–76
  naming tables and columns consistently
    for, 345–347
  with nested tables, 97–99
  null values and performance of, 322
  Optimizer hints in, 296
  sample, 68–69
  subqueries, 82, 86–87
  tips for writing good, 69–71
  using nested table, 97–99
  using SQL wrapper in SQL, 266–267
  using varrays, 100–101
  verifying indexes exist, 322
  viewing timing statistics for, 297–299
  wildcards and performance of, 323
  writing object-oriented SQL, 95–97
Quest Software tools, 381

• *R* •

Rathbone, Andy, 21
recovery logs, 272
Recovery Manager
  restoring data after hard disk
    crashes, 273
  restoring from full database export
    with, 272
redesigning columns and tables, 325–342
  changing columns, 325–326
  editing object tables in Schema Manager,
    340–342
  modifying column attributes, 329–333
  restructuring tables, 333–340, 352
  simple revisions to tables in Schema
    Manager, 327–329
REF object reference, 58
  creating index on column with, 320
  defining referenced objects, 190
referenced objects, 190
reformatting date with TO_CHAR, 76–77
Registry Crawler 2.0 (on CD-ROM), 382
relational databases, 44, 46–55, 123–136
  advantages of, 123–124
  concepts for, 44, 46–55
  connecting relational tables with objects,
    135–136
  creating index for, 320
  database keys, 124
  defined, 44, 371
  defining objects, 134–135
  importing foreign keys, 125–128
  making tree diagrams of, 137–140
  about object-relational databases,
    133–134
  overview, 46–47
  about relationships, 54–55
  setting up one to many relationships,
    132–133
  tables in, 49–52
  third normal form, 128–132
  types of database keys, 125
  users and roles in, 47–49
relational tables, 135–136

relationships, 54–55
  finding and correcting invalid foreign-key values, 363–364
  incorrectly identifying in tree diagrams, 139–140
  one to many, 142
  setting up one to many, 132–133
  in tree diagrams, 141
remote database, 371
removing
  columns, 333–340
  database elements during table restructuring, 334
  data from columns, 330
  foreign keys, 313–314
  indexes, 317–318, 321
  primary keys, 308–309
  roles, 113, 209
  tables, 178
  views, 223
RENAME command, 89
renaming columns, 333–340
reordering columns, 333–340
reorganizing, 372
reports
  choosing schema for WebDB, 247
  creating report page with WebDB, 246–252
  running from Web, 252
  setting display options for WebDB, 249, 250
  WebDB default, 251
repository, 31–34
reserved words, 51
RESOURCE role, 48, 49, 155
restoring
  data after hard disk crashes, 273
  data with ROLLBACK command, 330–331
  from full database export with Recovery Manager, 272
  primary key, 309
restructuring tables, 333–340, 352
  adding column between existing columns, 338, 339
  copying data to new table, 339

database elements removed when, 334
  modifying table structures, 352
  overview of changes for, 333–334
  removing columns, 338
  steps for, 334–340
Revert button, 22, 23
REVOKE command, 372
right-clicking, 4
roles. *See also* privileges
  adding, 113
  assigning, 114
  assigning privileges to, 210–212
  assigning to users, 161–162, 207–209, 212–215
  creating WebDB developer, 244, 245
  defined, 47, 372
  discovering users', 155–159
  granting table permissions to, 203–205
  in logical system, 48–49
  passwords assigned to, 209
  querying in SQL*Plus Worksheet for, 156
  in relational databases, 47–49
  removing, 113, 209
  with Security Manager, 205–212
  selecting authentication for, 206
  selecting on User Property page, 208
  shared read-only, 354
  with SQL, 212–215
  SQL creation of, 213
  for users, 153–155
  using general and theme-based roles for security, 355
  viewing available and assigned, 158
Role tab (Create User dialog box), 162
Role tab (Security Manager), 113–114, 158, 159
Role tab (User Property page), 209
ROLLBACK command
  commands that can't be undone with, 89
  defined, 372
  fixing mistakes with, 88
  restoring data to columns with, 330–331
  speeding up database testing with, 356
rollback segments, 112
row ID
  defined, 302, 372
  retrieving rows from table with, 315

`ROWID` pseudocolumn, 226
`ROWNUM` pseudocolumn, 226
rows
  choosing default detail row formatting
    for WebDB form, 255
  dangling refs in, 105
  defined, 52, 372
  deleting with `DELETE` command, 87–88
  deleting from nested table, 105–106
  deleting from object table, 105
  editing in Schema Manager, 119
  how Oracle adds to tables, 302
  illustrated, 53
  improving retrieval of, 315
  inserting into nested table, 104–105
  inserting into object table, 102–103
  inserting into varray, 103–104
  inserting with `INSERT` command, 85–87
  object types and, 57
  row ID and OID, 302
  searching for master, 255, 256
  selecting master row formatting for
    WebDB form, 253, 254
  specifying for WebDB Report Wizard,
    249, 250
  summing rows retrieved from nested
    table, 262
  updating in nested table, 102
`RULE` optimization mode, 295
rule-based mode, 292–293
running stored procedures from applet,
  267–268

• S •

saving
  data in holding tables, 330, 331–332
  initialization parameters when shutting
    down, 40, 41
Schema box (Create Attribute dialog box),
  189, 190
Schema Manager, 18–23, 115–120
  adding foreign key with, 309–312
  adding primary key in, 304–308
  choosing schemas, 116
  choosing Synonyms folder, 117–118

column changes in, 25–26
creating views with SQL versus, 229
defining object types in, 188–191
elements of window, 20, 21–22
looking at views with, 229
main menu and buttons on, 22–23
making hybrid tables in, 198–200
making object tables in, 196–198
making table types in, 191–194
navigating in, 20
Object window in, 19–21
overview of, 14
removing a primary key, 308–309
restructuring tables in, 333–340
starting and logging in, 18–23, 116
using Table Wizard Object Creation
  Wizard, 178–184
viewing and editing table data in, 119
viewing indexes in, 322
viewing tables with schemas, 118
Schema Manager Properties page, 319
Schema Manager toolbar, 20, 21–22
Schema Manager window, 117
schemas
  adding to new table, 180
  analyzing with `GATHER_SCHEMA_STATS`
    command, 293–294
  choosing for WebDB reports, 247
  defined, 372
  exporting selected, 277
Scott and Tiger, 30
scripts, 372
  `AMYOBJ_object_types.sql` script, 191,
    192, 195
  SQL scripts on CD-ROM, 379–380
security, 201–220. *See also* passwords;
  synonyms; views
  assigning profiles to user, 218–220
  creating profiles, 216–218
  designing, 204, 354–355
  granting table permissions to roles,
    203–205
  limiting access to information with
    views, 223–226
  limiting access with profiles, 216
  purpose of views, 222–223

security *(continued)*
  roles and privileges with Security
    Manager, 205–212
  roles and privileges with SQL, 212–215
  standard Oracle options for, 201–202
Security Manager, 112–115, 205–212
  assigning privileges to roles, 210–212
  assigning roles, 114
  assigning users to role, 207–209
  available and assigned roles in, 158
  changing user passwords in, 164–165
  closing, 115
  creating roles, 205–207
  creating users with, 159–162
  finding out user roles with, 157–159
  overview of, 14
  starting and logging in, 113
  viewing information about users in, 113,
    114
  viewing profiles in Profiles folder,
    114–115
Security Manager window, 114, 158
SELECT clause, 67
Selected tables box (Import Wizard dialog
  box), 281
selecting
  database for repository, 33
  with mouse, 4
semicolon (;)
  at end of SQL*Plus Worksheet com-
    mands, 26
  with SQL*Plus commands, 29
Server Manager, 17–18
Services window, 35
shared read-only roles, 354
Show/Hide SQL button, 22, 23
Shutdown Options dialog box, 41
shutting down Oracle8i
  on a desktop, 39–42
  on mainframe or network, 42
size
  adjusting for tablespaces, 111
  of buffer for exporting data, 283
  of tables, 51–52
software on CD-ROM, 381–382
  ColdFusion Studio 4.0 for Windows, 381

HomeSite 4.0, 381
  Registry Crawler 2.0, 382
  SQLab Xpert, 381
  SQLNavigator, 381
  TOAD, 381
sorting
  indexes and, 302
  list of indexes, 322
space usage table (Storage Manager), 110
SQL (Structured Query Language), 23–31,
  65–89
  assigning roles and privileges with,
    212–215
  closing SQL*Plus Worksheet, 27
  column changes in, 325–326
  combining tables, 73–76
  commands that cannot be undone, 89
  concatenating columns, 77–78
  creating roles in, 213
  date format in statements, 81
  defined, 372
  deleting rows with DELETE command,
    87–88
  developing views in Schema Manager
    versus, 229
  fixing mistakes with COMMIT and
    ROLLBACK commands, 88
  grouping and summarizing data, 78–79
  inserting rows with INSERT command,
    85–87
  making SQL wrapper for Java code,
    265–266
  manipulating data with SQL*Plus and
    SQL*Plus Worksheet, 24
  modifying data with UPDATE command,
    80–85
  queries in, 67–71
  querying object tables in, 94–101
  reformatting date with TO_CHAR, 76–77
  sample scripts on CD-ROM, 379–380
  starting SQL*Plus Worksheet, 24–27, 66,
    93–94
  starting and stopping SQL*Plus, 27–29
  using editor with SQL*Plus
    Worksheet, 71
  using Optimizer with, 292

using SQL wrapper in SQL query, 266–267
using table aliases, 72–73
SQL*Plus
defined, 23
overview of, 10, 11
starting and stopping on desktop, 27–28
starting and stopping on mainframe or network, 29
SQL*Plus window, 27–28
SQL*Plus Worksheet
changing user passwords in, 163–164
creating table with, 177–178
defined, 23
finding out user roles with, 155–157
looking at data-dictionary views, 150–152
overview of, 14
starting up, 24–27, 66, 93–94
using editor with, 71
SQL*Plus Worksheet window, illustrated, 25
SQLab Xpert (on CD-ROM), 381
SQLJ
JVM support for, 260
overview of, 261
using BAKERY schema in example, 261
writing Java code with embedded, 262–264
SQLNavigator (on CD-ROM), 381
starting
the Agent, 36
Enterprise Manager Console, 36–38
Enterprise Manager Server, 35
Oracle8i with Instance Manager, 15–16
Oracle8i using Server Manager, 17–18
Schema Manager, 18–23
SQL*Plus on desktop, 27–28
SQL*Plus Worksheet, 27, 66, 93–94
statistics
gathering for individual tables, 294–295
gathering for schemas, 293–294
viewing query timing, 297–299
stopping
SQL*Plus on desktop, 27–28
SQL*Plus Worksheet, 24–27

Storage Manager, 110–112
adjusting size of tablespaces, 111
closing, 112
overview of, 14
starting and logging in, 110
viewing and managing datafiles, 111
viewing and managing rollback segments, 112
storing backup files, 287–288
Structured Query Language. See SQL
subqueries
correlated, 83–85
inserting with INSERT command, 86–87
using with UPDATE command, 82, 83–85
switching user identity, 165–166
synonyms. See also views
advantages of, 238–239
assignment of privileges and public, 239
choosing Synonyms folder, 117–118
creating for objects in Schema Manager, 236–238
defined, 236, 372
public and private, 236, 237, 371
Synonyms folder, choosing, 117–118
syntax
of clauses in SQL query, 68
for creating index on nested table, 320
for GATHER_TABLE_STATS command, 294–295
of group function, 78
for grouping information from several tables with views, 227–228
for limiting view of table, 224
for Optimizer mode hint, 296
for SQL wrapper making function, 265
SYSDATE pseudocolumn, 226
system role, 48
system tables and data-dictionary views, 147
SYSTEM user name, 188

● T ●

table alias
defined, 72–73, 367
function in join queries, 73

table constraint properties
  adding to primary key, 305–307
  creating for foreign key, 310
Table Editor, 346, 347
table owners
  assigning extra privileges to tables,
    210–212
  defined, 154
  users and, 153–154
table permissions. *See also* privileges
  granting to roles, 203–205
table property page (Schema Manager,
    327–328
tables, 169–184
  adding foreign key to existing, 309
  analyzing performance of individual,
    294–295
  backing up, 271
  columns and rows on, 52–54
  combining, 73–76
  components of columns, 53–54
  compressing table data, 284
  connecting relational tables with
    objects, 58
  copying data from holding table to
    new, 339
  creating table with Schema Manager's
    wizard, 178–184
  creating with Table Wizard Object
    Creation Wizard, 180–184
  defined, 372
  defining columns in, 170–174
  DUAL, 225–226
  exporting, 277
  flattening nested, 97–98, 101
  granting table permissions to roles,
    203–205
  how Oracle adds rows to, 302
  hybrid, 92
  including owner prefix with table names
    in queries, 202
  integrity in relationships, 55
  making object tables, 196–198
  naming, 50, 180, 345–347
  nested, 59
  null values, 174–175, 176

primary key constraints on, 303
  primary key for, 52
  querying tables with columns versus
    relational, 96
  in relational databases, 49–52
  restructuring, 333–340, 352
  saving data in holding, 330, 331–332
  simple revisions to table structure,
    327–329
  size of, 51–52
  specifying datatypes for columns,
    170–174
  SQL creation of, 175–178
  table owners, 153–154
  tablespaces and, 169–170
  in tree diagrams, 140
  types of changes to structure of, 325–326
  using views with, 222–223, 227–228
  viewing and editing table data in Schema
    Manager, 119
  viewing with schemas, 118
tablespaces
  about, 169–170
  adjusting size of, 111
  backing up, 271–272
  checking space on, 110
  defined, 372
  reviewing datafiles making up, 111
  selecting repository user, 34
  selecting when creating new tables, 180
Tablespaces folder, 110
table types
  creating, 191–194
  defined, 188
Table Wizard Object Creation Wizard,
    180–184
  adding columns with, 180–182
  allowing null values in, 182
  defining foreign key in, 183
  defining primary key in, 182
  rearranging columns in, 182–183
temporary passwords, 161
terminology for databases, 43–45
test data, 355–356
theme-based roles for security, 355
third normal form, 128–132, 372

Tiger and Scott, 30
TIMING command, 297–299
timing statistics for queries, 297–299
title bar in Schema Manager window, 21
TOAD (on CD-ROM), 381
TO_CHAR command, 76–77
tree diagrams, 137–145
  adding objects to, 143–144
  components of, 140–143
  creating on paper, 137–140
  defined, 137, 372
  many-to-many relationships, 143
  one-to-many relationships, 142
  one-to-one relationships, 141–142
  relationships in, 141
  tables in, 141
  using UML type model diagram, 144–145
tuning queries, 291–299
  analyzing individual tables, 294–295
  analyzing schema, 293–294
  improving query performance, 297
  optimization modes for, 295–296
  about the Optimizer, 291–292
  rule-based and cost-based Optimizer
      modes, 292–293
  viewing timing statistics for queries,
      297–299
20 percent rule, 315
type model, 144–145
types. See also datatypes; object types;
      table types
  about, 187
  defined, 134
  object, array, and table, 187–188
  object SQL sample, 92–93

• U •

UML (Unified Modeling Language), 144,
      145
UNCLASSIFIED_AGENT view, 224
Unified Modeling Language (UML), 144
unique index, 314
UPDATE command, 80–85
  modifying data with, 80–85
  using correlated subqueries with, 83–85

using literals, 80–81
using subqueries, 82
updating
  objects in object tables, 102
  row in nested table, 102
user interface
  navigating in Schema Manager, 20
  for Schema Manager, 20, 21–22
User Manager page (WebDB), 245
User Property page, 207, 208
USER pseudocolumn, 225, 226
user-defined datatypes. See types
users, 153–166
  assigning for WebDB, 244–246
  assumptions about readers of this
      book, 2
  changing identity for, 165–166
  characteristics of database, 47
  choosing name for user ID, 160, 162
  creating, 159–162
  creating on User Manager page
      (WebDB), 245
  defined, 372
  designating for repository, 33
  determining existing roles, 155–159
  exporting selected, 277
  modifying passwords for, 163–165
  profiles assigned to, 218–220
  in relational databases, 47–49
  roles assigned to, 161–162, 207–209
  roles for, 153–155
  selecting status for new, 161
  SYSTEM, 188
  table owners and, 153–154
  using unique IDs for, 355
  viewing information about, 113, 114
using literals with UPDATE command,
      80–81

• V •

varrays
  datatypes for, 195
  defined, 60, 195
  inserting rows into, 103–104
  nested tables versus, 100
  using in queries, 100–101

viewing
  information about users, 113, 114
  list of indexes, 322
  timing statistics for queries, 297–299
  traffic light in Instance Manager, 16
views, 221–239. *See also* synonyms
  accessing multiple tables with, 227–228
  changing, 230
  creating object views, 221, 223, 229,
      231–236
  defined, 372
  limiting access to information with,
      223–226
  looking at with Schema Manager, 229
  overview, 221
  purpose of, 222–223
  removing, 223
  using data-dictionary, 148–150

• *W* •

Walsh, Aaron E., 259
Web Assistant Wizard, 360–361
Web page, 373
Web sites
  for Allaire Corporation Web design
      tools, 381
  for author, 382
  for 4Developers LLC, 382
  for Quest software tools, 381
WebDB, 241–258
  assigning developers for, 244–246
  creating report page with, 246–252
  downloading trial version of, 241
  form creation and testing, 252–258
  function and features of, 242–243
  installing, 243
  overview of, 10, 11, 12
WebDB Report Wizard, 247–251
  configuring joins, 247, 248, 253
  indicating columns, 249
  specifying rows, 249, 250
WebDB window, 243
WHERE clause, 68
wildcards, 323

windows
  components of Enterprise Manager,
      22, 23
  elements of Schema Manager, 20, 21–22
  navigating in, 20
  SQL*Plus, 28
  SQL*Plus Worksheet, 25
  starting Enterprise Manager Server in
      Services, 35
Windows control buttons, 21
World Wide Web, 373
writing good queries, 69–71

Notes

IDG Books Worldwide, Inc., End-User License Agreement

READ THIS. You should carefully read these terms and conditions before opening the software packet(s) included with this book ("Book"). This is a license agreement ("Agreement") between you and IDG Books Worldwide, Inc. ("IDGB"). By opening the accompanying software packet(s), you acknowledge that you have read and accept the following terms and conditions. If you do not agree and do not want to be bound by such terms and conditions, promptly return the Book and the unopened software packet(s) to the place you obtained them for a full refund.

1. **License Grant.** IDGB grants to you (either an individual or entity) a nonexclusive license to use one copy of the enclosed software program(s) (collectively, the "Software") solely for your own personal or business purposes on a single computer (whether a standard computer or a workstation component of a multiuser network). The Software is in use on a computer when it is loaded into temporary memory (RAM) or installed into permanent memory (hard disk, CD-ROM, or other storage device). IDGB reserves all rights not expressly granted herein.

2. **Ownership.** IDGB is the owner of all right, title, and interest, including copyright, in and to the compilation of the Software recorded on the disk(s) or CD-ROM ("Software Media"). Copyright to the individual programs recorded on the Software Media is owned by the author or other authorized copyright owner of each program. Ownership of the Software and all proprietary rights relating thereto remain with IDGB and its licensers.

3. **Restrictions on Use and Transfer.**

    (a) You may only (i) make one copy of the Software for backup or archival purposes, or (ii) transfer the Software to a single hard disk, provided that you keep the original for backup or archival purposes. You may not (i) rent or lease the Software, (ii) copy or reproduce the Software through a LAN or other network system or through any computer subscriber system or bulletin-board system, or (iii) modify, adapt, or create derivative works based on the Software.

    (b) You may not reverse engineer, decompile, or disassemble the Software. You may transfer the Software and user documentation on a permanent basis, provided that the transferee agrees to accept the terms and conditions of this Agreement and you retain no copies. If the Software is an update or has been updated, any transfer must include the most recent update and all prior versions.

4. **Restrictions on Use of Individual Programs.** You must follow the individual requirements and restrictions detailed for each individual program in the "About the CD" section of this Book. These limitations are also contained in the individual license agreements recorded on the Software Media. These limitations may include a requirement that after using the program for a specified period of time, the user must pay a registration fee or discontinue use. By opening the Software packet(s), you will be agreeing to abide by the licenses and restrictions for these individual programs that are detailed in the "About the CD" section and on the Software Media. None of the material on this Software Media or listed in this Book may ever be redistributed, in original or modified form, for commercial purposes.

5. **Limited Warranty.**

   (a) IDGB warrants that the Software and Software Media are free from defects in materials and workmanship under normal use for a period of sixty (60) days from the date of purchase of this Book. If IDGB receives notification within the warranty period of defects in materials or workmanship, IDGB will replace the defective Software Media.

   (b) **IDGB AND THE AUTHOR OF THE BOOK DISCLAIM ALL OTHER WARRANTIES, EXPRESS OR IMPLIED, INCLUDING WITHOUT LIMITATION IMPLIED WARRANTIES OF MERCHANTABILITY AND FITNESS FOR A PARTICULAR PURPOSE, WITH RESPECT TO THE SOFTWARE, THE PROGRAMS, THE SOURCE CODE CONTAINED THEREIN, AND/OR THE TECHNIQUES DESCRIBED IN THIS BOOK. IDGB DOES NOT WARRANT THAT THE FUNCTIONS CONTAINED IN THE SOFTWARE WILL MEET YOUR REQUIRE-MENTS OR THAT THE OPERATION OF THE SOFTWARE WILL BE ERROR FREE.**

   (c) This limited warranty gives you specific legal rights, and you may have other rights that vary from jurisdiction to jurisdiction.

6. **Remedies.**

   (a) IDGB's entire liability and your exclusive remedy for defects in materials and workmanship shall be limited to replacement of the Software Media, which may be returned to IDGB with a copy of your receipt at the following address: Software Media Fulfillment Department, Attn.: *Oracle8i For Dummies,* IDG Books Worldwide, Inc., 7260 Shadeland Station, Ste. 100, Indianapolis, IN 46256, or call 800-762-2974. Please allow three to four weeks for delivery. This Limited Warranty is void if failure of the Software Media has resulted from accident, abuse, or misapplication. Any replacement Software Media will be warranted for the remainder of the original warranty period or thirty (30) days, whichever is longer.

   (b) In no event shall IDGB or the author be liable for any damages whatsoever (including without limitation damages for loss of business profits, business interruption, loss of business information, or any other pecuniary loss) arising from the use of or inability to use the Book or the Software, even if IDGB has been advised of the possibility of such damages.

   (c) Because some jurisdictions do not allow the exclusion or limitation of liability for consequential or incidental damages, the above limitation or exclusion may not apply to you.

7. **U.S. Government Restricted Rights.** Use, duplication, or disclosure of the Software by the U.S. Government is subject to restrictions stated in paragraph (c)(1)(ii) of the Rights in Technical Data and Computer Software clause of DFARS 252.227-7013, and in subparagraphs (a) through (d) of the Commercial Computer–Restricted Rights clause at FAR 52.227-19, and in similar clauses in the NASA FAR supplement, when applicable.

8. **General.** This Agreement constitutes the entire understanding of the parties and revokes and supersedes all prior agreements, oral or written, between them and may not be modified or amended except in a writing signed by both parties hereto that specifically refers to this Agreement. This Agreement shall take precedence over any other documents that may be in conflict herewith. If any one or more provisions contained in this Agreement are held by any court or tribunal to be invalid, illegal, or otherwise unenforceable, each and every other provision shall remain in full force and effect.

CD-ROM Installation Information

● ●

*T*he CD-ROM contains the sample scripts and tables discussed throughout the book. The scripts are located in the Scripts folder at the root level of the CD. Within this folder, the scripts are organized by chapter. You can find the tables in the Tables folder at the root level of the CD. For instructions on installing the scripts and tables, see Appendix B.

The CD-ROM also contains some utility software that you may find useful. Each program has its own installer. For more details on installation, see Appendix B.

Discover Dummies™ Online!

The *Dummies* Web Site is your fun and friendly online resource for the latest information about ...*For Dummies*® books on all your favorite topics. From cars to computers, wine to Windows, and investing to the Internet, we've got a shelf full of ...*For Dummies* books waiting for you!

Ten Fun and Useful Things You Can Do at www.dummies.com

1. Register this book and win!
2. Find and buy the ...*For Dummies* books you want online.
3. Get ten great *Dummies Tips*™ every week.
4. Chat with your favorite ...*For Dummies* authors.
5. Subscribe free to *The Dummies Dispatch*™ newsletter.
6. Enter our sweepstakes and win cool stuff.
7. Send a free cartoon postcard to a friend.
8. Download free software.
9. Sample a book before you buy.
10. Talk to us. Make comments, ask questions, and get answers!

Jump online to these ten fun and useful things at
http://www.dummies.com/10useful

For other technology titles from IDG Books Worldwide, go to
www.idgbooks.com

Not online yet? It's easy to get started with *The Internet For Dummies*,® 5th Edition, or *Dummies 101*®: *The Internet For Windows*® 98, available at local retailers everywhere.

Find other ...*For Dummies* books on these topics:

Business • Careers • Databases • Food & Beverages • Games • Gardening • Graphics • Hardware
Health & Fitness • Internet and the World Wide Web • Networking • Office Suites
Operating Systems • Personal Finance • Pets • Programming • Recreation • Sports
Spreadsheets • Teacher Resources • Test Prep • Word Processing

IDG BOOKS WORLDWIDE BOOK REGISTRATION

We want to hear from you!

Visit **http://my2cents.dummies.com** to register this book and tell us how you liked it!

✔ Get entered in our monthly prize giveaway.

✔ Give us feedback about this book — tell us what you like best, what you like least, or maybe what you'd like to ask the author and us to change!

✔ Let us know any other ...*For Dummies*® topics that interest you.

Your feedback helps us determine what books to publish, tells us what coverage to add as we revise our books, and lets us know whether we're meeting your needs as a ...*For Dummies* reader. You're our most valuable resource, and what you have to say is important to us!

Not on the Web yet? It's easy to get started with *Dummies 101*®: *The Internet For Windows*® *98* or *The Internet For Dummies*®, 5th Edition, at local retailers everywhere.

Or let us know what you think by sending us a letter at the following address:

...*For Dummies* Book Registration
Dummies Press
7260 Shadeland Station, Suite 100
Indianapolis, IN 46256-3917
Fax 317-596-5498

BESTSELLING
BOOK SERIES